STEWART•M
SHOPGUIDE SERIES

Fret Work

STEP BY STEP

Dedication

Dedicated to **Irving Sloane**, **Hideo Kamimoto**, and *especially* to **Don Teeter**—"The Repairman's Repairman"

STEWART • MACDONALD'S
GUITAR SHOP SUPPLY

21 N. Shafer Street, Athens, OH 45701
Printed in USA.

Photography by Dan Erlewine and Pierre Chastain.

Stewart-MacDonald offers a free 104-page catalog four times each year. For repair shops all over the country and the world, the Guitar Shop Supply catalog is the source for tools, materials, and technical information. Each issue devotes several pages to Dan Erlewine's "Trade Secrets" newsletter. To receive your copy, call 1-800-848-2273 or write us at the address above.

If you're unfamiliar with GAL or ASIA, these well-organized trade guilds publish excellent quarterly journals. They hold semiannual conventions, on opposite years to accommodate membership in each group. Both welcome new members, so if you have an interest in luthiery, write them for information on how to join:

- Guild of American Luthiers (GAL), 8222 Park Ave., Tacoma, WA 98408
- Association of Stringed Instrument Artisans (ASIA), P.O. Box 341, Paul Smith's, NY 12970

ISBN: 0-9644752-1-9

Table of Contents

FretWork

Foreword

This book answers the hundreds of questions we receive about fretting... "Which tools are *must-haves?*" "What's the best rounding file?" "How do you folks put the frets in?" "Should I use glue to hold them in?" Even more so than *finish* work, fretting is the most asked-about subject in luthiery. These pages cover the fretting of four guitars and show a simple fret-dressing on a fifth. Each instrument starts from scratch, and many of the procedures are repeated; but each has its own unique twist because, since no two necks react alike, every fret job is different.

We've used over 800 photos to detail the "hows and whys" of fretting. Your teacher is Dan Erlewine. No one cares more about fretting than Dan. He's earned his fretting, teaching, and writing skills in the trenches, as:

■ editor of "Trade Secrets," an 8-page "book" on luthiery in each quarterly Guitar Shop Supply catalog
■ author of the definitive *Guitar Player Repair Guide,* now in a revised 1994 second edition
■ co-author of *Gibson's Fabulous Flat-Top Guitars—An Illustrated History and Guide* (Miller-Freeman Publishers, 1994)
■ monthly repair columnist for *Guitar Player* magazine, and author of repair and set-up features for *Bass Player* and *Guitar Player* magazines on a regular basis
■ producer of not only the *first* videotape series on guitar repair (nine two-hour tapes), but in 1983 they were some of the first educational videos on *any* subject (except maybe Jane Fonda)
■ teacher of the master repair seminars at the National Guitar Summer Workshops.

Dan also presents lectures, articles, and slide shows yearly at the Guild of American Luthiers (GAL) and Association of Stringed Instrument Artisans (ASIA) conventions, and contributes to both the GAL's *American Lutherie* and ASIA's *Guitarmaker* magazines. He does all of this while developing new tools, techniques, and new directions in guitar repair as a member of the R & B (repair & building) team for Stewart-MacDonald. Guitar Shop Supply is proud to have Dan as your teacher for this book.

Jay Hostetler
Vice-President
Stewart-MacDonald

Introduction

When I started out fretting with a hammer in 1963, there wasn't much information available on the subject. I struggled on my own for years, and always wondered "am I doing this right?" It was great when Irving Sloane published *Guitar Repair* in 1973, with a fretting chapter right out of the C.F. Martin repair shop, showing fretting traditions at their best. Then along came Don Teeter (1975) with *The Acoustic Guitar—Adjustment, Care, Maintenance, and Repair, Volume 1.* Fed up with trying to get frets to stay down in old worn-out fingerboards, Don had begun widening the fret slot with a Dremel router until he could press the frets in with finger pressure and hold them down with epoxy glue. All the fret tops were held perfectly flush with one another by a clamping caul as the glue set. His method was foolproof, and many of us adopted it with relish! In 1978 Hideo Kamimoto's *Complete Guitar Repair,* with its brief but concise chapter on traditional fretting, was another big help, although Mr. Kamimoto was (and is) disdainful of the use of glue—especially epoxy—for fretwork.

I used—and combined—all the fretting methods throughout the '60s, '70s, and '80s. In the summer of '93 I felt ready to offer my own in-depth "book" on fretting, so I revised and edited the *Guitar Player Repair Guide* to include a large detailed chapter on all styles of fretting. The *Repair Guide* revision prepared me for this book—the biggest and best of anything I've undertaken yet.

After spending a number of years using my own version of the epoxy method almost exclusively, by the late 1980s I'd returned to fretting with a hammer and/or a variety of *pressing* methods (check out the "Jaws" fret press in Lesson Five). I didn't abandon the glue-in method completely, but now I generally use hide glue or Titebond (although I use epoxy and superglue when needed).

I recommend the four above-mentioned books to anyone interested in fretting. They have the most complete fretting information of all the building and repair-related books previously published, and they'd certainly make a great accompaniment to this photo book. Add them to your library as your budget allows.

With the exception of an in-depth coverage of Don Teeter's "epoxy-method," and the "bar-style" fretting techniques used until the 1930s, all the other important fretting techniques are covered here in picture form. Don's methods are so well described in his first book that we needn't "re-invent the wheel," and "bar-style" fretwork is a bit too esoteric for this book. We do use Don's technique briefly, however, on the fretboard extension of an acoustic guitar where it's difficult to pound with a hammer in Lesson Three, and we give a "mini-lesson" in our version of the

Teeter style (see "To glue, or not to glue?"). And, there are a couple of bar-fretting tips in the "Fretwire shape, size, and hardness" section.

This book draws on the experience and knowledge of luthiery gained by our entire Guitar Shop Supply staff for over a quarter of a century. It's our hope that you'll find it to be a valuable reference, teaching aid, and all-around shop guide for years to come.

Dan Erlewine

OVERVIEW

THE MANY DIFFERENT STYLES OF FRETTING

HAMMERED, GLUED-IN, OR PRESSED-IN FRETS? (A FEW PROS & CONS)

For in-depth reviews and opinions from top repair professionals on the advantages and disadvantages of all the fretting methods, read our *Trade Secrets* book as well as the *Guitar Player Repair Guide.* But before starting this photo course, here are descriptions—in a nutshell—of the most popular fretting methods. Experiment with all of them.

HAMMER-IN METHOD

This is the traditional way of fretting: prep the slot, choose the wire and shape it, and then hammer the wire in until it's well seated. All fretters should develop their skills with a hammer before attempting (or forming opinions about) other techniques.

EPOXY, OR "GLUE-IN" METHOD

Dan Erlewine with Don Teeter

Developed by ace repairman Don Teeter, this technique, as mentioned above, involves widening the slot to accept the *outside* measurement of the sharp pointed barbs on the sides of the fret tang. With this method, the tang doesn't contact the fret slot walls—the points of the barb do. The remaining gap is filled with epoxy glue. This method can produce the cleanest-looking, most perfectly seated and leveled frets of all. The disadvantages are that it alters a vintage fretboard, and it's irreversible, since future refrets must follow the same procedure (unless complicated fret slot repair is done).

Schools arguing against the epoxy fret job also fear that the lack of fret compression weakens the neck, and that the use of epoxy is in itself harmful to tone. We can't judge that for you. However, Dan Erlewine, who used the epoxy method often for a number of years says: "Repair people whom I respect greatly use epoxy for fretwork and perform the Teeter-style epoxy fret job exclusively and successfully. Yet others, whom I respect equally, wouldn't touch the method (or the glue for fretwork) in a million years. These veterans have the skill, experience, intelligence, and ability to back critics of their methods, and each other, right into a corner. I've been beaten up in such arguments many times, and have supported both sides at different times during my career. Put me on record for saying the following:

"I no longer use the finger press-fit 'epoxy fret method' for these reasons: 1) I don't want to alter the fretboard any more than necessary; 2) Fretting with a saw, hammer and/or a press is much faster than a 'glue-in' job; 3) I like the sound of mechanically tight-fitting frets better than frets sitting in epoxy, although epoxied frets are certainly 'tight'; 4) Poorly-done epoxy fret jobs are more likely to weaken the neck than are poor hammer jobs (and epoxy jobs are much harder to re-do).

"I occasionally use epoxy for fretwork (both 24-hour and fast-cure epoxies). Most necks fretted with a finger-press fit in a properly-prepared fretboard, and using good epoxy glue, aren't weak."

PRESSED-IN FRET JOBS

Many of the larger manufacturers have used overhead presses (mainly "arbor presses") for years. With a press, you are limited by what you can rest under it, so bolt-on necks, removed from their bodies, are the easiest to "press-fret." All things being equal, pressed-in frets seat better than frets which are hammered in, because they're introduced into the wood smoothly and steadily. Hammer-blows tend to cause frets to react in opposition to the blow, causing springback, distortion of the radiused arch of the fret, flat spots, and loose "sprung" fret ends. Several variations of fret presses which you can buy or make yourself are shown in the specialty tool section of this book. Many professionals feel that pressed-in fret techniques produce the best fret job once they are mastered.

When talking "fast cure" epoxy, "five-minute" isn't the only thing going. Twenty, and thirty-minute versions are also available (and both have merit). —Dan Erlewine

Pressed-in frets—especially refrets—often hold better if some sort of glue is introduced. Titebond and hide glue are the easiest to use, although superglue and epoxy have their advantages too. Whenever glue is used for fretwork, it's very important to clean and degrease the fretwire beforehand.

ERLEWINE'S "MODERN GLUE-IN METHOD"

Dan calls this "his" method, while realizing that none of these techniques really "belong" to anyone—who knows what super-skilled repairwoman (or man) waits around the next corner, and with what space-age technique? The big difference between this method and Don Teeter's is that we pay strict attention to good fret compression. We *don't* widen the slot other than to *exactly* match (or be slightly less than) the thickness of a larger-tanged wire—a finger-press fit is considered too loose (drawing, right). Once a proper fret tang fit is achieved, we may remove some of the *barb* from the fret tang so that the frets go in more easily, but the *tang* still fills the slot tightly! So in most cases we're relying on the tang barbs to hold the fret into the slot, along with the glue.

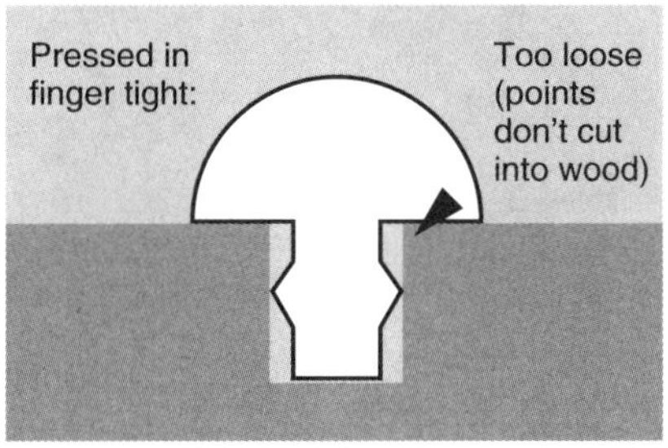

Q: THEN WHAT'S THE DIFFERENCE BETWEEN THE SO-CALLED "MODERN GLUE-IN METHOD," AND JUST USING A HAMMER?

A: Two things: 1) We use either a hammer or a *press* to push the frets in (a press is preferred); 2) We use glue! Not all hammer-fretters use glue, or even approve of it. We expect the glue to do *part* of the holding along with the barbs, but more importantly, we want the glue to fill all the air spaces around the fret to solidify the transmission of tone. We think the use of glue for fretwork improves the tone, if the tang and fret slot have a tight fit. And we remind you that the modern glue-in method is very similar to Don Teeter's method! The only difference between this and a traditional Teeter-style fret job, is that we hammer in the frets (not press them in with our fingers), and since we don't put all the frets in at once we use 5-minute epoxy rather than 24-hour cure. Because we won't go into the Teeter-style fret job in much detail (although we do use it in Lessons Three and Five), here's a "quickie" lesson in the modern glue-in method, using plexiglas cauls, so you'll be familiar with it when we come to it.

"MINI-LESSON" ON THE GLUE-IN FRET JOB

1 The frets are removed—heating the frets first makes removal easier...

2 ...excess glue and dirt is removed from the slot using a Dremel tool and a bit cutting a maximum of .024" (this widens the slot just a couple of thousandths to allow for a not-too-hard hammer-in fit). ...

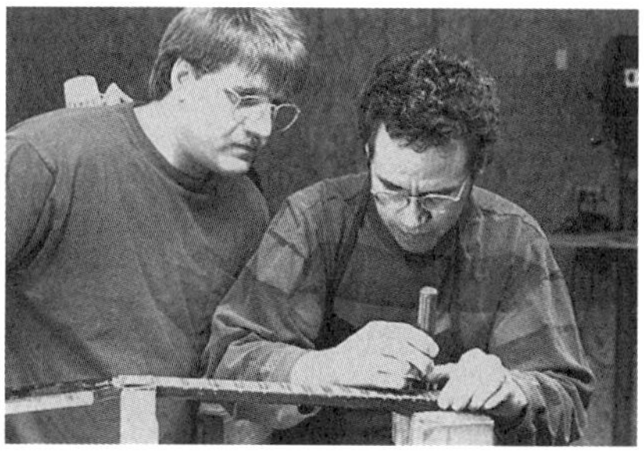

3 ...you may have to scrape the slots with an X-acto blade before, during, or after the Dremeling...

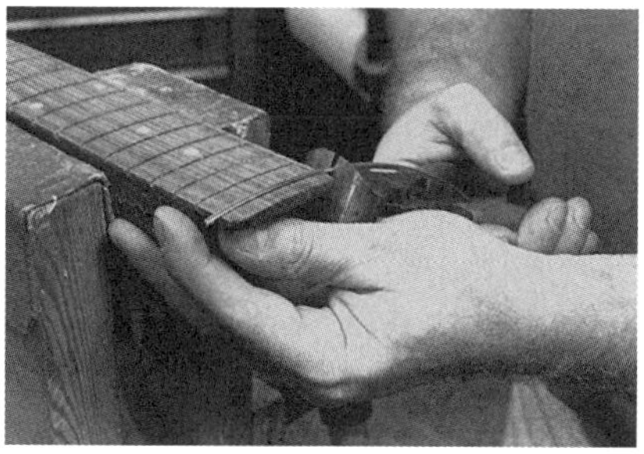

4 ...the frets are cut to length with a 3/16" overhang...

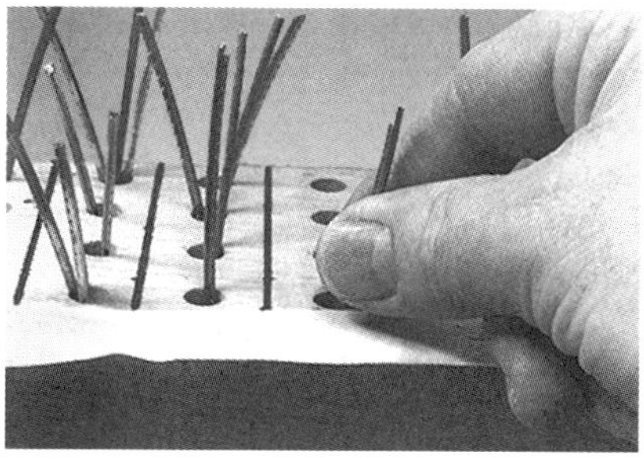

5 ...and stored in order.

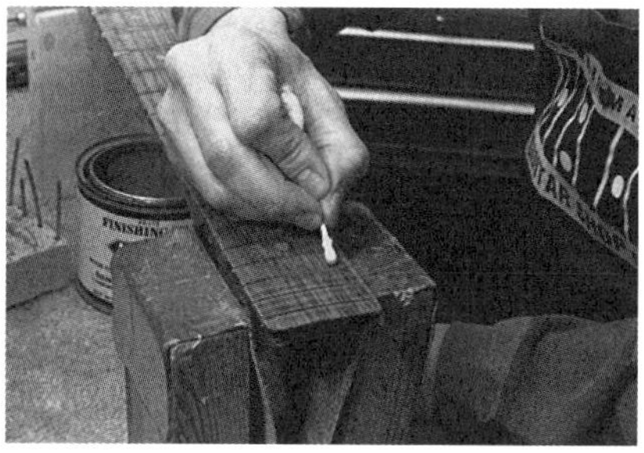

6 Wax carefully almost to the edge of the slot (leave a little clean dry area on each side of the slot for the fret to seat against). Let the wax dry.

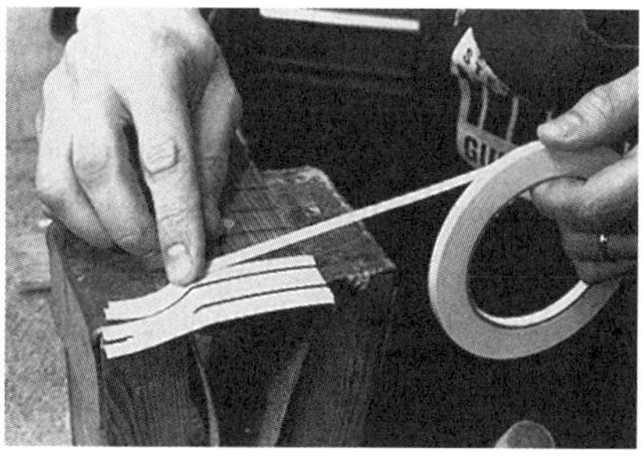

7 Tape off the fret slot on each side of the slot (we're doing three frets at a time here).

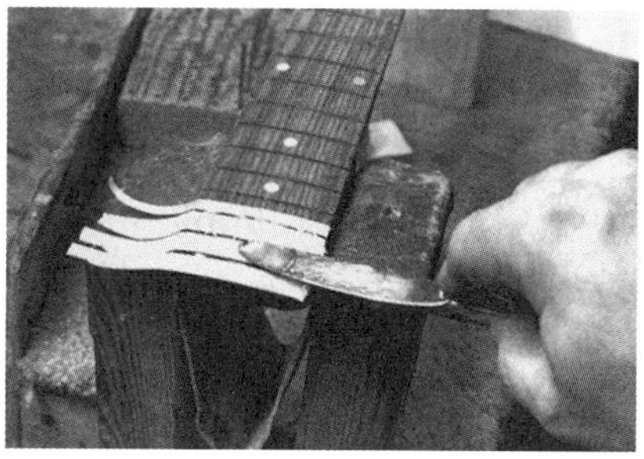

8 Apply well-mixed epoxy into the slots—this is five-minute epoxy.

Continued...

9 Remove the masking tape...

10 ...and hammer in the frets (watch for the glue squeeze-out)

11 ...the plexiglas caul is additional insurance that the frets are seated perfectly...

12 Trim the overhang after the glue is dry, and before removing the caul, to keep the fret from twisting under the cutter's pressure...

13 Chisel off the glue squeeze-out (the waxed board makes this easy) and you're done!

TO GLUE, OR NOT TO GLUE?

That's the question. There are arguments for and against using glue, so you'll have to make your own decision with each guitar on an individual basis. Here's some advice to help you...

■ The use of glue may depend on how well the fret tang fits the fret slot. With new work or extremely tight-fitting old work, the frets often don't *need* glue to hold them in.

■ Even with tight-fitting fret slots, many luthiers use glue to insure against the frets loosening because of fretboard shrinkage, expansion, and contraction. Again, we think glued-in frets sound better because the glue fills the air voids between the fret slot walls and the fret tang.

■ Of course you need glue if you're doing a Teeter-style fret job. The glue, not the tang, holds the fret, since the slot has been widened to accommodate the barbs as an easy press fit. In this case you should use epoxy, since it's the only glue which can fill the slots so rigidly without shrinking back.

■ Hide glue and Titebond are good choices because they're water-soluble and easy to clean up. When the guitar needs the *next* fret job, either can be removed from the fret slots more easily than epoxy or superglue.

■ Epoxy (both 24-hour and fast-cure) is good when mixed in correct proportions so that it dries hard and crystalline. Epoxy, like superglue, is not the best choice for certain vintage fret jobs because it can't be removed easily. You seldom need the strength and gap-filling qualities of epoxy unless you are doing the traditional epoxy fret job.

■ Superglue is great for gluing in frets—or just loose fret ends—but it can be messy and must be used with care around finished surfaces. As with epoxy, superglue is hard to remove from fret slots when the next fret job comes along. However, you can remove it with a Dremel tool and small cutter bits, which you have to clean after every slot since the glue loads the cutter bit up. (CAUTION: If you're routing slots glued with superglue, use good ventilation—superglue fumes generated by heat and friction are potentially dangerous.)

Many fretters have begun using superglue in every fret slot with either a hammer-in, press-in, or the glue-in Dremel tool method—as a substitute for hide glue, Titebond, or epoxy. Often, water-thin viscosity superglue is "floated" under the fret after it's installed. There's no doubt that superglue holds frets down beautifully, although some wonder if the glue will "break down" in the future. We doubt that it will.

Like epoxy, superglue may be overkill in many fretting situations, but it's the greatest for repairing fretboard chips, loose inlays, and building up the walls of rotten, worn-out, or overly-wide slots so that they'll accept a hammered-in fret.

FRET TERMINOLOGY: HERE ARE A FEW FRETTING TERMS THAT YOU SHOULD KNOW :

■ When sighting the neck with the body resting on its side in the playing position, the neck should be unsupported, so that you get a true reading of the neck's straightness and relief. The neck of a guitar laying on its back "reads" differently than it would if that same guitar were laying on its side in the playing position.

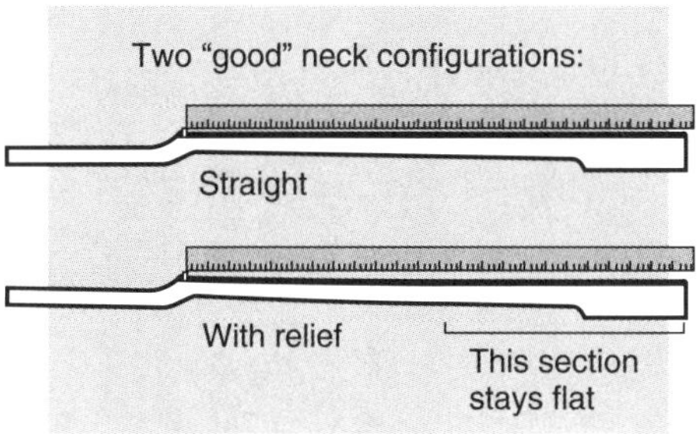

■ "Relief": Lay a straightedge on the fretted fingerboard in line with a string. "Relief" is the gap between the straightedge and the fret tops, measured approximately midway between the 1st fret and 12th or 13th fret. Relief occurs when the neck pulls forward from the tension of the strings. The amount of relief can be controlled by adjusting the truss rod.

■ Upbow: Another term for relief (neck pulling forward from string pull).

■ Backbow: When the neck bows backwards, away from the string pull. This can be the result of a truss rod which is too tight (loosen the rod and it straightens out), or it may be caused by a warped neck.

■ Warped neck: A neck which is twisted, backbowed, or upbowed in such a manner that the wood has taken a "set." A warp can't necessarily be removed with truss rod adjustment.

■ Drop-off: When one end of the fretboard (toward the nut, or at the body end) "drops off," or falls away from the straightedge. On a vintage Martin without an adjustable truss rod, look for drop-off between the nut and the fifth fret (with strings removed) so that the neck pulls straight under tension.

■ Fall-away: The drop-off on the body end of the fretboard is also known as "fall-away." A fall-away on the tongue (fretboard extension) of as much as .004" helps to avoid string "slap" (contact) and buzzing in that area. Fall-away isn't a *must* but it's good to have a little when the fingerboard thickness allows it. What you *don't* want is...

■ ...a "rising tongue" or hump on the fretboard extension. If the fretboard extension goes "uphill" you'll get buzzes. A rising tongue is one of the most common problems we run into!

■ "Hump" refers to any area on the fretboard where the wood rises up off an otherwise level plane.

■ Flex-test: Hold the peghead or the neck just under the nut—with the body resting on the workbench. Pull downward in the center of the fretboard where the neck is weakest. This tells you quickly how stiff the neck is, and whether or not you have a "rubber" neck.

Typical non-adjustable (Martin-style) neck configuration with strings removed. These pull into straightness under string pressure.

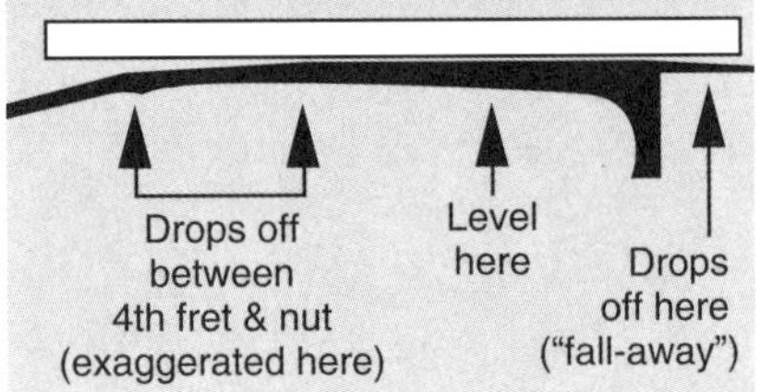

SET-UP TIPS FOR *ALL* FRETWORK

Here are some basic adjustment tips and some important theory to help you throughout this book:

■ **Neck adjusting pointers:** We'd assume that if you're interested in fret work you probably already know how to adjust necks and set action. Still, we give pointers throughout the book. Here are some neck-adjustment reminders just in case:

1 Most truss rods tighten (straightening the neck) by turning clockwise, and loosen counterclockwise.

2 Always *loosen* a truss rod before tightening it. It may already be as tight as it can go!

3 Lubricate a truss rod and its nut, and it will work better.

4 Our #977 two-way adjustable rod turns clockwise to straighten an upbowed neck, and counter-clockwise to introduce upbow to a backbowed neck. Note: our older two-way banjo truss rods worked in just the opposite directions!

HOW TO ADJUST A NECK BEFORE FRETWORK

The strings should be on when you adjust a neck and "read" the frets. Use the best and most accurate straightedges you can find to read the frets while you adjust the truss rod, preferably in the playing position. With the straightedge resting on the fret tops...

1 Loosen the truss rod nut completely (remove it, clean it and lube it), then tighten it until it's just snug. Make a mark on the rod so you know where you started from.

2 Experiment with the truss rod by tightening it as much as you dare to check its operation. **Note:** Most truss rods have done *all they can* before a half-turn is reached. A quarter-turn is usually all it takes to get a neck straight. Three-quarters of a turn is a lot, and a full turn is almost unheard of in all but the most hard to adjust necks.

3 Loosen the rod back to the starting point. Now, tighten the rod until the straightedge "rocks" around the 7th to 9th frets (the center of the neck), indicating that the truss rod has caused a backbow.

4 Next, loosen the rod until the rocking stops. Now the straightedge will be touching in at least two places, if not three—this is as straight as the neck will go, and where you should have it set during any fretboard leveling.

Alternate Adjustment For A "Bad" Neck

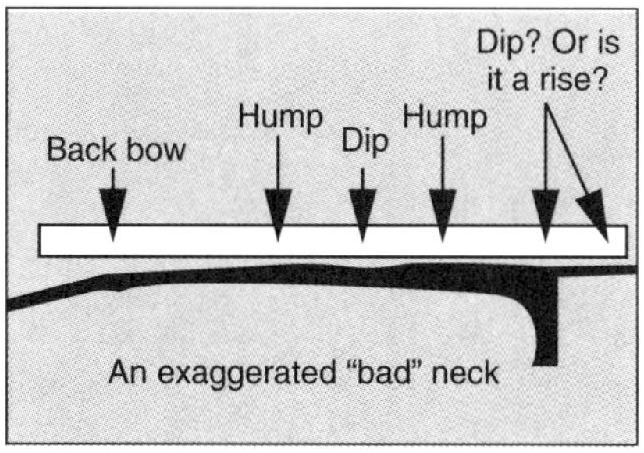

Not every truss rod works well (by "well" we mean that it can take the fretboard into a gentle smoothly-curved backbow, and cause the straightedge to rock). Instead, some rods will affect one area of the neck more than another, causing humps and twists. Adjust these necks by averaging out the best and the worst from end to end. The "bad neck" configuration, even at its optimum straight adjustment, looks something like the drawing at left.

1 The 1st (and maybe the 2nd) fret is backbowed, not even touching the straightedge. Notes played at the 1st, 2nd, and 3rd frets don't make a sound because they "fret-out."

2 Notes at the 4th and 5th frets start to play, and ring clearly until maybe the 9th, when they fret-out again because of what can be perceived as either a hump at the 9th fret or a "dip" or low spot from the 9th fret to the body—depending upon how you choose to look at it.

3 Or it may be seen as a rising tongue (the fretboard over the body is humped or runs uphill). It might be a dip *and* a rising tongue!

So, if you have a neck that looks like the drawing, the best approach is to adjust the neck (in the playing position) until, when comparing the frets to the straightedge, you have the same amount of gap showing at the 1st fret as at the 9th fret. You want the "valleys" equal, and the "humps" (the 4th/5th, the 9th, and the tongue) all on the same plane. Thus you'll take off the least amount of wood from the fretboard because you averaged out the problem areas.

Two Aspects of Fretwork: Installation and Dressing

Fret installation of course refers to new work or the replacement of worn frets during a refret. **Fret dressing** describes the leveling (re-rounding, or "crowning") of the fret tops—new or old. You can dress frets until they're too low for enjoyable playing (.025" is as low a fret as most of us prefer). Whether dressing or fretting, approach fretwork with the following considerations in mind...

1 Is the neck adjustable, and if so, how *well* does the truss rod work? Under string tension, an ideal neck will adjust straight, tighten into a backbow, or loosen into relief (upbow). In general, the object is to adjust a neck so that it will be as straight (flat from end to end) as possible for leveling either the fretboard (during a refret) or the fret tops (during a dressing). Especially when fretting, it's important to know where to adjust the neck during the installa-

tion so that it doesn't backbow, warp, or have too much relief.

2 Is the fretboard flat or radiused? Most modern steel-string guitars, and even some classicals, have some sort of fretboard radius. What is the radius (if any), and is it constant from one end to the other (a cylinder), or does it gradually flatten as you go towards the body (a cone, or "compound" radius)? You may approach a cylinder-shaped fretboard with different tools than you would a cone (see the section on cylinder vs. cone-shaped fretboards).

3 How stiff is the neck? How much flex does it have if you give it the "flex-test" (you'll see the flex-test in every lesson). Weak necks can be stiffened with heavy-tanged fretwire during a refret.

4 If you're dressing a worn-out factory fret job, it's usually because there's a complaint of buzzing. When the buzz is isolated in one area (commonly the first three or four frets), consider a partial refret—you replace only the most worn frets, instead of replacing all the frets just because five are worn. Likewise, you wouldn't dress all the remaining frets down as low as the most worn ones just to get the fret tops level. So always consider a partial refret!

FRETWIRE SHAPE, SIZE, AND HARDNESS

At one time, a "thin" fretwire of medium height was used for most American steel-string guitars, acoustic or electric (excluding the bar fretwire on vintage Martins, of course). Then in the late '50s Gibson began using "wide oval" or "jumbo" wire on everything from Les Pauls to J-45s—this was *wide* wire of medium height. In the '70s, most of the new electric guitar manufacturers favored a wide *tall* fretwire even bigger than Gibson's (Dunlop #6100, and DiMarzio wide oval became the rage). Nowadays, repairmen and players have become knowledgeable enough about fretwire to make an intelligent fretwire choice based on the player's style and playing attack.

To us, "thin" fretwire is .080" and thinner; "medium" begins around .082" and runs to .100", and "wide" is anything above .100". The original "wide" Gibson wire of the late '50s was actually a medium width by our standards. It measured around .098" or .100" until sometime during the '60s, when it changed to .103". The .103" "Gibson" wire lasted until well into the late '70s, when .108" became the norm.

You may see fretwire available in three shapes or "profiles," rounded, squared, and triangular. The round wire is by far the most common. Fretwire is manufactured in low, medium, and tall heights; the low (.034" and under) isn't very popular. By the time frets are installed and leveled, it's easy to lose from .004" to .010" in height—especially if you're learning.

Tall fretwire (.048" and up) offers the same advantages as medium, only more so. However, many players don't like the "railroad tie" feel as they move up and down the neck. Players should at least try a guitar with .050" or taller frets to find out if they're missing anything. There are fewer sizes of "tall" fretwire available than medium. Some feel they offer more sustain not only

Medium-height fretwire (.036" to .048") is preferable to lower wires because:
■ They can be dressed more times between refrets
■ They offer a better sustained note
■ They're easier for a player to bend on
■ They level and dress easier than low frets

because of their greater mass, but because the string isn't damped by as much finger/fingerboard contact, which draws away a bit of tone, volume, and sustain. Tall wire gives you better hammer-ons and pull-offs, and it outlasts medium fret (more fret dressings are possible between refrets).

A fret's hardness is determined by its composition. The most common choice is the hard 18% nickel/silver, although some classical builders prefer softer 12% wire, feeling that it's gentler on nylon or gut strings. The percentage—12% or 18%—refers to the amount of *nickel* in a given wire, not *silver*. Fretwire *looks* silver, but it's actually made of copper, nickel, and zinc, with no silver at all. The alloy mix for an 18% wire is 65% copper, 18% nickel, and 17% zinc. In the U.S., a 12% wire is considered soft, while the industry standard 18% wire is comparatively hard. Stick with the hardest wire you're offered—it wears longer.

Fretwire begins as a semi-hard round wire that is heated to anneal (soften) it, and is then allowed to cool. It becomes "work-hardened" from being drawn through roller dies that compress the wire into a shaped fret. Once drawn, there's no practical way at the manufacturing end to increase fret hardness (in experiments, manufacturers found that rolling a too-hard wire, or a wire with nickel content over 18%, caused breakdowns in the machinery).

If you're serious about fret work, you should buy samples of any wire that arouses your curiosity, and check it out for yourself.

THE CONE-SHAPED VS. CYLINDRICAL FRETBOARD

Here's an excerpt from Dan Erlewine's new* Guitar Player Repair Guide. *Thanks to GPI Publications for letting us reprint this important information.

COMPARING THE COMPOUND RADIUS TO THE CYLINDER

Understanding the difference between a cylindrical and a cone-shaped, or "compound" fretboard may be the most subtle—and important—fretting task you'll face. The ability to use this knowledge during fret dressing or refretting separates the novice from the professional, and the clean playing note from a buzz—yet I've never seen it explained!

In my opinion, radiused fretboards are more comfortable for playing chords than are flat fretboards, because they follow the natural curve of the hand. A player choosing a guitar should have the fretboard radius in mind. The most heavily-radiused fretboards are Rickenbacker and Fender, but for some reason we always refer to Fender when describing the problems associated with low action and a radiused fretboard—like the vintage Fender 7-1/4" radius. This radius is very comfortable to chord on, but when you bend the high *E*- string (and to a lesser degree the *B*) the string will often "note out." The solution is to raise the strings (which doesn't please most players), or come to grips with the compound radius. If you're a player who never bends strings, or doesn't bend very far, then even a vintage Fender Strat or Tele with a 7-1/4" radius can have a fairly low action without buzz, and you needn't mess with compound fretwork at all.

A flatter fretboard radius offers fewer problems to string benders. Gibson's traditional 12" radius has always been good for blues-bending, and Martin's 16", too. But the flatter you get the radius, the less chord-comfort you have. So an "in-between" radius like a 9" or 10" may be just right. For some, a combination of radii—the compound radius—is the answer.

Most fretboards are radiused (they have a side to side arc). A machine cutter creates a perfect cylindrically-shaped radius the length of the board. When the fingerboard gets "profiled," or cut to the tapered width of the neck (viewed from above) the fingerboard is much narrower at the nut than at the very last fret. Looking down from above, notice that the outer two *E*-strings follow the taper (profile) of the fingerboard—they are not parallel to the fingerboard's length or centerline. The remaining four strings follow the same taper but gradually become more parallel to the centerline, with the space between the *D* & *G*-strings being on dead-center.

Imagine this profiled cylinder-shaped fretboard glued to a neck adjusted perfectly straight. A straightedge set on the board in the "lie" of the strings (the individual string's line between the nut and saddle), especially the outside *E*-strings, will rock from end to end because the *only way a straight line can be in full contact with the surface of a cylinder is when it is parallel to the center.* Take a cylinder—a water glass—and set your straightedge in full contact with the glass' surface lengthwise. As soon as you slant the straightedge to the centerline (out of parallel) it loses contact from end to end and rocks on the "hill" in the center.

A fret surface which was machine-radiused at Fender in 1957 was not touched before being fretted. The board and the fret tops are a cylinder. The string, following the profile (or being at an angle to the cylinder's centerline) is going to "rock" in the center on the high spot, like the water glass—especially when the high *E* or *B* is pushed at an even greater angle (out of parallel) to the centerline during string bends. This is why Fender began offering a 9" and 12" radius, keeping the 7-1/4" radius only on vintage models.

The only way to avoid this rocking in the center is to shape the fretboard (or the water glass) into a cone. A cone-shaped fretboard simply means that the radius at the nut will be more curved than at the last fret—the fingerboard radius will flatten gradually from end to end. In repairshops we have been compounding fretboards for years, when applicable, to give customers low action with blues-bending capabilities and minimal buzz. Some manufacturers who use, or have used, a compound radius include Warmoth, Jackson, Collings, Taylor, and Martin.

When preparing the fretboard for a fret job you will sand, file, or scrape the surface until it's straight from end to end across the radius of the board. Note: *If you check your progress with a straightedge resting in the six individual string lies (which is the most common method), you are shaping a slight compound taper into the fretboard.* In the case of a refret on many factory guitars (Fender, Gibson, Guild, and Martin after '93) you're altering the machine-made cylinder which was never intended to have a taper or "profile."

Vintage Martins were compounded this way. They started out with a 16" machine-shaped cylindrical fretboard, which became tapered to 20" at the end because Martin hand-leveled the board in the lie of the strings. Martin guitars made after 1993 have cylindrical fretboards with no taper, because they changed their fretboard preparation technique. They realized that for a 16" or higher radius, a compound fretboard wasn't too great an issue, especially on an acoustic guitar. As a general rule, the radius of an average compound fingerboard flattens out about 3" or 4" toward the end of the fingerboard.

A QUICK FIX FOR A VINTAGE BUZZ:

The quickest fix (although I'm not suggesting it's necessary) for vintage Fenders that buzz when you bend, is to re-level the existing frets until the straightedge sits flat on the top three string lies (the *E*, *B*, & *G*-string lies). You don't need to worry about the bass side because the strings are heavier, higher, and you don't bend them much. You'll be removing the most metal on the edges (*E* & *B*-strings) where the string taper is greatest. The first and last few frets will hardly get filed at all, because they aren't part of the "hill" which is causing the problem. You're creating a slight compound radius on the fret tops themselves.

After compounding, some frets will be taller than others, but if the frets were fairly tall to begin with, the lowest ones usually aren't uncomfortably low. Coupled with the traditionally higher action normally accepted with a vintage Strat, you can now get the blues bends you're after. This solution is only worthwhile on a vintage axe that still has plenty of fret to work with, however, and that's not too common.

A better solution is to put the compound radius into the fretboard itself—prep the board's *surface* that way. Now the tops of the newly installed frets will touch the straightedge (after a normal light fret leveling) because the frets will follow the compound radius from end to end and the fret height will be uniform. This "compound leveling" is common during a refret. I fretted guitars like that for years before realizing that what I'd been doing had a "name." You can't compound a vintage maple neck without removing most (or all) of the finish however, and neither can you reshape thin "veneer" rosewood Fender boards (there's not enough wood to remove). In all cases—especially the most radiused boards—you have to take inlays and fingerboard side dots into consideration.

It's easy to run into side dots, especially on Fenders. Since Gibson sometimes starts out at 12", you have less chance of hitting side dots, but it's still possible. Because of side dots, inlays, and the fretboard's thickness, look, and feel, a "partial" compound job may be the answer. In other words, you don't go *all the way* (following the formula which is given later), but simply in the *direction* of a somewhat flatter board.

Knowing that I generally "read" and prep a fretboard with my straightedges resting on the lie of the string, creating a cone, I wanted to know what radius I should look for at the fretboard end, and—perhaps even more important to final set-up—what is the projected radius when it meets the bridge saddle? I asked my good friend Don MacRostie, head of R&D at Stewart-MacDonald. Working with two other interested luthiers, Gila Eban and Dana Bourgeois, Don worked out three basic fingerboard radius formulas.

The purpose of these formulas is to keep us from removing more wood than necessary while attempting to get the straightedge to sit flat on the fretboard during a refret. The amount of wood to be removed is more subtle than some realize, and is determined by the fingerboard's taper (width of the nut and 12th fret), scale length, and starting radius at the nut. With the formula, you can find out what the radius must be at the end of the fingerboard, at any point along the fingerboard (for checking your accuracy with radius gauges as you work), and determine the projected radius at the bridge saddle. It's very useful information!

DON MACROSTIE'S "FORMULA FOR CONE HEADS" (HOW TO DETERMINE A RADIUS AT ANY POINT ON A FRETBOARD)

MEMO

To: Dan
From: Don

Don MacRostie lecturing at the 1992 GAL Convention

Dan: Here you are. Anyone doing a fret job who doesn't understand the difference between a cylinder and a cone is working "blind." If they understand it and choose to ignore it, that's a different story!

Straight lines that run lengthwise on a cylinder and are in full contact with its surface must be parallel, and could never be tapered to each other as guitar strings on a fingerboard are. I have drawn out three formulas for dealing with the phenomenon of string spread over a curved surface. Whenever straight lines eventually converge on a point (the fingerboard tapering from the body toward the nut), and those straight lines lie in full contact with a radiused surface, then the shape of that surface must be conical or some portion of a cone. First we must determine where the lines (strings) converge. I've defined the following:

X = Distance from the nut to the Origin (focal point)

T = Distance from the nut to the 12th fret

Sn = String spread at the nut

St = String spread at the 12th fret

Rn = Fingerboard radius at the nut

Rd = Fingerboard radius at "D" (a certain distance from nut)

D – Arbitrary distance from the nut

1

$$\frac{T}{\frac{St}{Sn} - 1}$$

2

$$Rd = \frac{Rn\,(X + D)}{X}$$

3

$$D = \frac{Rd \times X}{Rn} - X$$

1) Using the spacing of the two *E*-strings at the nut and 12th fret, extend the lines until they converge. (See illustration below.) Measure from the point of convergence to the nut and you will have "X" or the focal length. X is then used in the remaining formulas. The formula is shown at left.

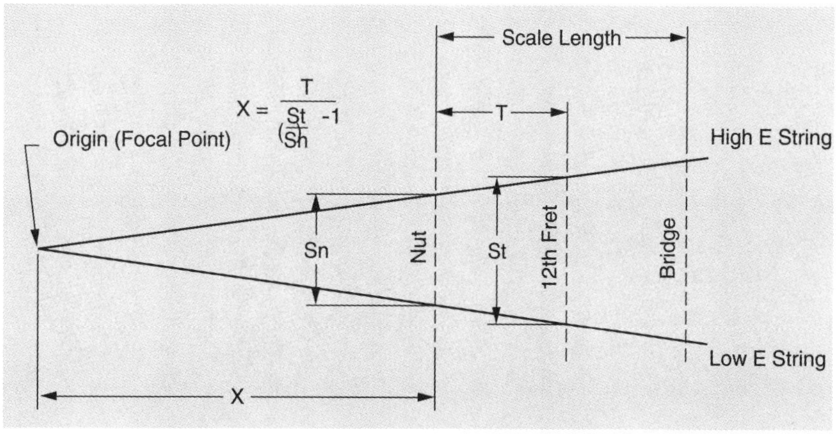

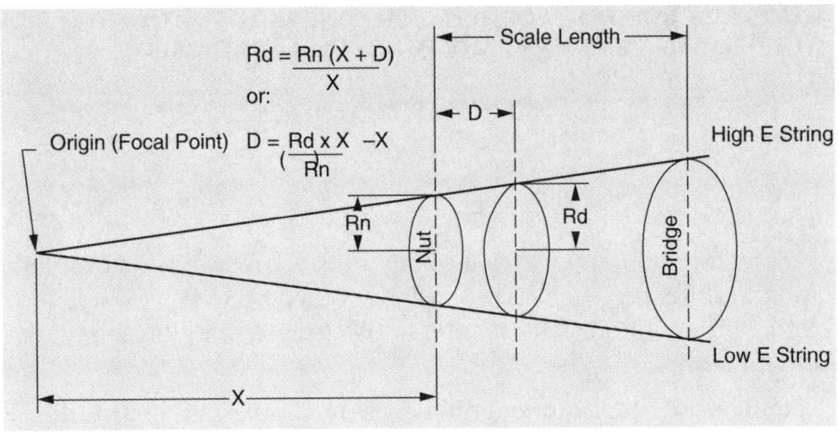

2) The second formula assumes that you have already determined X, the location of the Origin of the cone. This solves for the radius at any point along the fingerboard represented by the value D.

3) The third formula, to find the point D where the radius equals a known value, is written as #3.

All of these formulas are linear and relatively easy to solve and rearrange. What's the bottom line? When you check the fretboard radius, if it measures the same at the nut as at the last fret, you have a cylinder-shaped board (*a la* Fender and Gibson). If the radius is flatter at the last fret than it is at the nut, then you have a "compound," "cone-shaped," or "tapered-radius" fretboard.

Note: Two similar formulas, overlooked by us, were published in the GAL's American Lutherie *magazine: "In Search Of The Perfect Cone" written by Tim Earls—Vol. 30 (Summer '92, page 44); and "Conical Radius Fretboard Formula" by Elaine Hartstein—Vol. 34 (Summer 93, page 46) Check your back issues, or contact the GAL for those articles.*

"COMPRESSION FRETTING" USING REFRET WIRE WITH UNDERSIZE OR OVERSIZE TANGS

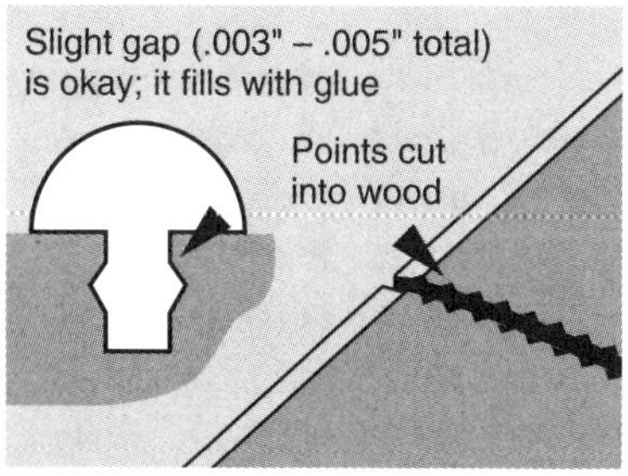

Although the replacement wire is listed in half-thousanth (.005") increments, no fretwire could be that accurate! So don't worry if the wire you purchase doesn't measure **exactly** ***on the money—you'll figure it out after using it awhile.***

Take any guitar, remove the frets, and string it to pitch. What happens? The fretboard will upbow drastically, toward the pull of the strings, because the empty fret slots act like any kerfed piece of wood. Even an adjustable truss rod couldn't remove all the bow. This demonstrates how important the fit of the fret tang to the slot is—too loose gives you upbow, too tight can backbow a neck. It's our opinion that the fret tang, excluding the "barbs" (the pointed diamonds on the sides of the tang), should match the slot *exactly*—filling up the wood so that *no* air space exists. When the tang fits the slot tightly, the fingerboard *can't* upbow from string pressure because the fret slots are filled with metal—the tang of each fret. Fret slots which aren't filled with the tang allow the neck to upbow—sometimes way too much (as shown in Lesson Four).

Realistically, from one to three thousandths of tolerance (gap, or air space) around the fret is acceptable, but not preferred, and *no* gap is far better! Using a Dremel router, sawblades, and a good selection of fretwire, we'll show you how to match the fret to the slot. We'll even use a homemade tool, the "Tang-Sizer," to control the size of the fret tang barbs (see Lesson Three).

But the most important factor with any fretwork, whether it be new work or a refret, is the careful matching of the fret tang to the slot. Known as "fret compression," the fit of the tang has always been crucial during manufacture as a means of keeping necks stiff, straight, and producing good tone. Not only do weak, "rubbery" necks suffer upbow or warp from string tension, resulting in high action, but they don't "drive" the soundbox well either. Weak, unstiff necks can cause an otherwise fine instrument to lack that big-time sound.

Most "rubber" necks can be straightened, or *repaired*, by carefully matching the size of a replacement fretwire's tang to the fret slot. Nicknamed "compression fretting," this method was developed by the Martin repair staff as a means of straightening non-adjustable necks, in particular certain Martin necks built with the "hollow square tube" truss rods from 1967 until 1985. After several years of being strung to pitch, some "square-tube" necks developed very high action and ended up back at the factory for straightening.

Martin switched from the old "bar" frets (solid wire with no tang) to the modern "T-fret" in 1934. By the early '70s, when "weak" square-bar neck problems first began to surface, Martin's repair staff had almost 40 years of experience using T-wire for refretting. They'd learned even in the 1930s to keep several larger-than-standard fret tang sizes handy for everyday refrets. But those Martin necks made from 1934 until 1967 were reinforced with the very solid steel T-Bar. Those necks seldom warped, and are still exceptionally stiff (see Lesson Two—the "perfect" neck). Faced with the new (and relatively few, considering the number of Martin guitars built between 1967 and 1985) neck-stiffness problems of the hollow-tube era, Martin's *fretmeisters* quickly produced *eight* oversize-tang wires, from .018" to .027", to handle the subtle task of controlling neck stiffness—with great results. They were able to straighten—and stiffen—problem necks, simply by using a fretwire with a larger tang for the refret (or in some situations by using a combination of fret tang size and careful "trueing" of the fretboard). The techniques they developed are widely used today for refretting *all* guitars, even those with adjustable truss rods.

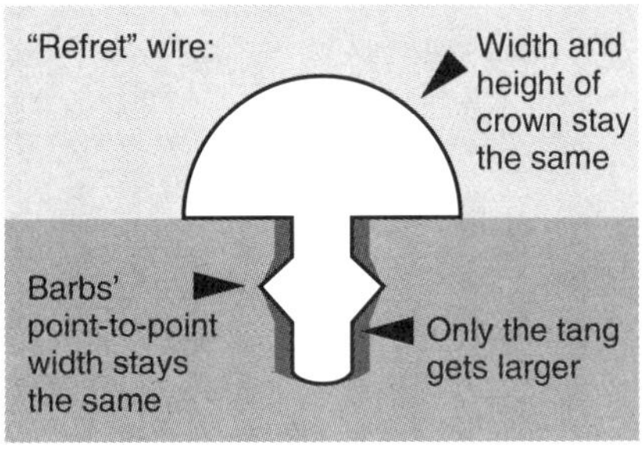

All of our standard fretwire has different sized tangs, but we can't mix and match it during refrets to control neck stiffness because the *crowns* all differ in width and height, too. That's why the specialized undersized and oversized-tang "refret" wire is so valuable—both the crown (head, or bead), and the point to point measurement of the barbs remain the same (meaning some barbs are smaller than others), while only the thickness of the tang changes. "Refret" wire comes in increments of .019", .020", .021", .022", .023", .024", and .025", and then skips to the largest, which is .028". The only drawback to using "refret" wire is that there is only one crown size available (.080" x .036"), so you've got to like the size. However, if you can do clean fret work, and not remove much metal during leveling, a .036" crown is more than adequate for most fretwork.

Although "replacement" wire is listed in thousandths increments, no fretwire could be that accurate. So don't worry if the fretwire you purchase doesn't measure exactly on the money—you'll figure it out after you've used it for a while.

FACTORS WHICH AFFECT FRETWIRE-TO-FRETSLOT CHOICE

When you're choosing a tang size to match a given slot, consider all of the following points:

- The *type* of fretboard. Maple, ebony, and rosewood are the most common. Brazilian rosewood is normally much harder than Indian rosewood, so don't just lump them together as "rosewoods."
- The condition of the fretboard wood. Dirt, decay, moisture, and poor care can make some fingerboards "rotten," pithy, and less able to hold a fret.
- Is the truss rod adjustable or not? How well does it work?
- Quality and strength of the neck wood.
- Is it new work or a refret? How many times has it been refretted? Each time you refret a guitar, the slot is less able to hold the same size fretwire, although to switch to the next size tang may be *too* much.

If you pull the original fretwire from a guitar, but don't have the right size to replace it,* don't do the fret job until you have the proper fretwire! *One of the biggest ways good necks are ruined is by being fretted with the wrong size fretwire.

MATCHING THE TANG TO THE SLOT

There are two ways to approach compression fretting: 1) To maintain stiffness and straightness in a good neck; 2) To add or return stiffness and straightness to a weak or fatigued neck. Using Martin guitars as an example, and understanding that most Martin fret slots measure .020"-.022", follow these compression principles with *any* fret job (but refret jobs in particular):

- For new work, begin with as close a match of the slot to the

Fret wire chart:

There are a number of different fretwires available—and we aren't the only supplier. But we offer a good selection of the best sizes for most fretwork, and you should be able to please most customers with our fretwire alone. Follow this chart:

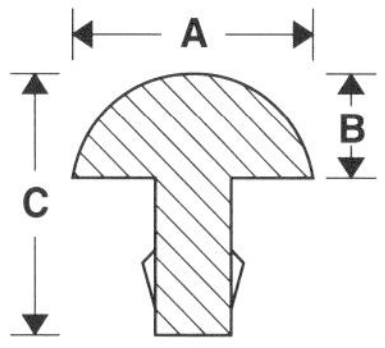

DIMENSIONS LISTED BELOW

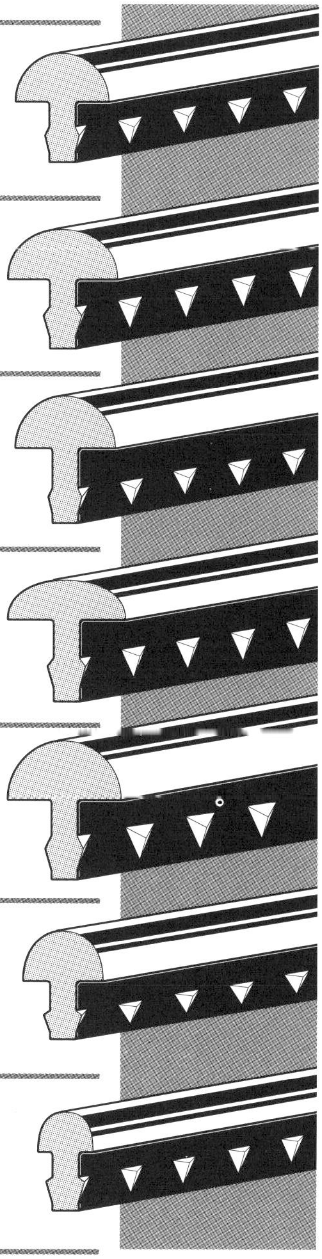

#148 Thin wire for electrics or acoustics (vintage Fender, Gibson, and Martin). A very popular wire, suitable for refretting Martins, Fenders, Guilds, Gibsons and most guitars requiring a "standard" medium size wire. This is a bit wider than the #147 banjo / small guitar wire.

A. Width above fingerboard .... **.085″**
B. Height above fingerboard .... **.041″**
C. Overall height .... **.100″**
Fret slot width required: .022″

#149 Standard wide frets (vintage "wide oval" Gibson). This "wide-oval" wire is similar to older Gibson "jumbo" fretwire, but is slightly taller. The small extra height permits the leveling of newly installed frets with plenty of metal remaining for a traditional jumbo feel.

A. Width above fingerboard ..... **.103″**
B. Height above fingerboard .. **.046″**
C. Overall height .... **.110″**
Fret slot width required: .022″

#141 Medium width and medium/tall height (Fender "Stevie Ray" size. A versatile size that's "in-between" medium fretwire and the larger electric guitar sizes. Somewhat narrower than #149 "wide" fretwire, it can be redressed without becoming too flat.

A. Width above fingerboard .... **.095″**
B. Height above fingerboard .. **.045″**
C. Overall height .... **.118″**
Fret slot width required: .022″

#146 Low/wide electric guitar. As wide as modern jumbo rock frets, but considerably lower in height. This is a good choice for partial refretting jobs (to match large frets that are worn or which have been filed down), or for players who prefer a lower fret height.

A. Width above fingerboard ..... **.106″**
B. Height above fingerboard .. **.036″**
C. Overall height .... **.110″**
Fret slot width required: .022″

#150 Extra tall and wide (modern heavy-metal wire). "Rock Jumbo" fretwire in the modern standard size. Plenty of height and width for rock, metal and blues styles, string bending and advanced tremolo work. Choose this wire for Kramer, Jackson, Ibanez and similar rock guitars.

A. Width above fingerboard ..... **.110″**
B. Height above fingerboard .. **.055″**
C. Overall height .... **.130″**
Fret slot width required: .022″

#147 Banjo wire. This is the standard fretwire used by modern banjo builders, and is only slightly smaller than pre-war Martin guitar wire. It has a bit more bulk than the smaller, flatter fretwire used on many banjos in the '20s and '30s.

A. Width above fingerboard .... **.078″**
B. Height above fingerboard .... **.041″**
C. Overall height .... **.100″**
Fret slot width required: .022″

#764 Mandolin wire. We have offered this wire for many years. It is more durable and comfortable than the small flat wire used on mandolins early in the century. Banjo purists sometimes choose this size for approximating old style banjo wire.

A. Width above fingerboard .... **.053″**
B. Height above fingerboard .. **.032″**
C. Overall height .... **.090″**
Fret slot width required: .022″

Medium width and tall: Stew-Mac #3391 Width above fingerboard: .092″. Height above fingerboard: .048″

"Refret" wire with oversize tangs. Our refret wire is available in tang width increments of .019″, .020″, .021″, .022″, .023″, .024″, .025″, and .028″. The crown (the portion above the fingerboard) measures .080″ wide and .036″ high.

"Bar" frets: No, this isn't the wire used for guitars which get hard use in bars and nightclubs. This old-style wire was used before the modern "T-fret" became popular in the '30s. We don't stock this wire, but it's available from Martin.

tang as possible. Test a piece, and if it holds, go with it. Use glue as a helper if you wish.

■ For refret work, we recommend replacement wire with a tang one size larger than the original fretwire you removed from ebony, and two sizes up for rosewood—but this is not a hard and fast rule by any means!

■ The "one size larger" is measured in half-thousandths, since tangs are manufactured in half-thousandth increments.

■ Don't expect to remove more than .010" to .020" of unwanted relief or upbow with oversize tangs alone. As often as not, you'll need to resurface the board as well.

■ Don't just start at the nut end (or the body end going toward the nut) and pound frets in all the way down the length of the fretboard. Instead, put in the 3rd, 5th, 7th, and 9th frets to get a feel for how the compression is affecting the neck's overall straightness and stiffness.

■ With Martin necks, or any neck without a truss rod—and even some with truss rods—you would normally see a backbow in the fretboard when the strings are removed. Under string tension the neck pulls straight, or into a slight upbow or "relief."

■ Always "test" the fretwire you plan on using. Try your first fret on the area over the body joint where compression isn't a factor, and don't use a whole fret—use a piece 1/2" long to get the feel of how it's holding.

Chart Of Fret Sizes And Shapes

Our fret chart (on the previous page) offers a selection of fretwire in sizes and shapes carefully chosen to work in the greatest number of fretting situations (both new and old work), and to satisfy most players. The first goal in selecting a fretwire is to satisfy the player's needs, and as long as the wire you choose keeps the integrity of the neck (or adds to it), any fretwire choice is fine. But—and this is very important—unless you keep a wide selection of fretwire in stock, you may have to custom-order it for certain jobs.

Bar Fretting

Bar fret jobs are not easy to do, so don't ruin a good instrument by experimenting. There's a good section on bar-fretting in the *Guitar Player Repair Guide.* On these pages are some quick bar fret pointers.

Bar frets are the best way to refret Martin instruments made before 1934 (the year Martin switched to modern T-frets). Other makers used bar fretwire, too; you see it often in turn-of-the-century instruments. Some shops fill bar fret slots with wood and recut for T-frets, but it's no longer considered historically acceptable to devalue a vintage instrument this way. Also, many players like the height and feel of bar frets—even more, they love the tone of a bar-fretted guitar. The heavy mass and tight fit stiffen a neck, which directs the strings' energy toward the soundbox.

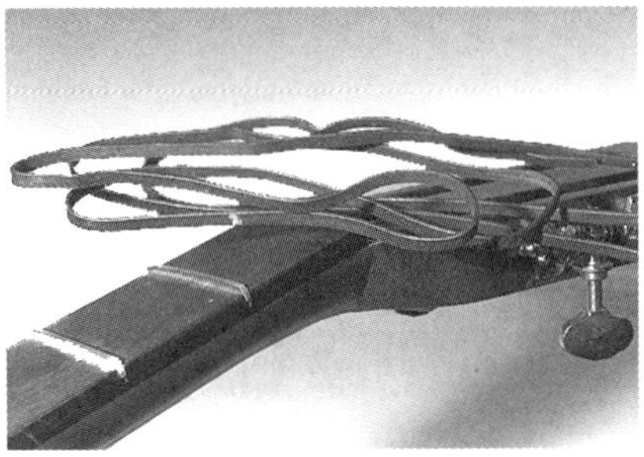

Be glad that new bar fretwire is available. When you ordered it in the 1960s it arrived looking like ribbon candy—what a mess!

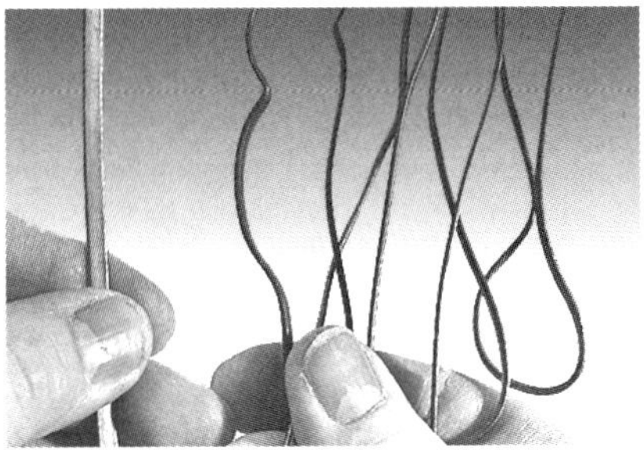

On the left is Martin's "new" bar fretwire. It's flat and true.

T. J. passed out* Bar Fret Basics *during his lecture/ demonstration on bar-style refretting at the 1993 ASIA Symposium in Amherst, Massachusetts. You can see T. J. in action on the live videotape of that lecture, "Masters of Repair." To me, T. J. is the "King of the Bar Fret Job." —Dan Erlewine

The new bar wire comes coiled sideways. A good way to straighten it is to run it through the FretBender "backwards"—a tip from T.J. Thompson.

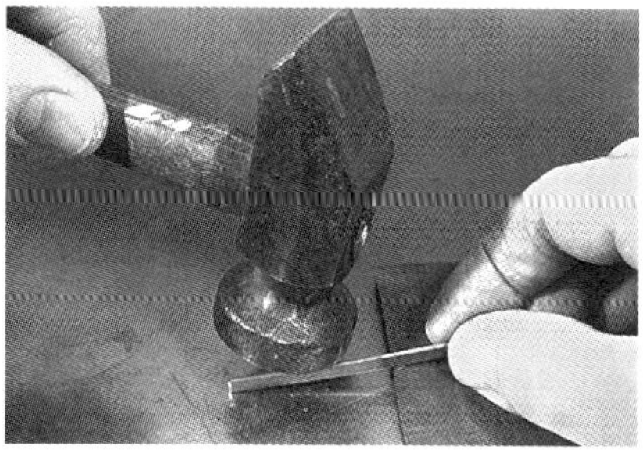

Bar wire is very hard, and difficult to bend to a fretboard radius with either the FretBender or by hand. To arch bar fretwire, stand the wire on edge, shimmed up by a block of hardwood, and hammer a radius into the wire.

T.J. taught us this neat trick for notching bar fretwire to overhang binding: Grab the wire with your fret nippers held vertically and place the face of the nippers against a steel "filing block". Then simply file the notch until the file contacts the block (as one stop) and the side of the nippers (as the other stop).

BAR FRET BASICS *BY T. J. THOMPSON*

Bar fret wire went out of fashion in the 1930s when steel neck reinforcement came into fashion, This important detail is often overlooked. It's incorrect to say that the early guitars had no neck reinforcement, because the frets keep the neck straight. If the frets are too loose, the neck bows forward, If the frets are too tight, the neck bows backwards.

Whether you're fretting a new guitar or refretting a vintage guitar, there are five (hundred) important factors to keep in mind. If you leave one out, or try to cut a corner, you'll be longing for your old familiar T-frets.

1 C. F. Martin & Co. sells two gauges of bar fretwire—.057" and .051"—by the pound in perfectly gauged rolls. They also have a third, lighter gauge wire. (.045").

2 Buy or make a selection of cutters which range from .002" smaller than the finest gauge wire you are using to .002" wider than the heaviest gauge. I used dental burrs ground to different diameters. The .002" (undersized) cutter will be used to cut the fret slots in the middle of the neck (maybe frets 4–8); the oversized cutter will be used over the extension where fret compression is undesirable.

3 Leave the fret wire about .050" above the level of the fingerboard. In other words, since the fret wire is .160" tall, cut your fret slot .110" deep. Don't forget to tap the fret wire flat, and to radius it to match the fingerboard.

4 Don't grind the fret ends off at a 45° angle, or the string will end up falling off the edge of the fret. The fret ends should be dressed with a very slight angle, almost perpendicular to the edge of the board. This makes dressing the frets an exciting challenge.

5 Dress the sides of the frets carefully with a three-corner file, taking your time. If this part of the job doesn't seem weird and like it's taking forever, you're probably doing it wrong. Sand and then steel wool each fret, making certain you knock off any sharp edges that would cause bleeding (just kidding!).

Good luck!

T. J. Thompson
Thompson Guitar Company

A GUIDE TO FRETTING TOOLS

Here are descriptions and photos of the tools used throughout the book, so that when you see them in use, you'll be familiar with them. Most of these tools are available in our catalog.

MEASURING TOOLS

Waverly precision straightedge set: Make *this* your starter set. The 15" edge is long enough to read most neck situations, the 8" is good for reading the tongue (or any shorter length of the board), and the 2" and 3" are excellent "fret rockers" to isolate individual fret problems. All four have a bevelled edge for accuracy.

Deluxe 24" stainless straightedge: Long enough to read any neck completely from end to end—including long scale basses. It's got a million other uses around the shop, too (for example, we use it in Lesson Four to scribe a long mark on the side of the fretboard binding).

Notched straightedge: This is the greatest tool ever, because with it you can read the fretboard while the frets are still in it! The notched straightedge is a typical brainstorm from Don MacRostie of our Stew-Mac "R & B" team. Don's a veteran luthier, woodworker, and machinist.

Luthier's dial caliper: Our Luthier's Dial Caliper has a clearance slot in one jaw which accepts the fret tang and lets you measure the height of any fretwire in moments. This is also a good quality stainless steel dial caliper. (Trade Secret: Don MacRostie grinds the *tip* of the jaws on his caliper to thin them for measuring the tang in *between* the barbs).

Radius gauge: Although they hardly need mentioning, radius gauges are a necessity for any fret work or set-up work—ours have eight radii and are white on one side and black on the other, so they're easy to read against light or dark fretboards.

LEVELING TOOLS FOR FINGERBOARDS & FRET TOPS

There are a variety of tools for leveling the tops of frets so that none is left higher or lower than its neighbor, and/or for leveling the wood surface of the fretboard before a fret job begins. Most tools you'll need are available commercially, although we do use a few tools which you'd have to make yourself. Some of these tools double for use on the fretboard as well as on the frets, and may be used before, during, or after a fret job.

Fret planes: These glass-bottomed tools (for flatness) are used to remove scratches from fret tops after the frets have been leveled, and/or to prepare the wood surfaces of fretboards. The spring-clips allow for rapid sandpaper changing. Long (13-1/2") and short (8") versions are available.

Radius sanding blocks: These blocks, faced with "Stikit" self-adhesive sandpaper, impart a perfect cylinder-shaped radius to the

1 Waverly Precision Straightedge Set. Finding high spots with the short "fret rocker" and marking them with a white pencil.

2 One edge is surface ground and bevelled for accuracy.

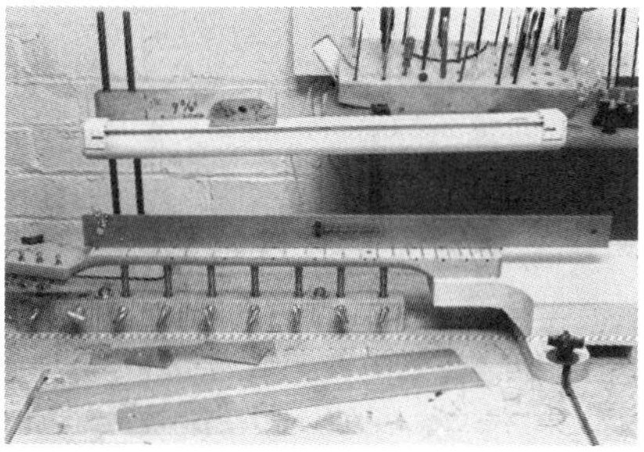

3 Deluxe 24" Stainless Straight Edge. The 24" spans the entire fretboard of a guitar or an electric bass.

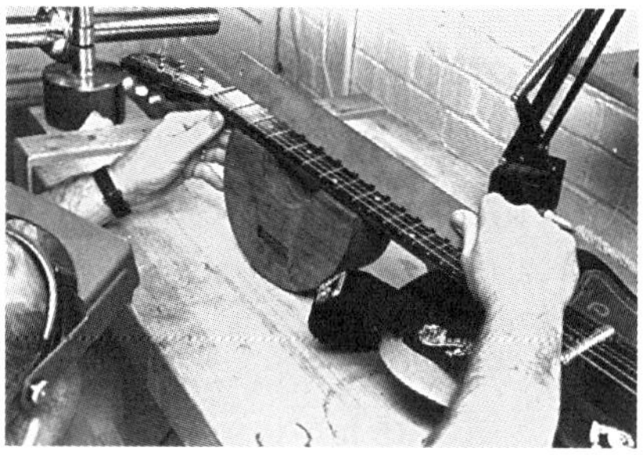

4 Notched Straightedge. Designed by Don MacRostie, the notched straightedge deserves a place next to the FretBender and Tang Nipper in the "Fretting Hall of Fame"...

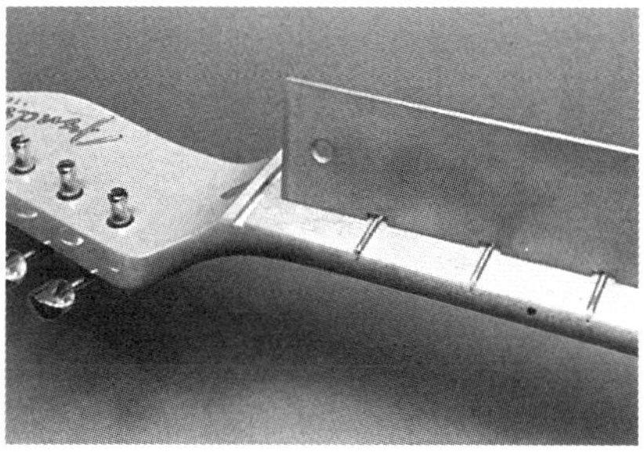

5 ...it reads the fret*board*—not the frets themselves!

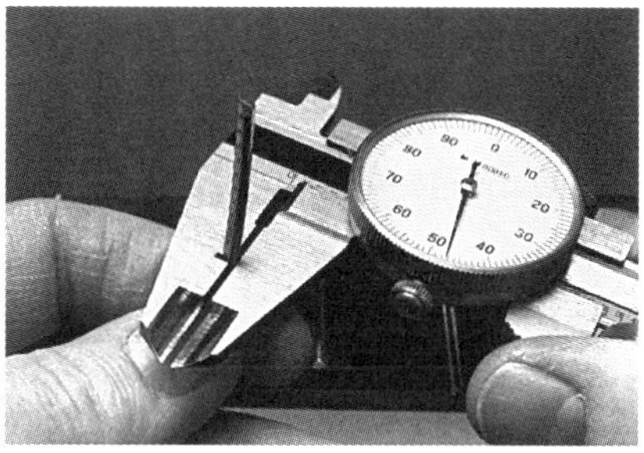

6 Our Luthier's Dial Caliper has a clearance slot in one jaw for measuring fret height.

7 Don MacRostie put a grinder to the *tip* of the jaws on his caliper to thin them for measuring the tang in *between* the barbs.

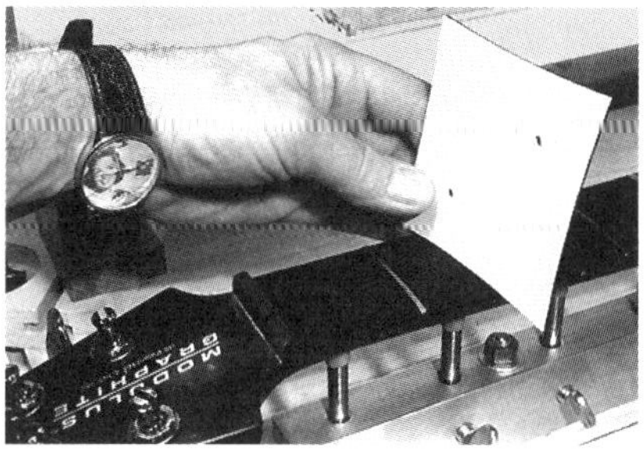

8 Our Radius Gauges are a necessity for any fretwork—white on one side, and black on the other, they're easy to read against light or dark fretboards.

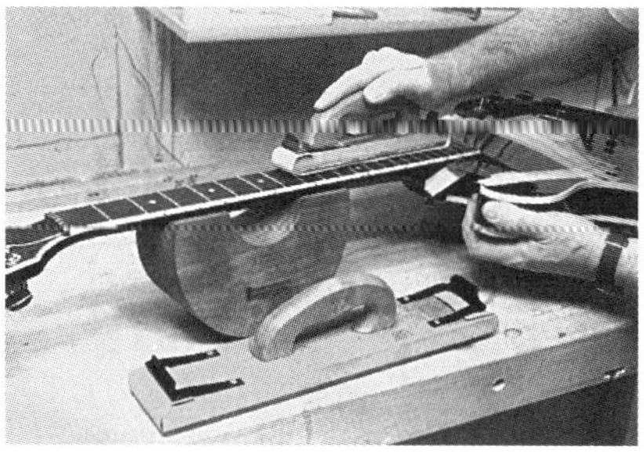

9 The glass-bottomed "Fret Planes" hold the sandpaper with quick-change spring clips, and are a relatively inexpensive leveling tool (when compared to our Diamond Leveler).

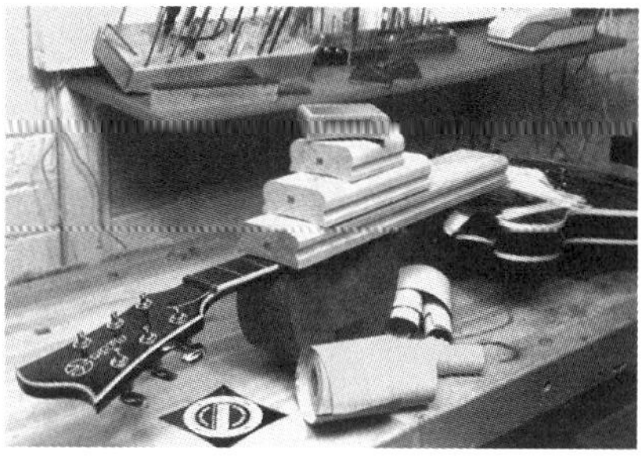

10 Available in wood, or 'Deluxe' cast-resin (top of the pile), Radius Sanding Blocks create—or control—the radius of any fretboard.

11 Our wood blocks are longer than the Deluxe blocks. This is handy in situations where you want to be contacting a longer area of the fretboard at once...

12 ...the Deluxe blocks will do the same fret-leveling job as the wooden ones, however (except for the first few frets of an electric bass)...

13 Radius blocks powder the tops of the frets at once!

fretboard. We offer two versions: 1) GSS blocks made from maple; 2) A Deluxe set of cast resin blocks is available, as a set only, in 3" lengths. The advantages and disadvantages of each are...

GSS wooden blocks: At 4" and 8" they're longer than the Deluxe set, so they can level frets on a long neck bass easier. And on guitar necks, they'll span more fretboard length than the shorter Deluxe blocks (when contacting more of the surface is desirable). These blocks are less expensive, and available individually.

The wood blocks must have protection on the wood surface to keep from being marred by the metal frets if you use them as clamping cauls (thin .018" pickguard plastic, or stainless steel, double-stick taped to the face of the blocks allows them to be used as cauls).

Generally speaking, we use the longer 8" block—preferring to rest on more surface than with either the 4" (wooden) or 3" Deluxe blocks. In fact, you can wrap the 8" block with a shorter length of sandpaper to level just one area.

Deluxe blocks: These 3" long blocks were originally designed to be used on the fretboard—not the frets. They rough in the shape during the preparation stage by creating or changing a radius, so the ability to sit on top of the frets wasn't a concern in their design. They make good fret levelers though, except that they barely span the first few frets of a 34" scale electric bass.

They won't warp, and are hard enough to be used as cauls for clamping frets in place. Even so, we recommend protecting the face of the blocks if you do intend to use them as cauls. The deluxe blocks aren't available individually.

Waverly fret levelers: The fret levelers have a custom made tooth with an exaggerated long angle and a single cut. Used correctly, they don't leave harsh "chatter" marks as most files do, but you need to sand or stone the fret tops after leveling them with a file. The 3" and 6" lengths are good for spot filing in localized areas, or for leveling high spots along the full length of the fretboard in preparation for sanding tools (radius blocks and sandpaper, fret planes, etc.).

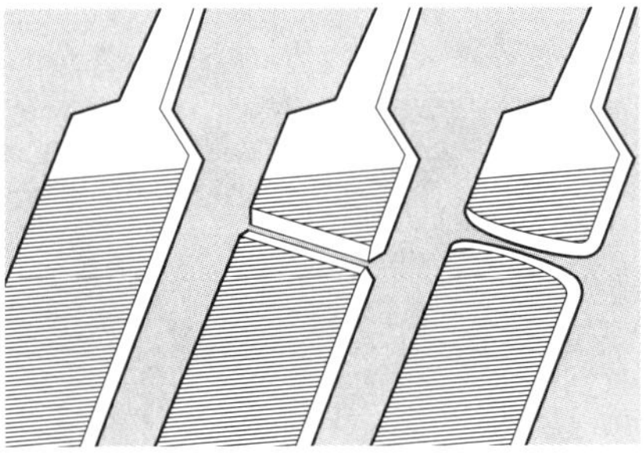

10" or 12" smooth mill file: You'll see this homemade leveling file in several of the chapters—it's never the *only* tool being used, but just one of them. Waverly doesn't make this one because it's hard for file manufacturers to guarantee a consistant supply of longer files which are flat from end-to-end. Take your straightedge to the hardware store and shop for yourself—eventually you'll find one which is flat enough for fret leveling. Cut off the tang and the tip and glue a wooden handle to it. A 12" smooth mill file is long enough to accurately level fret tops (although Dan's diamond leveler is better). If you can't find a flat 12" file, shop for a good 10" one.

Waverly fingerboard leveler: This double cut 6" file removes ebony, rosewood, and pearl with ease during fretboard leveling, and leaves hardly a mark! Use it to smooth inlays or remove stubborn high spots. With its strong, rough cut, this file is also

14 And the Deluxe blocks make great gluing cauls.

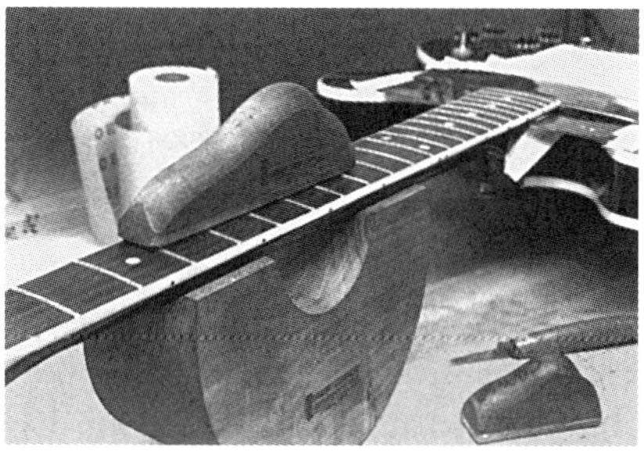
15 Waverly 3" and 6" Fret Levelers: just because you have both of these leveling files...

16 ...doesn't mean you won't want a homemade 10" or 12" fret leveler...

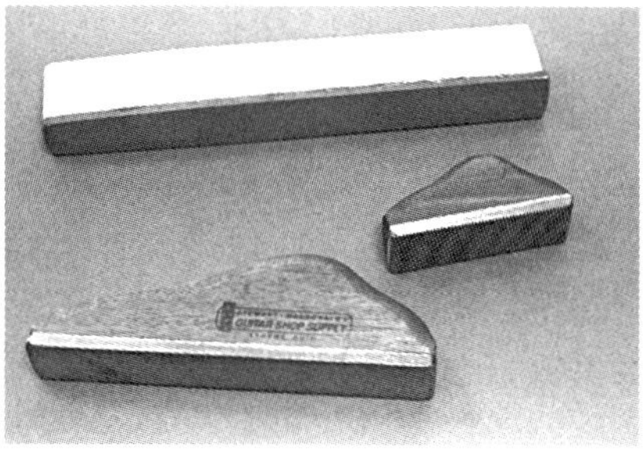
17 ...the homemade leveler doesn't have the long-angle teeth that the Waverly's do, however (and you can almost see that in this photo!)

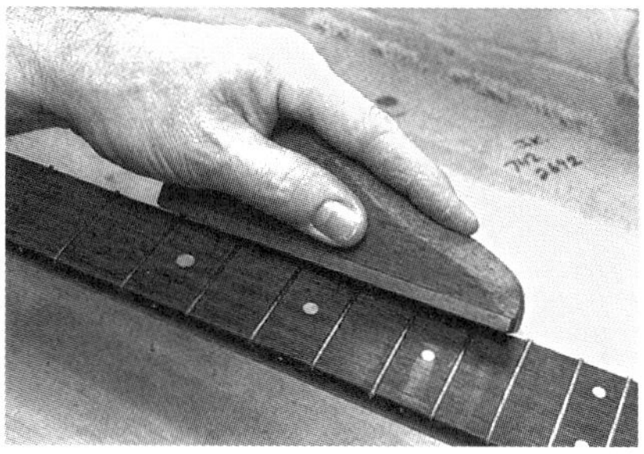
18 The 6" fret leveler is great for bevelling the fret ends, too.

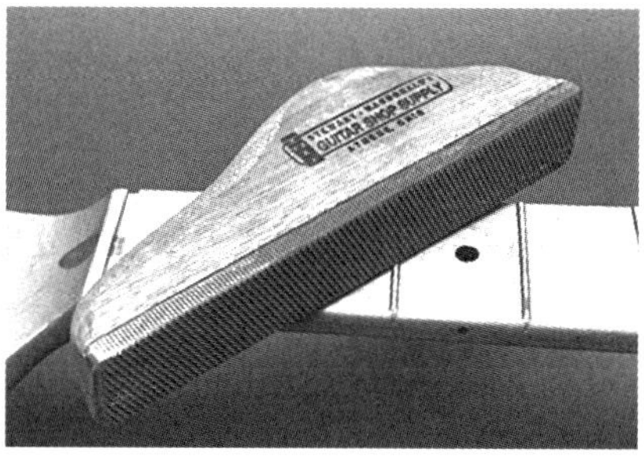
19 Waverly 6" Fingerboard Leveler: the coarse cut of this file can trim pearl inlays flush to the fretboard in seconds—but it doesn't leave scratches.

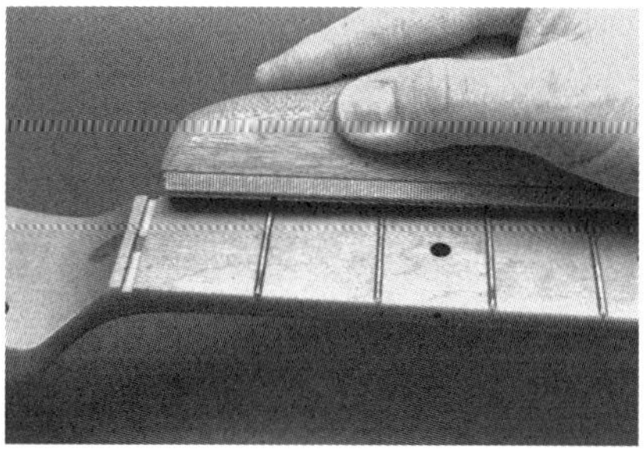
20 It's also great for "roughing-in" the fret end bevel and the ends of the fret tang on new fretwork (to prepare the ends for smoothing with the Waverly Fret Levelers).

21 The diamond leveler: this is for professional use—a lifetime investment for the serious "fretmeister."

22 It powders the fret tops perfectly.

23 Whetstone: C.F. Martin fret specialist Carl Frantz uses his whetstone on the narrow edge.

24 Fret slotting saw: you can use the standard fret slotting saw to deepen or clean existing slots, but it's more often used to *cut* fret slots...

great for roughing-off the fret tang ends protruding from the fret slots, and for the initial bevelling of the fret ends after a fret job. Switch to the 6" fret leveler to finish the bevelling and smooth things out.

Diamond leveling "file": This is for leveling the tops of frets after a fret job or during a fret dressing. It replaces any flat leveling tools (files, files wrapped with sandpaper, sanding blocks, and the fret planes) for the serious professional. 24" long, it will rest on all the frets at once—even on long-scale electric bass necks—and will level uniformly from end to end, with no question of error. If you like a shorter leveler you can cut this quite easily with a hacksaw. We cut one into two shorter lengths, 16" and 8", for leveling mandolins and for spot-leveling.

The diamond leveler was still in the R & D stage as this book was nearing its deadline. The idea of a long flat tool for leveling the fretboard is nothing new, but try finding a source for a 24" x 2" x 1" piece of steel that:
- ***is lightweight enough to handle easily***
- ***is surface ground on two edges***
- ***has one edge coated with diamond dust***

That's hard to find! We think it's too good a tool to go unmentioned; check your latest Guitar Shop Supply catalog for availability.

Even diamonds leave a few marks which need to be removed. By using Stikit sandpaper, you can convert the ground diamond edge to a long, flat sander for removing any leveling marks from frets, or for flattening the wood surface of any fingerboard before a refret.

Whetstone: A good flat whetstone, 8" or longer, makes a good inexpensive "fret-hone," or leveler. An excellent one, preferred by the C.F. Martin company, is the Crystolon "Fine" Benchstone—FJB8. The whetstone is good for removing marks from frets which are already leveled (we think it's a little short, and its cut too mild, for removing too much excess metal quickly). As Martin uses it in controlled situations on level, professional factory fret jobs, it's excellent. During the dressing or rounding stage, you need to round off the "flats" created by the stone.

Flat chunk of wood: If you have access to a jointer, or can flatten a length of wood with hand tools, the edge of a hardwood board faced with Stikit sandpaper makes a good fret or fretboard leveler. Use a 1" wide piece slightly longer than the fretboard, and you'll have a homemade version of our Diamond Leveler.

TOOLS FOR CUTTING, CLEANING OR ENLARGING THE FRET SLOT

Fret slotting saw: This saw, with its .022" blade, is intended to be used for slotting a fretboard for the first time. It also works well for sawing out existing slots to a greater depth, or to remove residue, if you need a .022" slot. For thinner slots use the Blitz Saw.

Blitz saw: This a smaller version of the fret slotting saw. It's still a "backsaw," with a ridge of support along one edge of the blade. It comes with interchangeable blades in six sizes: **.015", .020", .024", .029", .032", and .040".** Check out the customized Blitz Saw used throughout this book.

Dremel tool: The main use of these miniature routers in fretwork is to clean glue and other residue out of the fret slots, to make room for the fret tang during refrets. You'll see it used here to slightly enlarge the slots on the fretboard extension of acoustic guitars so that the frets will hammer in easily. We also use it to re-inlay pearl fret markers removed during the fretboard leveling in

25 …whereas the Blitz Saw, with its many (smaller) blades, is excellent for sizing and cleaning a variety of fret slot sizes.

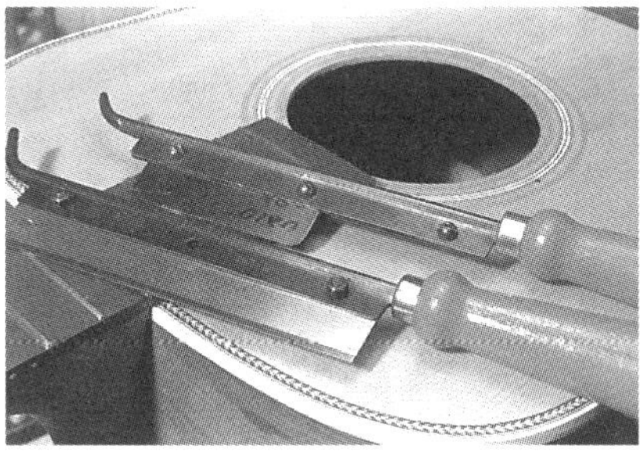

26 You'll see many adaptations of the Blitz sawblades throughout this book!

27 Dremel tool bits: when widening fret slots with the Dremel tool, we often custom-grind our bits to make them smaller by pressing the bit (under power) against a whetstone…

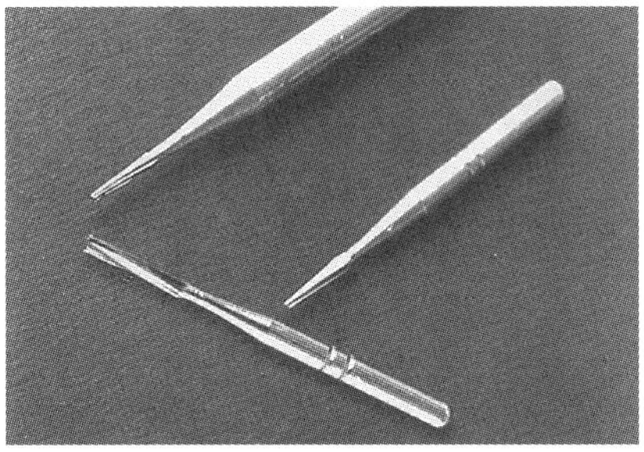

28 If you're doing the "Teeter-Style" fret job, you want the slots wide, so grinding down the bit isn't necessary. Most Dremel-fretters mix and match our long-shanked bits with the shorter shanked bits used by dentists.

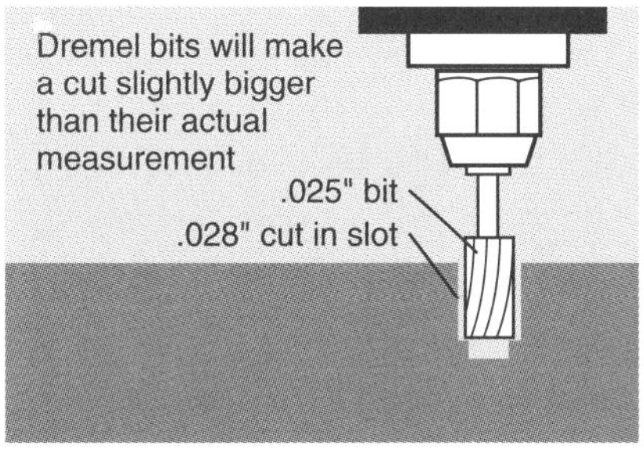

29 Any Dremel tool will widen a fret slot somewhat bigger than the size of the bit, so experiment by cutting fret slots in scrap and widening them.

30 The leading edge of your Dremel tool base should be 3/8" away from the center of the bit if you want to use it for fret slots, because you want the base to be well supported on the fretboard as the cutter bit enters the slot.

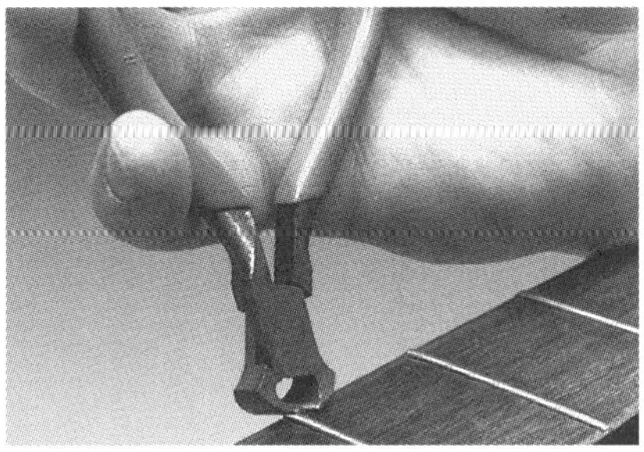

31 Fret pullers: although they *are* miniature end-nippers, don't cut anything with your pullers…

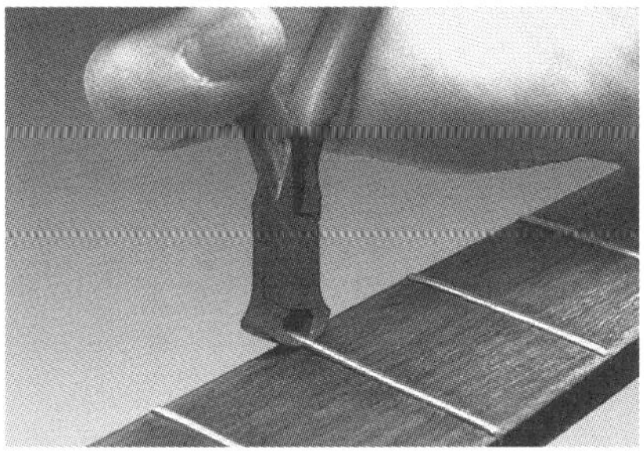

32 …use them only to get under the fret…

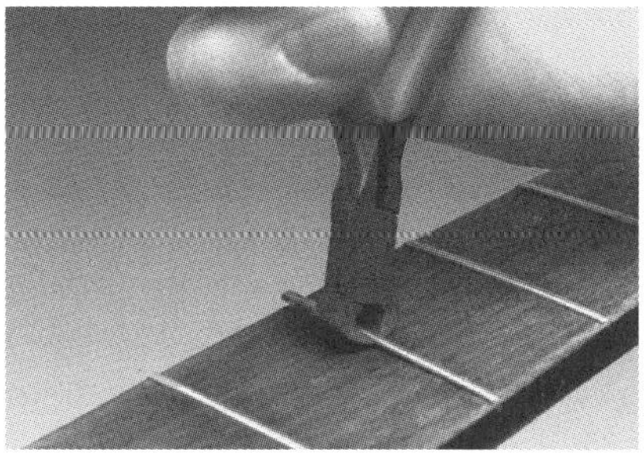

33 thru 36 …and "walk" the fret out across the board.

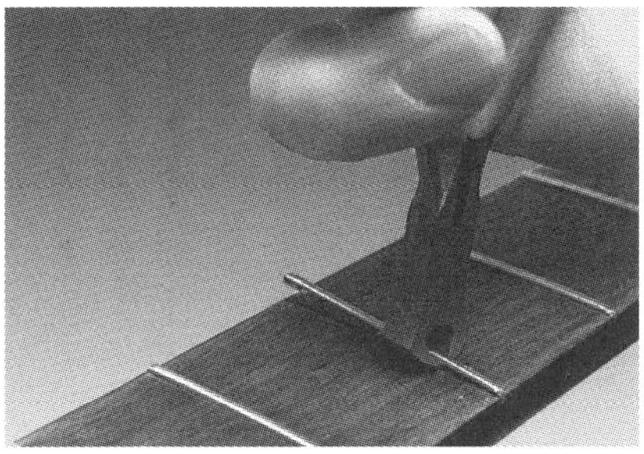

34

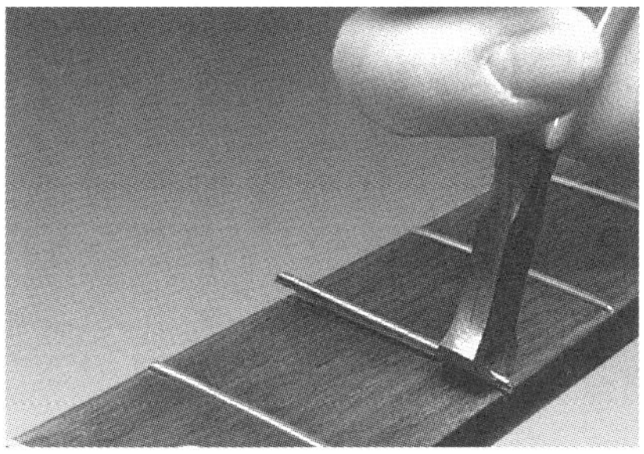

35

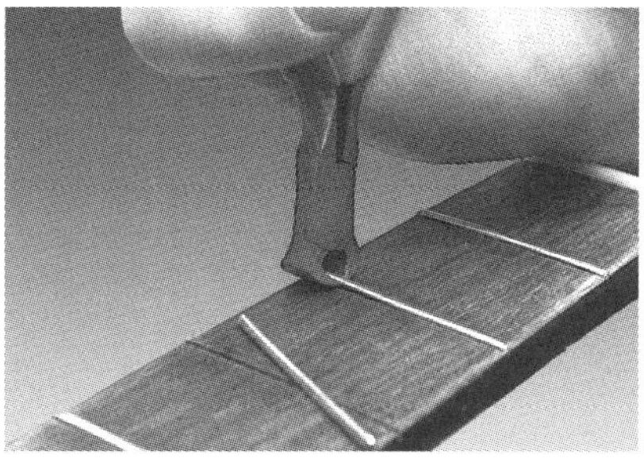

36

Lesson Four. You can do a lot of fret jobs without a Dremel tool, but sooner or later you'll have to get one, especially for the "Teeter Method" of fretting (see page 5).

Another big use for the Dremel tool is to widen the slot just enough to match a fret tang which is slightly larger than the normal .020" to .022". In other words, if you have a fretwire with a tang thickness of .024" (like our No. 3391 wire), you might not want to pound that into a .020"-.022" slot, because it could backbow the neck. In this case you use the Dremel tool to match the slot to the tang.

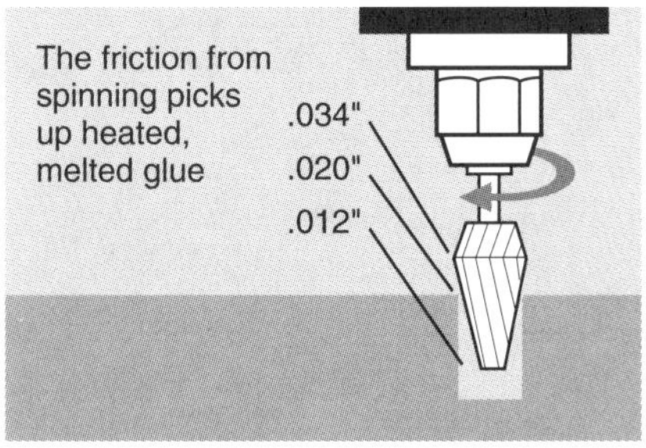

Dremel cutting bits: For fret slot widening or cleaning, our No. 1187 (1/32" cut), and No. 1189 (tapering from .034" to .010" in a .150" length) bits will usually do, but not exactly as they come out of the box. You'll need to touch the No. 1187 straight-fluted cutter against a diamond-stone or whetstone, to bring the cutter down from .031" close to the size you want. The No. 1187 runs out of teeth at about .022" or .023", so that's as small as you can get.

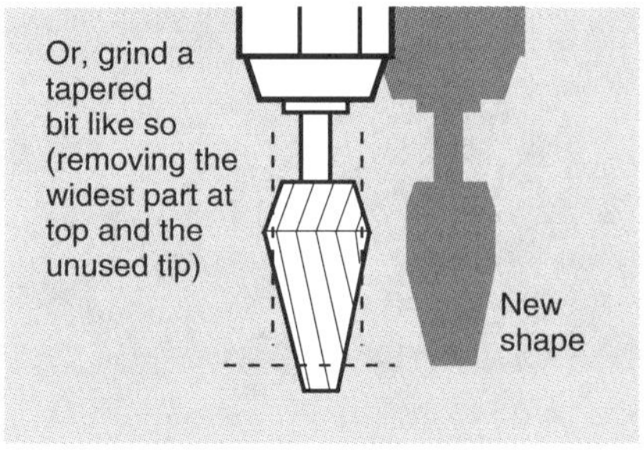

The tapered No. 1189 bit can be used from the small end up to .020" (upper drawing, right) without widening the slot, while still heating, pulling, and removing glue and residue. Or, it can be reground as in the lower drawing.

FRET INSTALLATION AND REMOVAL TOOLS

Many tools used in this book (regardless of whether we have them in our catalog) are common to any woodworking or guitar repair shop and aren't special to fret work. Such items as Titebond and hide glue, bar clamps, neck vises, etc. get no mention here. However, there are a bunch of tools that you should know about before starting:

Fret pullers: These are actually miniature "nippers," but don't nip with them! Their reground edges can't take the pressure. Use them solely for getting under frets easily and pulling them out for a refret. Since the jaws aren't very wide (1/2" vs. 1-1/8") you can get under frets on a radiused fretboard easily. Start on the edge of the fretboard, under the first 1/4" of fret; once you get under the fret the face of the jaws holds the wood down as the shape of the jaw pulls out the fret. Walk the nippers from one side to the other and the fret will come out easily.

Most of us use a soldering iron to heat the frets before removal, and a steel guard to protect the fretboard. This heat drives oils out of the surrounding wood to lubricate the fret removal, as well as to release any glue used in previous fretting.

Fret nippers: This larger version of the fret puller is a pair of end-nippers carefully ground by Waverly to cut fretwire without crushing it. We use these for pulling frets, too (often, in conjunction with the smaller Fret Puller). The Fret Nippers will last quite a while if you only use them for cutting frets (no guitar strings). In a busy shop, however, this is a tool which needs to be replaced from time to time.

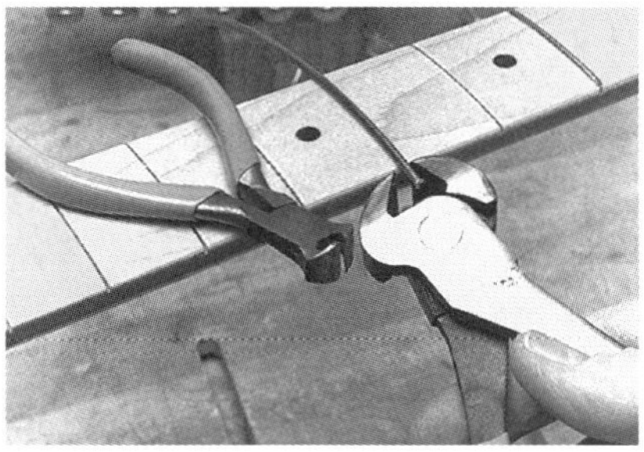

37 Fret nippers: unlike their little brother, these *are* big enough to handle cutting frets (but don't use them on anything but fretwire!).

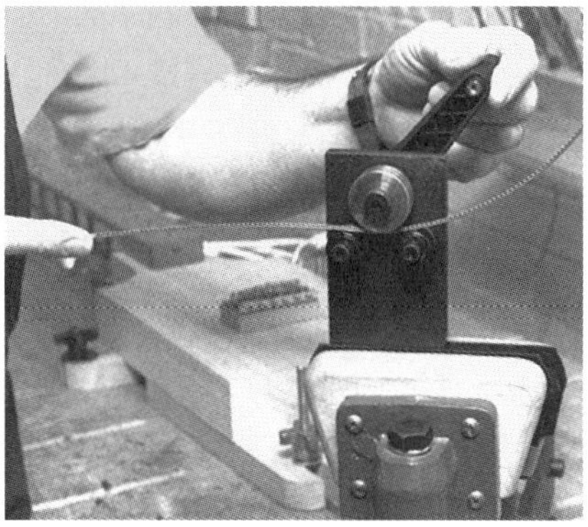

38 The FretBender is a joy to use…

39 …and it's adjustable for any radius.

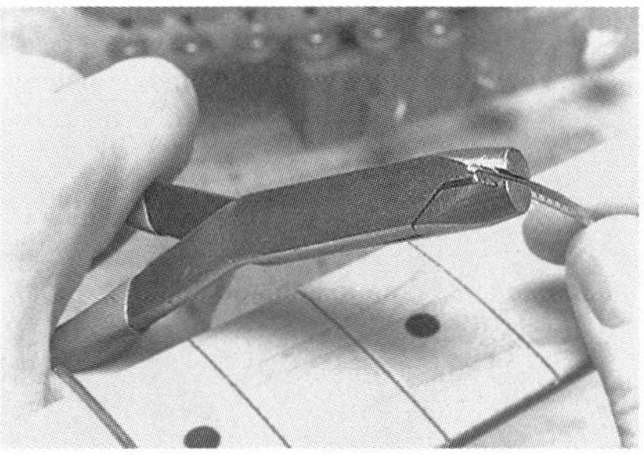

40 Fret bending pliers: even with a FretBender we still use the "old-fashioned" method of bending frets.

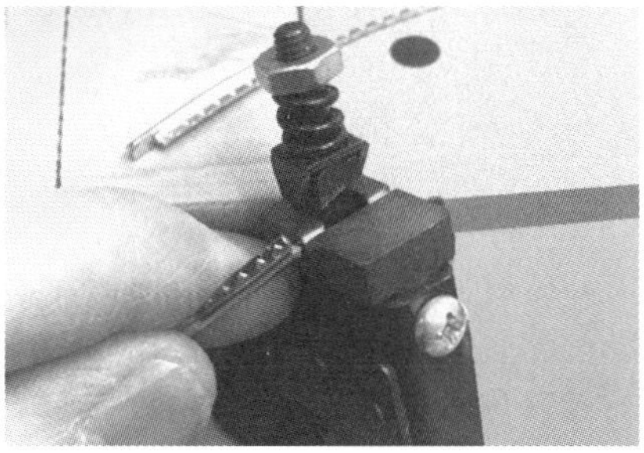

41 The fret tang nipper is the only tool as cool as the FretBender—cutting a clean notch for overhanging binding…

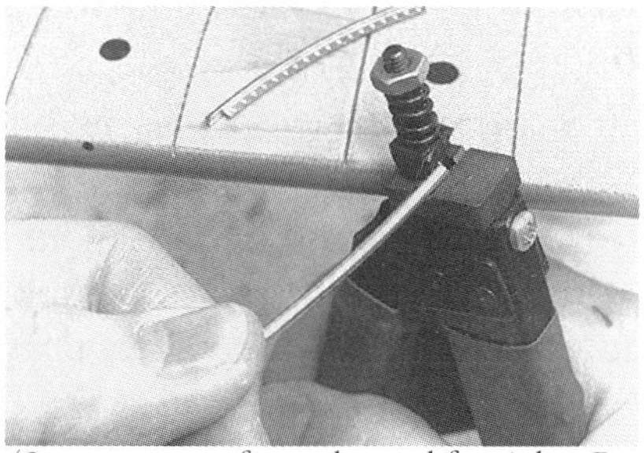

42 …or even for unbound fret jobs. By trimming the tang to length before fretting, the crown overhang clips off easily after the fret is installed.

43 Fretting arbor: if you have a drill press, arbor press, or milling machine, these steel fret pressers are tremendous…

44 …for pressing in frets evenly and accurately. We don't use the arbor press in any of the lessons (although we do some pressing with "Jaws" in Lesson Five).

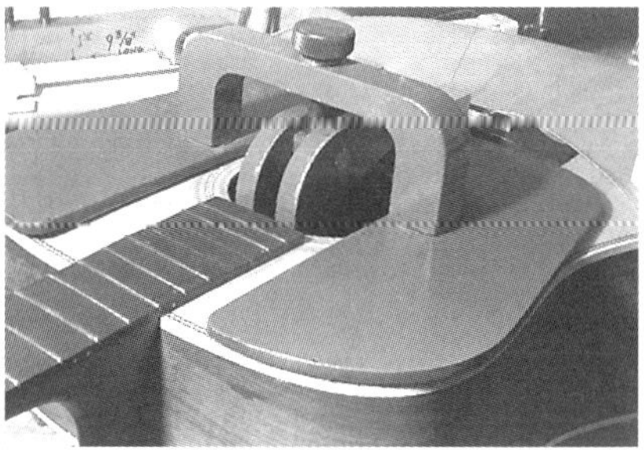

45 The Fret Buck reaches through the soundhole and supports the fretboard extension while you hammer in the frets.

46 Another "tool" in use at the Taylor Guitar factory is a 25 lb. bag of buckshot, and we use it too. Dan is wearing ear protection—good advice if you do many fret jobs (and would like to keep your hearing).

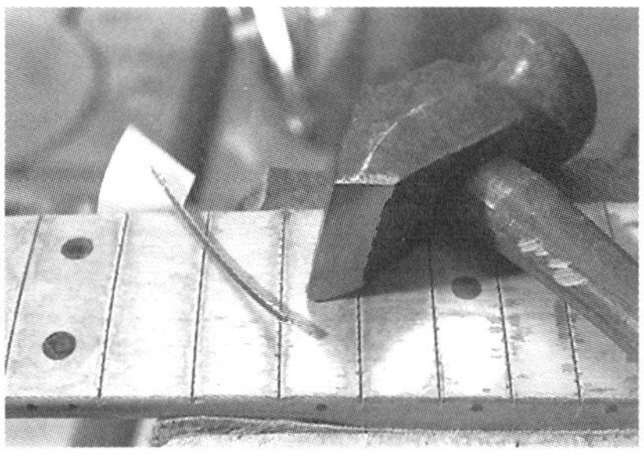

47 This is Dan's version of Martin's "chasing hammer"—it's a "flea market" brand cobbler's hammer with its back ground to a sharp point…

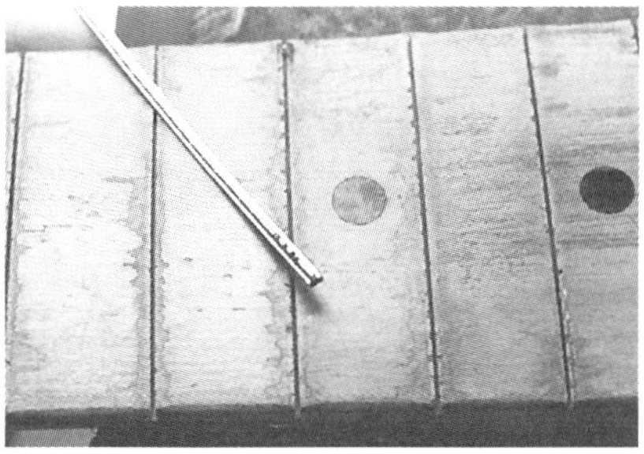

48 …for denting and "mushrooming" the bottom of the tang to oversize it when a fret won't hold.

FretBender: This is a tool professionals really appreciate! You can adjust the roller wheels from straight to any radius in seconds, and the curve put into a fretwire is perfect—hard to duplicate by hand.

Fret bending pliers: These are ground to the shape of a fret—a "crown" in the top jaw and a "tang-slot" in the bottom. Ordinary pliers tend to slip on frets and ding them up. Even if you own a FretBender you'll still want bending pliers for individual pieces and custom adjustments (the FretBender doesn't roll wire shorter than 4" or 6" too easily).

Fret tang nipper: The Tang Nipper, like the FretBender, has been much appreciated by professionals. It cuts the notch in the fret tang, which allows the fret to overhang the binding on bound-fingerboard guitars.

Fretting arbor press: These fret presses fit into your drill press chuck, converting it to an arbor press of sorts. This is an easy way to install frets on any intrument that you can get under (or onto) your drill press. We don't use it in this book, but we may in a future edition! To use a fret press correctly you must have a good feel for the fit of the fret tang to the fret slot. There are a several other pressing tools (homemade) in the "neck-jig" and "specialty tools" section.

Fret buck: This cast iron tool is lined with padding to protect a guitar's finish as it rests on the guitar's shoulders. It reaches through the soundhole to give tremendous support to the fretboard extension ("tongue") as you hammer in the frets. Designed by Bob Taylor of Taylor Guitars, it's in constant use at their factory. No other support method compares! One technique for fretting the fretboard extension of acoustic guitars (especially delicate vintage guitars) has been to enlarge the slots with a Dremel tool so they'll accept the fretwire more easily. With the Fret Buck this isn't necessary, and the frets can be hammered in with ease.

We now install it *before* fretting any acoustic guitar because of the rigidity it adds to the entire job—even out on the neck. It absorbs the energy from hammer blows, cuts down on noise, and helps the frets go in—and stay down—better.

Speaking of "fretting noise," that's no joke—fretting is loud! We got the idea from Elderly Instruments' repairman Joe Konkoly to wear ear protection when fretting—the hammer blows and Dremel tools are rough on the ear drums... What did you say?

Hammers: brass/nylon, dead blow, etc... You'll see several hammers used in the lessons, and they all work well. For a single choice, use either the "Dead-blow," or the "Brass/Nylon" hammer. They both work well, and there's less chance of damaging the fret or the board with them if you slip. The Brass hammer can be used for other jobs around the shop, but the Dead-Blow has a little more ooomph! Get 'em both.

Another hammer (shown in Lesson Four) is an antique cobbler's hammer that belongs to Dan: "It's really no *better* than the others, although it is a little heavier, and I like the weight. And it just looks cool—sort of like the 'chasing hammers' Martin uses. The 'claw' part of it is sharpened for tapping the underside of the tang to 'mushroom' or enlarge it when the wire isn't quite holding down

49 Fretting hammers, from left to right: 1) homemade brass, 2) the old "rawhide" hammer—once popular but never very good; 3) the Deadblow shot-filled fretting hammer; 4) cobbler's hammer; 5) Brass/nylon combo.

50 Martin's "chasing" hammer

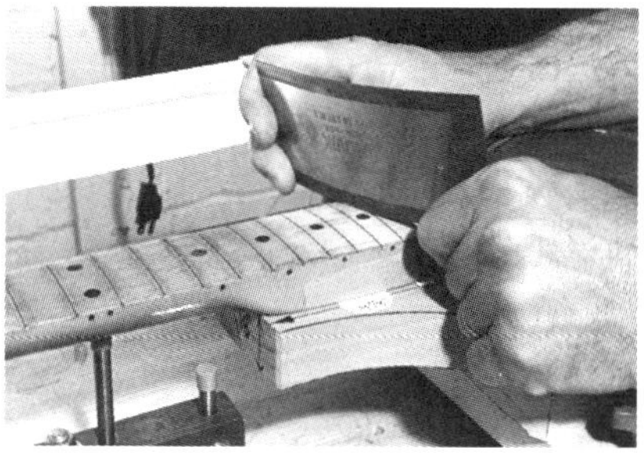

51 For many of us the scraper plays a big role in fretwork—the Sandvik, with its specially treated edge, is superior to most.

52 Fret end shaper and de-burring file: actually this is the same as our 1/8" Fender nut-seating file…

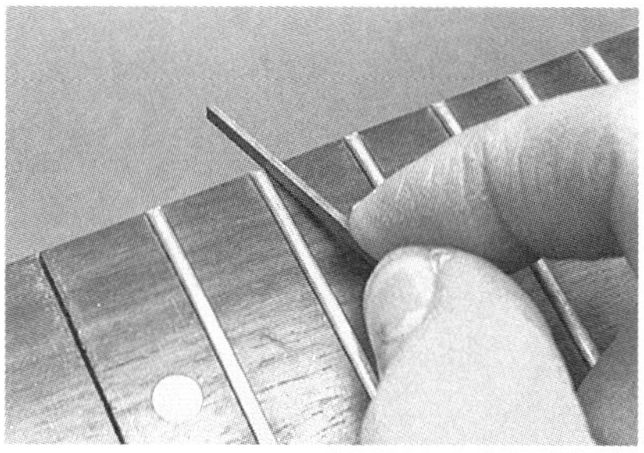

53 …it's just perfect for this job too.

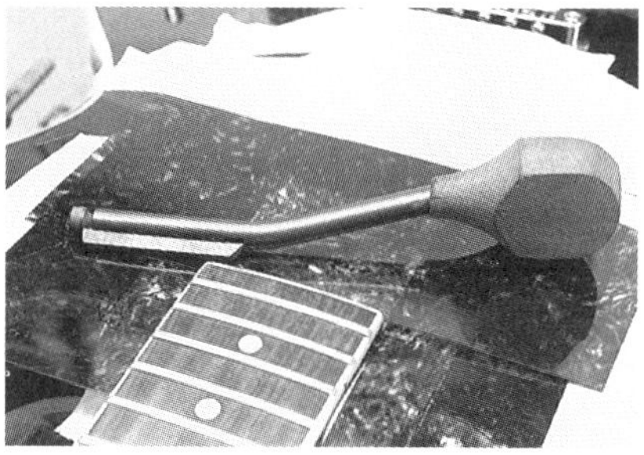

54 Waverly offset handle file: the Waverly 'Three-in-One' rounding file has an offset which keeps the operator's knuckles from hitting the soundboard…

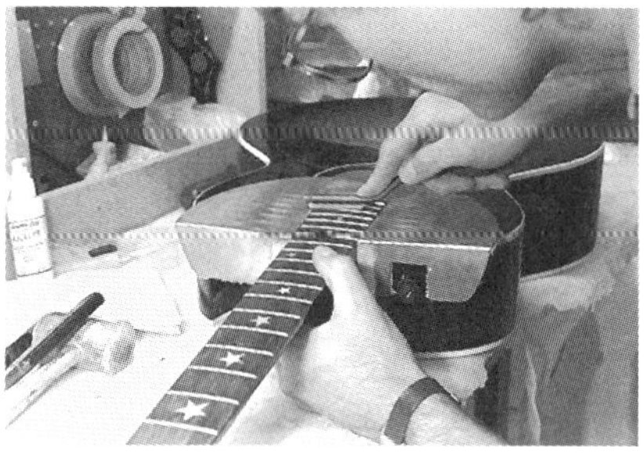

55 …as Gibson Montana's Eric Lang shows us here.

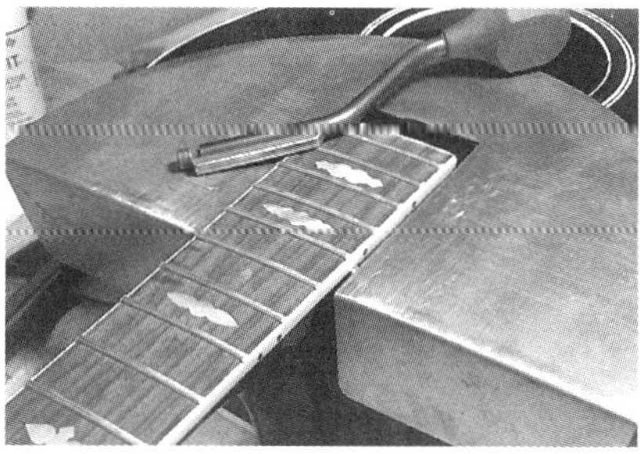

56 How's this for a deluxe top protector? Solid brass, it keeps chips off the guitar's face and protects against a possible slip.

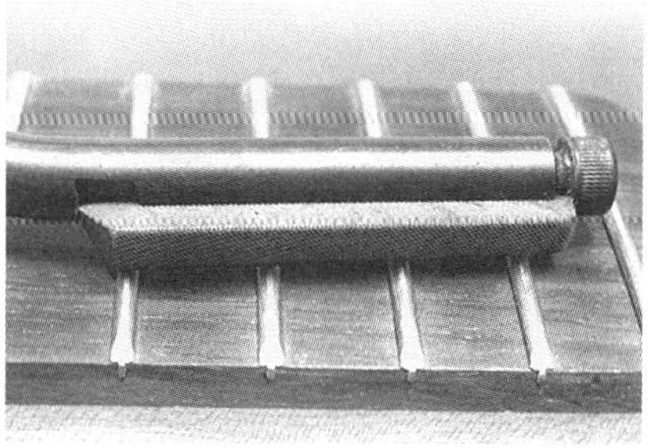

57 Here's a "Trade Secret": Grind a short piece of 3-corner file (large or small—this is the large) so that it fits the Waverly handle—then you'll have a Waverly 'Four-in-One' file!

58 The Waverly 3-Corner file is a small delicate version of an old standby…

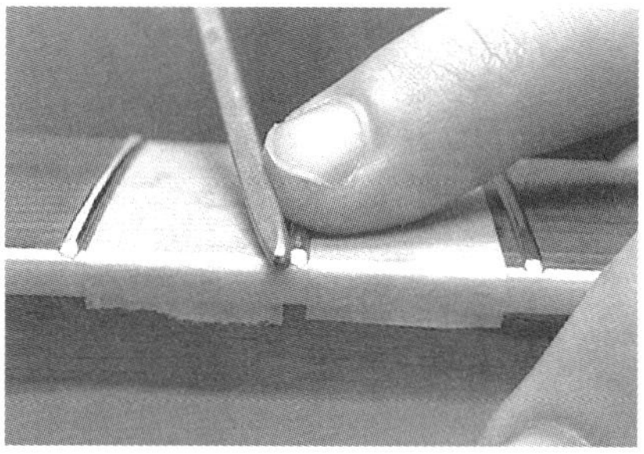

59 …it's good for final-rounding and "kissing off" the last of a flat fret top, and especially for shaping ends (you can get in close with it).

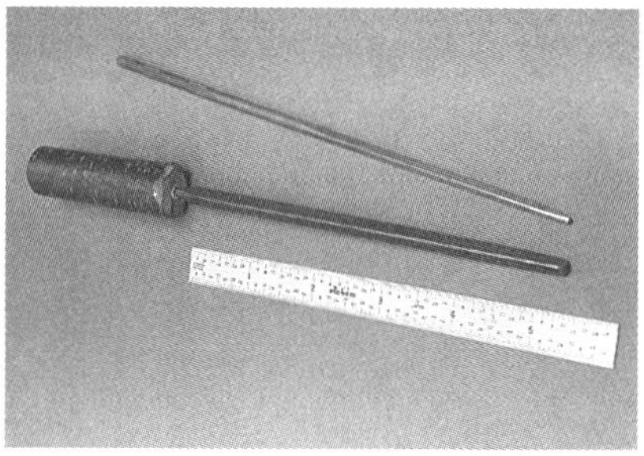

60 Waverly's large size 3-Corner File next to the small one for comparison

well enough. I also use a hammer with a solid brass head, which I made from a 4" x 1" length of brass bar-stock. It has a 3/8" brass shank threaded into it and a turned maple handle—it's great. I also like a mid-sized ball peen hammer, with a 3-1/8" long x 1" diameter head."

Scraper: A simple steel cabinet scraper is a very important fretboard leveling tool. You can use it to level individual high spots in seconds, or working across the fretboard width you can straighten the entire fingerboard, smoothing in the "flats" created with other levelers such as files or sanding tools.

Fret Rounding Tools—for use after the frets have been installed and leveled

After the fret tops are leveled—during a fret dressing or an entire refret—you must finish the job by rounding them to center, and shaping the fret ends along the fretboard edge. Here are the tools we use in the book.

Fret end file: Actually this is our 1/8" Fender "nut-seating" file. It just happens to be perfect for cleaning the bevel on fret ends, removing fret end burr, and for a certain amount of fret end shaping too.

Waverly 'Three-in-One' rounding file: This file has an offset handle which keeps the operator's knuckles from hitting the soundboard. It's "Three-in-One" because it comes with three file sizes, for thin, medium, and jumbo width wires. (Trade Secret: Dan took a length of a standard large-sized 3-corner file and adapted it to the Waverly handle.)

Waverly 3-corner file: A small thin triangle file that's great for the final rounding of flat fret tops, and for shaping and rounding the fret ends. The edges and "nose" of the file have been carefully ground to make them safe.

3-Corner file: This is the big brother to our smaller Waverly 3-Corner File. The smaller Waverly is for light, final shaping of fret ends or fret tops, but this larger 6" version hogs metal off in a hurry. It's the first file that most us learned to dress with, and we all still use it, along with the others.

Double-edge fret files: These are the toothed files made for rounding fret tops left flat after leveling. For years these toothed-edge rounding files were the only kid on the block. If you grew tired of dressing with a 3-Corner file, you could choose from a variety of toothed-edge rounding files in different widths, sizes, and shapes—all "double-edge"—with a small and large cut. They remove metal faster than the diamond files, and as fast (perhaps faster) as the large 3-corner file while rounding the fret from both sides to center. You must clean them often, because when they become clogged with metal they make scratches in the fret that are difficult (sometimes impossible) to remove. Most serious fretters have all the rounding files they can get their hands on, *plus* the Waverly diamond files. If you want to start with just one rounding file, get the diamond file.

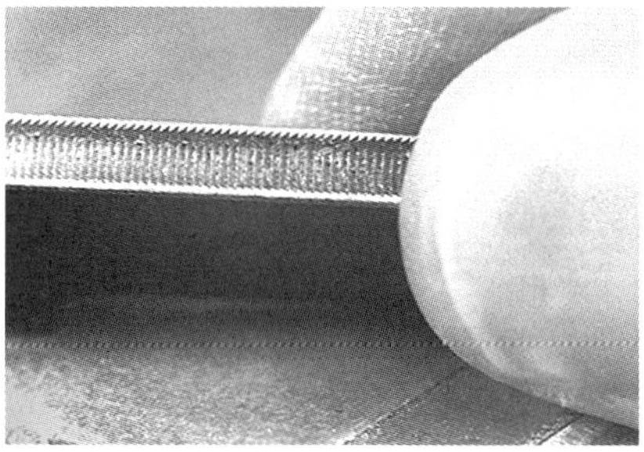

61 Most "rounding" fret files have teeth cut into a radiused blank for shaping the fret tops…

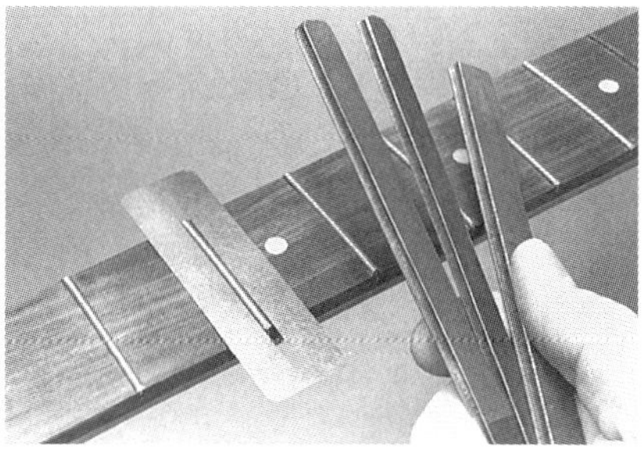

62 …they come in a variety of sizes and are double-edged (a large and small radius).

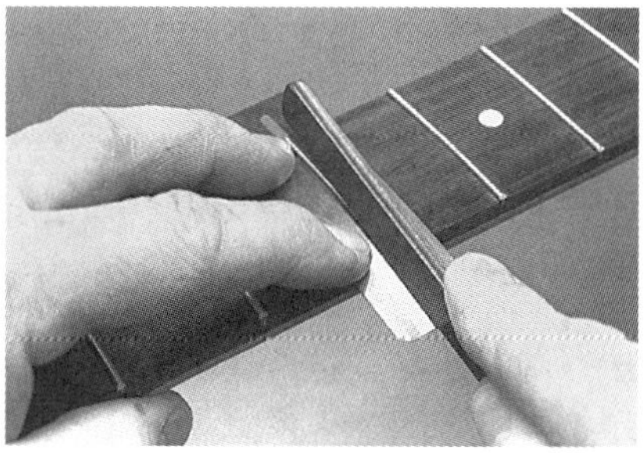

63 Use masking tape or the stainless steel fret guard with these tools to keep from marring the fretboard.

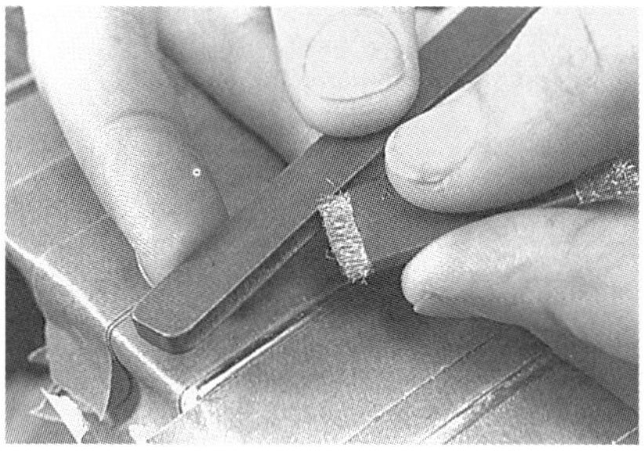

64 Toothed files should be cleaned every few minutes—the miniature brass-bristle brush is the only one small enough to clean the small specialty files used by luthiers.

65 The 'Pro-Cut' cutting lubricant we use on pearl-cutting jeweler's sawblades is good for lubricating the teeth of a rounding file (it helps keep the teeth from clogging).

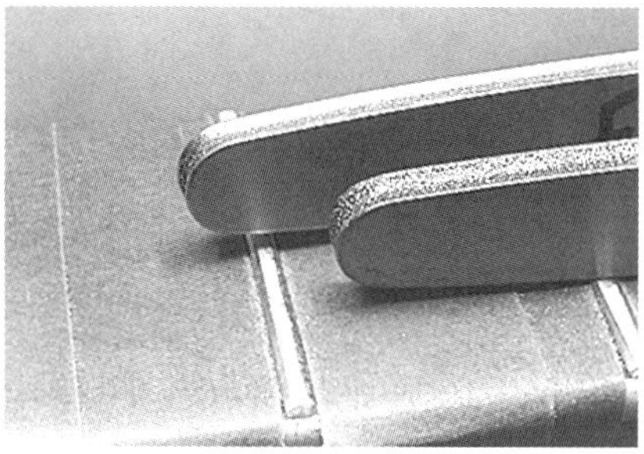

66 Our Diamond rounding file is available in coarse and fine grits, and with no "teeth," there's no clogging problem…

67 …these smooth cutting "files" leave fewer scratches than toothed files, and the rounded nose lets you "spot-file" on end.

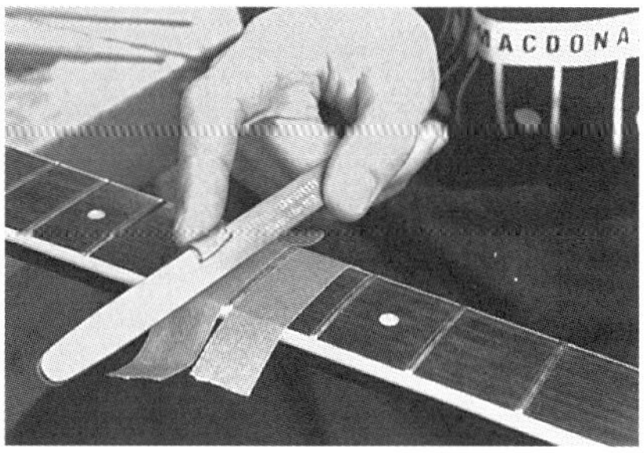

68 The diamond file will also cut in both directions—not just on the push stroke—try putting a piece of plastic hose over the unused edge as a finger protector.

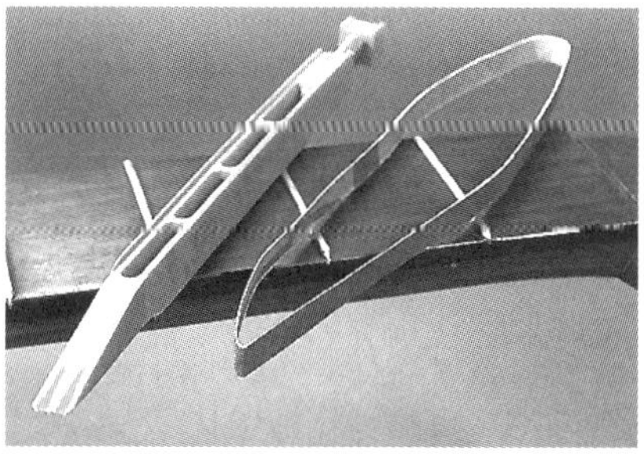

69 Sanding sticks: This tool, with it's spring loaded quick-change belts, is perfect for sanding frets smooth…

70 ….we grind several grooves in the tip to hug the fret contour (there's a single groove in the *center* of the opposite side).

Fret protector: You must use something to protect the fretboard from being scratched by your tools. Masking tape will do, but our stainless steel Fret Protector is even better!

Diamond rounding file: Three advantages of our diamond fret files over the toothed variety are:

- They cut on both the forward and backward strokes.
- They don't leave hard-to-remove scratches in the fret, as toothed files sometimes do.
- With their rounded "nose" you can spot-file in a small area.

We have two grits available—a coarse 150-grit and a fine 300-grit. Start with the coarse (don't worry, it isn't that coarse), because it removes metal the fastest. Later, as you can afford it, add the fine grit to your tools. It's great for fine-rounding and "kissing-off" that last little bit of flat fret top. Diamond files can be cleaned with a pencil eraser.

Sanding sticks: These durable plastic spring-loaded "Sand Stiks" are like miniature belt sanders. The sanding belt can be rotated to constantly expose fresh grit at the working tip. Nothing surpasses these tools for removing the final scratches left by the fret rounding operation, and for shaping fret ends. Use the 320, 400, and 600-grits (the 320-grit doesn't get used *too* often, but...). The serious professional will want three Sanding Sticks, one for each grit.

Specialized Tools and Fixtures

Here are several unique tools and fixtures that aren't shown in much detail (or at all) in the lessons.

The Neck-Jig: The neck-jig is an important tool, and anyone would benefit from knowing what it does and how to operate it. In Lesson Five, "Bolt-On Necks," we refret a Fender Telecaster using the "neck-jig" and "surrogate-body" attachments of Stewart-MacDonald's "Luthier's Workstation." We manufactured the Workstation for three years, and several hundred of our neck-jigs are used in shops around the country. Plans for the Workstation are available, and we still offer the neck-jig in our catalog. For those interested in the neck-jig (and since we receive questions about it regularly), here's some additional information....

Dan developed the first neck-jig in 1975—as a means of gaining further control and accuracy over the fretboard while doing "Teeter-style" refrets. Bryan Galloup helped him refine it in '83 when they worked together at Dan Erlewine's Guitar Hospital in Big Rapids, Michigan (Dan came to Stewart-MacDonald in 1986). The neck-jig is a string simulation device which helps re-create the neck's configuration—in the "playing position"—as it is when the strings are installed at pitch.

The workstation is a revolving-top workbench equipped with special "hold-downs" for clamping a guitar (or other stringed instrument) onto the top. Also clamped to the top, under the backside of the guitar's neck, is the neck-jig. The neck-jig has a number of small plastic-capped metal rods which raise up and touch the back of the neck and are fastened firmly with set screws. Before setting the jig rods, the table top is rotated into the "playing position" (perpendicular to the floor). Resting on its side, a guitar neck is less affected by its own weight, the weight of the tuners, and most importantly—by gravity itself (all factors which make the fretboard surface "read" differently than when checked in the horizontal "working" position).

The jig rods are set, the bench is spun back to level, and the strings are removed. Because of the truss rod's back-bowing effect on a neck, most necks will raise up off the jig rods when the string pressure is removed, until the truss rod is loosened (this lets the neck sit back down on the rods). In this "jigged" position, the neck can be planed, leveled, fretted, and dressed with great accuracy and little loss of fretboard thickness. Guitars *without* adjustable truss rods can be fretted in the jig also, using specialized fixtures which pull the neck back down onto the jig rods. See the videotape *Don't Fret* shot by Dan Erlewine at Bryan Galloup's Guitar Hospital & Guitar Repair Training School for in-depth instruction on the neck-jig.

"Surrogate" body: One nice thing about the neck-jig as we use it here is the "surrogate body"—a block of wood equipped to

1 This is the Luthier's Workstation. The table top tilts (it actually rotates 360°).

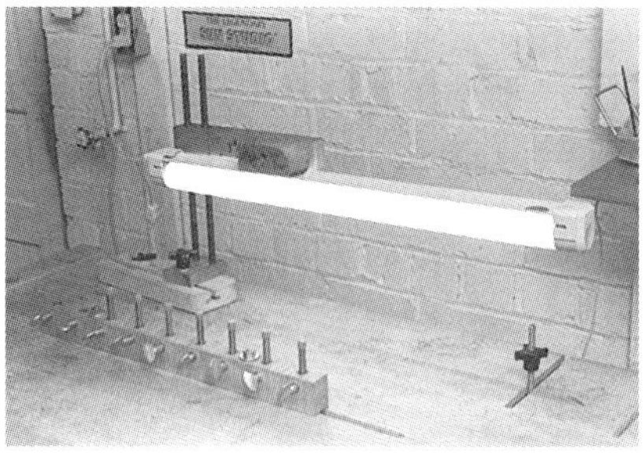

2 The removable neck-jig bolts to the table top. The "Brite-Stick" light in the background slides up and down, tilts, and gives great back-light for a straight-edge reading.

3 Guitars with glued-in (set) necks are clamped to the table top with "hold-down clamps).

4 With bolt-on neck guitars we bolt the neck into a temporary body (a "surrogate" body) and clamp that to the table.

5 The surrogate body is simply a block (or blocks) of wood that bolts into the table. This version has a "hard-tail" non-tremolo Stratocaster bridge...

6 ...and Tele-style rear mount ferrules for mounting the strings. You can make a surrogate-body a million ways.

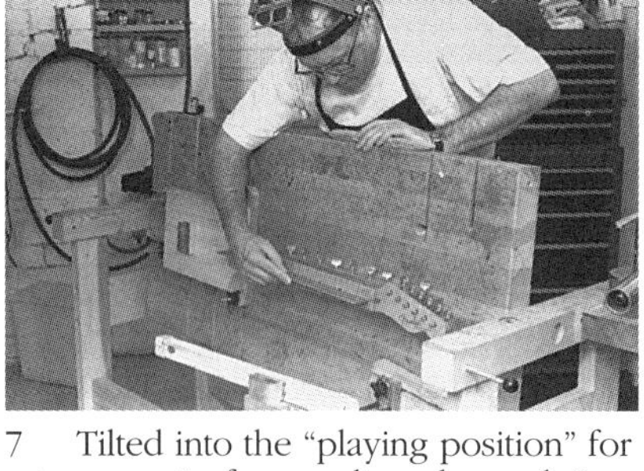

7 Tilted into the "playing position" for a true, gravity-free reading, the neck-jig rods are set in this position, then the table will be rotated back to horizontal for working.

8 Bryan Galloup's neck-jig is a permanent built-in—he calls it the "battleship." Here he tightens the machinist-style "hold-downs" clamping the body onto padded tapered shims which keep it level and protected from scratches.

accept bolt-on necks (instead of having to clamp the guitar body into the bench as well). This leaves the customer's guitar clean and protected in the case during all fretwork (even nut-making and final neck adjusting if you like), and the surrogate block bolts easily onto the table top. Another benefit is that since the block has no "neck pocket" you can get directly at the truss rod adjusting nut on vintage Fender instruments (a great feature). Even if you never expect to use a neck-jig, you'd be wise to consider building a surrogate body just to fret bolt-on necks!

A handy "mini-jig/surrogate body combo" is shown in photo 16 on page 40. Built by Brian Galloup for use in his school, it's a "wafer-board" box with a hole on one side for access to the neck-jig (which is bolted to the underside of the top). A surrogate body bolts onto the top. Instead of spinning the table top, you just set the box over on its side! For bolt-on necks this works great, and it's easy to make (we still make the neck-jig—just build a box and buy some bolts!).

Fret Pressing And Clamping Tools: In Lesson Three we use a radius-sanding block as a "caul" to clamp some frets in on the fretboard extension of an acoustic guitar; then in Lesson Five "Jaws" *squeezes* frets into a Telecaster neck. But we don't go into clamping or pressing frets in much detail. There are a number of ways to press in frets. Here are several good ones, in the order that Dan learned them, starting with Don Teeter's version from 1975.

Teeter-style fret clamp: It was in Volume One of his *Acoustic Guitar—Adjustment, Care, Maintenance, And Repair* that Don Teeter taught his revolutionary fretting technique. After routing the fret slots to accept frets with a finger-press fit, Don glues all the frets in at once using steel dowel rods to press the ends down—clamped from above with a board and a number of clamps to spread the pressure evenly (photo 25, page 44). If you clamp too hard this method can cause the center of the fret to rise up. To prevent this, we've made a number of variations, like the wooden U-clamp with a center hold-down strip shown.

Variation of the Teeter clamp (Photo 26, page 44)**:** The two outside edges of this U-shaped wooden press (like runners on a sled) hold the edges of the frets down, and the wooden center insert keeps the centers of the frets down when the thumbscrews are tightened. The clamp is shaped to match an average finger-board taper, and the bottom is radiused (actually the clamp is made up to two long wooden radius-sanding blocks cut, glued, drilled, and rabbeted as you see here.) This clamp can have the *opposite* effect of Don Teeter's, however (over-tightening the bolts can cause the outside rails to rise up, leaving the fret ends loose). Also, Teeter's simple clamp is adjustable to any width and fretboard taper.

Plexiglas fret caul (Erlewine-style) (Photo 27, page 44)**:** These cauls—like Don Teeter's—are not intended to clamp, install, or press the frets in—they're for holding the frets down against the fretboard while the glue dries during an "epoxy" fret job. Of all the

9 The heavy-duty frame remains solid, while the table top inside the frame tilts…

10 …like so, into the "playing position." In the tilted position, Brian adjusts the neck.

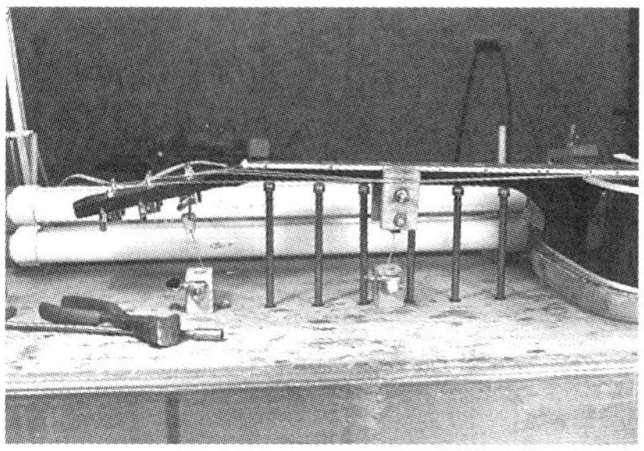

11 With strings removed, some necks won't sit back down on the studs as well as others (especially necks without adjustable truss rods). This "pull-down" fixture bolts to the table, and clamps to the edge of the fretboard. It uses a guitar tuner, low *E*-string, and a bent hook to *pull* the clamp (and the neck) down onto the studs. The second "pull-down," under the peghead, can simulate the tightening of a truss rod on non-adjustable necks, and is used for pulling down on the peghead to further control a neck during fretwork. The use of both these pull-downs (and both Dan's and Bryan's neck-jigs) is well taught in our video *Don't Fret.*

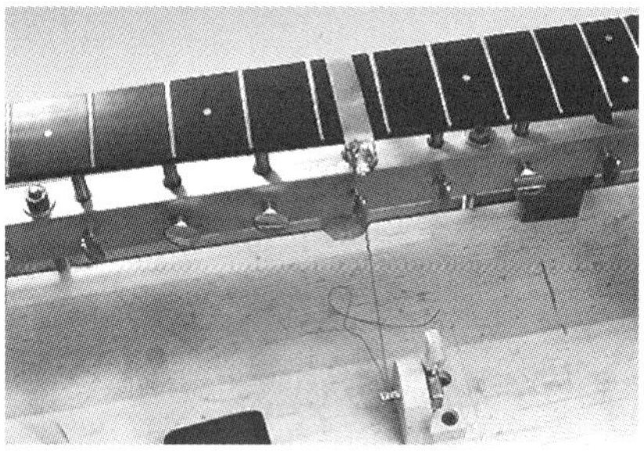

12 Here's another style of "pull-down"—pulling this non-adjustable Modulus Graphite bass neck down onto the studs. It's like a "saddle" made of thin brass sheet (shim-stock) with a guitar string soldered to each end. Bolt the string to the table on the treble side, and run the bass side string into the little guitar tuner clamp screwed to the table. The brass shim-stock, at .012", is far thinner than the height of the frets so it doesn't get in the way. It's easier to make than Bryan's version, but of course you can't use it for installing frets because it lays on top of the surface. (But you can use this pull down for refretting fingerboards with no binding by running a guitar string through a fret slot, doing the fret job, and then pulling out the string for the very last fret).

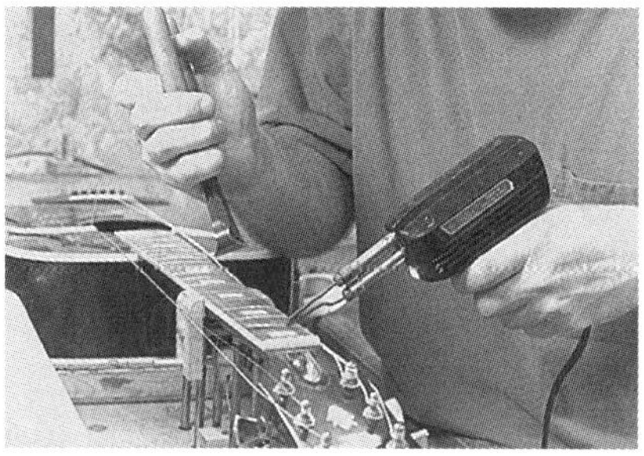

13 Back in the horizontal "working" position, the frets are removed…

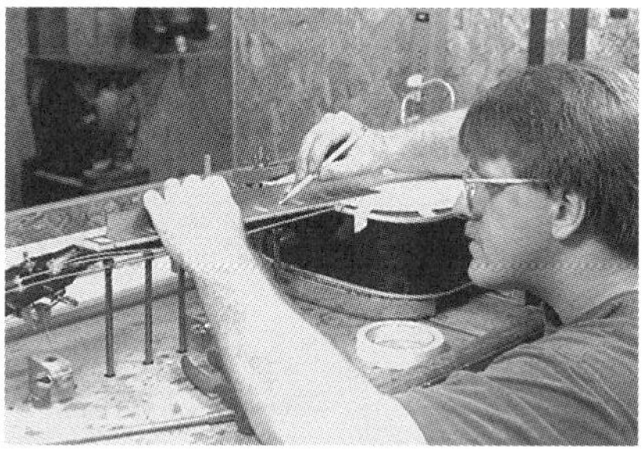

14 …and the fretboard prepped (you can get a better view of the peghead hold-down in this photo). Bryan's marking out high spots…

15 …which are removed with a variety of tools—the long wooden radius-sanding block in this case.

16 (Right) Sitting on top of Dan's workbench is Bryan's *portable* table-top neck-jig for fretting bolt-on-necks in a surrogate body.

many cauls we've tried, these work the best for us because the curve of the bottom plexiglas sheet holds the entire fret smoothly against the board and the center never rises up. The secret to this caul's success is that one contact surface between the dowel rod and the bottom sheet is not glued. The unglued "slip-joint" allows the pressing sheet to slip as it clamps into a curve—so one clamp fits any radius.

For these clamps to work, you must rout the fret slots to some extent—not necessarily for a finger-press fit, but at least wide enough so that a hammer can tap them in easily (once the fret is in, and down against the board, the clamp has plenty of strength to keep the fret from popping up—especially on the ends). We make these cauls in long lengths and cut them into shorter lengths as needed. When we do a "glue-in" fret job, we seldom install all the frets at once the way Don Teeter and others do—so shorter cauls that span two, three, or four frets at a time work well.

You could make these cauls out of wood, steel, or aluminum as well, but plexiglas was handy and easy to "weld." The thick top is 1/2" plexiglas, the dowel rods are 3/16", and the pressing sheet is 1/8". One of the greatest uses for these cauls is to hold down superglued fret ends because they clamp into place so quickly!

"Jaws," the fret clamp from Hell: This was described in detail in the Winter '94 "Trade Secrets" (Vol. 15) section of our catalog, showing how to make the tool. It's also in our new "Trade Secrets" book. On page 46 are a couple photos to give you an idea how you might make one from a similar tool. We used a "Facom" brand Lock-Grip Plier, Model F516.

Big Bessey (photo 31, page 44)**:** Brian Galloup came up with this clamp setup in answer to Dan's "Jaws" tool. This one is made from a Bessey flat bar clamp (other brands don't have the strength). With this tool you *can* clamp frets in without enlarging the fretslot. The pressing arm slides over the Bessey clamp's bar, and is pinned into the holes drilled in the bar (for height adjustment). The pressing "shoe" pins into a slot milled into the bar on a 45° angle, so that the clamp clears the body when pressing frets in over the neck block. You need a set of shoes radiused to match all the different fretboard radii from 7-1/4" (Fender) to 20" (Martin). The bottom of the radiused "shoes" are grooved to help center them on the fret as the clamp is tightened.

Fixture for "clamping around the heel": Another Galloup "box" original that we really like clamps onto the neck, and offers a clamping surface for bar-clamps when you're clamp-pressing frets. It eliminates the need to stack up a variety of curved cauls and blocks of wood. (See photos 28-30, page 44.)

Fret Tang Sizer: Here's another homemade tool which has lots of merit, and we use it here in Lesson Three. The tang sizer shown on page 45 removes some (or all) or the fret tang barb to help control excess fret compression—in particular, to avoid backbow in a fretboard. Imagine a fret job where the tang thickness is a

17 It's a box with an aluminum Stew-Mac neck-jig bolted permanently to the top's underside. Bryan has cut a hole in the side for setting the jig-rods...

18 ...and a single aluminum channel is rabbetted into the top. The channel accepts a 'T' nut, all-thread rod, and pronged knob to fasten the cute little surrogate body firmly to the 2" thick...

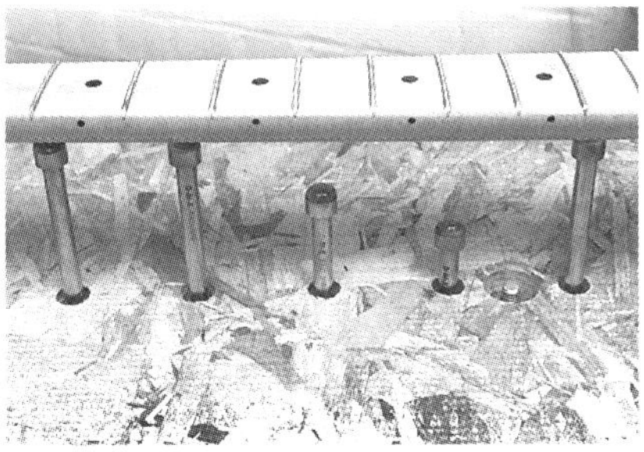

19 ...top of flake-board, glued and screwed to solid pine 2 x 12s. The box has a sturdy 2 x 4 frame. He uses ultra-smooth working (and longer) tempered 5/16" "injector pins" in place of the steel rods supplied with Stew-Mac's neck jig.

20 Just set the box over on its side—easy to make, easy to use!

21 Another Galloup original is this "student" jig. It spins like its big brother, but is only for accepting a surrogate body and bolt-on neck. Here Bryan shows student Jack Fortner how to use the jig.

22 When Bryan gets confused he always goes back to Dan's book (just kidding—he's using the book's fretting section to help Jack).

23 After preparing the board Bryan removes the guitar from the neck-jig for fretting and then "re-jigs" for leveling before dressing. Dan Erlewine usually does the entire operation in the jig, and removes the guitar to final-round the frets. Although Dan prefers to press his frets in, for occasions where he has to hammer in the neck jig, he uses a curved neck caul/jack stand underneath to keep the hammer blows from affecting the neck rods.

24 ...Like any proud father!

We'd like to give special thanks to Don MacRostie and Bryan Galloup for their help in our ongoing fretwork research. But there are so many others who deserve praise too, that we couldn't begin to mention you all. You'll see many* people's ideas in this book, and in the "Trade Secrets"** ***section of our catalog. Thanks to all of you—professional and novice alike—for your willingness to share your secrets with us. We're passing your tips, drawings, and photos on to the people who appreciate them most!
—Dan Erlewine

Speaking of trade secrets, please send in your ideas to share in **"Trade Secrets"—** ***our 8-page repair newsletter in each Guitar Shop Supply catalog.***

perfect fit, but the added presence of the barbs is just a *little* too much—by removing some of the barb the fret will still hold in the slot, but not exert as much of a wedging effect on the fret slots. The tang sizer is a big help for sizing fretwire for the fretboard extension ("tongue").

The tool is a slotted block of aluminum with two set-screws tapped into the side. Take two lengths of file and remove the teeth from one edge, and then round the edge lengthwise on a grinder. Set the two file pieces into the block, and with feeler gauges as spacers to hold the files apart (so that the teeth don't touch each other) clamp the files tight with the set screws. By controlling the number and size of the feeler gauges, you can shave the barbs off a fret tang by pulling the frewire through the files against the cut of the teeth. You could also use a small drill press vise to hold the files instead of the metal block.

Under-The-String 'T'-Leveler: Don't be afraid to experiment (but not on your customers' guitars). As Don Teeter says, "Don't just sit there contemplating your navel!" Here's a crazy little technique—what you might call one of Dan's "new repair directions." Soon it may be a "Trade Secret," who knows?

Don MacRostie and Dan have experimented with fret compression using hammers, "Jaws," and other techniques. As an experiment in fret compression, Don actually *fretted* a guitar with the strings on, using Jaws and a pressing-caul *notched* to clear the strings. Going one fret at a time, Don measured his progress with the notched straightedge. Soon afterward, Bryan Galloup experimented with leveling the fretboard with the strings on. He used a steel "radius-sanding block" made of .090" steel—thin enough to fit under the strings easily while still being strong.

Brian pulls the frets, strings up the guitar with a wood dowel in the nut slot to raise the strings a little, and (adjusting the truss rod while he works) sands, shapes, and preps the fretboard very quickly and accurately—in or out of the neck jig! He says, "I'd never quit using the jig completely, especially not for real problem necks. But I'm now doing at least half of my fret jobs using the new "strings-on method" (not in the jig at all and very fast) and with great results!"

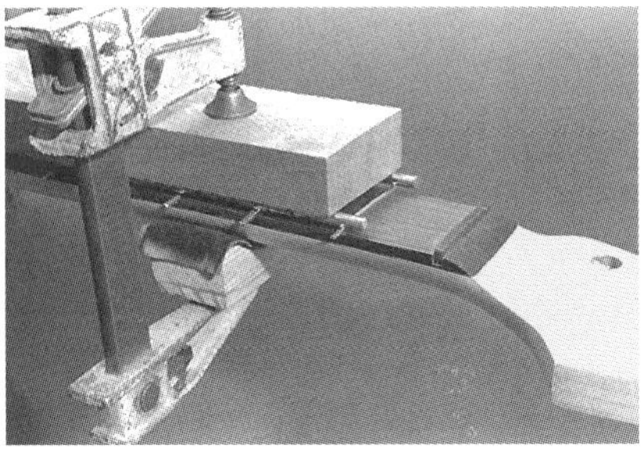

FRET CLAMPING FIXTURES:
25 Don Teeter's original fret clamping setup: two steel rods topped with a piece of plywood and clamped just tight enough to hold the ends down, but not so tight as to cause the center to rise.

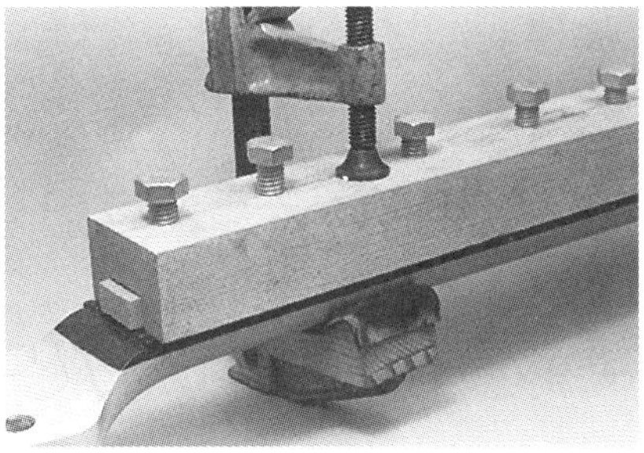

26 A variation of the Teeter-style, this one presses on the center as well. It was made from two long radius-sanding blocks.

27 This is the plexiglas caul that Dan devised—the bottom plate "slips" to follow the radius ...

28 This "clamping box" has a long curved caul to fit the back of the neck...

29 ...to spread the clamping pressure over a large area. Brian's clamping press is pretty cool—it's his answer to "Jaws."

30 The clamping box eliminates the need to stack up a variety of curved cauls and blocks of wood. The bar clamp in the center is clamping the frets, the other two are just holding the whole rig in place.

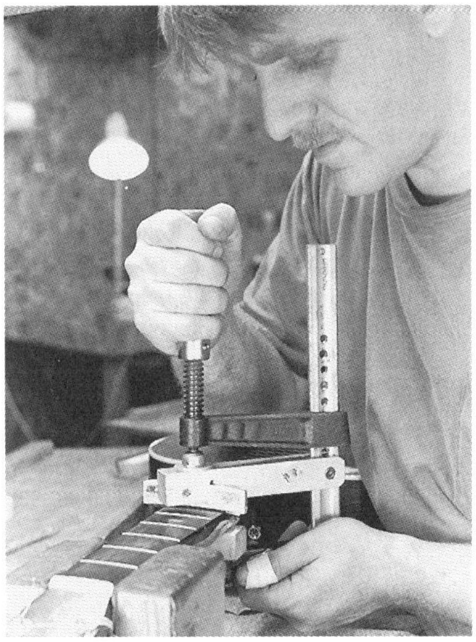

31 Brian's version of Dan Erlewine's "Jaws" is a Bessey flat bar-clamp with a series of holes in the bar to accommodate the adjustble fret press which pins into it.

32 He uses a good-fitting caul on the back of the neck for the areas where the clamping-box isn't needed. The reason for the angle of the "press" to the bar of the clamp is...

33 ...to accommodate fretting on the body past the neck joint and over the neck block (it keeps the clamp away from the body).

34 Brian also has a "T" or right angle clamp for coming in through the soundhole but he says "since I've got the Fret Buck I don't clamp through the soundhole anymore."

THE TANG SIZER

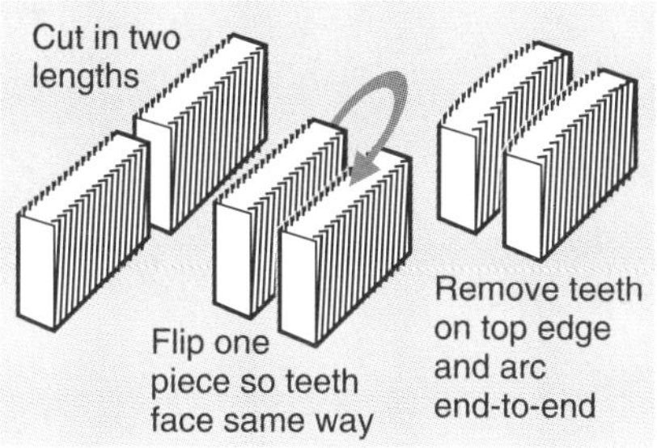

35 The tang sizer uses two 2-1/2" sections of our #864 fret leveling file faced together as shown. The top edges are smoothed and given a slightly arced shaped.

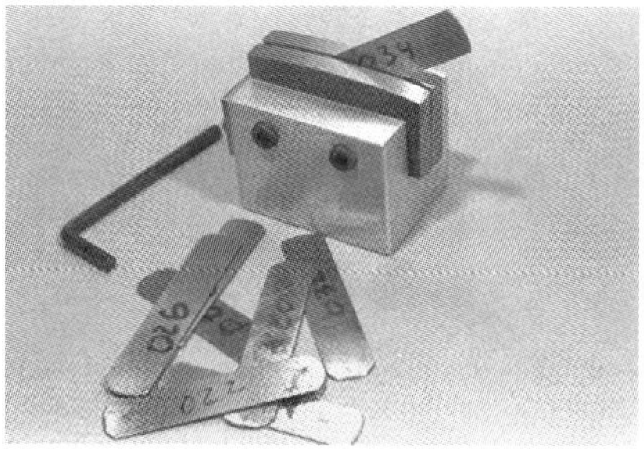

36 The file pieces are clamped into a U-shaped aluminum block with a feeler gauge (the gauge sits at the bottom of the block as in photo 38). Set-screws hold the files and feeler gauge tight.

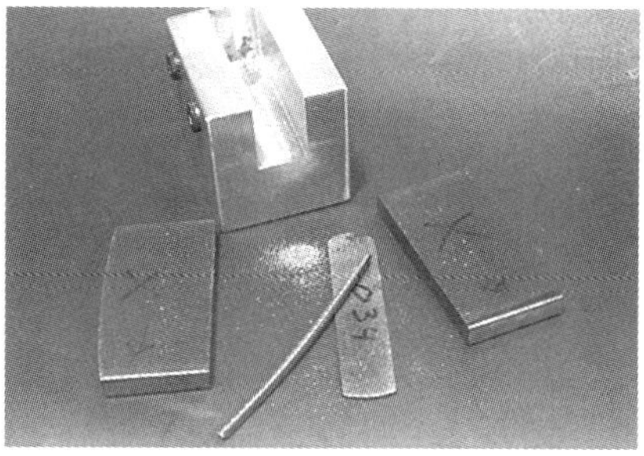

37 By controlling the number and size of the feeler gauges, you can shave the barbs off quickly. See the pile of metal dust?

38 A miniature "drill press vise" makes a good file holder too, instead of the aluminum block.

T-PLATE SANDER/LEVELER

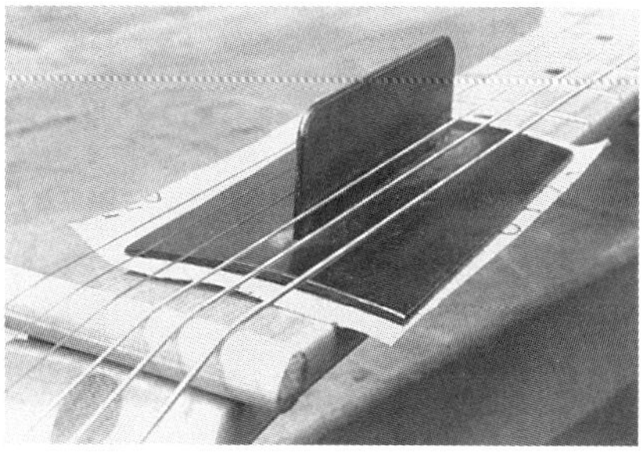

39 Thin steel radius-sanding block slides under the strings (the strings are propped up at the nut). The steel handle rides between the *D* and *G*-strings.

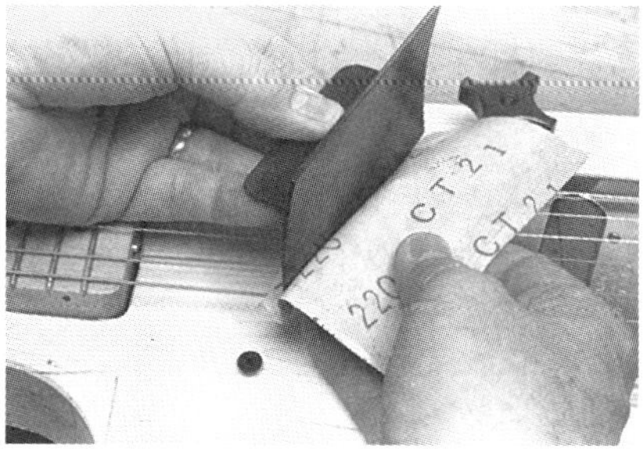

40 You can prep the fretboard or the frets with it, and it removes easily at the body end for changing the paper.

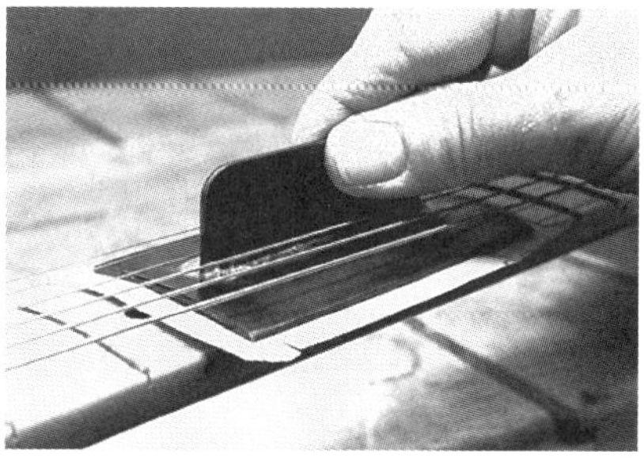

41 As of this writing, this technique is still somewhat experimental—but who knows?

"JAWS"
THE FRET PRESS FROM HELL

42 The early Jaws had a pressing shoe slotted into the upper jaw, and a simple padded curved wood caul on the bottom…

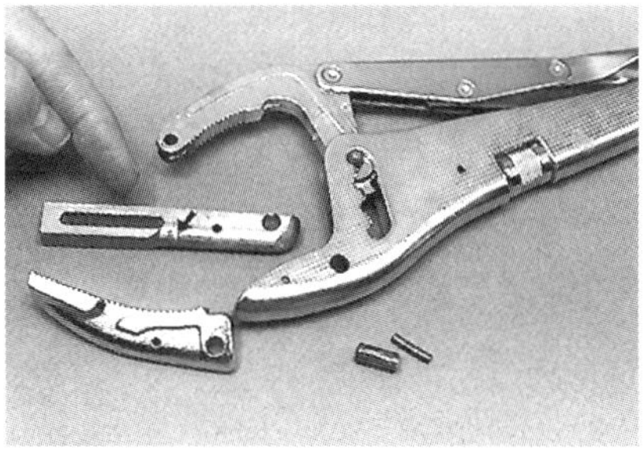

43 Then we replaced the bottom jaw with this handmade piece of brass, drilled and shaped to fit the tool…

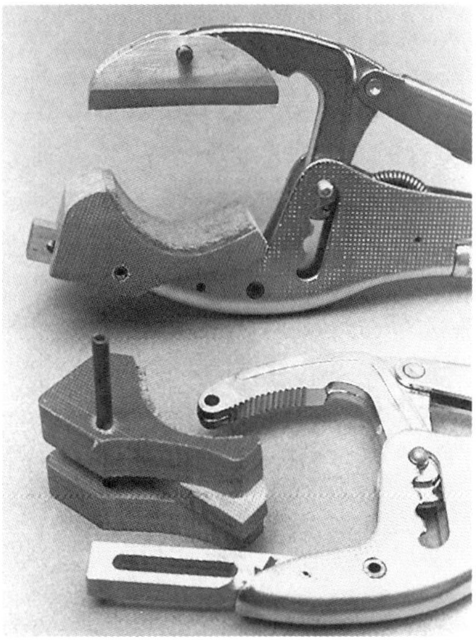

44 …and we attached this sliding curved bottom jaw—so that it would center itself to the top jaw automatically.

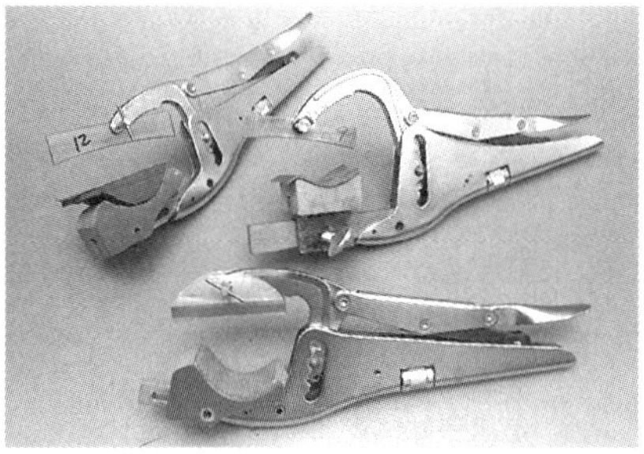

45 A trio of Jaws prototypes.

LESSON 1

FRET DRESSING

Fret dressing refers to the leveling and re-rounding (or "crowning") of high, low, or worn spots on frets; these can cause buzzes and "noting out"—notes that won't play cleanly. Basically, here's what's involved in the process: Leveling is first done with a smooth, flat mill file, followed by #22-, #32-, and #400-grit sandpaper for smoothing. Next, the fret tops left flat by the leveling operation are re-rounded with a small triangular file or a fret-rounding file. Any jagged fret ends along the fingerboard's edge are rounded now, too. Finally, a good polishing with fine sandpaper and steel wool gives smooth, buzz-free frets that are a dream to bend on.

Most of us learn to dress frets before attempting a refret, so that's where we'll begin. Some fret dresses are as simple as one, two, three: 1) get the neck straight; 2) level the tops of the frets; 3) round or "crown" the fret tops. But more typically, fret dressing will throw you a curve or two. Such is the case with this Elektra semi-hollow body—a couple of loose frets, and a hard-to-adjust neck made this one more fun! Before starting, here's an excerpt from the "Fret Dressing" chapter of the new *Guitar Player Repair Guide* —a good simple explanation of how to prepare for a fret dress…

THE LEVELING POSITION

Using the neck evaluation and truss rod adjustment section of the Getting Started chapter as a guide, adjust your truss rod to remove any relief. Get the neck straight from the 1st fret to the 12th, using a metal straightedge for comparison. Then duplicate this straight, or "leveling," position with the strings removed. Lay a towel or pad on the table top, covering it and the entire work surface with newspaper to catch any metal filings. Rest the guitar's body on the padded part of the work surface, and cradle the back of the neck on a stack of books or anything else that can serve as a support (I like the "neck rocker" used by repairman Pete Towers in Chesterton, Cambridge, UK. It's fantastic!).

Any neck support should be padded, and covered with paper as well, because filings will scratch the lacquer on the back of the neck. (To avoid scratching, vacuum or remove the filings often.) Check with your straightedge again to be sure that the neck support hasn't altered your neck straightness. If it has, move the support to a different part of the neck and/or make a slight truss rod adjustment.

Note: Even with the strings removed and the truss rod loose, some necks may tend to backbow slightly. These necks gain relief from string tension alone. In this case, support the headstock, not the back of the neck, and later you may either put slight pressure on the body or pull down on the neck's heel to straighten the neck as you file.

A better way than pulling down on the heel to get the neck into the "playing," or straight position was shown to me by Rich Starkey at the Martin repair department. For simulating string tension on a neck—whether refretting or dressing—Rich supports the peghead and then sets two 6 lb. weights on either side of the fretboard on the shoulders of the guitar. For a non-flat top (like a Les Paul), use a sandbag or sack of buckshot. The weights add just enough pressure to get the neck of a non-adjustable Martin (or any guitar) into the perfect leveling position.

TAPING OFF THE FRETS FOR "DRESSING"

To avoid marring the wood, tape off the fretboard on each side of the frets for any type of filing, sanding, or steel-wooling. You may prefer to tape-off the entire board before you start, and then go right to buffing (plus you'll save time if you don't have to get out the X-acto knife and tape each time you get to a new fret). Some fretters just tape off one fret at a time—steel-wooling and polishing each fret by hand as they progress. If the whole fretboard is taped off, you can buff the frets on a power buffer, or by hand with liquid compounds, without buffing the fretboard. Some fretters *like* to buff the fretboard because it gives a polished, "waxy" look; others prefer the unbuffed look. Try both methods and see which suits you.

The best tape to use is "drafting" tape—a low-tack tape designed to remove from paper without tearing it. In the same fashion, we don't want to pull finish from the fretboard edges (or wood and inlays from the fretboard itself). Drafting tape can be covered with heavier-duty tape if you feel it is too thin.

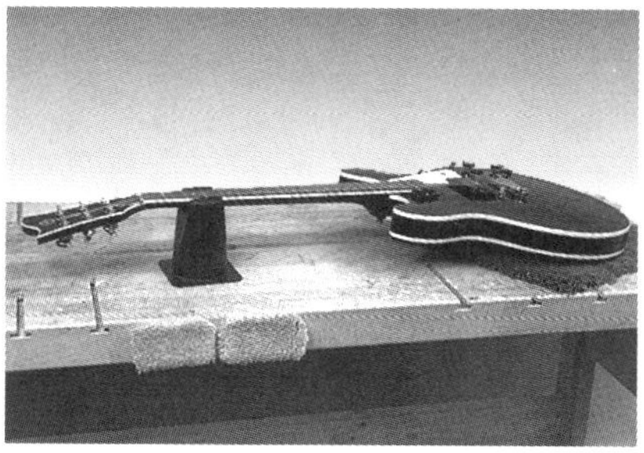

1 You need a "neck rest," or some way to support the neck as you work.

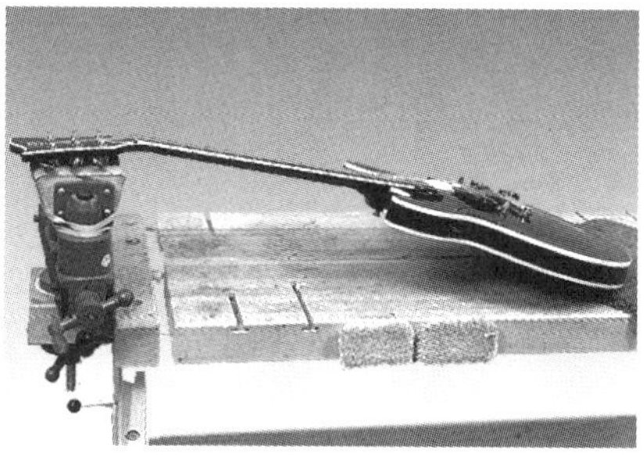

2 For a quick leveling, at least on a good straight neck, you can simply prop up the peghead for the leveling part.

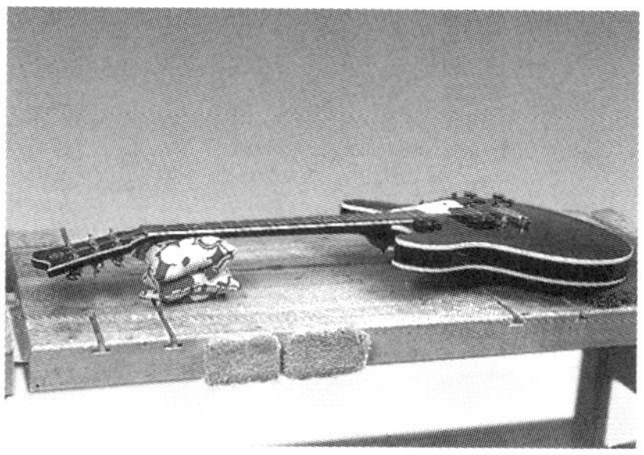

3 Cloth bags filled with buckshot or sand work well, too.

4 We'll use the neck rocker.

5 This is the "flex-test"—support the peghead and pull down on the neck (somewhere near its center) to see how much "give" there is. This one's a little weak, but maybe by adjusting the truss rod we can stiffen it up a little.

6 Make a mark on the truss rod to let you know where the truss rod adjustment was when you started (you may want to return to that exact position later).

7 Always loosen the rod first, in case it's already quite tight! Besides, you should clean the threads on the nut and rod and lubricate them lightly…

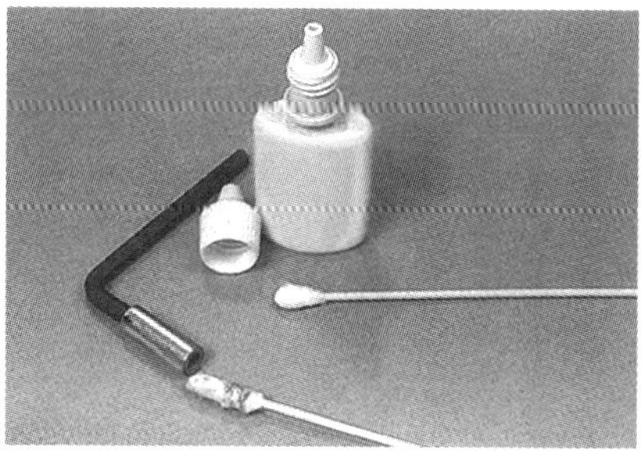

8 …with a little teflon lube, graphite, light machine oil, etc.

9 Strung to pitch and in the "playing position," check for straightness using a straightedge as long as the fretboard. A white background makes it easier.

10 This neck has way too much upbow or "relief," and simply tightening the rod isn't getting it straight. Put a notched wood block over the strings at each end of the neck…

11 …and with the truss rod loose, *clamp* the neck straight (or even into a slight backbow).

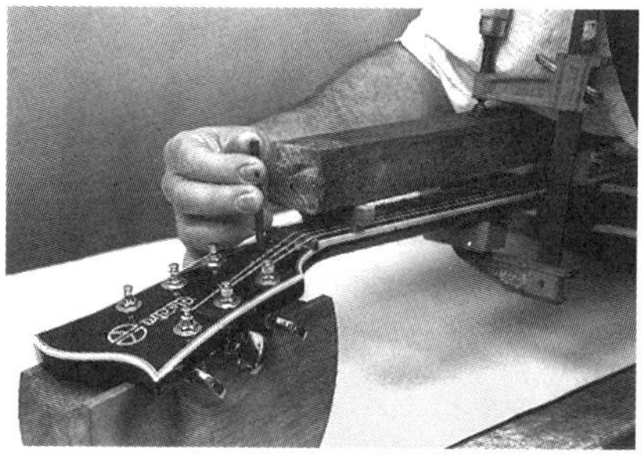

12 Now when you tighten the truss rod it doesn't have to fight the neck—it's being "helped" by the clamping. This isn't necessary with most necks, but it's often a good trick on an electric bass.

13 This neck straightened out almost perfectly—there's only .003" of relief—we can remove .003" from the frets during the leveling and end up with all the fret tops level with one another.

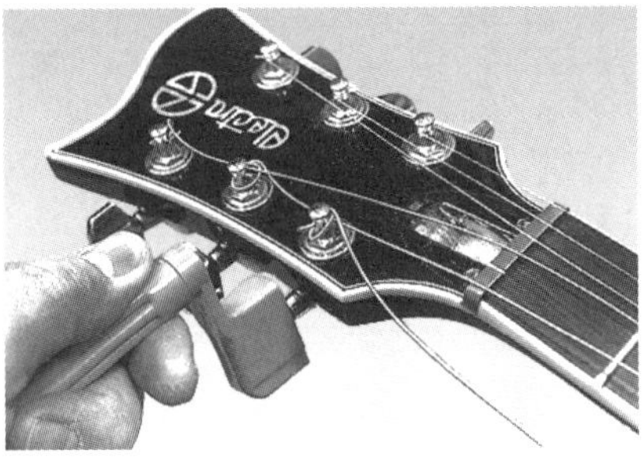

14 Remove the strings…

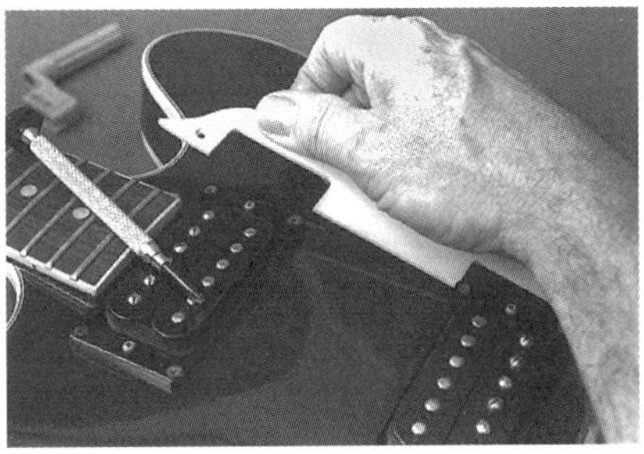

15 …the pickguard…

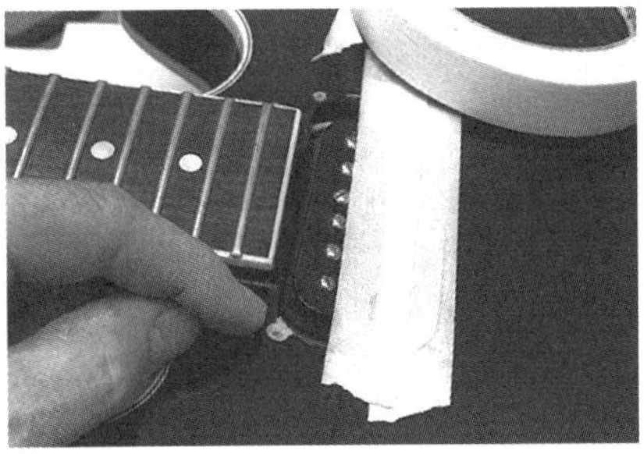

16 …and the mounting ring, and drop the pickup into its cavity—to be protected with light-tack "draftsman's tape." Take note of that finish chip when you peel off the tape later!

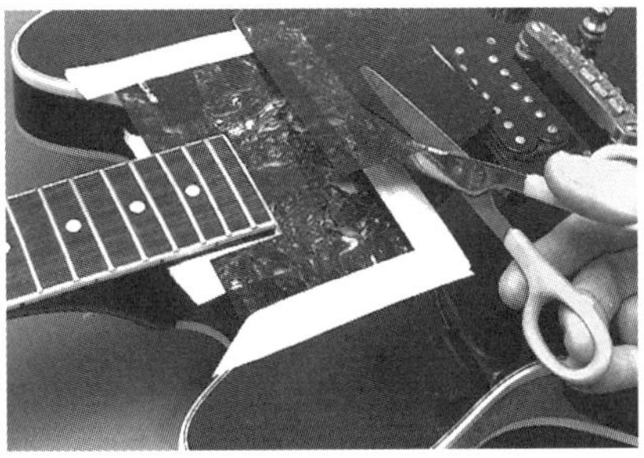

17 Thin .018" pickguard material makes an easy-to-trim protector for the guitar and finish.

18 Now loosen the rod (the neck has backbowed without the string pressure) until the neck is straight—note the white background.

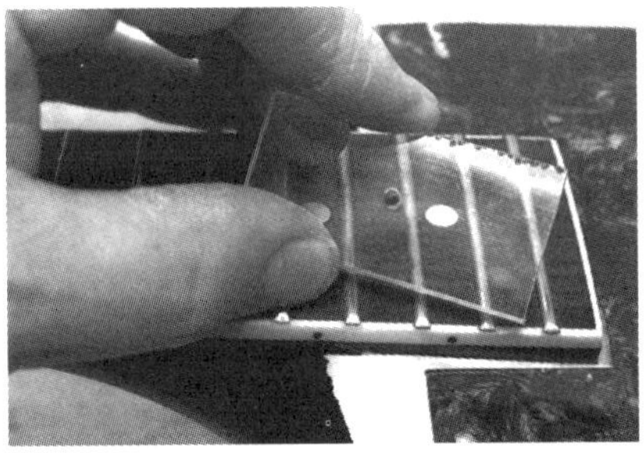

19 It's nice to know how tall the existing frets are. Lay a piece of plexiglas with a small hole drilled in it over the frets…

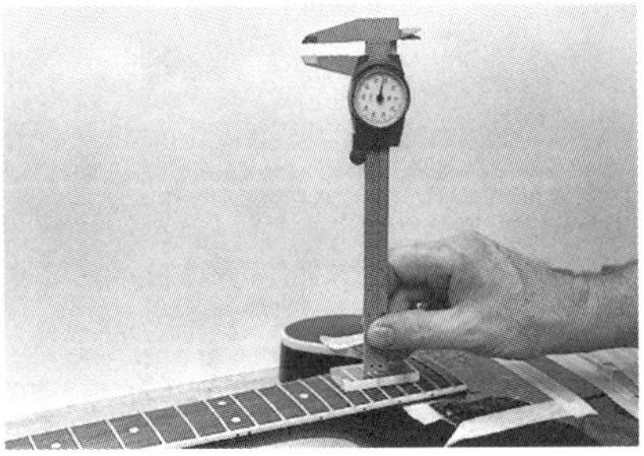

20 …and measure down through it to the fretboard…

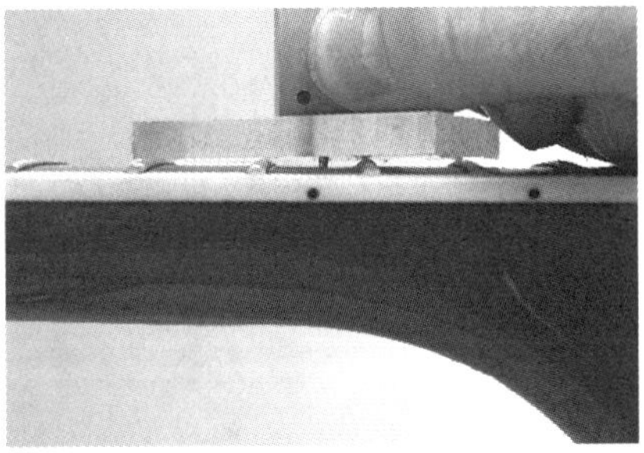

21 …using the depth gauge end of a micrometer.

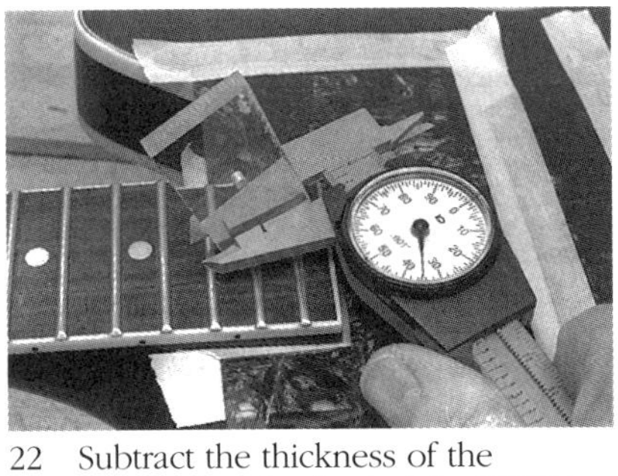

22 Subtract the thickness of the plexiglas to find the fret height (.034" is plenty tall to dress). As a rule, frets lower than .25" are better off being replaced than dressed.

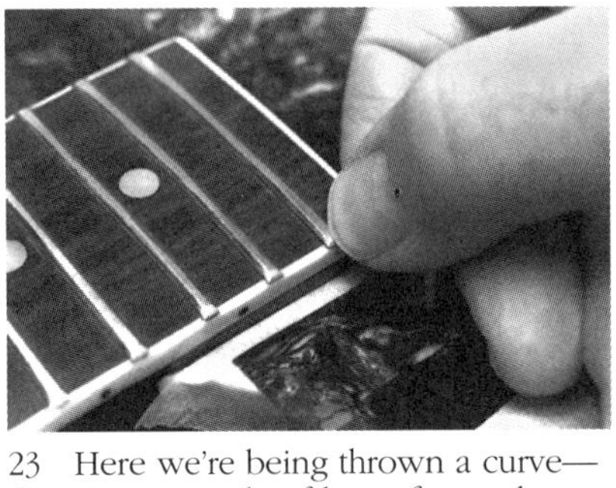

23 Here we're being thrown a curve—there are a couple of loose fret ends.

24 Get some paste wax on a Q-tip (wipe off any excess lumps on a rag or paper towel)…

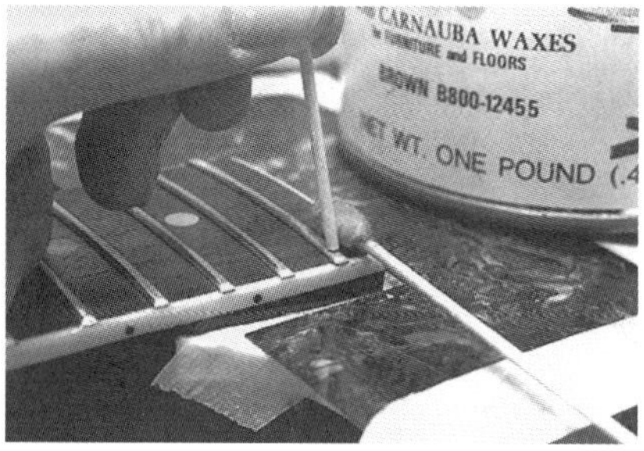

25 Hold down the fret and wax the fretboard thoroughly on each side.

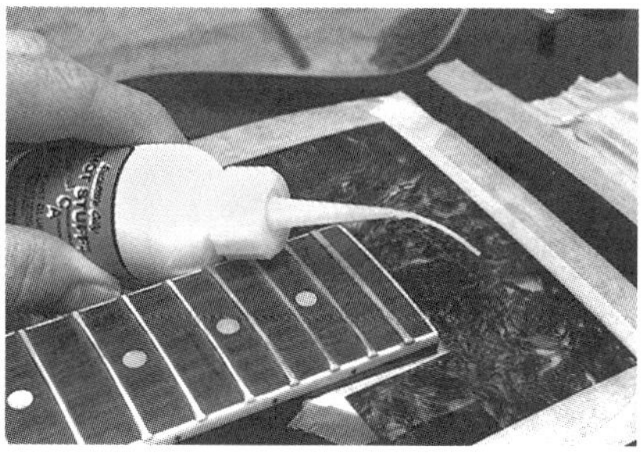

26 Using the red label (water-thin) "Hot-Stuff" and the small #1170 applicator tubing...

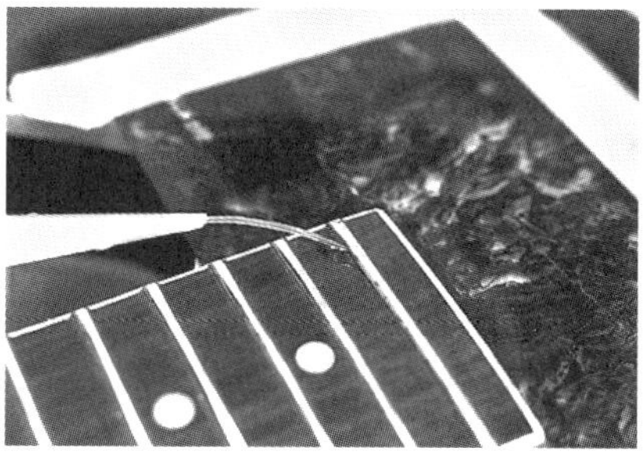

27 ...run a bead of superglue under the fret. It disappears as it runs under the fret and down into the slot.

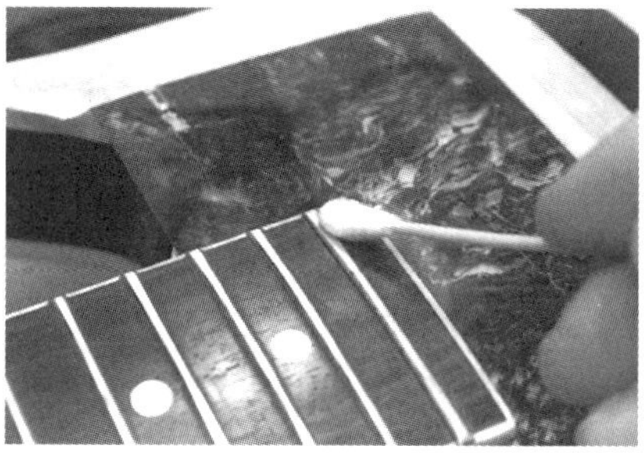

28 Quickly swab up the excess...

29 ...and hold the fret end level with the surrounding frets. A small steel straightedge is perfect—you can see (and feel) when it's level.

30 The glue squeeze-out removes easily because the board was waxed. These small "micro-chisels" have many uses—from cleaning nut slots (or saddle slots on an acoustic bridge), to removing glue during fretwork.

31 Check the fretboard radius with a radius gauge...

32 ...and be sure to check it at both ends. Some fretboards are cone-shaped rather than cylindrical. This one is a cylinder, and we want to keep it that way (cylinders are easiest to level).

33 We're going to remove these pits by leveling the fret tops. By taking a little extra off at each end of the fretboard, we "average" the unwanted relief, and all the fret tops will contact the straightedge (a "straight neck").

34 'Marks-A-Lot' blue felt-tip markers are the best for highlighting the fret tops so you can *see* what you're filing.

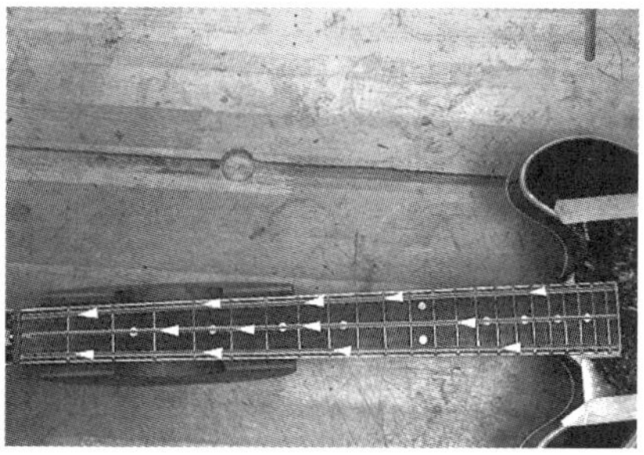

35 These lines and arrows show that the "lie of the strings" follows the taper of the fretboard's width, as was explained in the compound/cylinder section.

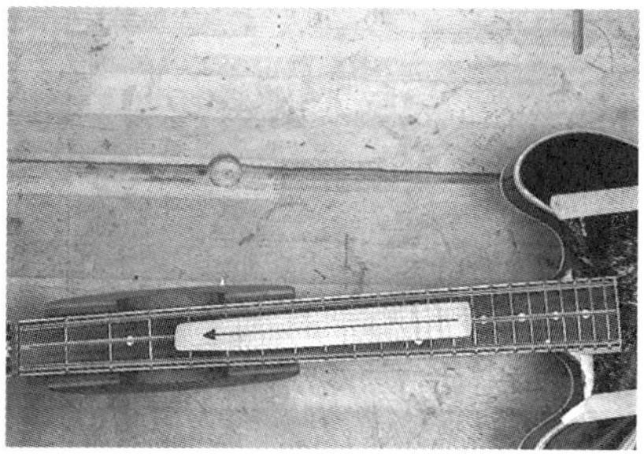

36 A common method of leveling the fret tops is with a file—like this flat 10" smooth mill file glued to a wooden handle. It's easy to file straight when you're on center...

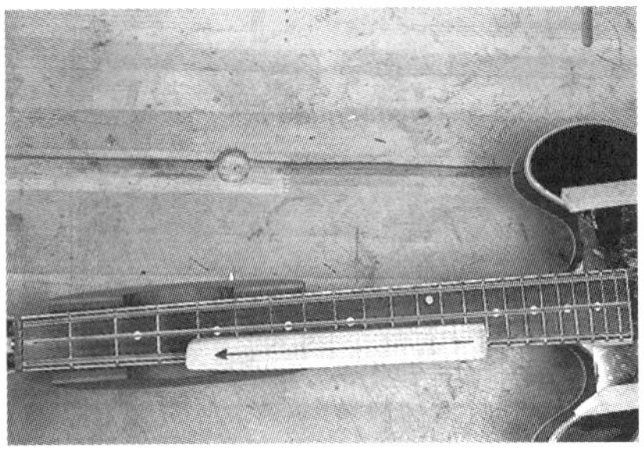

37 …but the tendency is to follow the "lie of the string" as you work toward the edges. This would create a cone-shaped radius into the cylinder-shaped board! (That's not bad, but we don't want the cone in this case.)

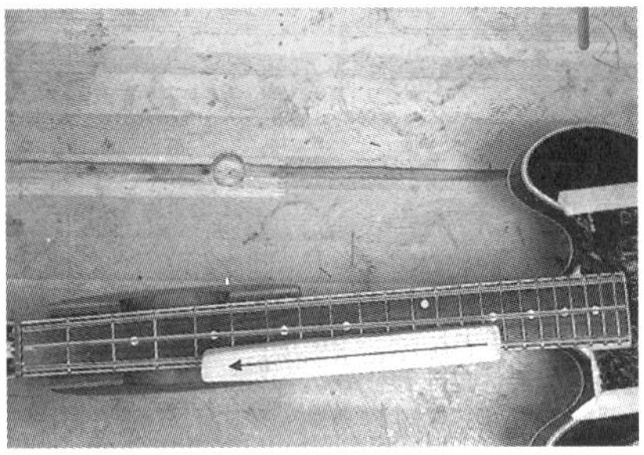

38 You must file parallel to the center line in order to keep the cylinder. As you cover the fretboard from side to side you'll create a series of flats to be removed with sandpaper later.

39 Filing down the center…

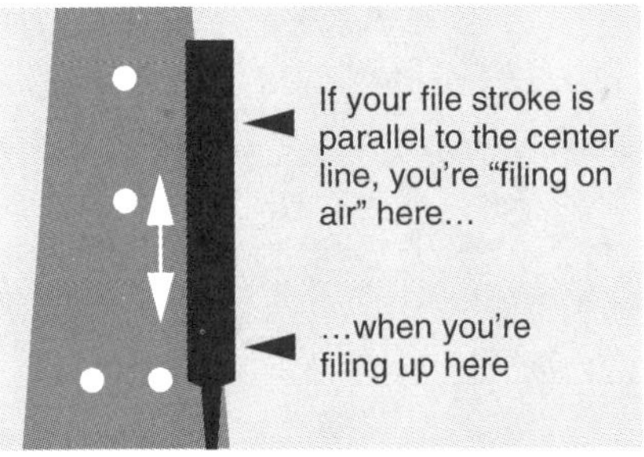

40 …filing "parallel" down the edge. Part of the file is "filing on air" while the other part is on the wider area of the board.

41 Here's a different type of leveler. It's as long as the fretboard, machined flat, and coated with diamond dust.

42 You still need to stay parallel with it if you're trying to keep a cylinder!

43 It won't leave "chatter-marks" like files do…

44 …the diamonds "powder" the metal instead.

45 Regardless of which tool you level with, it's good to remove the nut if you can. Not a must, but nice because…

46 …you can finish your stroke off the fretboard end.

47 Be careful not to dip, and hit the tops of the tuners!

48 Leveling Tip: An advanced length-wise leveling stroke ("cross-stroke") avoids creating a series of flats across the fretboard. File across the board in smooth unbroken strokes while going forward at the same time.

49 The tiniest of pits is left—time to switch to sandpaper.

50 Re-blue the tops...

51 To smooth the series of "flats" created by the leveling, use 220- and then 320-grit "Stikit" sandpaper and a radius block—the radius block rounds the entire board at once edge-to-edge.

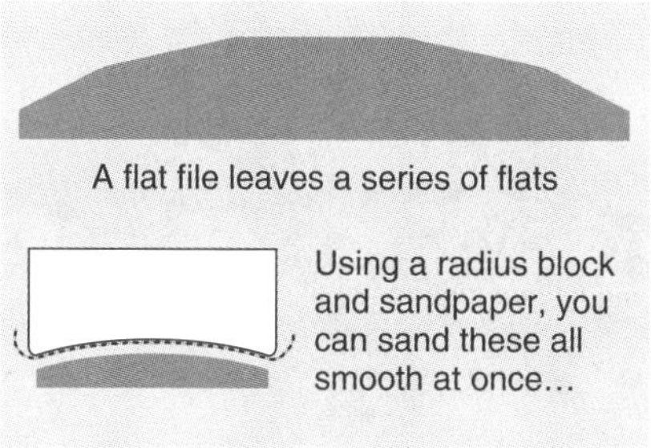

52 Use a radius block for sanding, or...

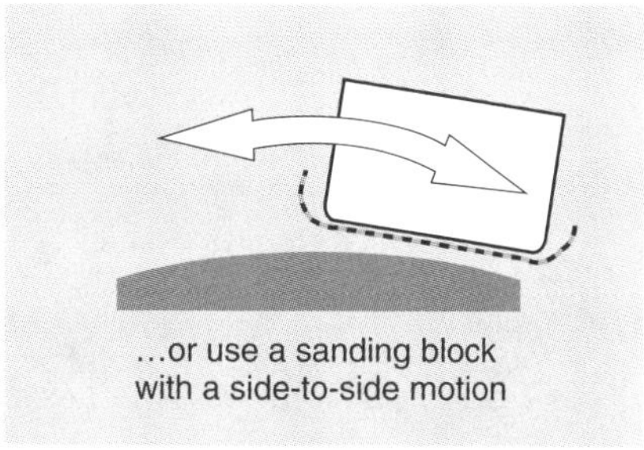

53 ...wrap sandpaper around your file (or a block of wood) and move from side to side across the fretboard *while going lengthwise*. Another technique is to move across the fretboard at a long angle while going forward (fig. 48).

54 The radius block covers the whole width of the board at once. You could have used it for the entire job, but it doesn't level as quickly as a file or diamonds (to remove that .003").

55 By watching the dust piles, you know when the all the frets have been touched. There's one small area which has been missed up on the body...

56 ...you can see on the sanding block which part of the sandpaper is still fresh.

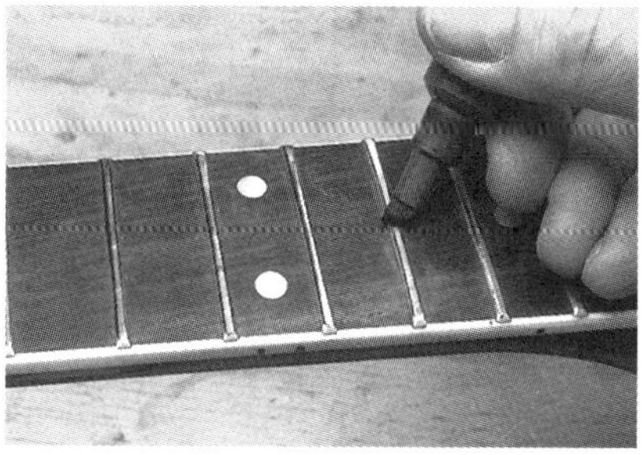

57 Re-blue (just on the upper frets)...

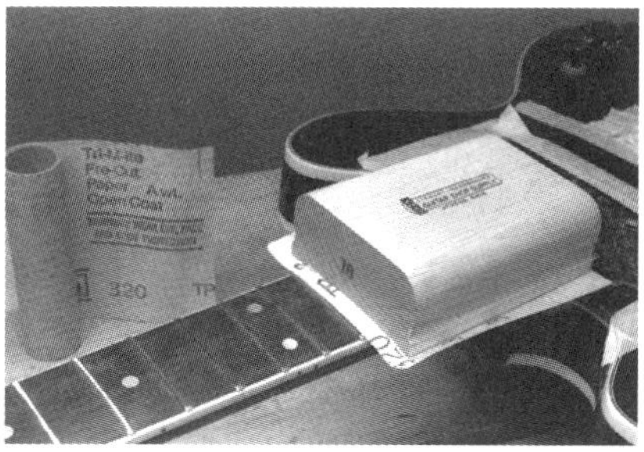

58 ...change paper, and sand one more time.

59 Now we've got it!

60 The fret tops after leveling.

61 With most fret dresses, there's not *too* much shaping to be done on the ends because they were filed at the factory. But we'll clean them up a little.

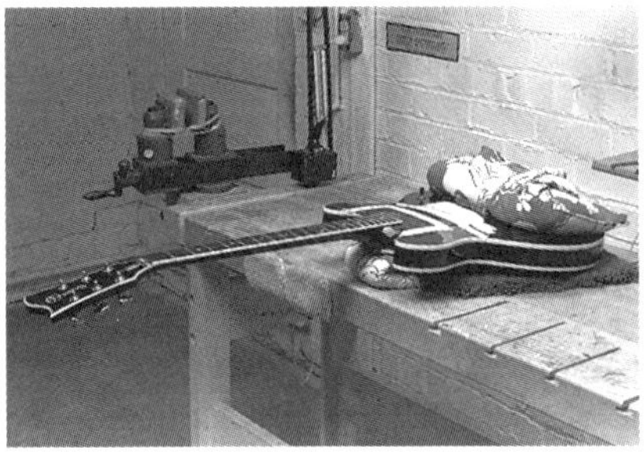

62 Here's an effective, easy way to dress, that allows access to both sides. Carpet underneath and a few bags of sand for ballast.

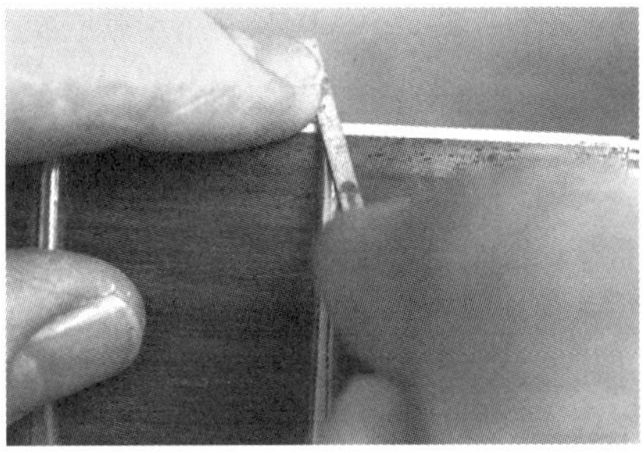

63 To be sure the bevel on the ends is clean, take a couple of light downstrokes on the flat of the bevel. This is the 1/8" "nut seating file." It works well on the ends.

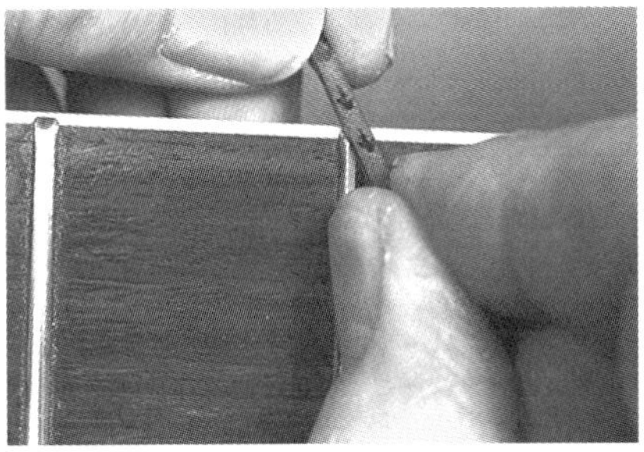

64 Sometimes an "up-stroke" is called for to push any fret burr out where you can...

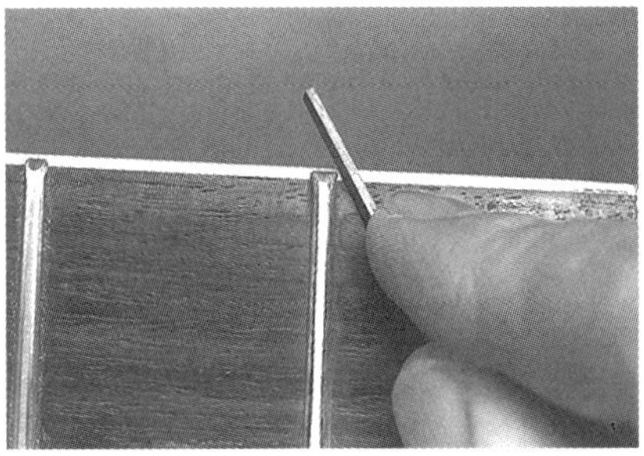

65 ...remove it with the same file held on edge. Be careful not to cut into the wood or binding (be gentle).

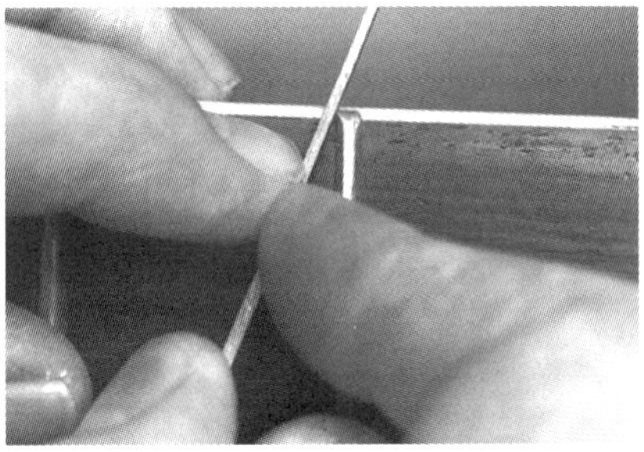

66 Kiss off any burr on the other side—"kiss" is the right word—you don't use much pressure!

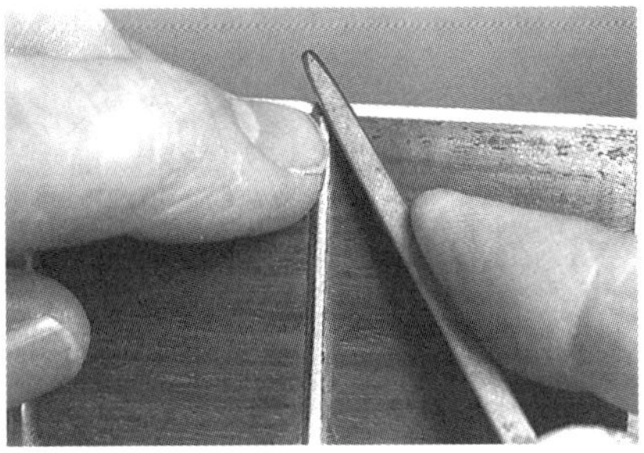

67 The smooth-edged miniature Waverly "3-Corner File" is perfect to smooth, polish, round, and finish up the ends. Start on one edge...

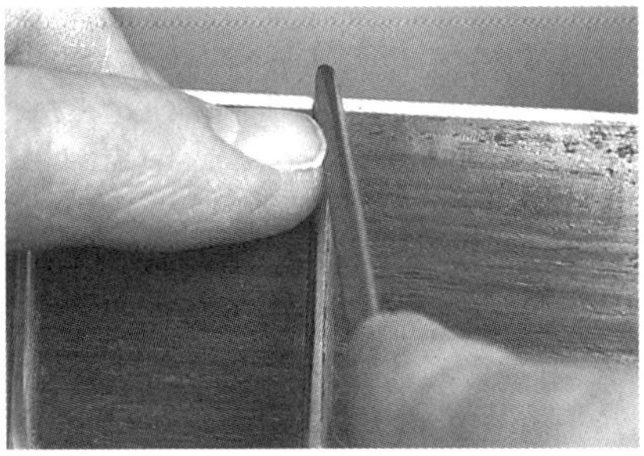

68 ...and round the end with short downstrokes...

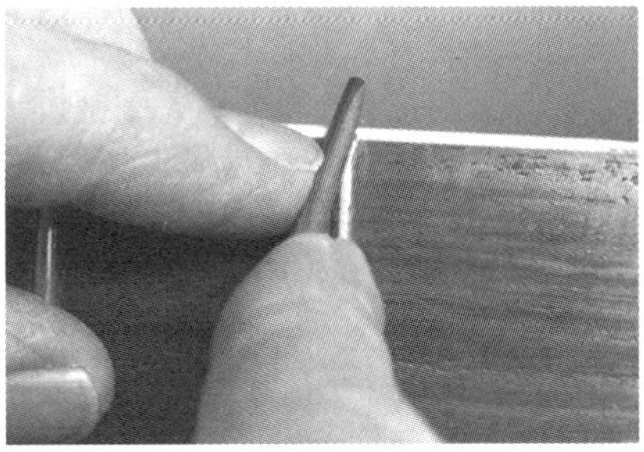

69 ...as you roll to the other side.

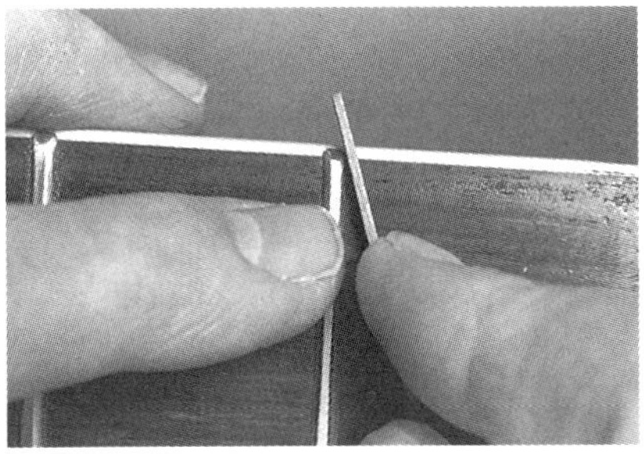

70 Another way to shape, de-burr, and round the ends is to use the 1/8" seating file, starting on its edge...

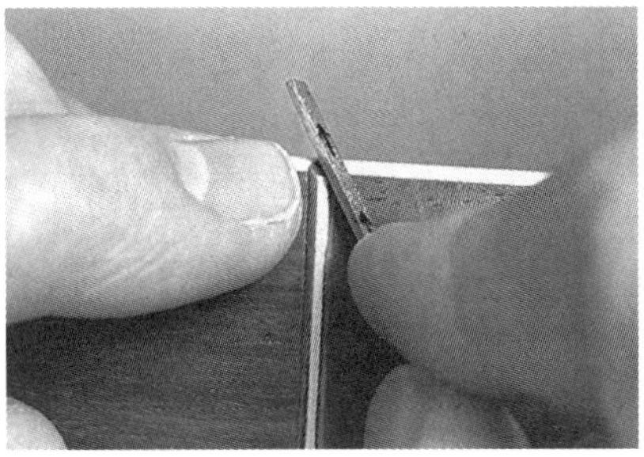

71 ...and roll-stroking toward center...

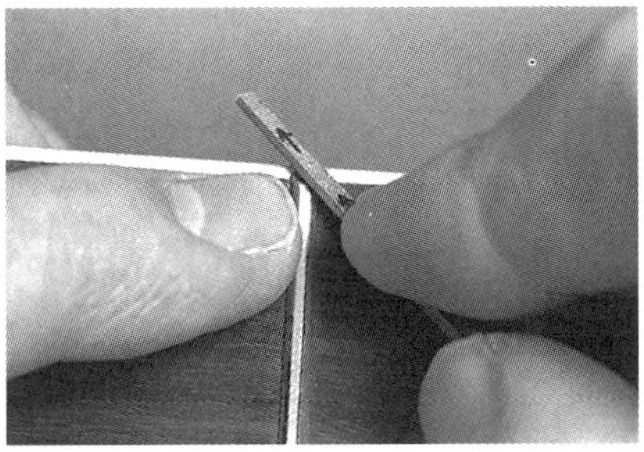

72 ...to accomplish the same fret end shaping.

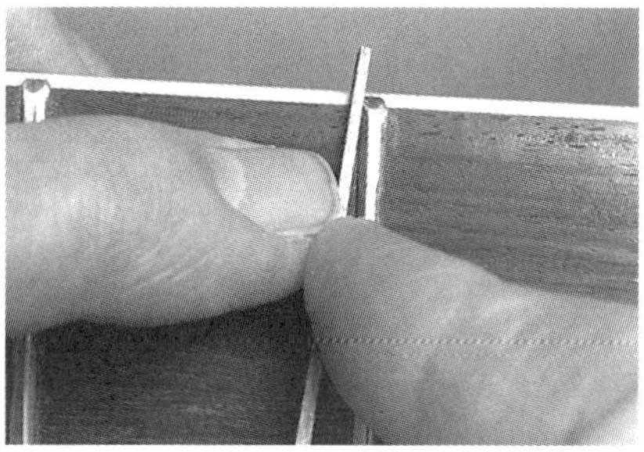

73 Here's the same stroke…

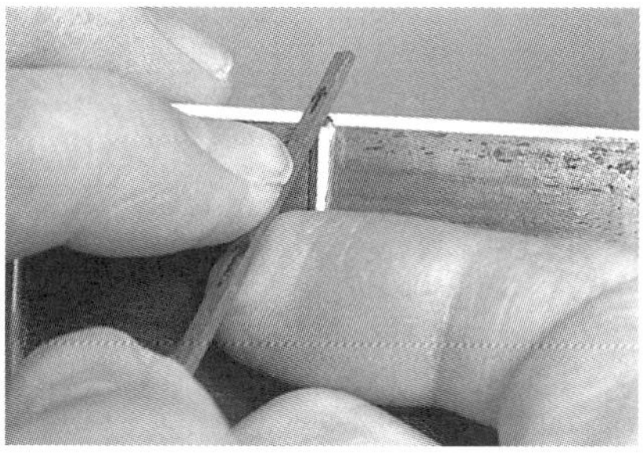

74 …working from the left side…

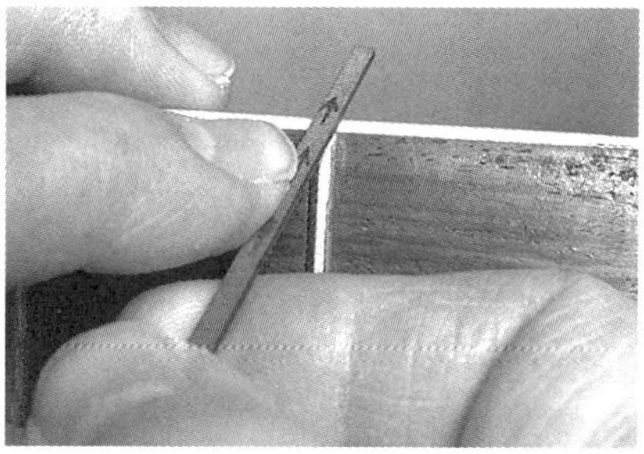

75 …toward center.

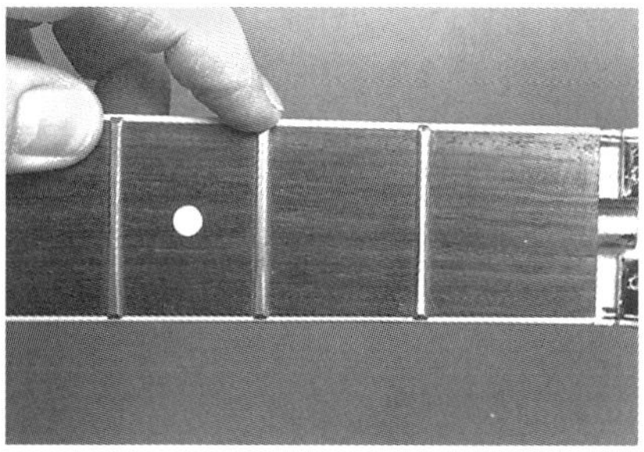

76 The fret ends are correct when they're well-shaped and you cannot feel a "picky" burr when you pass your fingertip along the edge (do this with your eyes closed—you'll feel a burr better).

77 OK—here's a play-by-play of fret rounding, using the Waverly 3-Corner file. Starting on the right hand side of the fret, watch the arrow on the file…

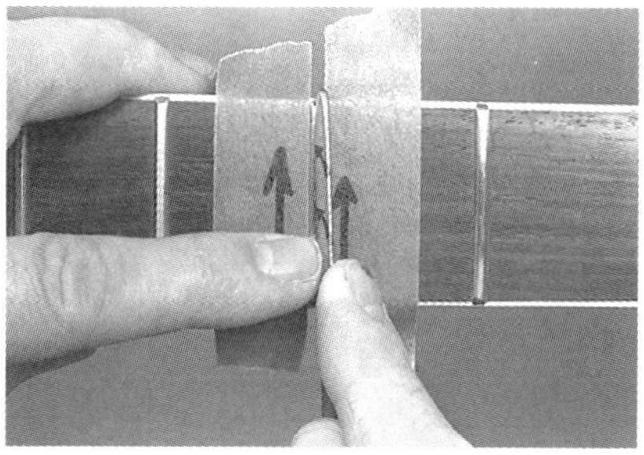

78 …as it rolls…

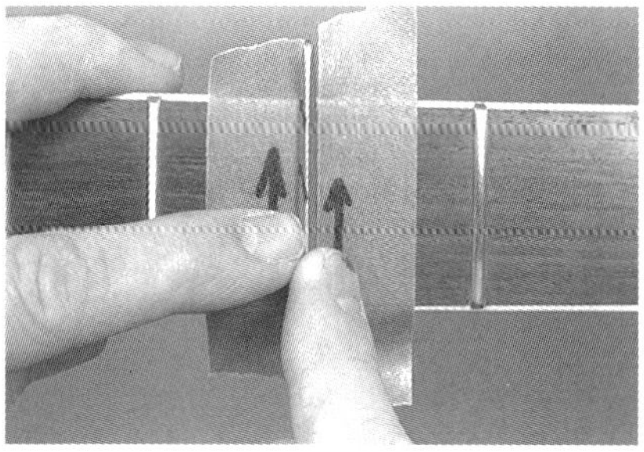

79 …over the top and passes center.

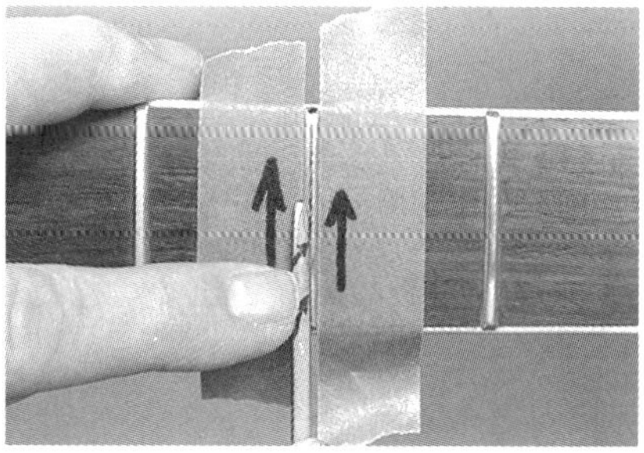

80 Then switch to the left, coming onto the fret filing in a straight, forward stroke as you roll…

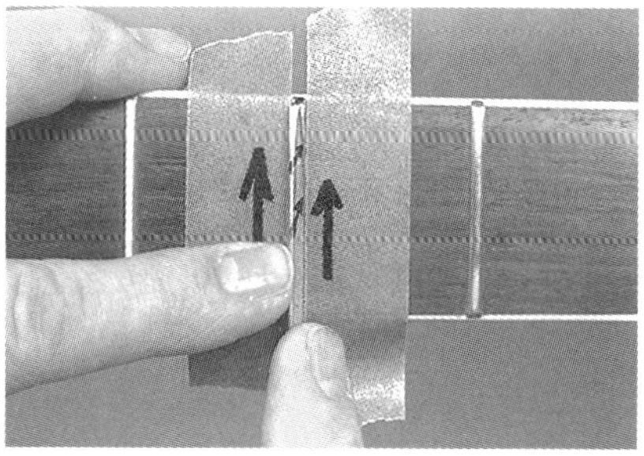

81 …toward center…

82 …rolling over the top as the file continues in a forward stroke…

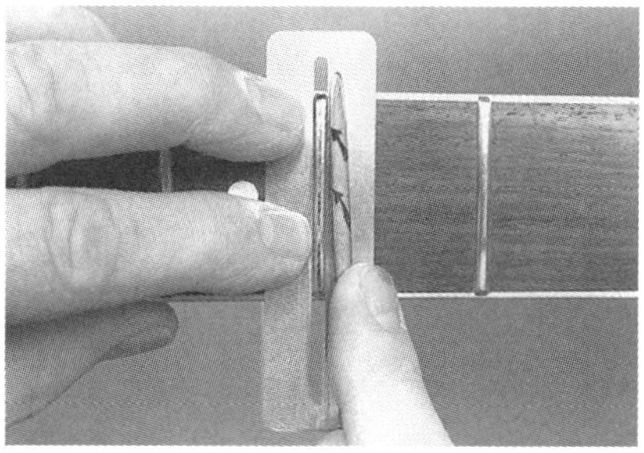

83 These thin stainless steel fretboard guards are great, by the way (you'll see them throughout the book).

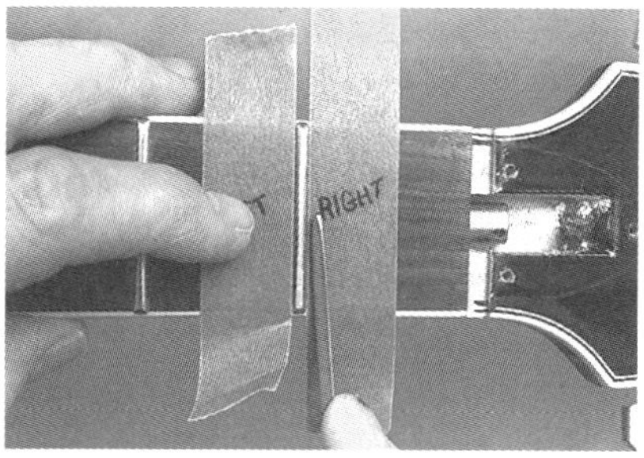

84 And you'll see several types of tape. This is brown "flatback" tape—very strong, quite thick, and protective (but it's very sticky—could pull finish off). This is the right hand stroke…

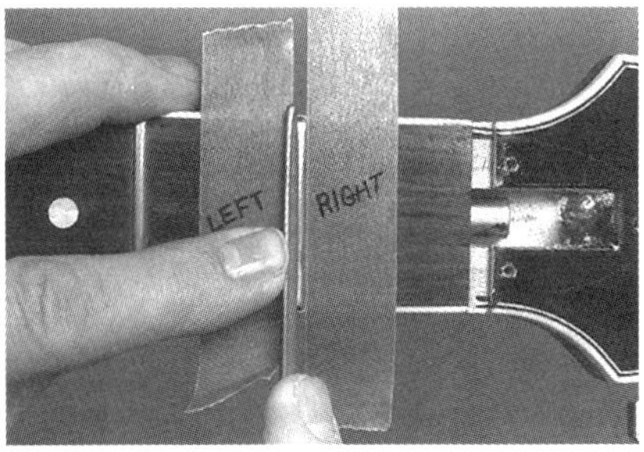

85 …and this is the left hand stroke (and the other hand's fingertip keeps the file on course).

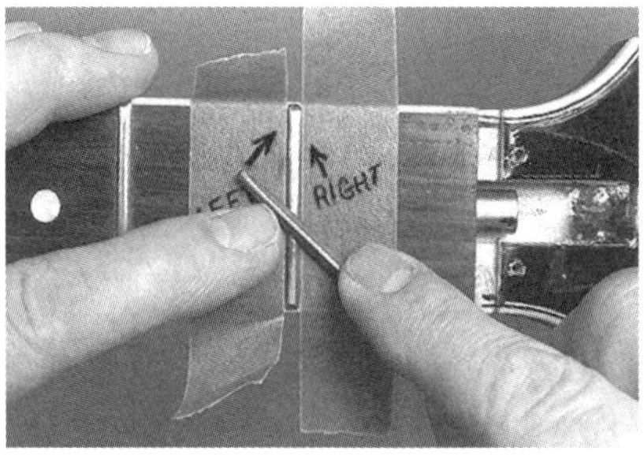

86 If there's one little "shiny spot" left on top, but the rest of the flat has disappeared, hold the file at an angle to "spot-file."

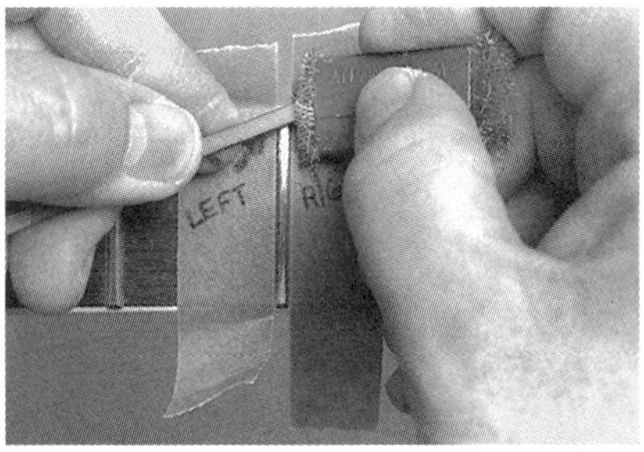

87 Clean your file often. This little brush is the only file cleaner we've seen that can clean such fine-toothed files.

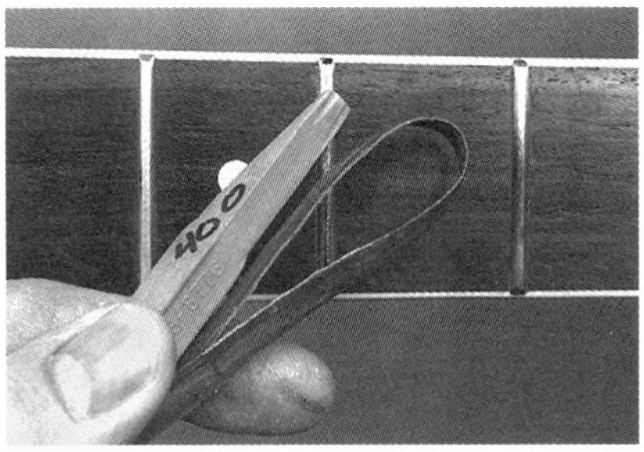

88 To remove any scratches left by the files, use the Sanding Stick. File two grooves on one side of the Sanding Stick…

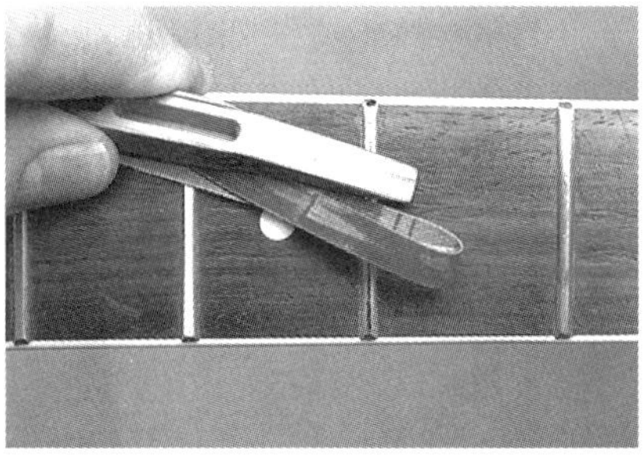

89 …and one on the other. The center groove sands the fret top, and the outer grooves sand the sides (right and left). You use the full width of the sandpaper this way, too.

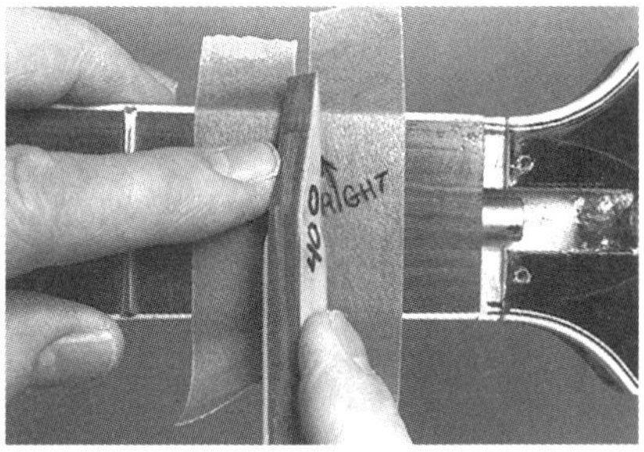

90 The Sanding Sticks remove the last thin strip of flat, or "land," from the center of the fret top using #400 and #600 sandpaper.

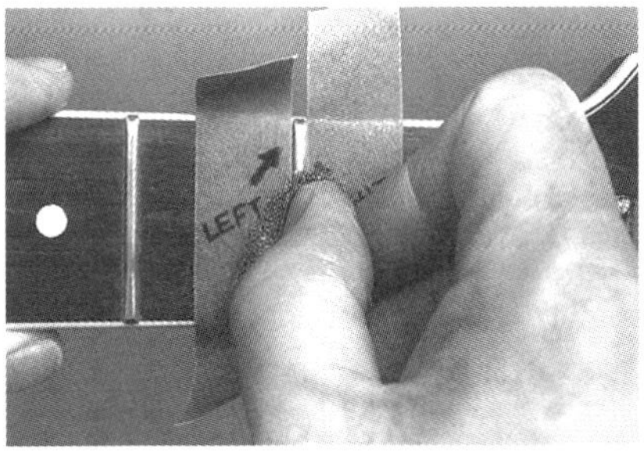

91 Final-polish the fret—still taped off—with #0000 steel wool.

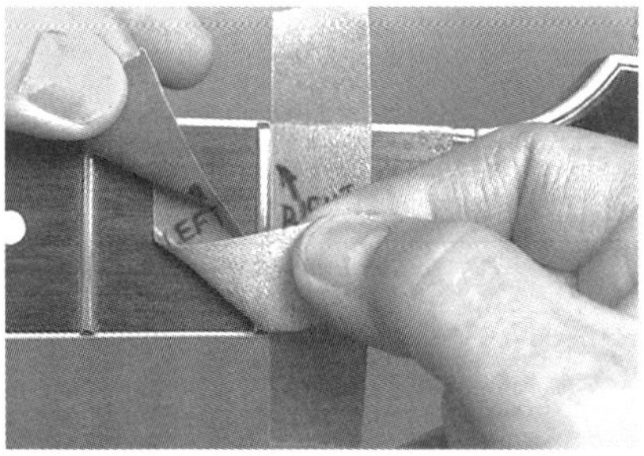

92 When you remove the protective tape, do it like this—peeling each end in, toward center. This avoids pulling lacquer off the fretboard edge!

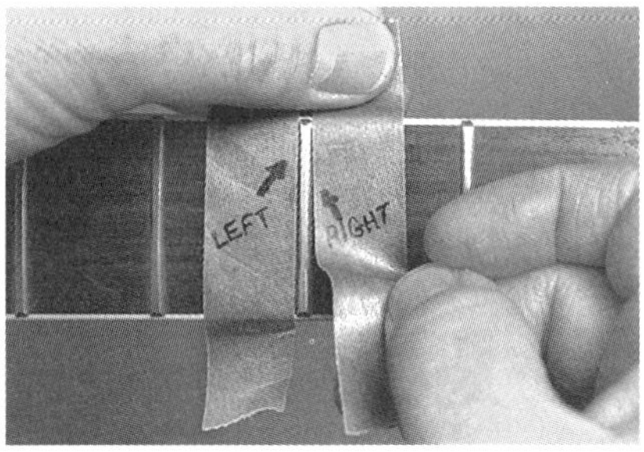

93 Move on to another fret. You can use the same strips of tape for at least several frets until they wear out (another choice is to tape off the entire board—you'll see that later).

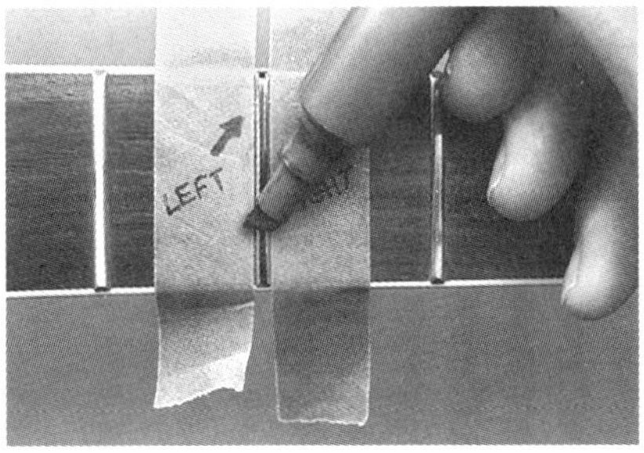

94 The blue marker works for dressing the frets too, letting you know when your rounding work has reached the center.

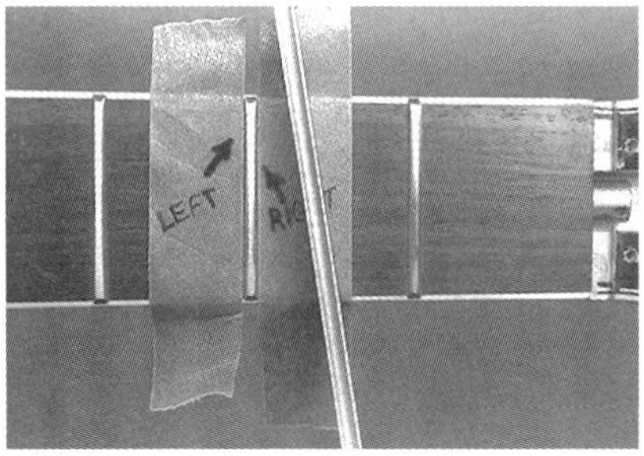

95 Here's another way to round the fret tops—with the Diamond Rounding File (this is the fine grit).

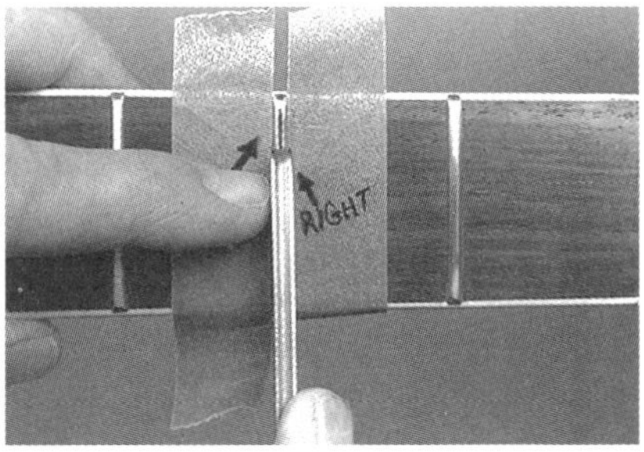

96 Choose the appropriate side of the file to do the rounding (there's a wide and a narrow radius). If you didn't remove much metal during the leveling operation, the fine grit is all you need…

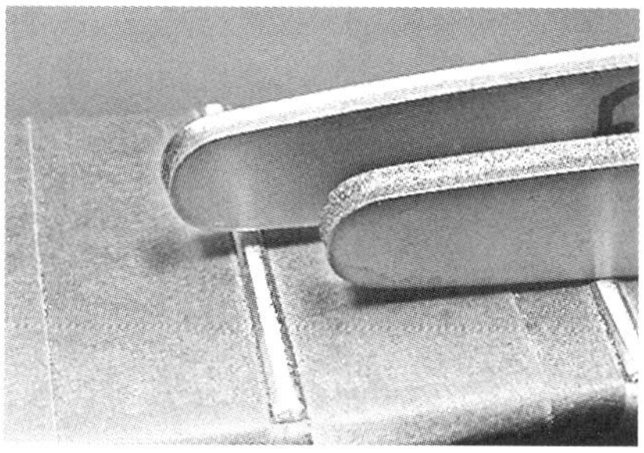
97 Both grits side by side. The coarse grit may leave some marks lengthwise which need to be sanded out later, but if the fret tops are quite broad and flat—like this—start with the coarse file.

98 A big advantage of the diamond file is its rounded tip or "nose" which can spot-file small areas without contacting the entire fret.

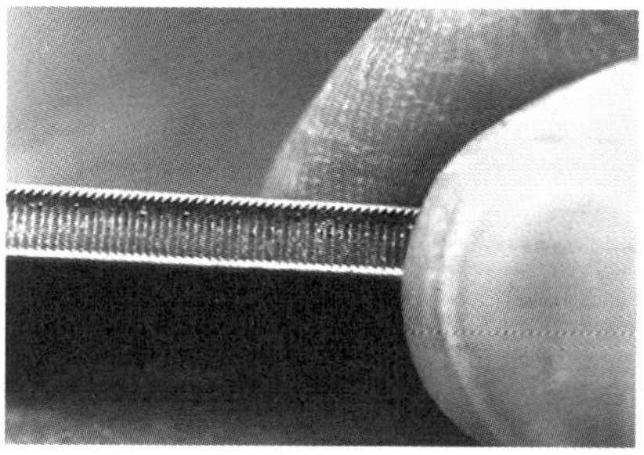
99 Before the diamond files became available, all rounding or "crowning" files had teeth…

100 …and many still prefer to use the toothed files because they hog metal off faster, and perhaps get you where you're headed a little quicker than diamonds.

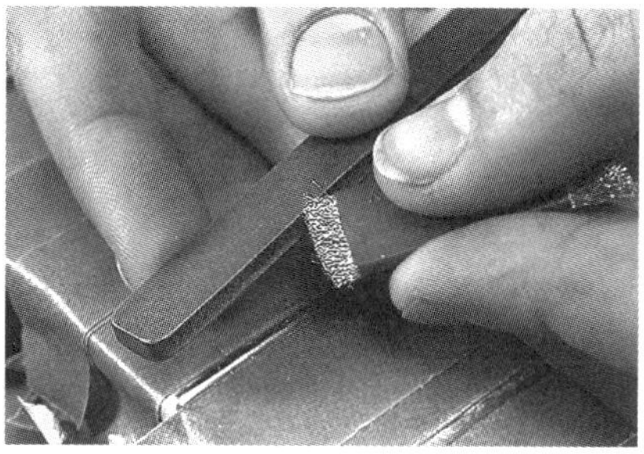
101 When you're using a toothed file, clean it often with this little brass-bristle file cleaner. Metal filings will build up in the teeth and scratch the sides of the frets if the file isn't clean!

102 Wipe paraffin on toothed files, and they'll clog less and cut smoother. Our Cutting Lubricant works well for this purpose.

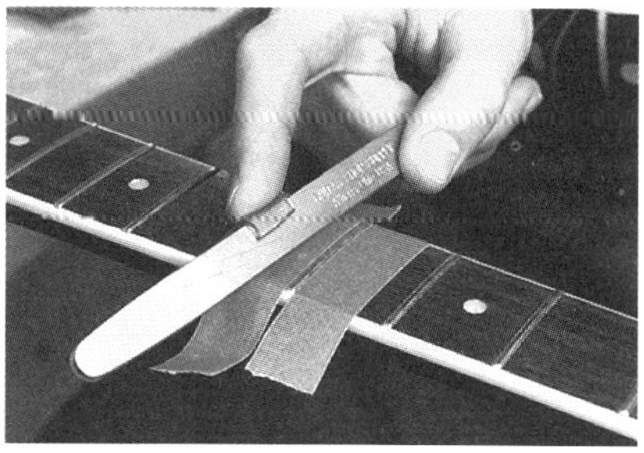
103 Unlike toothed files, diamond files will cut on both the forward and the backstroke. A piece of plastic tubing, sliced and pressed over one edge of the file protects your finger.

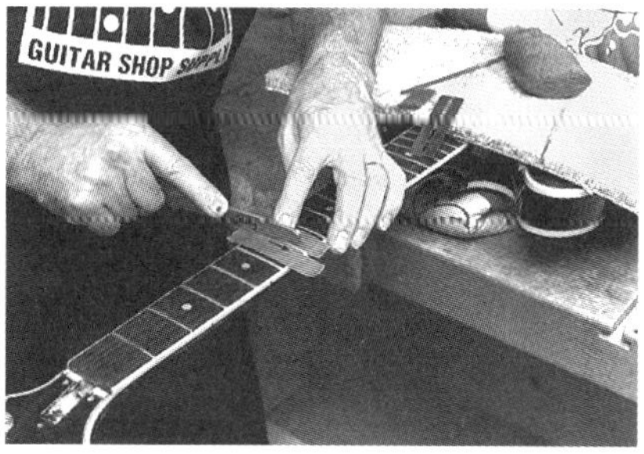

104 A carpet scrap resting on the guitar makes a great "tool-chest."

105 You must have good lighting (*and* plenty of room to move the light around) so you can catch the light off the fret tops to see the fine edge of "land" as it disappears.

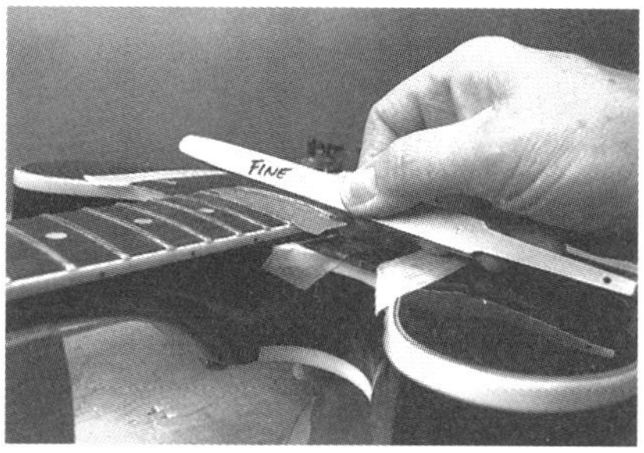

106 A problem with all files is that you hit the body with the handle and/or your own hand when you try to work up on the body extension.

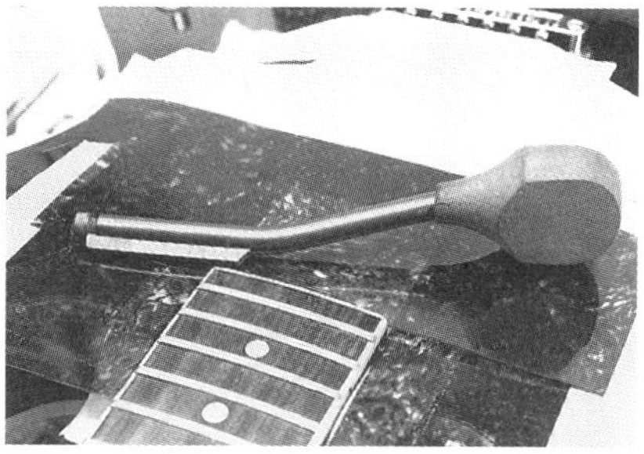
107 One solution is the Waverly Three-in-One (offset handle) file. It has three different-sized toothed edges which are interchangeable…

108 …it lets you work with your hand and knuckles free of the body.

109 Here the whole board is taped off with drafting tape for the final steel wooling...

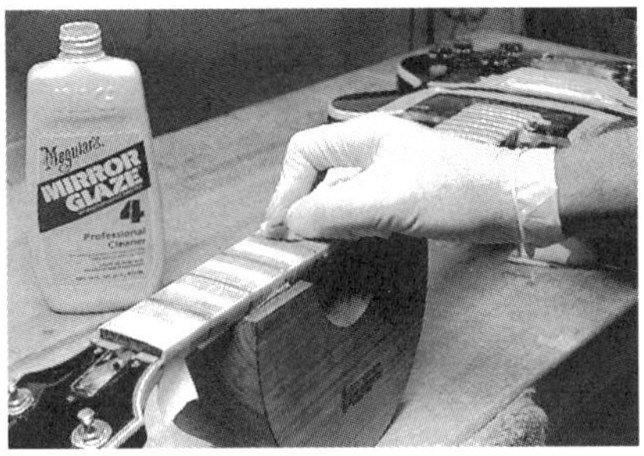

110 ...and polishing. Mirror Glaze No. 4 does a great job—as does the "X-Treem" Metal Polish.

111 Most of us polished by hand for years until...

112 ...we found this affordable stationary buffer.

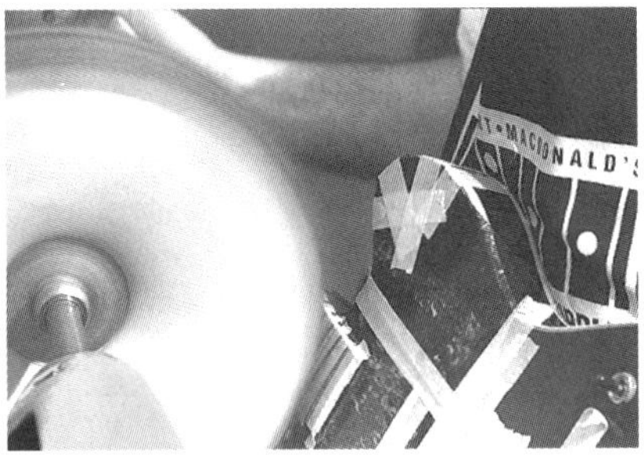

113 When you're buffing on the wheel, buff from the center down (don't catch the top edge of the fretboard or you'll throw the guitar!).

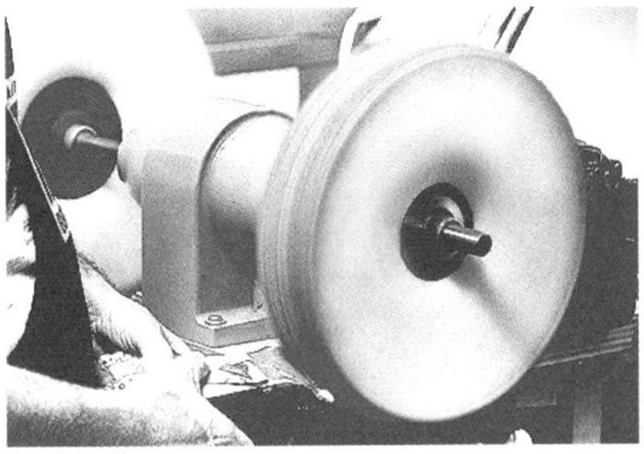

114 Frets should be buffed on the coarse ("brown") wheel. This is the brown stick compound being applied to the buffer.

115 This buffer is big enough for anything, yet small enough to be stored out of the way in a small shop. You don't *need* a buffer to polish frets, but it does add the professional look.

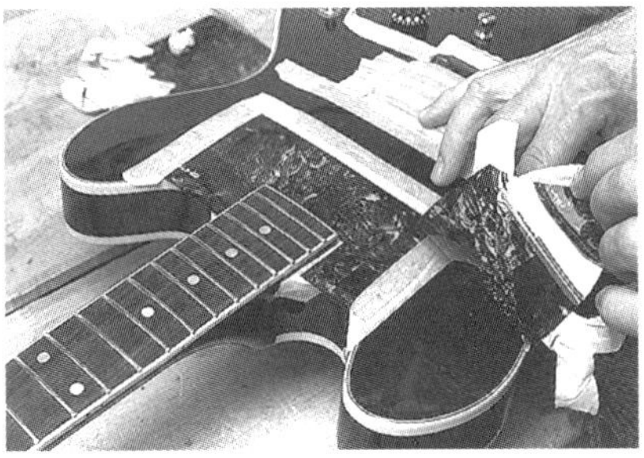

116 Carefully remove all the guards and tape...

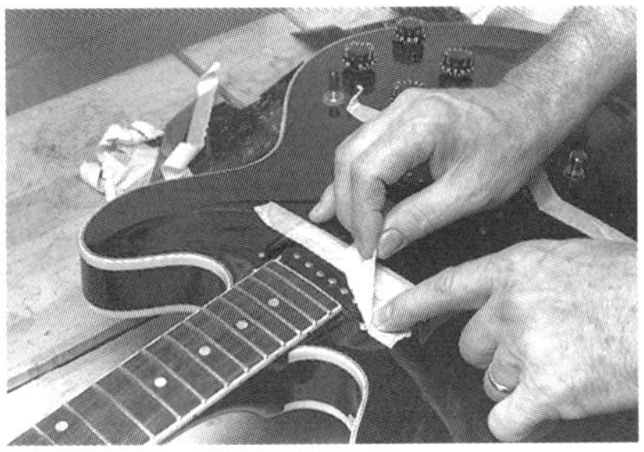

117 ...careful of that chip! You don't want to pull off the finish.

118 Re-adjust that truss rod...

119 ...and string 'er up.
This baby's done!

LESSON 2

A "SIMPLE" REFRET JOB
(NO BINDING, AND A GOOD STRAIGHT NECK)

We knew that this 1957 OO-18 Martin would be an "easy" refret because it had such a straight, stiff, "perfect" neck. An easy refret is one that requires no major leveling of the fretboard, needs no inlays (position markers) removed, has no binding, and in some cases doesn't even have an adjustable truss rod. This was a case where we could pretty much just "yank 'em out and put 'em in."

1 In general, '50s Martins usually have very good necks—stiff and straight—because of the old style deep (1/2") T-Bar non-adjustable truss rod.

2 And this one's no exception. In the playing position the neck looks almost straight…

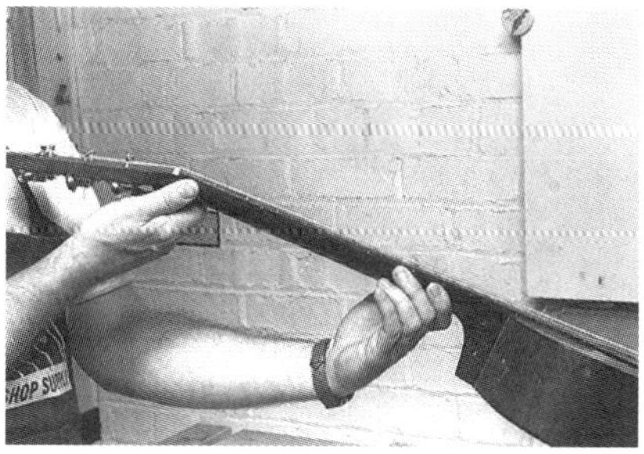

3 …and the flex test can't make it budge!

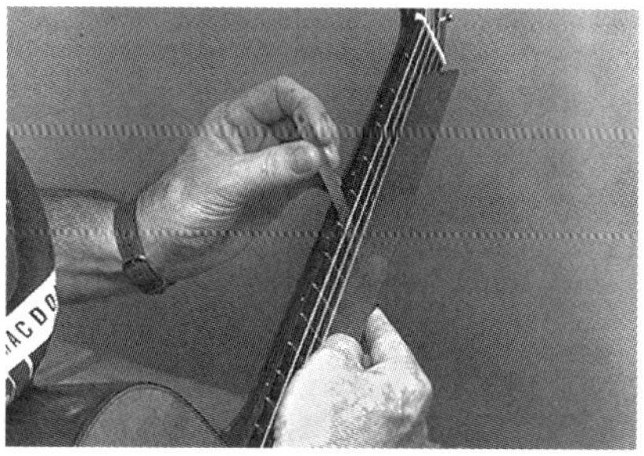

4 Under string tension this neck shows .004" of relief, which is almost nothing. In fact, it's the perfect amount!

5 This one shows .006" of "fall-away" or "drop-off" on the tongue, which is somewhat unusual for a guitar which has never had a neck reset.

6 Even laying on its back with the neck on a rest the neck remains the same. In other words, this is a very stable neck and should be easy to refret.

7 Take off the strings…

8 …and even without the strings, the neck is straight (most necks would back-bow).

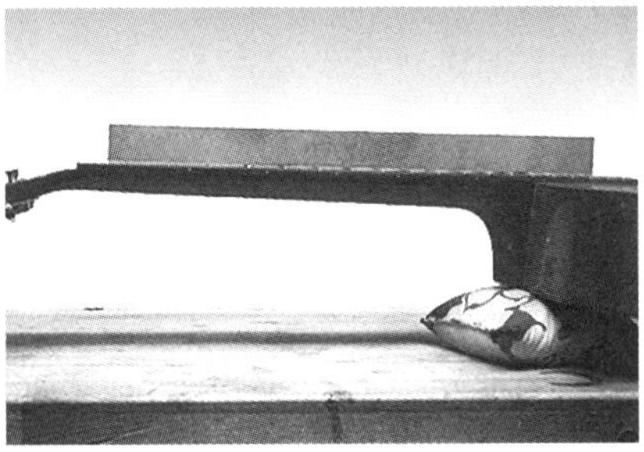

9 Even with the neck resting free—totally unsupported—the neck is straight…

10 …it simply needs new frets.

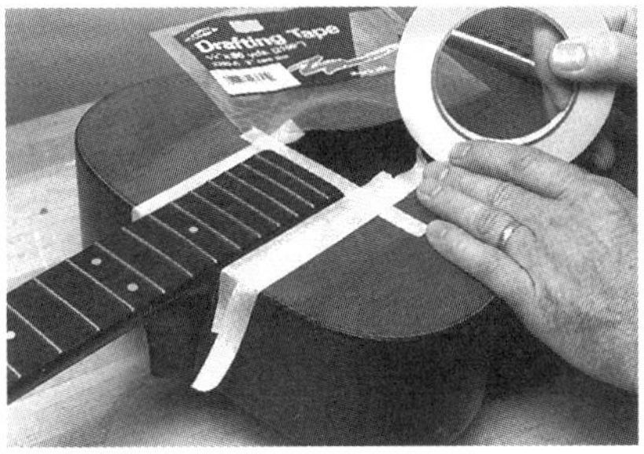

11 For top protection, start by taping off around the fingerboard with draftsman's tape (it has a very low "tack," or stickiness, and won't pull off brittle old finish as easily as other tapes).

12 Then you can use stronger masking tape to tape your top guards onto the drafting tape (these guards are pieces of .018" tortoise pickguard material scrap).

13 Heat the frets with a soldering iron; the metal fret guard is *the best tool* for protecting against slips!

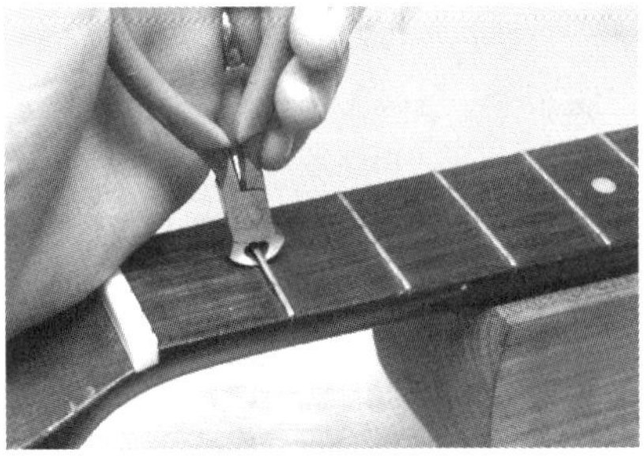

14 The little fret pullers get under a fret more easily than large ones (see "Guide To Tools, page 29)…

15 …and when combined with heat, can pull frets with virtually no chipping, if you're careful.

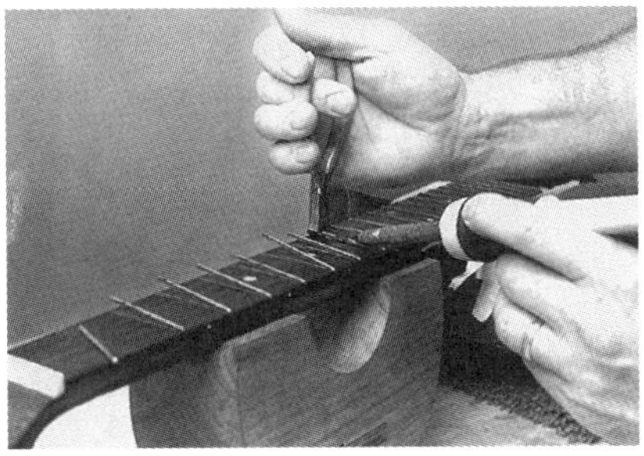

16 The neck rocker is great for immobilizing the neck during removal.

17 These slots measure .020"—typical for a Martin of this vintage. Now check the wire that was taken out (and record the measurements).

18 The original frets have a tang width of .021" or .0215" (frankly, it's pretty hard to measure frets in half-thousandth sizes)…

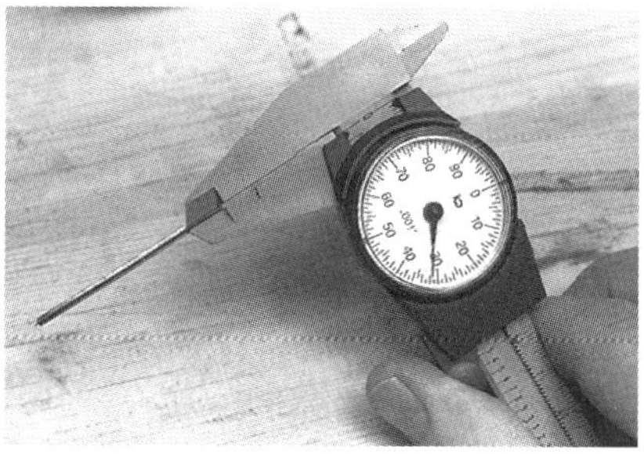

19 …a bead or barb width of .0315" (or so)…

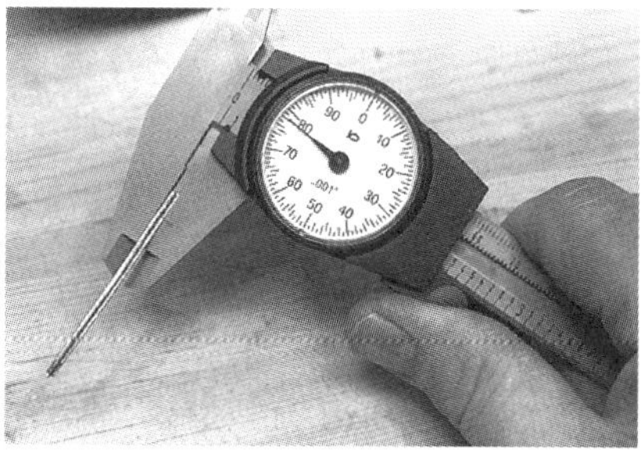

20 …the crown is .078" wide.

21 The total height of a worn fret is .090"…

22 …the worn crown measures .027". The difference between the two (.090" minus .027") gives an actual tang depth or (height) of .063".

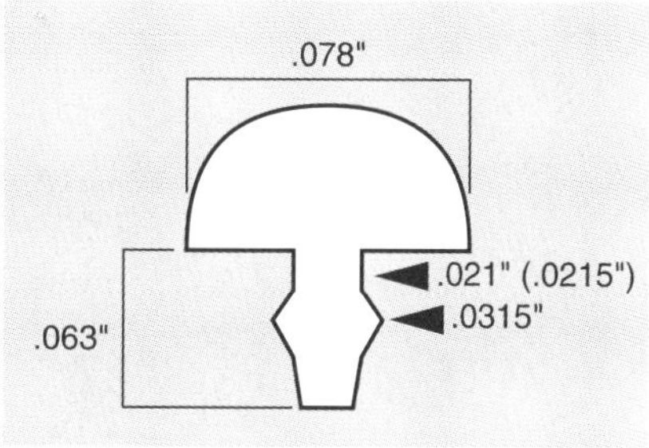

23 The original frets looked like this drawing…

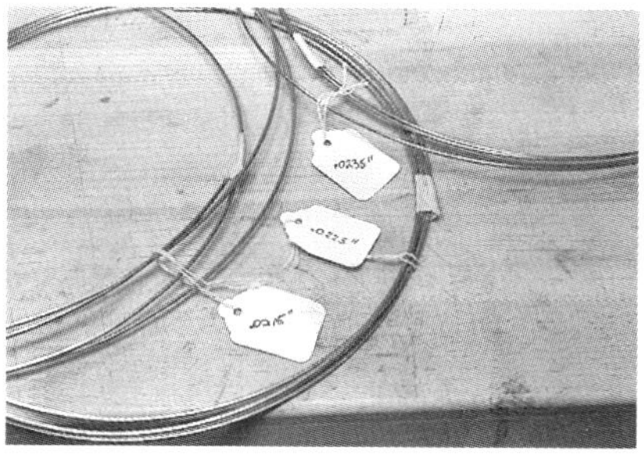

24 Normally with a refret in rosewood you use a tang from one to two sizes bigger than the original. If the original was .021", a suitable replacement would be .0225" or .0235".

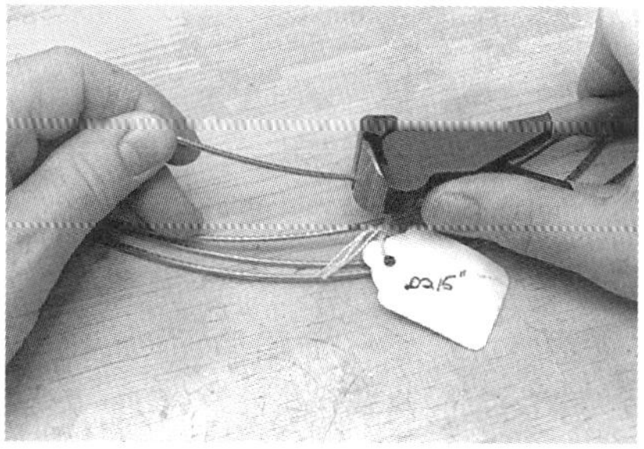

25 However, this neck was so stiff that it made sense to at least *try* the original wire size (the .0215"). When a Brazilian rosewood fingerboard is dense and hard, the fret slots' width is hardly affected by the factory fret job.

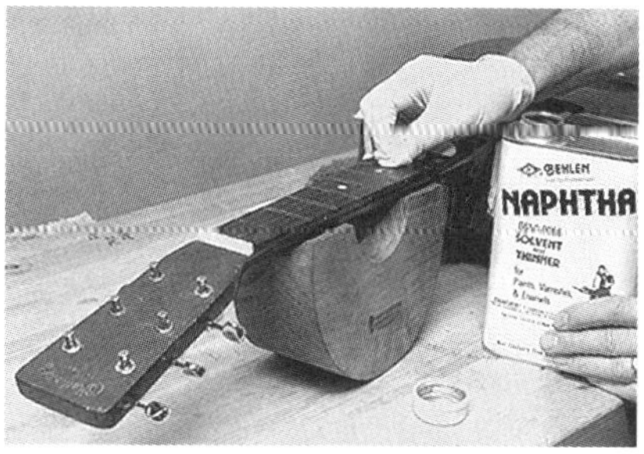

26 One thing was for sure—the fretboard was filthy. Naphtha cut the grease and buildup quickly (this was done in a room with good fresh air ventilation).

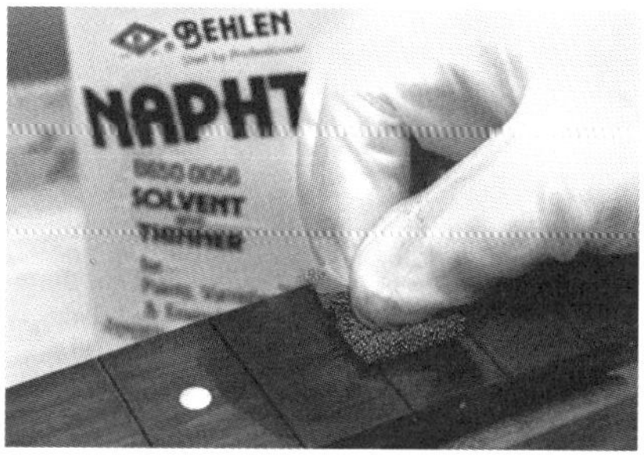

27 It took Scotch-brite pads soaked in naphtha to loosen the crud…

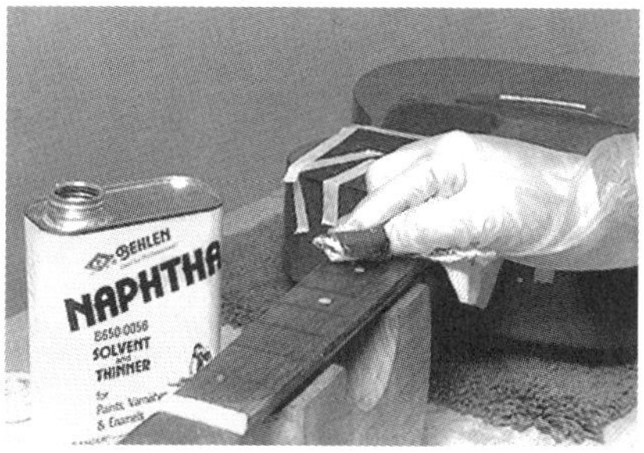

28 …and several actual washings with a Naphtha-soaked rag to wash it up.

29 A clean, dry fretboard—original and unsanded. This neck is so good that we could fret it without sanding or re-shaping at all (just pull 'em out and put 'em back in).

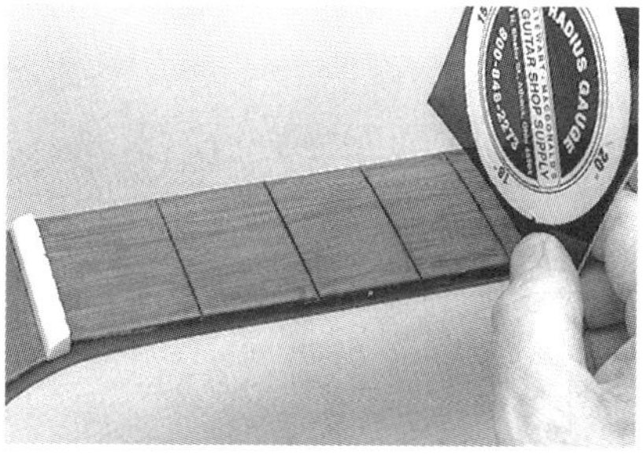

30 Typical of most vintage Martins, the fretboard radius is 16" at the nut…

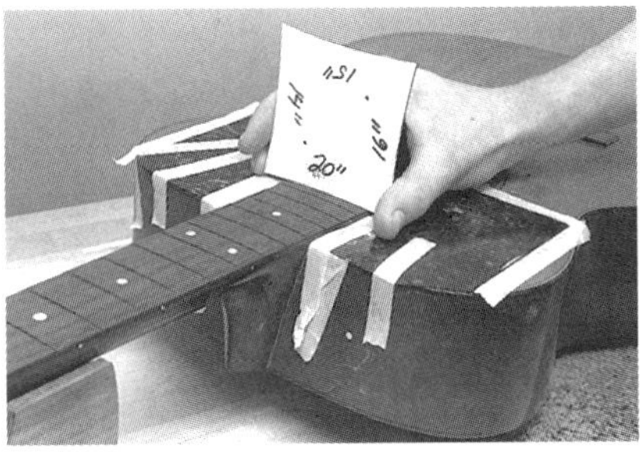

31 ... and ends at 20" near the soundhole.

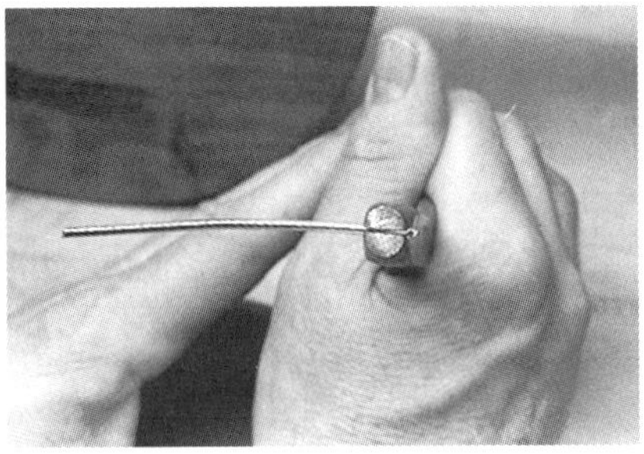

32 Always check your fretwire for end-to-end tang straightness; this wire has a kink in it. Hold it by the end with the fret bending pliers, looking at the underside...

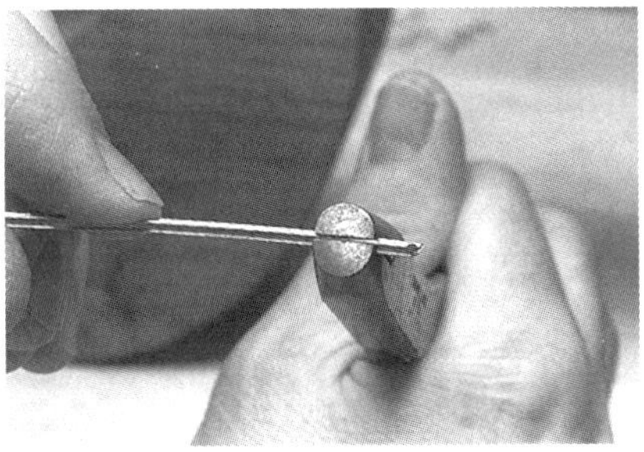

33 ...but you don't necessarily put the re-bend at the point where the kink is. Put your index finger toward the center as a fulcrum...

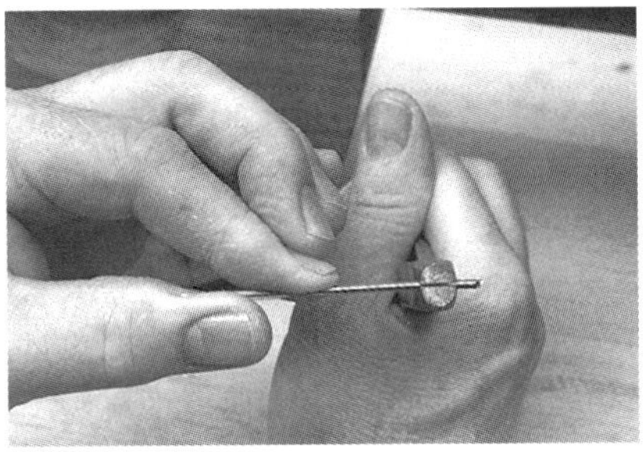

34 ...and with the thumb holding the bottom, put a little "reverse bend" in the wire.

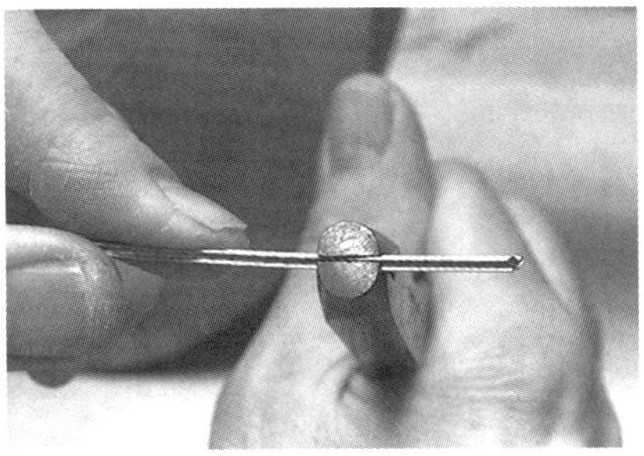

35 Move the bending pliers along the fret's length...

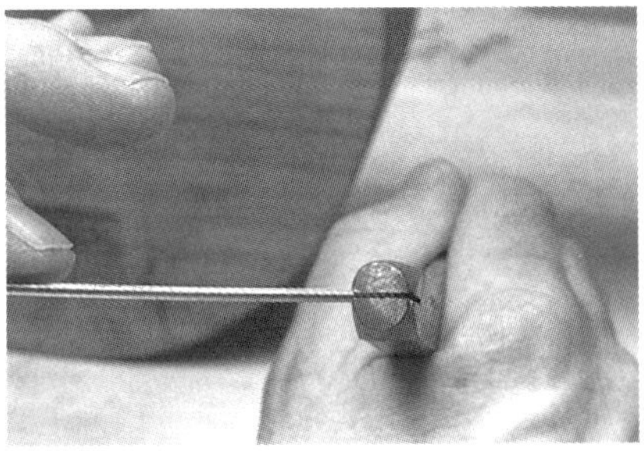

36 ...and continue the bend.

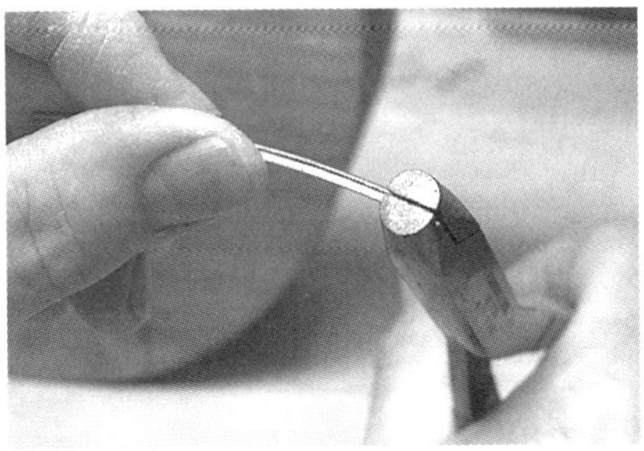

37 Once the wire's straight end-for-end, bend it to the curve of the fretboard. Grab it on the end (the pliers are notched for this job)...

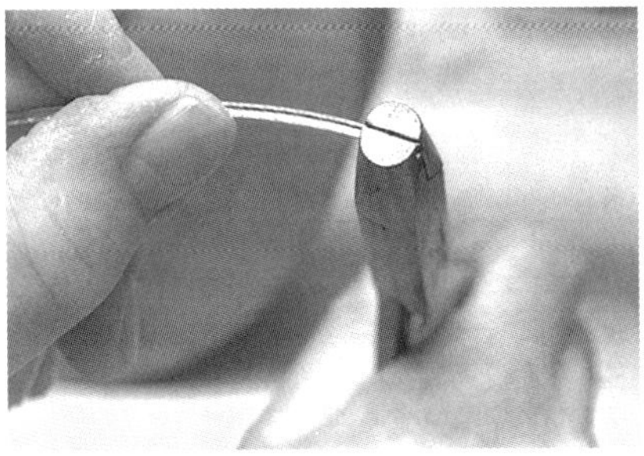

38 ...and again use your thumb to apply the bending pressure.

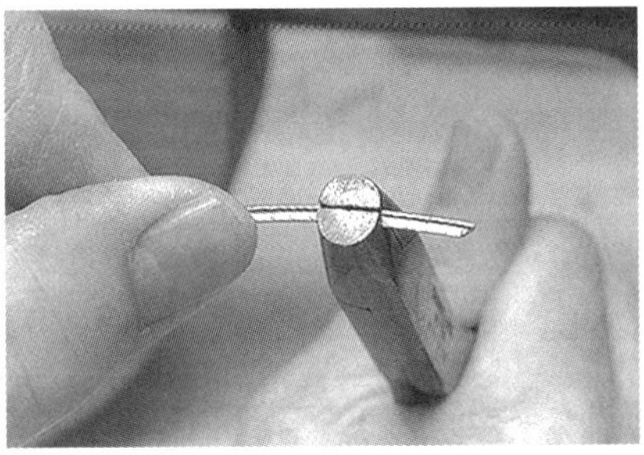

39 Move the nippers along the length, bending as you go...

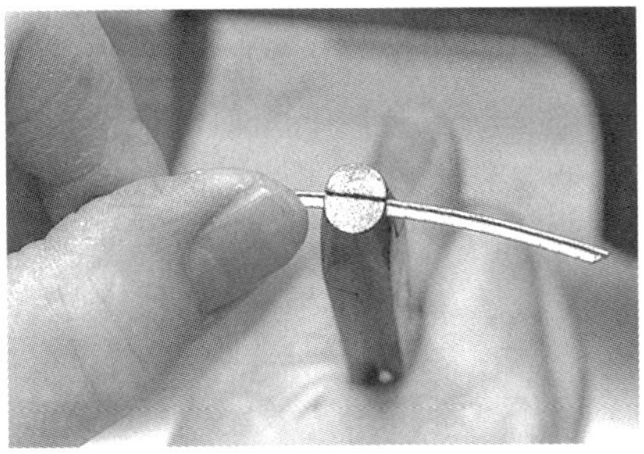

40 ...until near the middle you'll stop...

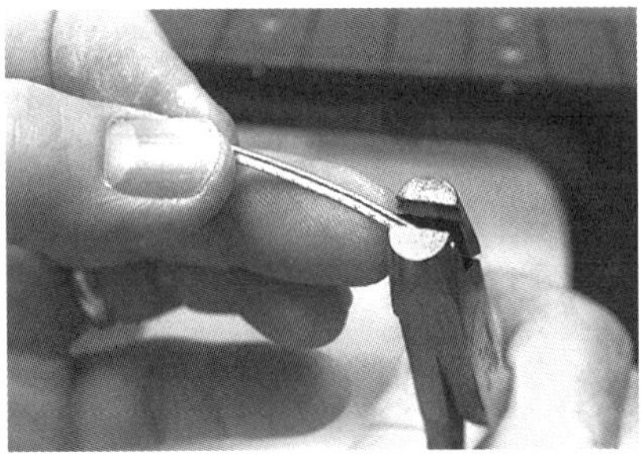

41 ...flip or "spin" the fret...

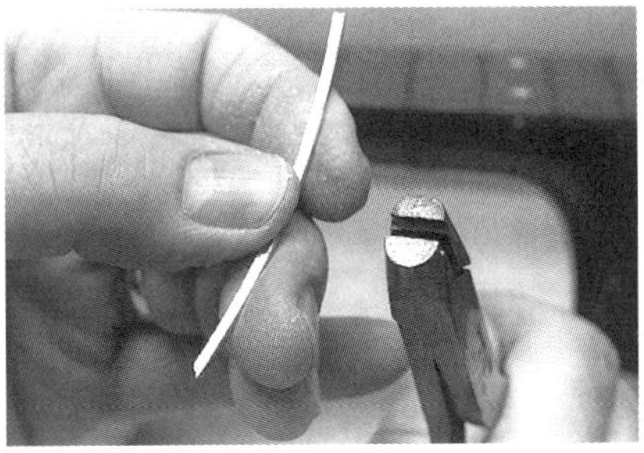

42 ...end for end...

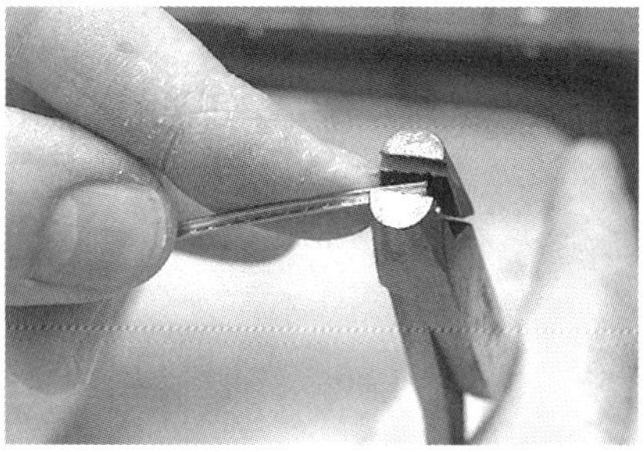

43 ...and repeat the bending process...

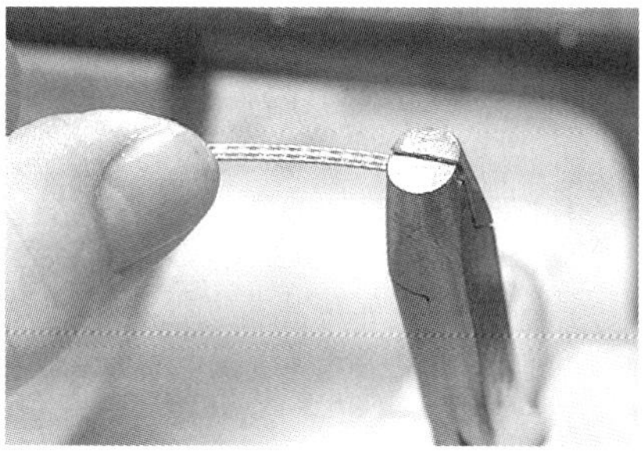

44 ...starting on the other end...

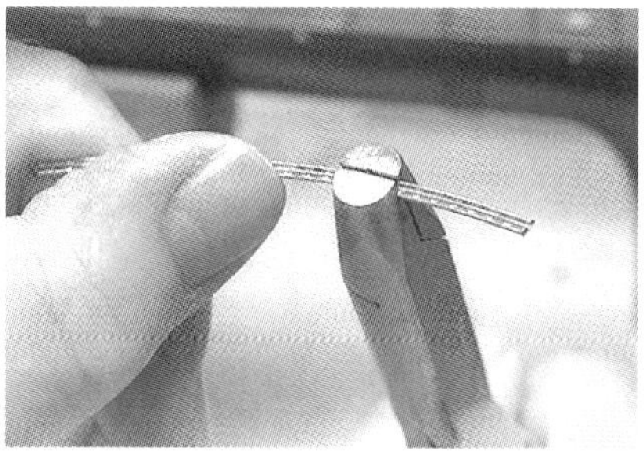

45 ...and bending until you reach the center.

46 Side view of the fret bending pliers showing the notches ground into the jaws.

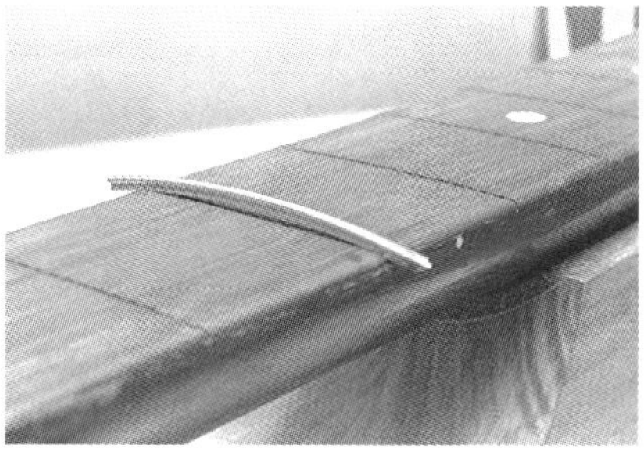

47 The frets should be overbent at least this much (sometimes more).

48 The frets will go in easily if you slightly chamfer (bevel) the top of the fret slot (this helps the tang guide itself into the slot).

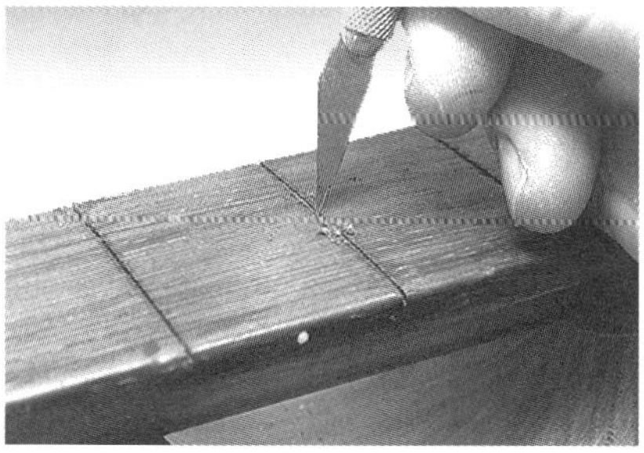

49 Use a #11 X-acto blade to scrape sawdust, dirt, glue, or sweaty crud residue from the slot. Only remove whatever can be scraped away freely—not widening the slot!

50 This .020" Blitz sawblade will guarantee a clean slot with a clean bottom. But on radiused fretboards, be careful not to accidentally cut at 'B' (top of the slot)...

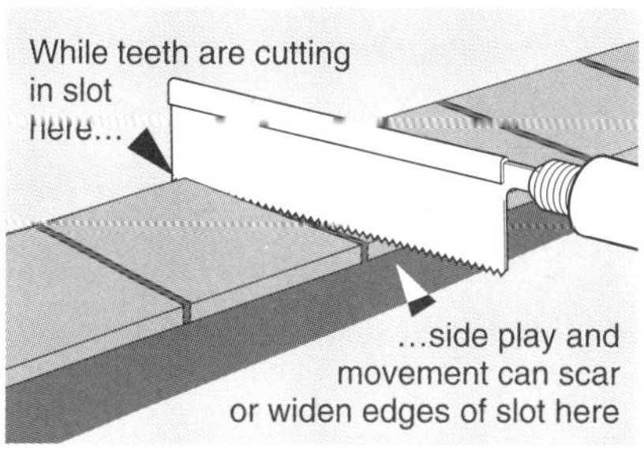

...when the other end is cutting down in the slot as at 'A' (as shown in drawing above).

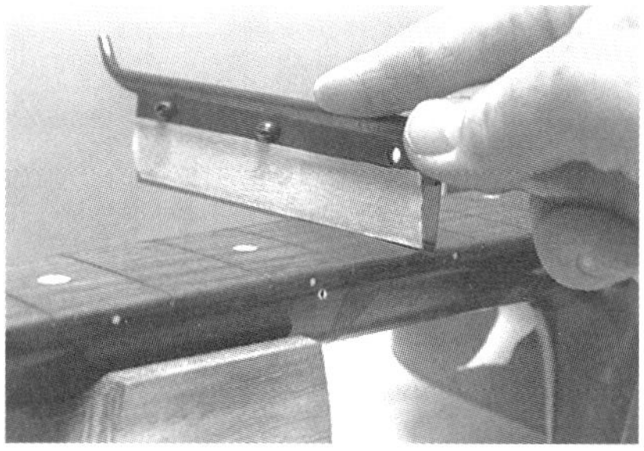

51 Masking tape works as a depth guide to keep from going too deep. (Check the short saw and depth guide in Lesson Three, photo 41). These slots don't need to be deepened because we're not taking off any wood...

52 ...Martin fret slots are usually plenty deep anyhow. And just because you might use the saw doesn't mean that you wouldn't check every slot with the knife...

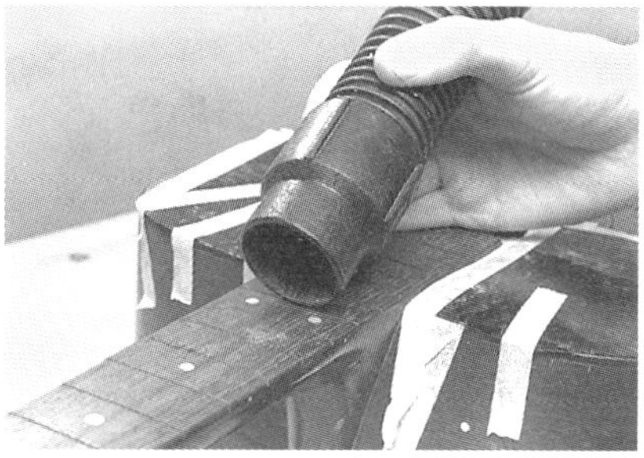

53 ...and then vaccum up any dust and blow the slots out with compressed air if it's available.

54 Hammer in a short test piece of the chosen wire (.0215") at the 14th or 15th fret (it's over the neck block and real solid—making for easy hammering).

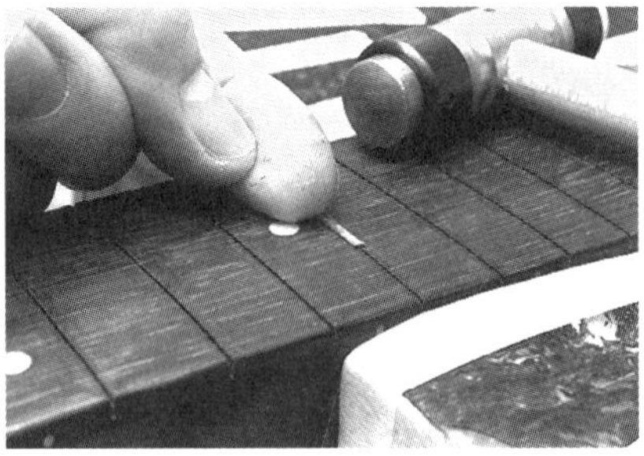

55 Try to see how easily it will lift out when you pry with your fingernail (the "fingernail test"). If you can pry it out with your fingernail or thumbnail, go to the next size up!

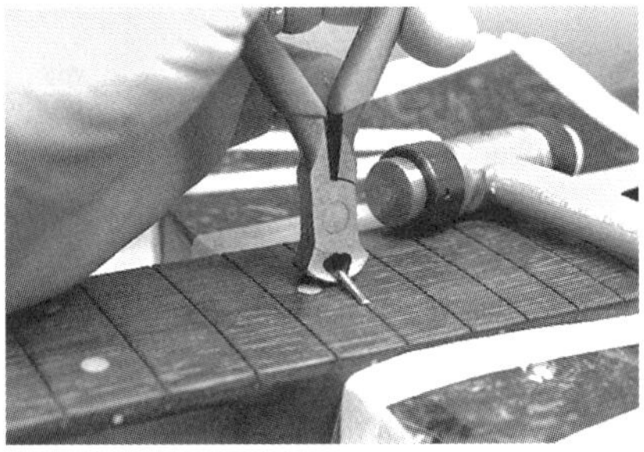

56 It's well seated and needs the fret pullers to get it out. So we're replacing the frets with the same size wire we removed—because this particular rosewood is so dense (as mentioned before).

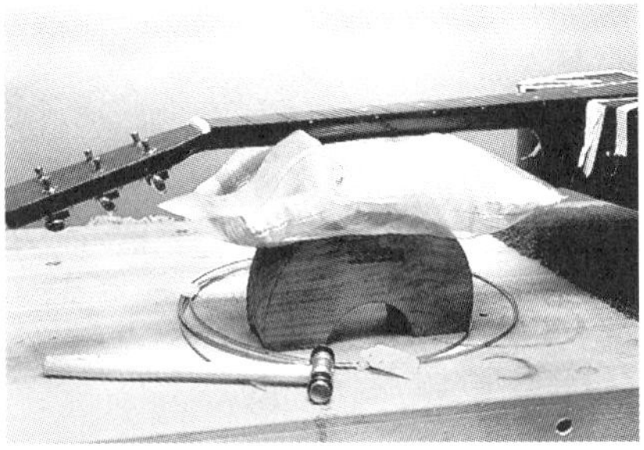

57 We're ready to fret. The neck rocker, upside down and with a 25 lb. bag of buckshot laying on it, makes a great anvil to hammer against.

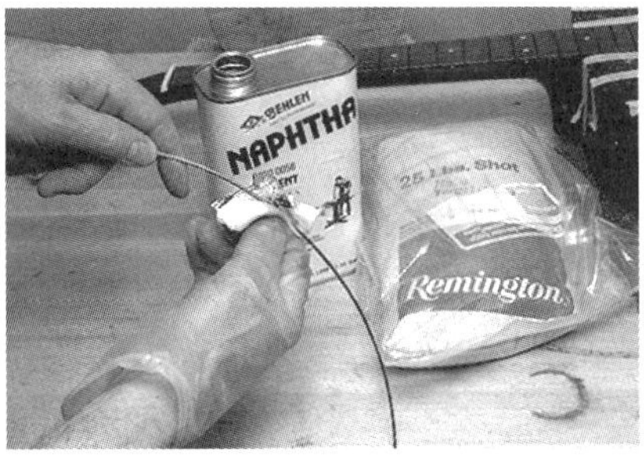

58 Fretwire is greasy; clean it with Naphtha or other solvent before using it. Wear gloves, work in a well-ventilated area, and wipe until black grease no longer comes off (especially on the tang).

59 For straight fretwire lengths, we slide it into this PVC "cleaning tube" to de-grease it. The bottom is permanently closed by a glued-on cap…

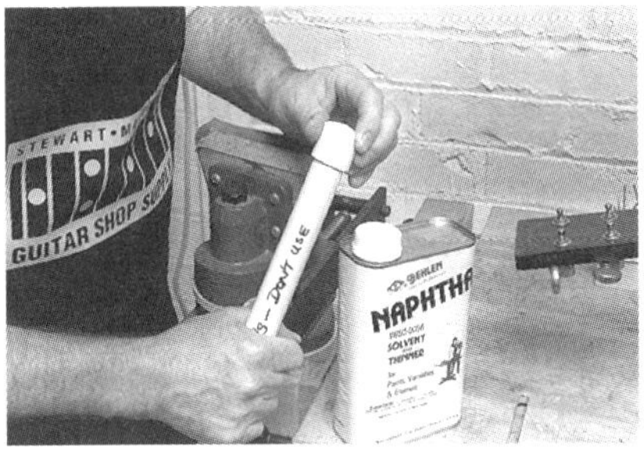

60 …after putting enough straight lengths of wire in the tube, fill it with Naphtha and put on an unglued cap (they fit so tight that there's no evaporation).

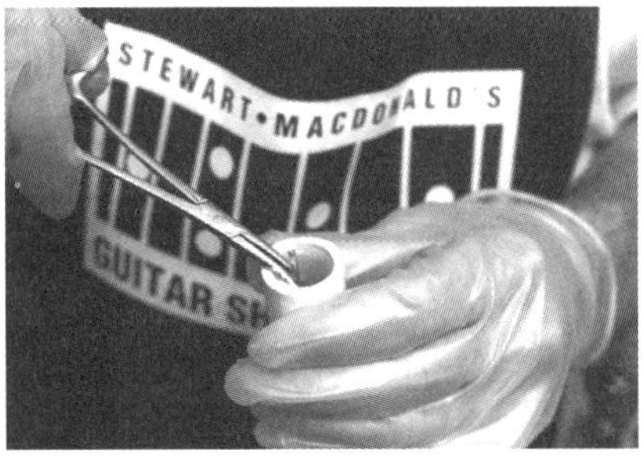

61 Later, when you pull the pieces out, most of the grease remains in the solvent…

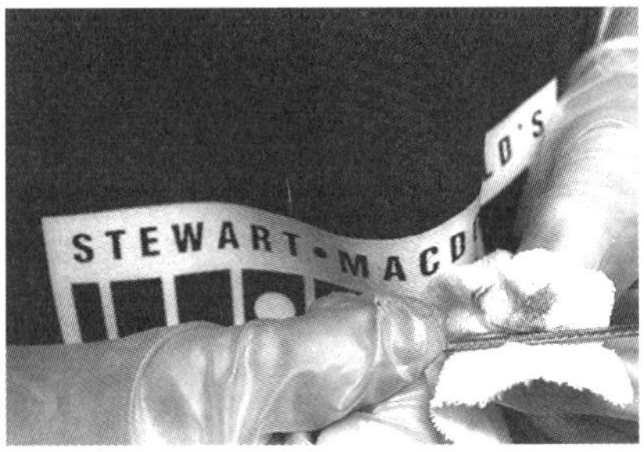

62 …and the rest wipes off easily. Fretwire must be degreased before using it (especially if you plan to use glue in the slots).

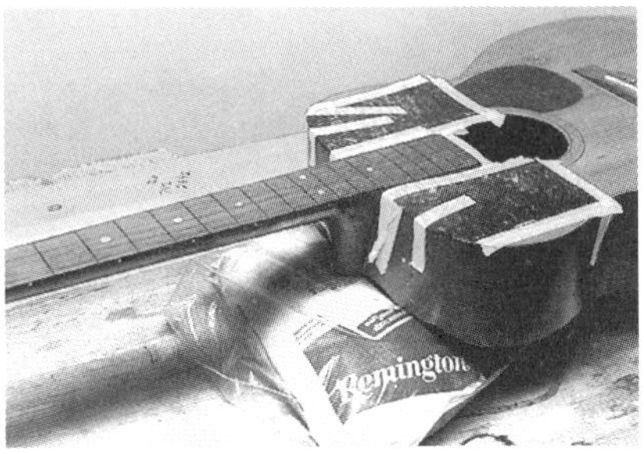

63 We put the first fret in up on the body joint to get a feel for the frets' holding power in an area that wouldn't affect the neck's flex or stiffness. Rest the guitar's shoulders on the buckshot for rigidity.

64 Dab a little warm water on the slot to swell up the wood—the fret will go in easier with this lubrication, and the swelled wood will grab the fret better.

65 Use plenty of over-bend…

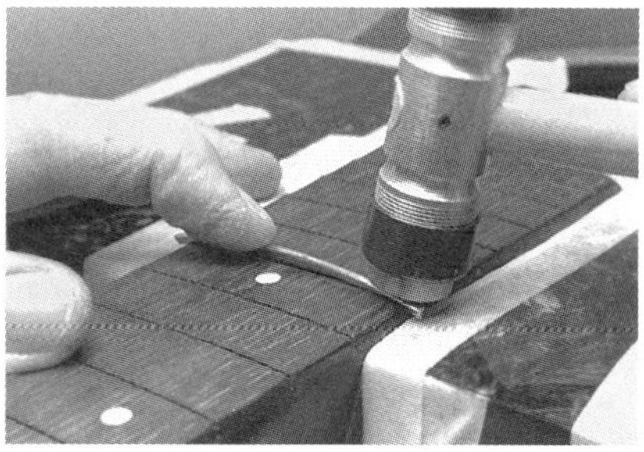

66 ...and hammer the ends down first (not completely home, but definitely seat them). Do one side...

67 ...then the other...

68 ...and then hammer home the whole fret, going back and forth along the fret length...

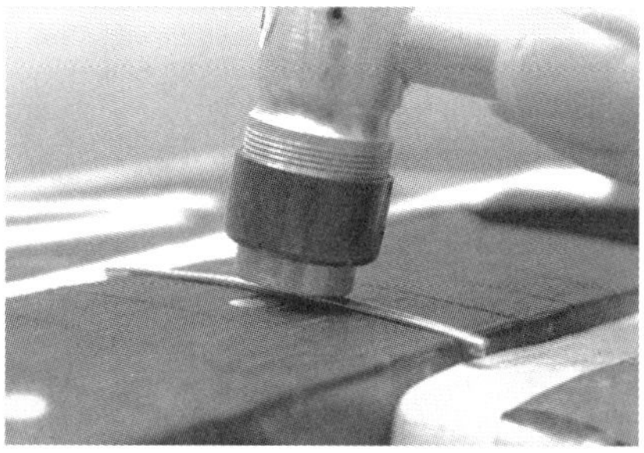

69 ...so that the fret seats uniformly.

70 The brass face of this fretting hammer is soft enough that it won't mark the fretwire.

71 Try the thumbnail test on the fret end overhang...

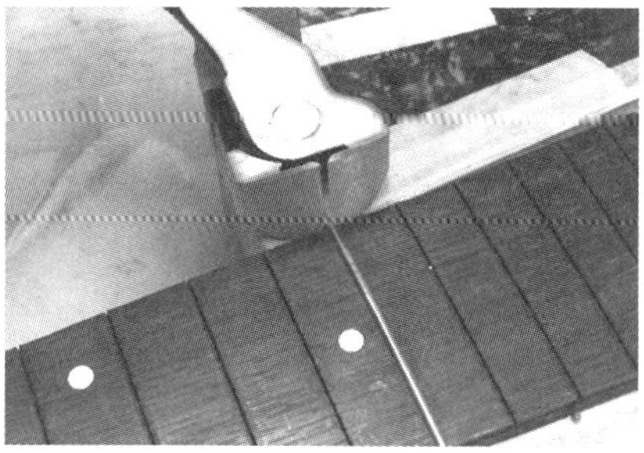

72 ...and if it doesn't pull up, the fit is tight. Go ahead and clip off the overhang with your nippers (you will see other methods of dealing with the overhang later in this book).

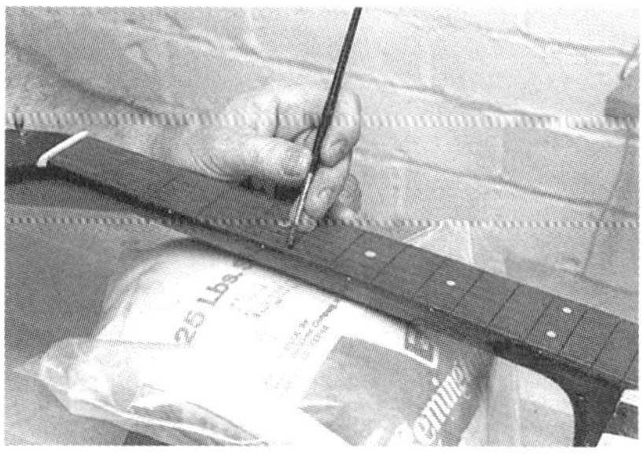

73 This fretboard holds frets well without glue—the water helps them go in. If there was any doubt about the frets staying seated, for more holding power we'd use glue (hide glue or Titebond work well).

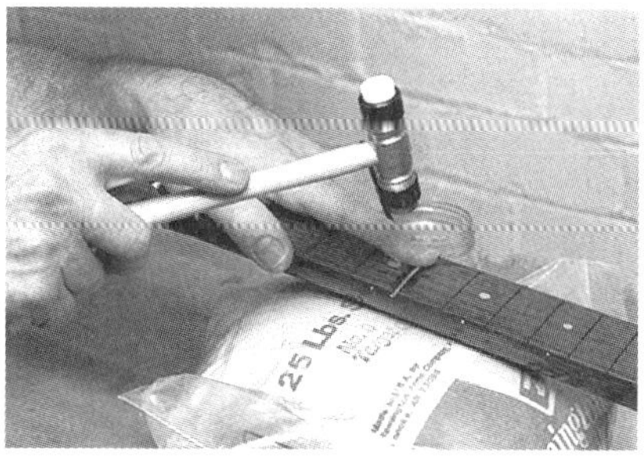

74 Try one fret (the 5th is good) to test the fit out on the main fretboard. Hold the fret steady...

75 ...while you tap in first one end...

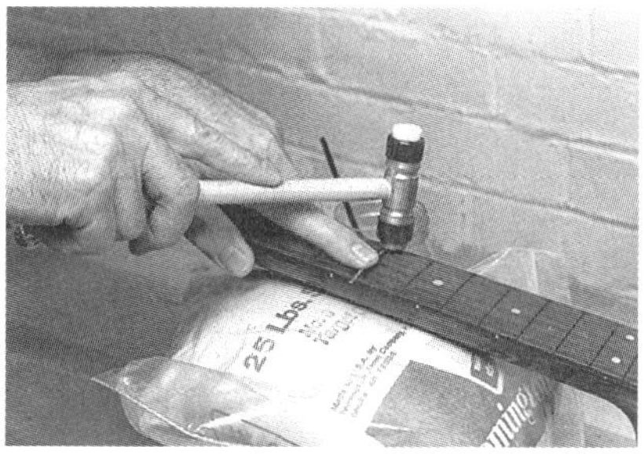

76 ...and then the other. Holding the fret steady until it gets started keeps the fret from tipping or falling over sideways and popping a chip of wood out of the fretboard.

77 You don't need to hold the fret once both ends are started. This fret is holding in well. That's good news, because if a larger fret tang were needed to hold the fret in the slot...

78 …the already straight neck might backbow from the cumulative wedging effect of oversized fret tangs (we'll use this "compression" to our advantage on guitars coming up). Go ahead and cut frets 1 thru 12 to length.

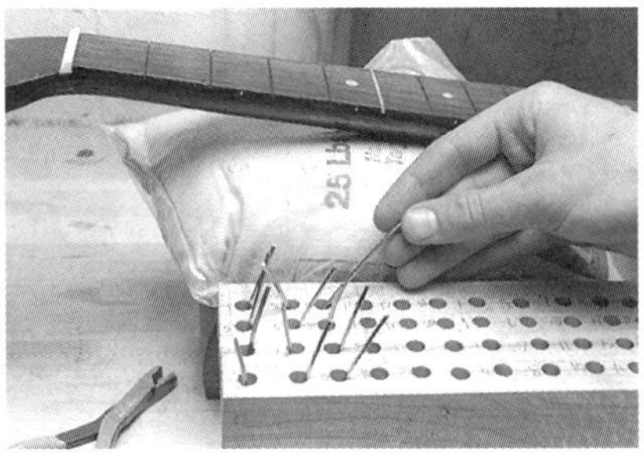

79 Store the cut-to-length frets in order in a block of wood…

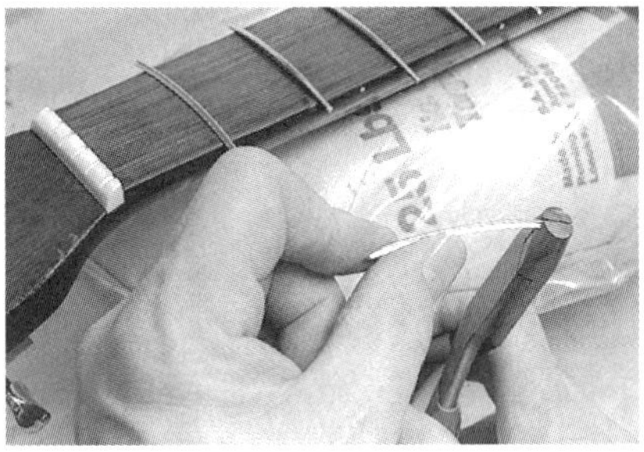

80 …remove them one at a time and bend them to the contour of the board (over-bend them, that is). For years most of us bent fretwire like this—with fret bending pliers—before the FretBender was available (shown on page 31).

81 Don't do all the frets; try the 1st and 3rd (to go with the 5th)…

82 …and the 7th and 9th if they're going in well and holding down…

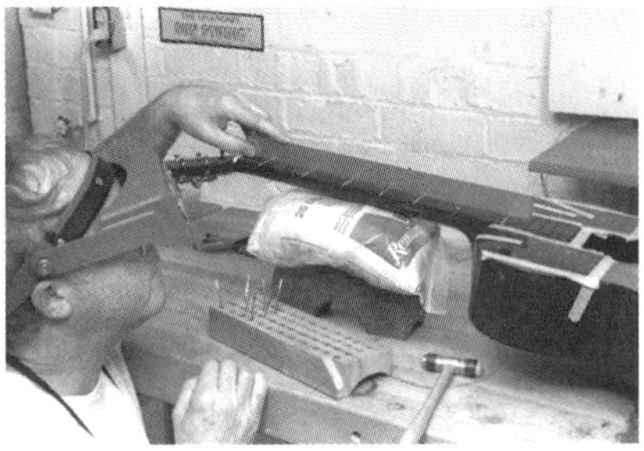

83 …then give the neck a quick check to be sure it's not backbowing. This neck was so strong and straight that a backbow might never pull out! The notched straightedge makes checking the fretboard—not the frets—possible.

84 The neck is still nice and straight (all fret jobs aren't this easy), so the remainder of frets 1 thru 12 are installed. The more typical problems will be discovered in the next guitar (coming up).

85 The neck still retains its shape—a remarkably strong neck (it's because of a good piece of rosewood, excellent mahogany, and the iron T-bar used in vintage Martin construction).

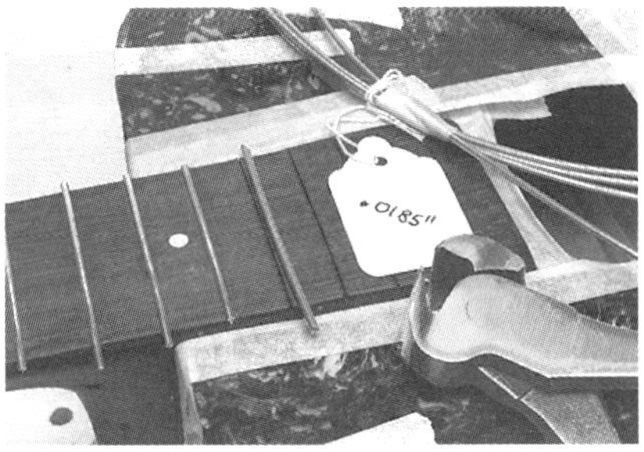

86 When you get to the "tongue" (fretboard extension over the body), change to a smaller wire that will hammer in easily and gently. An .0185" wire is about right if it will hold down.

87 Hold a chunk of steel or a bag of sand or buckshot inside (reaching through the soundhole) to support the tongue…

88 …while you hammer.

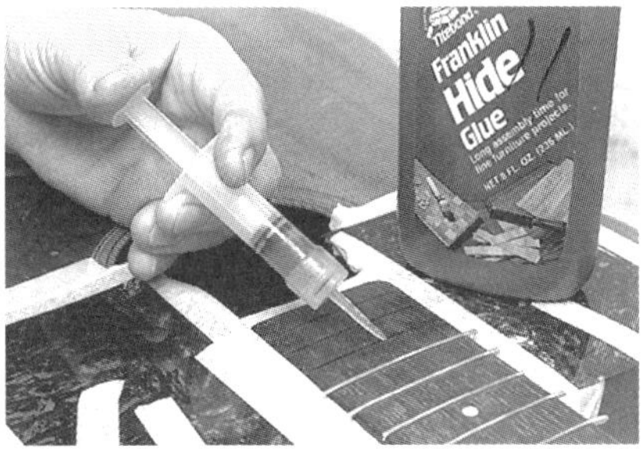

89 Since the smaller-tanged fret isn't going to hold as well as the larger .0215" tang did, a little glue in the slot is probably good insurance. Hide glue is excellent for fretwork.

90 Clean up the glue squeeze-out...

91 ...and hammer the rest in. This is a bag of buckshot held through the soundhole to absorb the blow. It's a good idea to wear ear-protection while you hammer, by the way!.

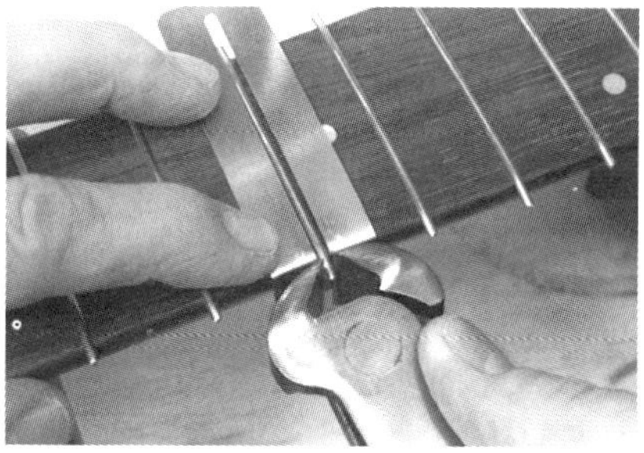

92 If you fret with glue and have time, let it dry overnight before clipping the ends flush to the fretboard edge. The thin steel fret protector, bent over the edge, allows you to cut without damaging the finish.

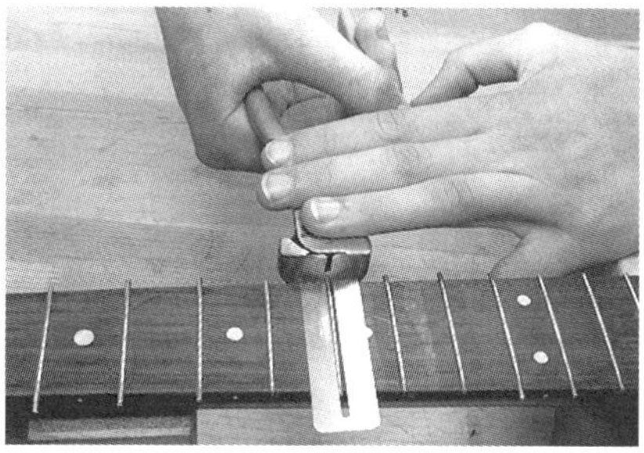

93 Glue or no glue, hold the nipper level as you cut (don't let it twist the fret end in the slot and loosen it), and press firmly downward with your fingers...

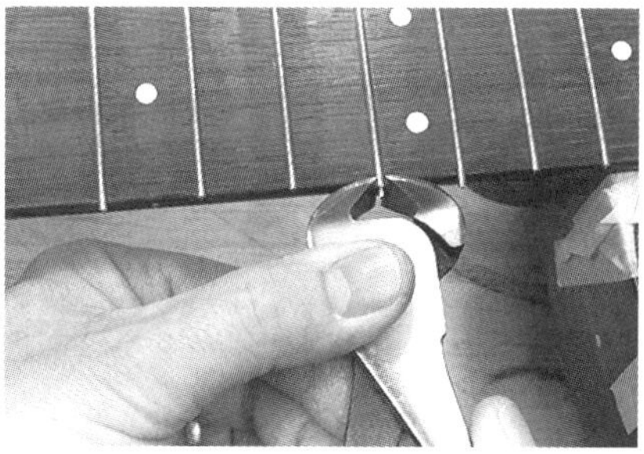

94 ...or your thumb.

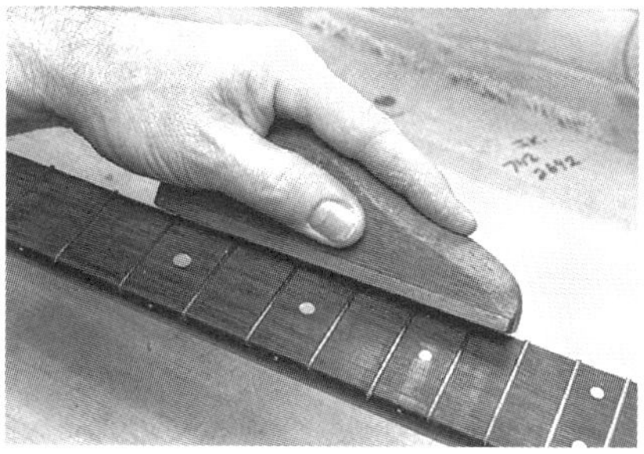

95 The 6" fret leveler, held at an angle, is good for smoothing the bevel and removing the marks left from the nipping operation. You must be careful not to slip up onto the new frets!

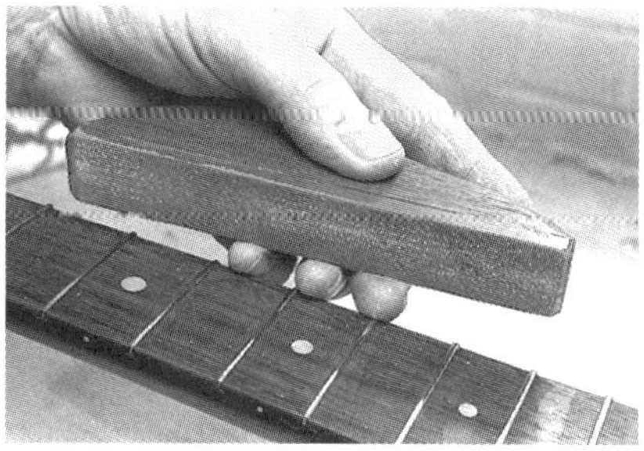

96 Use the ball ends of your fingertips as a guide along the fretboard edge to keep your hand (and the file) from slipping.

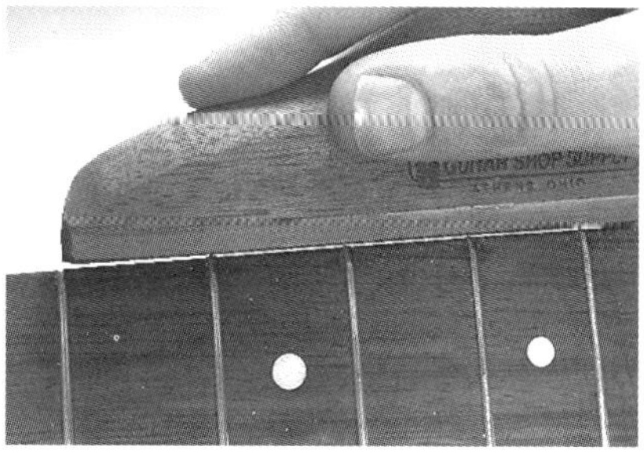

97 Hold the file at the bevel you prefer (we use about a 60° bevel), and file until you can't see light anymore.

98 This simple holding setup will make the beveling and the fret top leveling much easier—the guitar must be held firm while you file.

99 Once again the neck rocker becomes a useful tool as it contacts the peghead firmly and holds it in place. An angled, leather-padded clamping block doesn't hurt the peghead at all.

100 And the whole deal really helps with the filing.

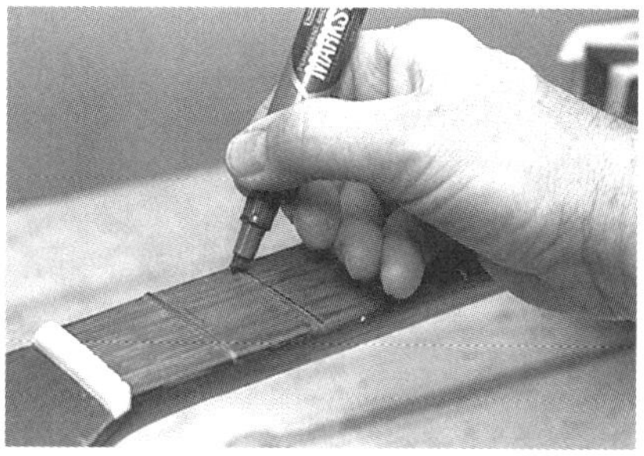

101 With the bevels done, use a blue marker for highlighting the tops of the new frets, so you can see what you're filing during the leveling operation.

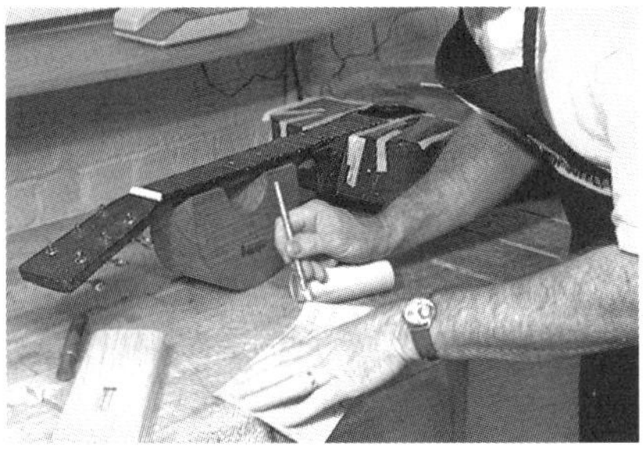

102 To make all the fret tops level with each other, I'm using a 16"-radius sanding block (8" long) with #220-grit self-stick paper. The sanding block, having a 16" radius, will change the upper-end 20" radius slightly…

103 …but it's no big deal. It simply means that the ends of the frets up in the 20" area will have a little more metal removed than the others (the factory fretboard is cone-shaped, but we're making the fret tops a cylinder).

104 Unlike flat sanding blocks or files, the radius block contacts the whole fret at once—leveling them quickly. By watching the remaining blue marker, and the pile of fret "dust," you can tell where you've made contact.

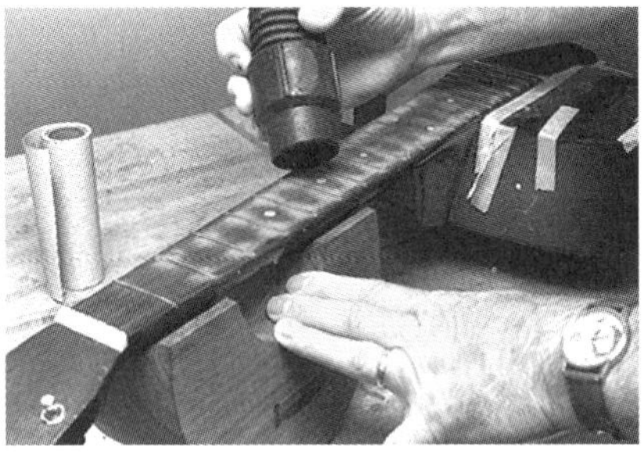

105 Vacuum well, and often…

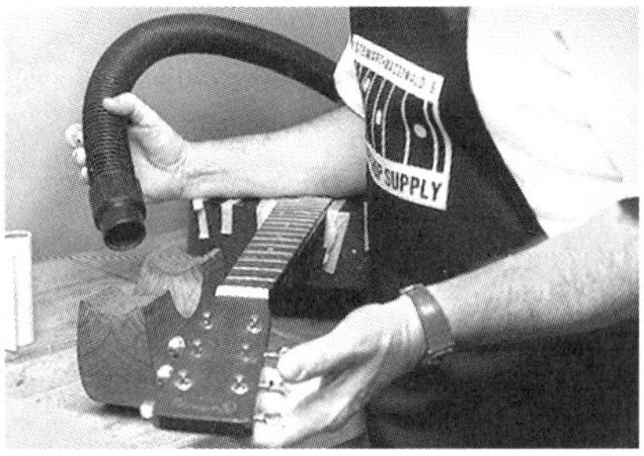

106 …including vacuuming the neck rest and anything that might contact the guitar and its finish (the metal fret dust will scratch like crazy).

107 Re-blue with the marker pen and switch to 320-grit sandpaper (Fre-Cut "Open Coat" sandpaper works well).

108 During any fretboard leveling, assume a strong steady stance, and hold your arms and shoulders rigid. The peghead clamp is a help…

109 Support the heel and body if there's any "give" from the pressure of sanding, so that the neck remains straight.

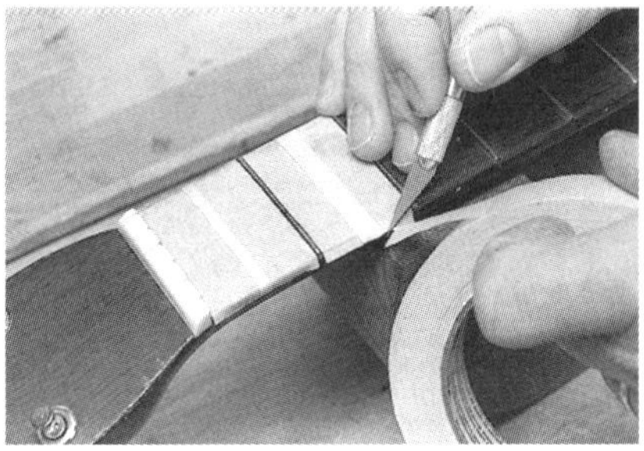

110 When the fret tops show no blue, you're ready to "dress," rounding the fret tops, and shaping the fret ends. One way to do this is to tape off all the frets at once before starting.

111 Draftsman's masking tape has a lower "tack" than others and is less likely to pull finish off upon removal. Cut 6 or 7 pieces and stick them to your benchtop…

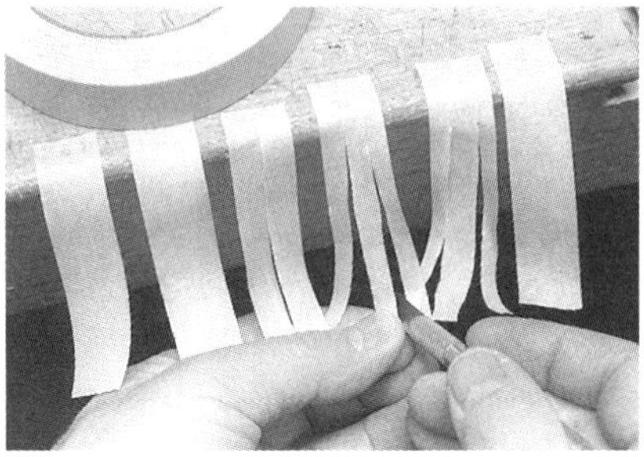

112 …and strip it like so. The outside of each stripped piece will have a straight "factory" edge…

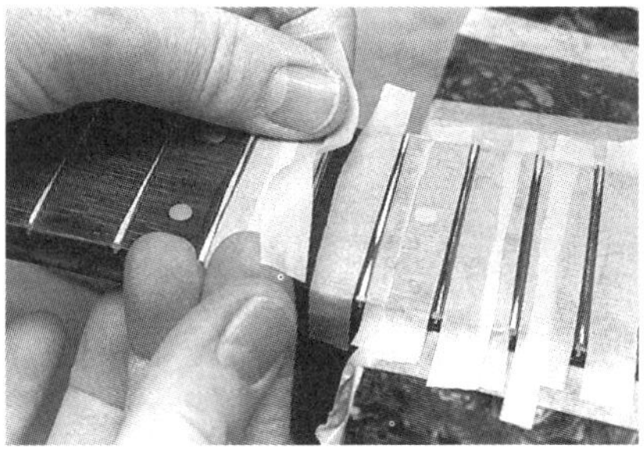

113 …and the small pieces will fit in between the frets—factory-edge against the fret.

114 The tape protects the fretboard from your tools.

115 A simple "quickie" method of rounding the fret tops is to wrap self-sticking sandpaper around your fingers and sand (press hard) lengthwise with the fingerboard (protective cloth gloves are a help).

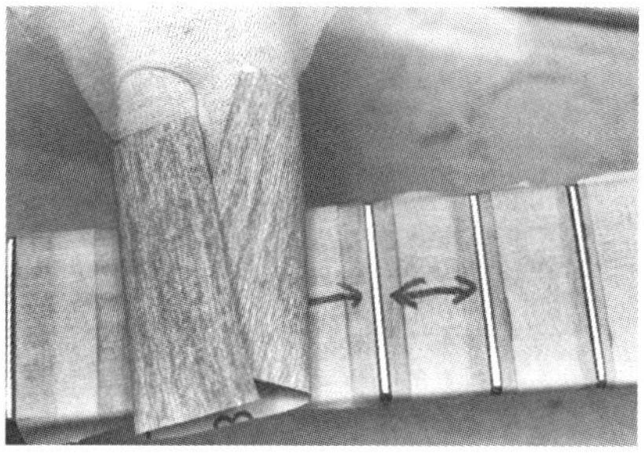
116 This simple method does OK, but it's not really fret dressing—there will still be marks left in the fret tops, which we'll remove shortly.

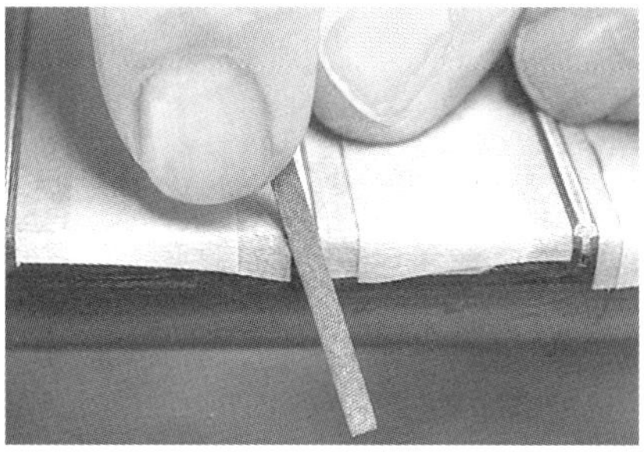
117 Use the 1/8" nut-seating file to smooth the bevel and remove any scratches left from the beveling. Because of its size it won't mar the wood or finish of the neck, unless you slip.

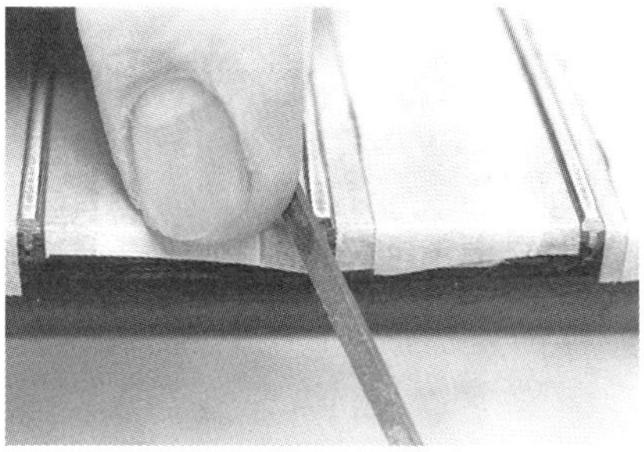
118 This same file is excellent for knocking off the sharp burr-like corners of the fret ends (these are caused by the lengthwise stroke of the beveling operation). Get the burr on one side…

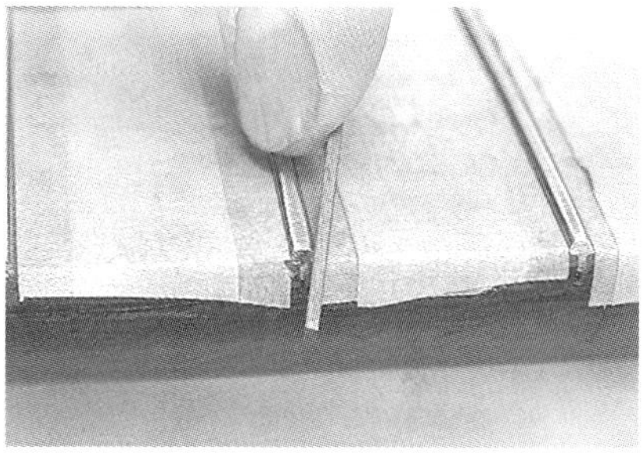
119 …and then the other. There is no "safe edge" on the 1/8" file—the thin edge has no teeth, but it's sharp on the corner.

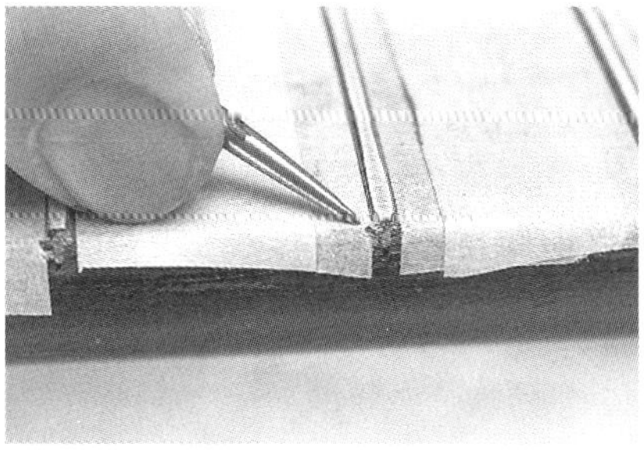
120 Without the protective tape here, the file could have made quite a mark in the wood or finish. Notice the rough marks in the fret tops—they still look flat, too!

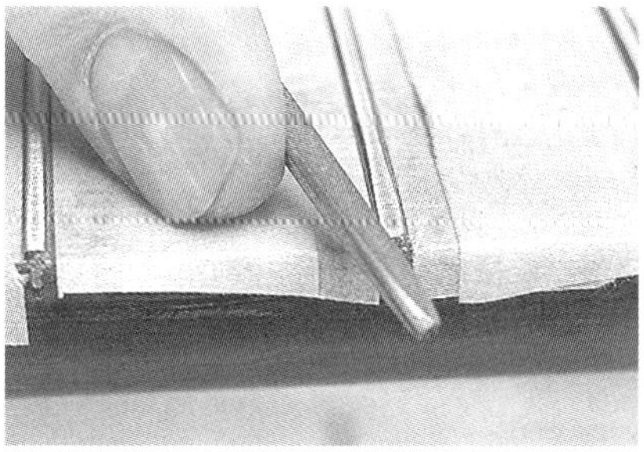
121 As soon as the slightest mark shows on the fretboard edge, switch to the 3-corner file. It *does* have ground, "safe" edges.

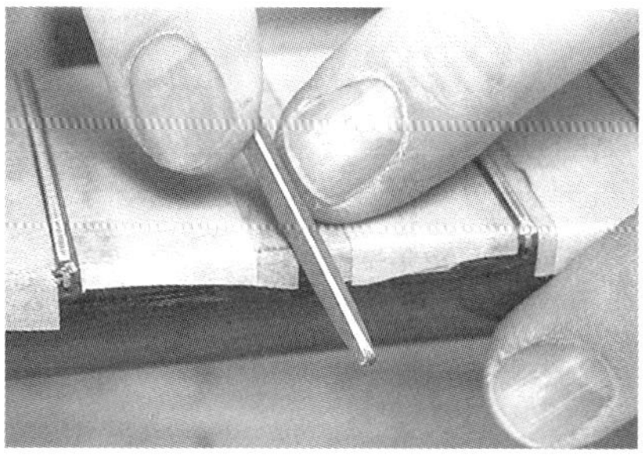
122 Working in short downward strokes, roll the file over the end…

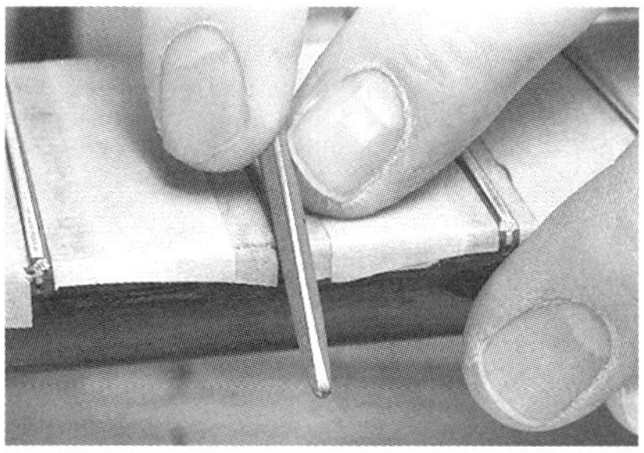
123 …to create the blunt, smooth rounded end which makes playing comfortable.

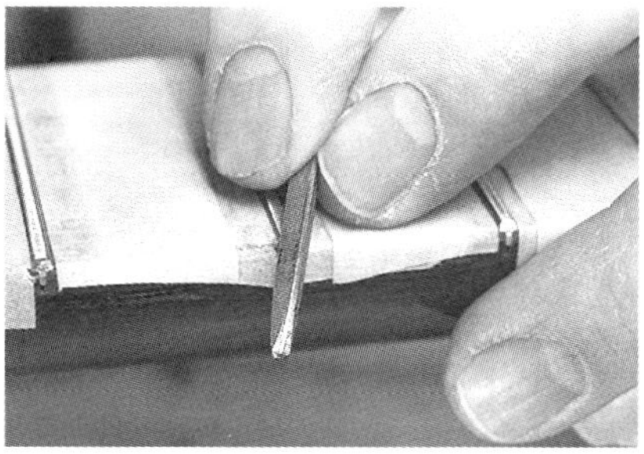
124 You can use the same 3-corner file to round the fret top as well, of course.

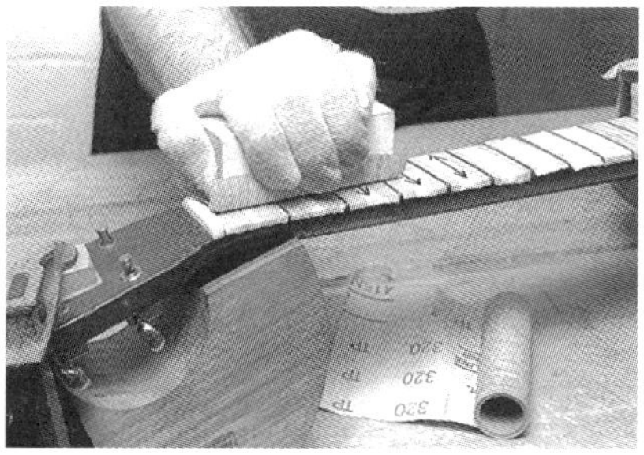
125 Here's a technique for getting rid of the harsh lengthwise leveling marks we mentioned a moment ago. Remove them, or at least get them going *sideways* in the direction of a bent string, using a 4" to 5" wood block wrapped with #220-grit sandpaper…

126 …by sanding sideways we mean in the lengthwise direction of the fret (across the fingerboard).

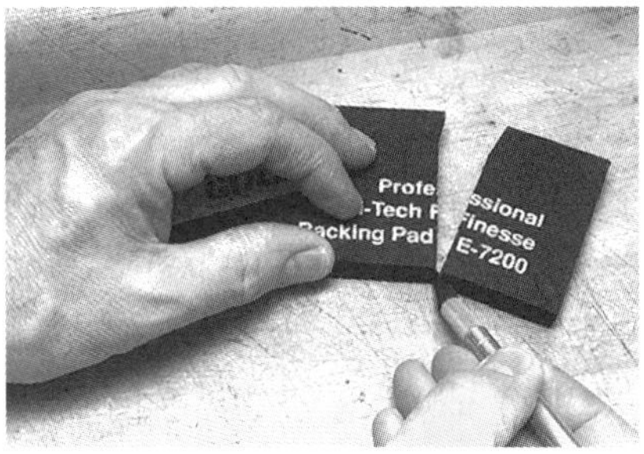

127 Here's a "quickie" rounding method that *does* work—especially if the harsh marks are already removed and all you need to do is impart roundness to the frets. Cut a piece off a Meguiar's rubber sanding pad…

128 …you can use soft wood, folded leather, cardboard, or a number of other materials for this, but we choose the Meguiar's rubber sanding pad—it's the perfect resiliency. Cut off the sharp corners…

129 …round the sharp edges a bit (these Sandplate "Steel Sandpaper" files will cut anything—even rubber)…

130 …wrap with sandpaper…

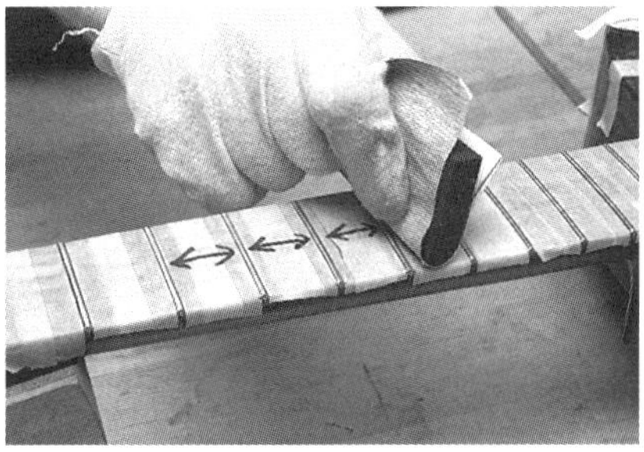

131 …and go end-to-end. This rounds the frets better than your fingers wrapped with sandpaper ever could.

132 Hold the burnisher at an angle in the direction of your stroke.

133 Go at least to #500-grit…

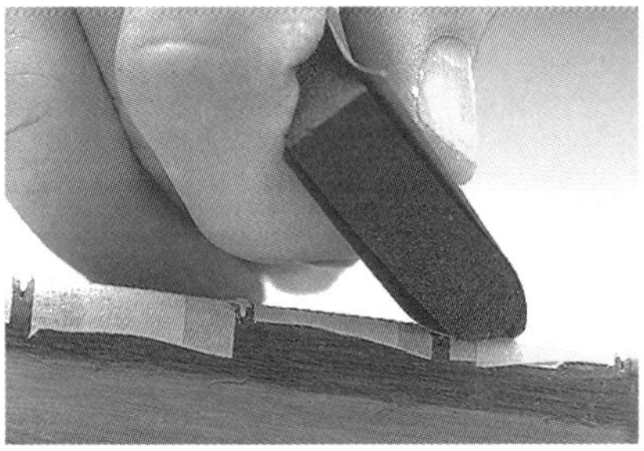

134 And hold it at an angle to burnish the round shape of the ends.

135 0000-steel wool gives almost the final polish…

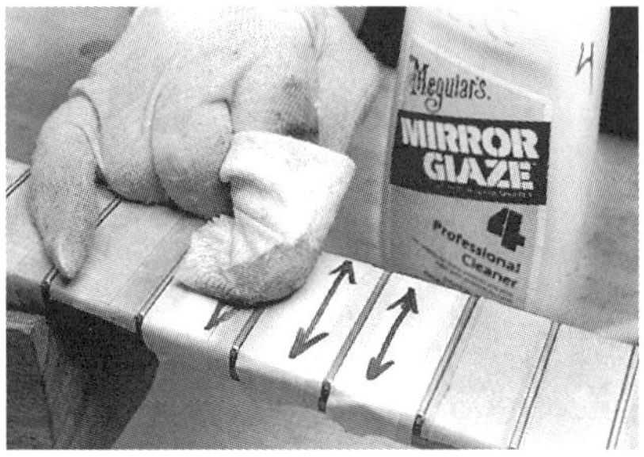

136 …and the coarse No. 4 Mirror Glaze rubbing compound gives the final buff.

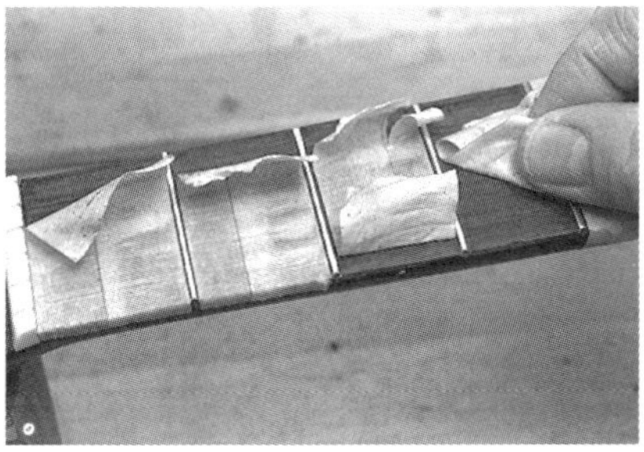

137 As always, peel the tape toward center—from the outside edges in…

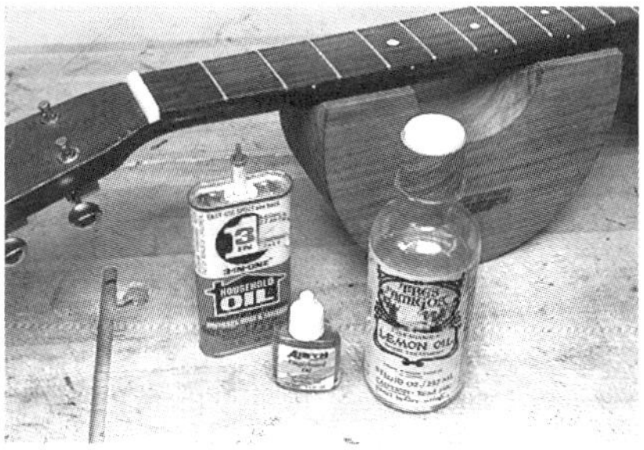

138 Using the Naphtha to clean this filthy board leached the moisture from the rosewood. Use machine-oil, lemon oil, linseed oil, etc. to add moisture.

140 With strings installed and strung to pitch, this neck is just like it was—straight as an arrow—but with nice new frets. Let's get on with the job—there's another Martin fret job coming up.

LESSON 3
A LITTLE TOUGHER REFRET JOB

(A SOMEWHAT FLEXIBLE, NON-ADJUSTABLE MARTIN D-28 WITH A HOLLOW SQUARE-TUBE ROD)

1 Here's a good D-28 but the neck is weak—not like the '57 Martin 00-18 we did earlier. The truss rod in this one is the later square-tube (hollow) that was used from around '68 until '85. You can see a *lot* of relief!

2 The "flex-test" (holding the peghead and pulling down on the center of the neck) shows a lot of movement, and...

3 ...over .018" of relief (the feeler gauge is loose) at the 7th fret. Martin's maximum spec on relief is .010" (I prefer .004"). This neck has too much upbow; the notched straightedge shows this by reading the fretboard, not the frets!

4 Take off the strings and see if the neck straightens, or backbows, without string pressure. (It should do one or the other—see "drop-off" on page 9.) However, sometimes a neck takes a permanent "set" in the upbow position!

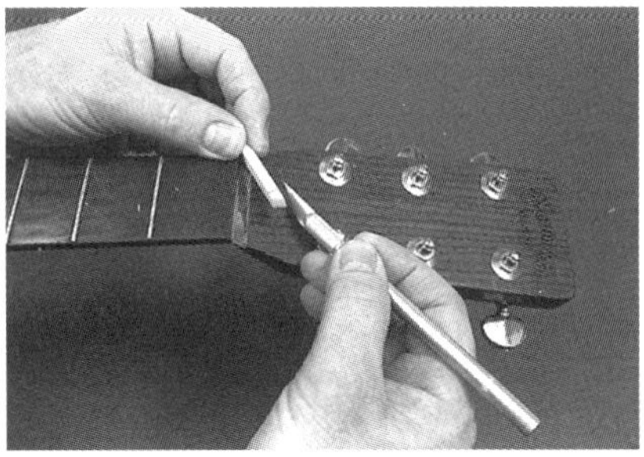

5 We'll remove the nut in this case because we'll be doing a lot of wood-working at the nut end of the neck.

6 In the playing position (strings removed) the neck goes into a *slight* backbow as it should, but not enough (the backbow pulls out when strung to pitch). This neck has taken a "set."

7 The notched straightedge lets you read the backbow (some call it "drop-off") without having to remove the frets.

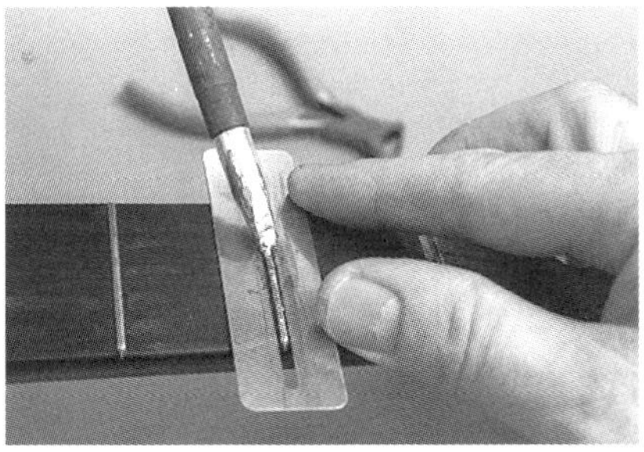

8 Take out the frets. Heat the fret lightly, and it can be removed more easily.

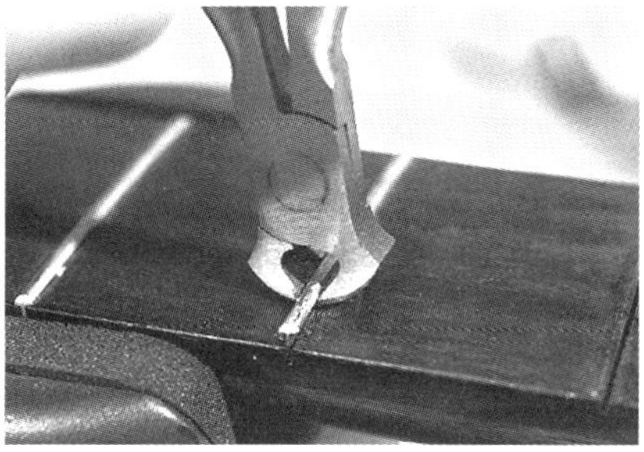

9 The small fret pullers can get under a fret more easily than the large ones, and tend to chip the fretboard less…

10 …but some boards are "chippier" than others. Fix the chips as they happen, so you don't forget about them (or have trouble finding them later).

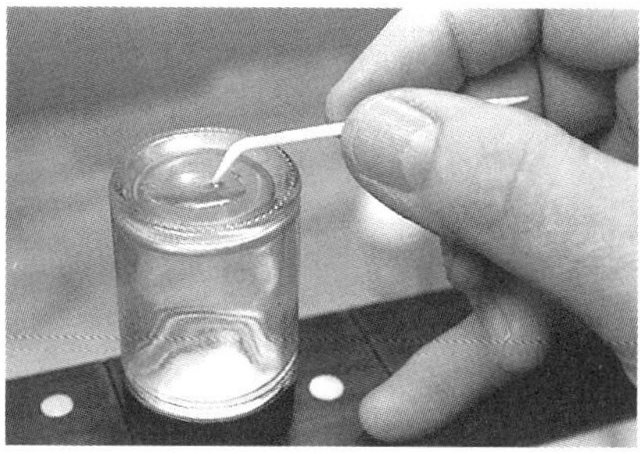

11 A little medium viscosity (yellow-label "Super T") superglue will fix the chip in a hurry. The bottom of a small glass jar makes a good palette…

12 …and a toothpick can put it right where you want it.

13 Wipe off any squeeze-out, and "burnish" or rub the chip to press it down tight as it sets (about 10 or 15 seconds)…

14 …the 3-corner Waverly fret file can smooth the edges without marring the board (and the chip is invisible).

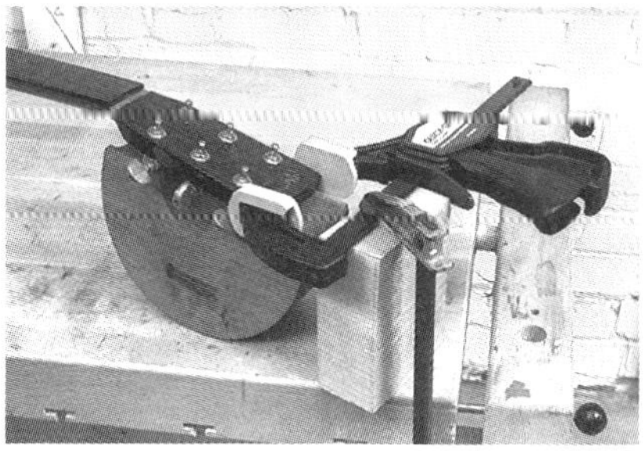

15 To hold the guitar while you work, rest the peghead on a support (again, the neck rocker is perfect), clamp the peghead with padded jaws, and then clamp *that clamp* to the bench.

16 This is a stainless steel guard taped around the fretboard to protect the top (use draftsman's tape).

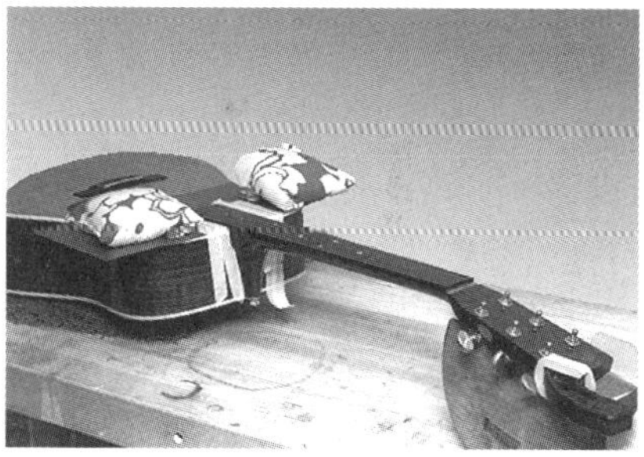

17 Two 6 lb. bags of buckshot or sand resting on the shoulders simulate the neck under string tension. (In the Martin repair shop, they use a 6 lb. weight on each shoulder this way.)

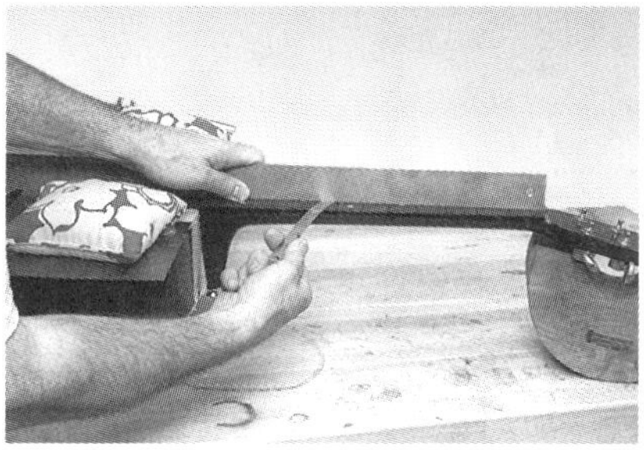

18 Now we have the same .018" relief with the strings off, and we're ready to level the board. Once again, you must decide at this point if you're treating the fretboard radius as a cylinder or a cone.

19 Martins made before 1992 typically have a slightly conical radius since they were prepped by hand with a flat sanding block. This one starts at about 14"–15" near the nut…

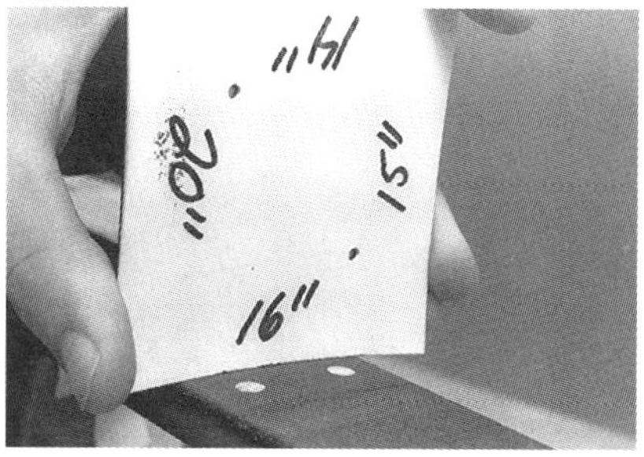

20 …graduates quickly to 16" and remains so for most of the board…

21 ...and hits 20" at the fretboard's end. We may change the whole radius to a 16" cylinder (the average), but for now to remove that excessive upbow, and regardless of the radius...

22 ...a lot of wood's coming off at this end—mark the high spots between the 5th fret and the nut with white pencil...

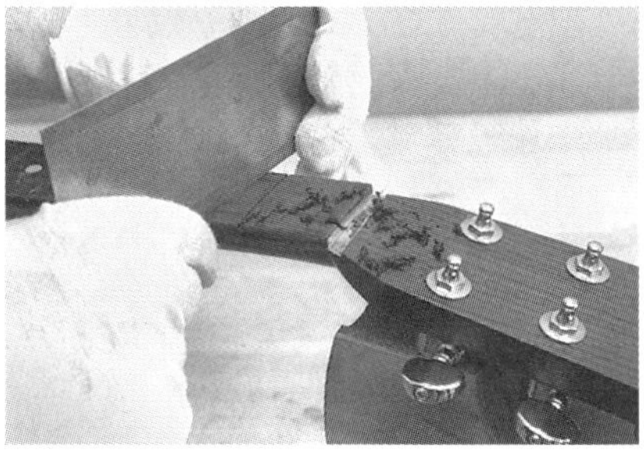

23 ...and have at it with a sharp scraper—these Sandvik scrapers hold an edge well. You want the fretboard to be *more* than just flat from the 5th to the nut...

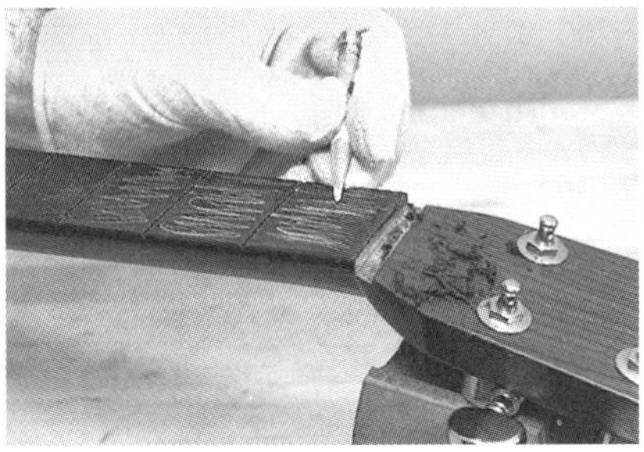

24 ...you need to plane-in some more backbow or "drop-off." Obviously the amount of wood to remove can only be guessed at, and experience is a big help. White it again...

25 ...and take off more wood—sometimes a rough-toothed file is as good as a scraper. Check repeatedly with a radius gauge to see that you're at least holding the factory radius!

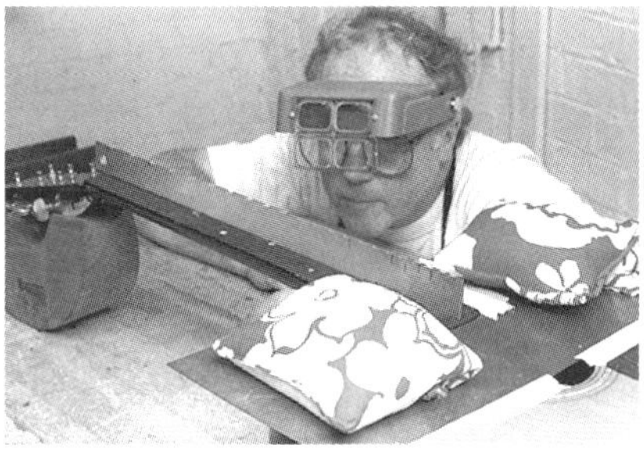

26 Now the straightedge sits flat under the simulated string tension, and hopefully by carefully choosing a fret tang, we can fret the neck and keep it straight (even though it's flat, it's still weak).

27 We laid out white lines from end-to-end. Watch the progress as we convert the fretboard to a 16" cylindrical radius from end to end.

28 We worked down the tongue area first...

29 ...and then from the 5th to the nut. See how the central area, which was 16" to begin with, has remained untouched.

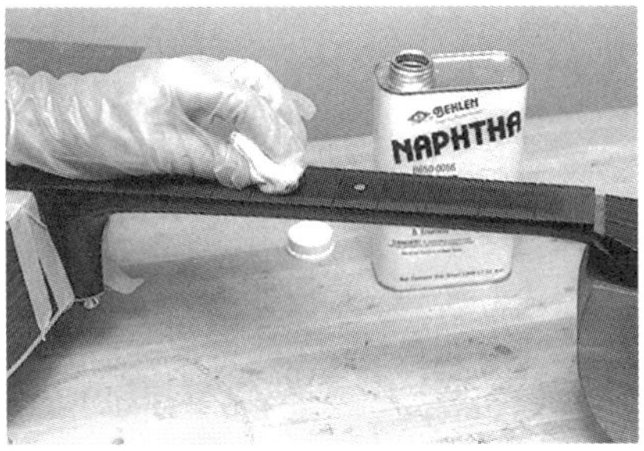

30 Dampen the fretboard to raise the grain—if using water on a fretboard makes you nervous, use Naphtha instead—it'll do much the same thing (you need good ventilation, though).

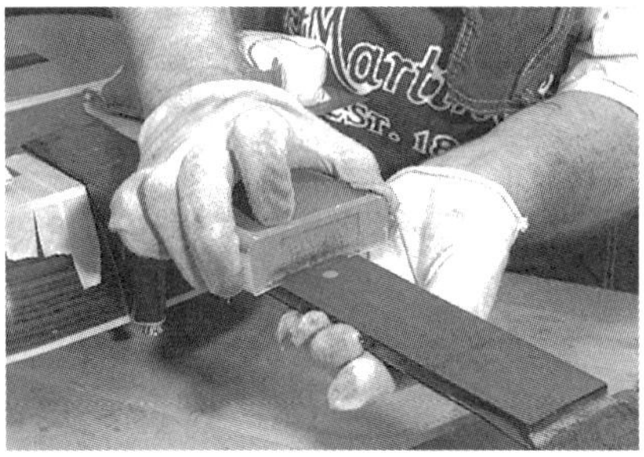

31 Now blend both ends in with the center.

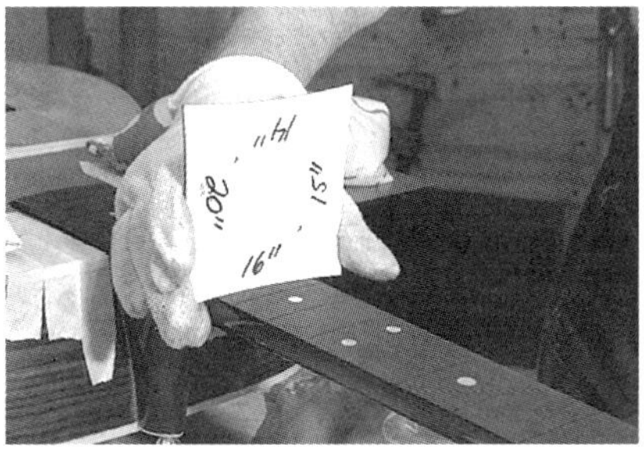

32 There we have a pretty nice 16" cylinder-shaped board (like the modern-day Martins of the '90s).

33 Now, with the neck unclamped and the simulation weight removed, we have a good looking unstrung neck with a "dropoff" at each end…

34 …even with the frets removed there's a good .010" dropoff from the 5th fret to the nut…

35 …and .005" of "fall-away" up on the tongue. Now it's time to choose a fretwire (refer to the fretwire chart up front). Remember: fallaway isn't a "must" (see page 10).

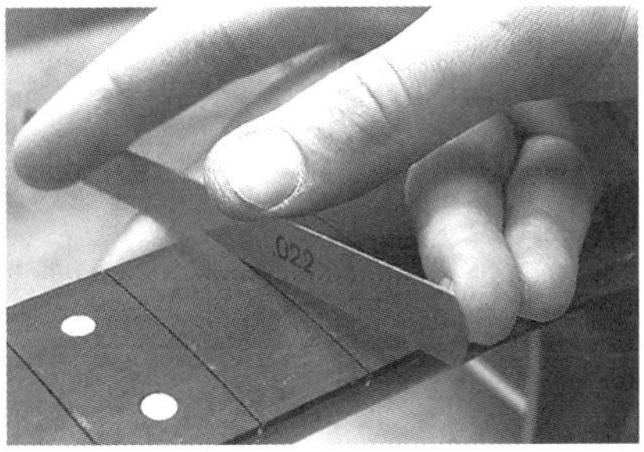

36 Well-vacuumed, the slots measure .022". The fret tang slot ratios given on pages 20 and 22 suggest that—for ebony—a tang one size up (.0225") might keep the neck stiff and straight…

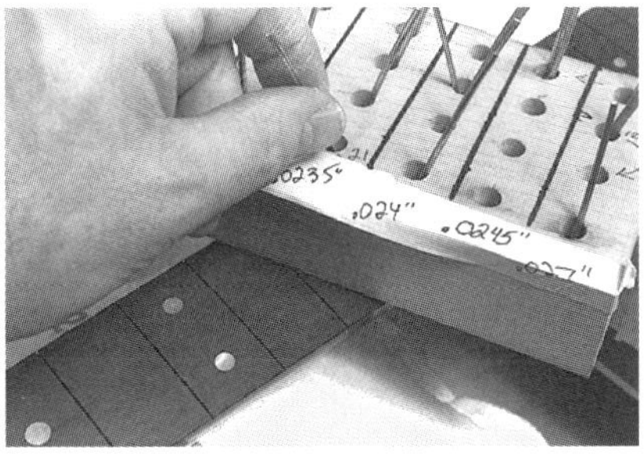

37 …and prevent upbowing again. But since this neck was so weak, we chose to go two sizes up (.0235") for extra stiffness. We'll see what happens.

38 Oddly enough, the 4th fret slot measured .024"…

39 …and the 3rd measured .025"! We made a note of those two slots for later.

40 Slightly bevel the top edges of the fret slot with a file and the fret goes in easier.

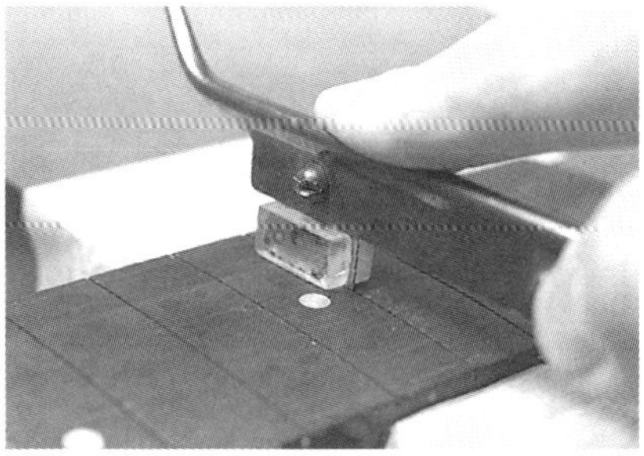

41 After all that fretboard leveling, be sure that *all* the slots are still deep enough for the tang. This little saw is a 3/4" piece of .020" Blitz sawblade with plexiglas runners superglued on as depth-stops…

42 We started using a shortened sawblade (2-1/2") up on the tongue in order to saw without cutting into the top, and eventually we found that a short blade is all you need—especially for depth (or if you just use it to remove debris).

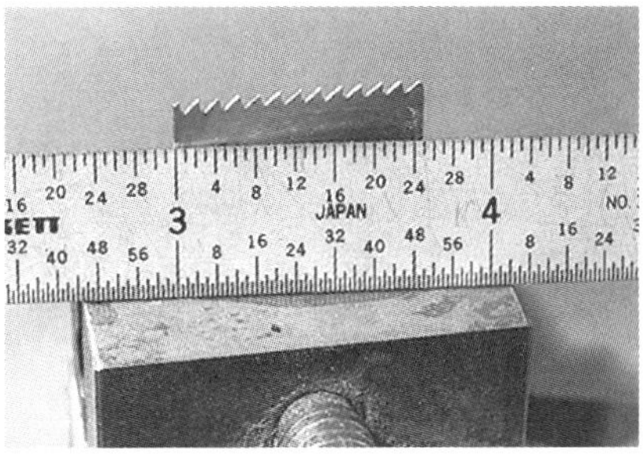

43 Break off a 3/4" length of Blitz sawblade by clamping it into a vise and snapping it (wear protective safety glasses!).

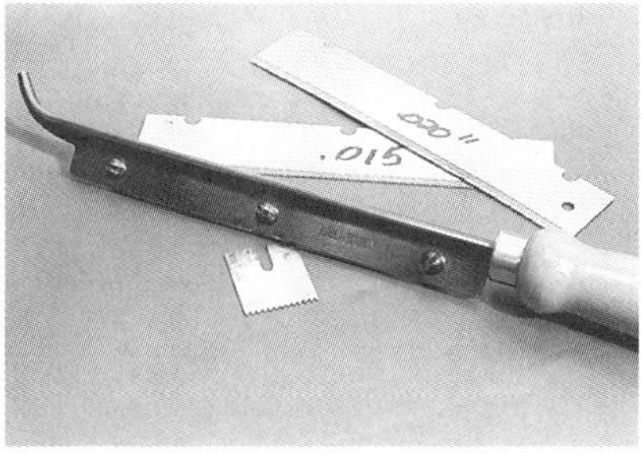

44 Blitz sawblades come in six sizes: .015", .020", .024", .029", .032", and .040". You can do a lot of fret slot sizing with these blades!

45 You can sharpen the teeth with any small fine-toothed file.

46 .062" is a little deeper than the tang…

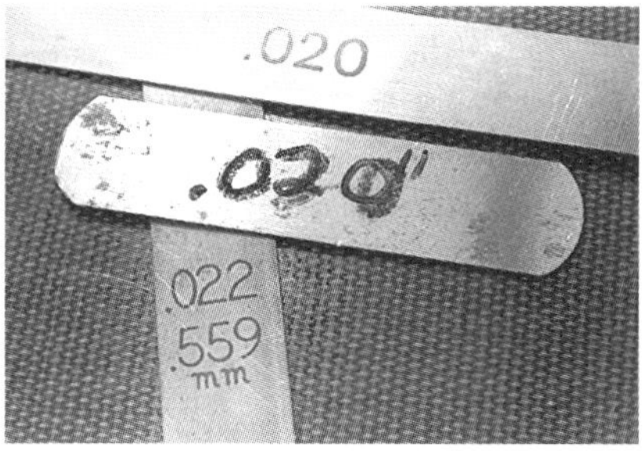

47 …and you can set the depth guides by stacking up .062" worth of feeler gauges…

48 …to shim up the plexiglas stops to the correct depth while you super glue them on.

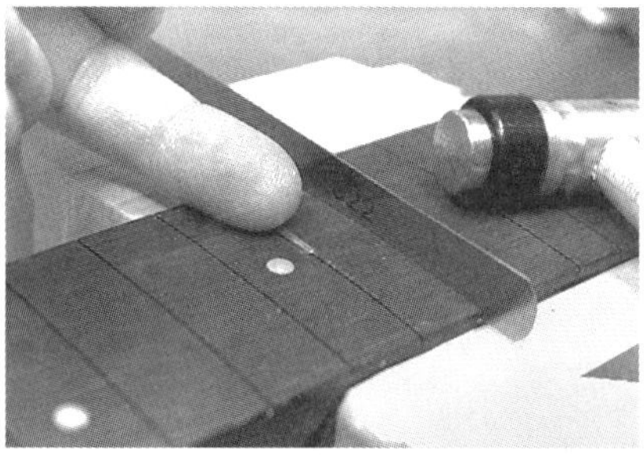

49 This is a short length of the .0235" wire hammered in over the neck block area where it's solid. Give it the "fingernail" test—see if you can lift the wire. Seems tight, so we'll try a whole one out on the board at the 6th fret…

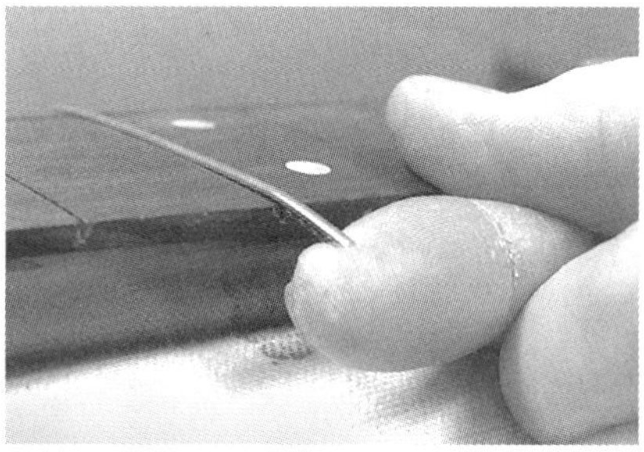

50 …when you push up on the overhang it gives a little—not a good fit after all. Not all ebony is super-dense.

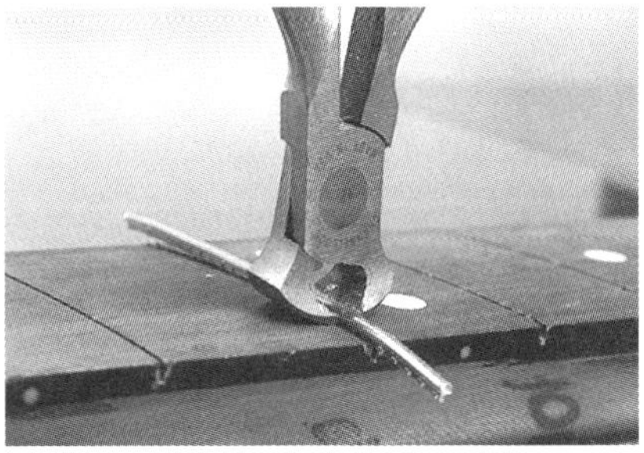

51 We'll pull that one and try the next size up (.0245") in a different slot—the 5th fret.

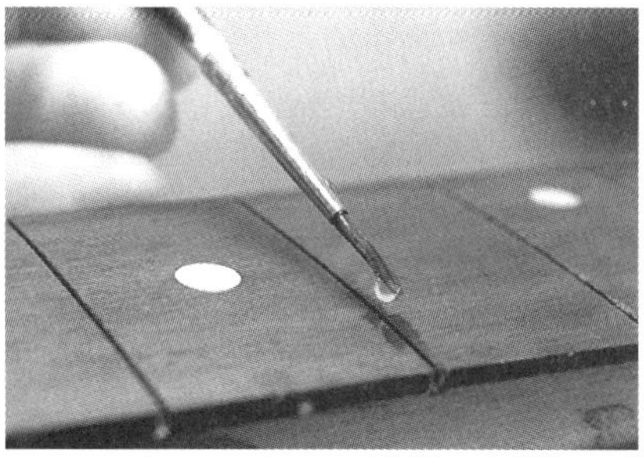

52 You'll recall that a bit of water and/ or glue in the slot lubricates the wood and makes the wire go in easier, and also swells the wood and holds the fret a little better.

53 Use an over-radiused wire of course, and hammer the ends down first…

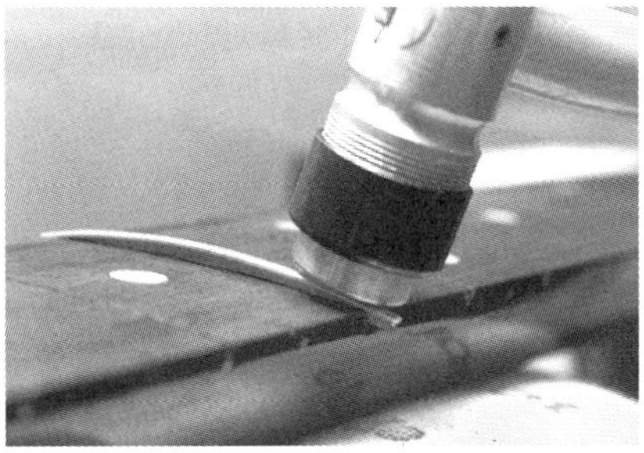

54 …tap them down pretty well—almost "home" as they say…

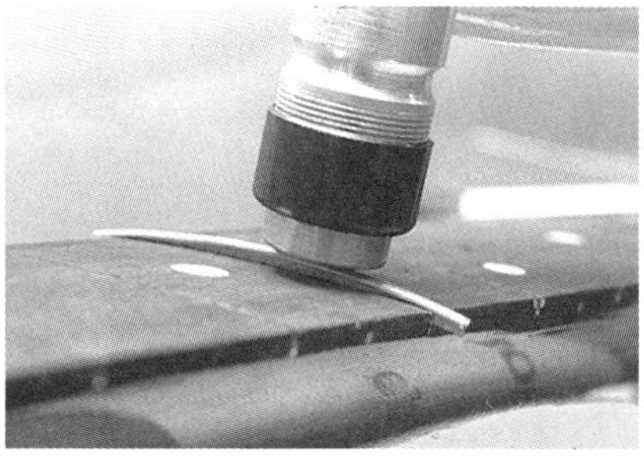

55 …and then work the center out toward both ends. This causes the fret barbs to press sideways through the slot slightly and hold the fret better.

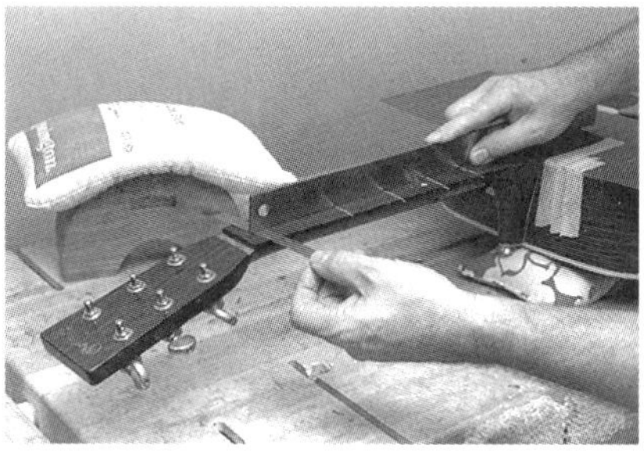

56 With a 25 lb. bag of buckshot resting on the neck rocker as an anvil, we put in frets 1, 3, 5, 7, and 9 using the .0245" wire.

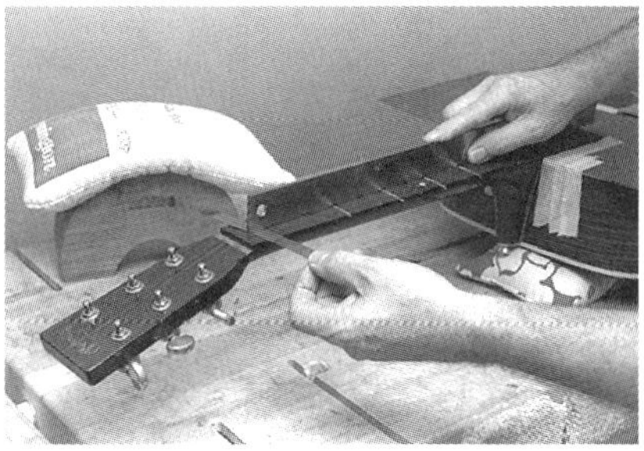

57 Next, check the unsupported neck with the notched straightedge and a .010" feeler gauge to be sure that the frets aren't backbowing the neck.

58 Check the supported neck too, with the string simulation weights on.

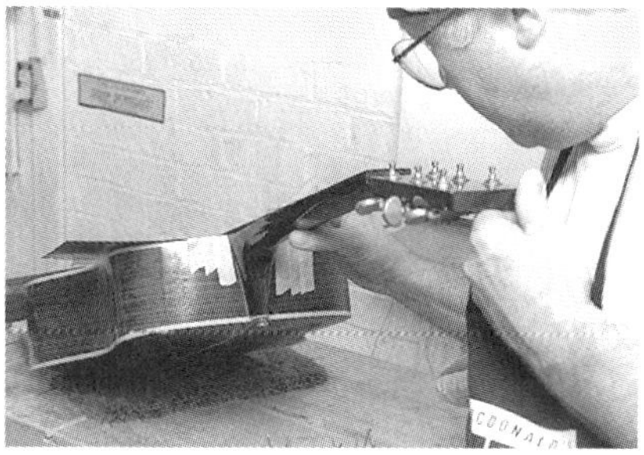

59 Give the flex test from time to time—even with all those frets in place the neck may still be weak—in fact, it is. Remember the 3rd and 4th frets with the .025" slots?

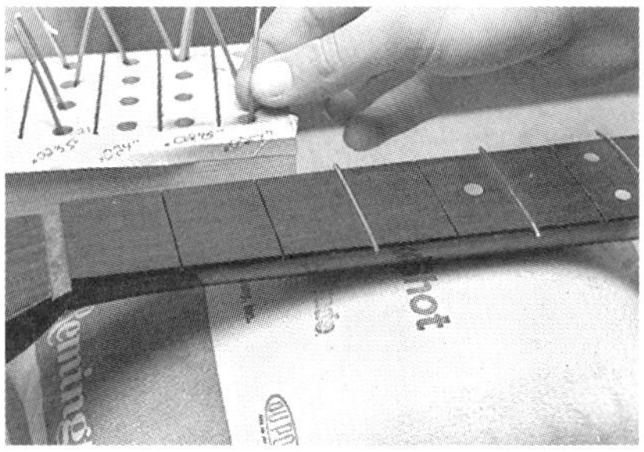

60 Put a .027" tang wire in those slots for extra stiffness and holding power. Now fret the tongue, remembering to use a smaller wire as we did on the Martin earlier (photo 86, page 66).

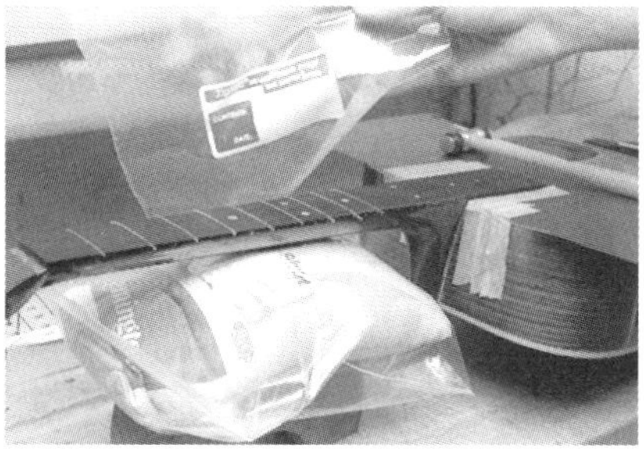

61 By the way, if you're using lead buckshot, put the canvas bag inside a ziplock plastic bag to contain any lead dust.

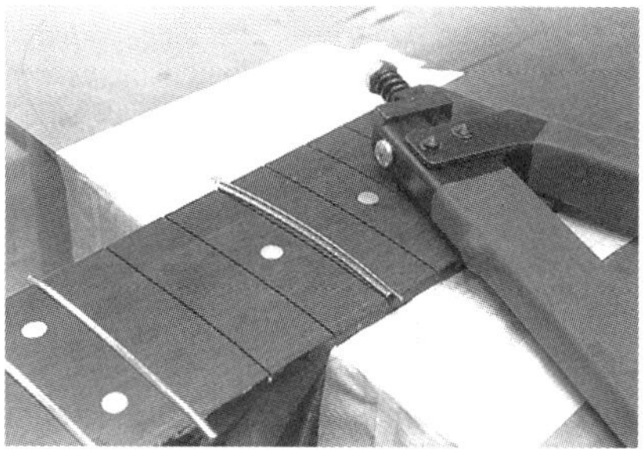

62 On the tongue, if you clip the tang part of the fret end overhang before hammering it in, you'll avoid twisting and unseating the fret when you clip it later, because there's less metal to cut (see next page, photo 78).

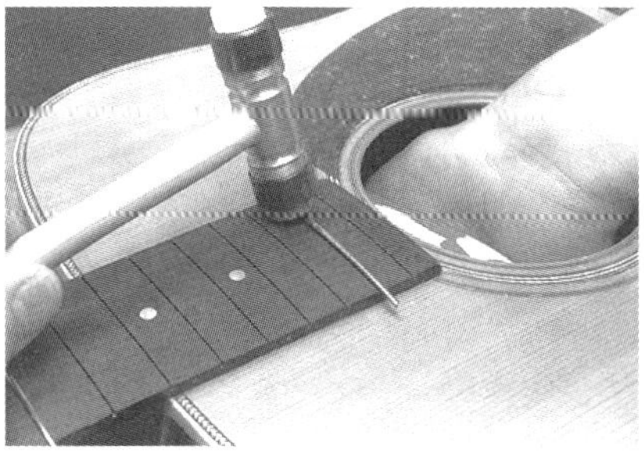

63 Start with the smallest tang size (.0185") since it will go in easily—as long as it holds down, you're OK. Hold a bag of sand or buckshot, or a chunk of steel, through the soundhole to support the tongue as you hammer.

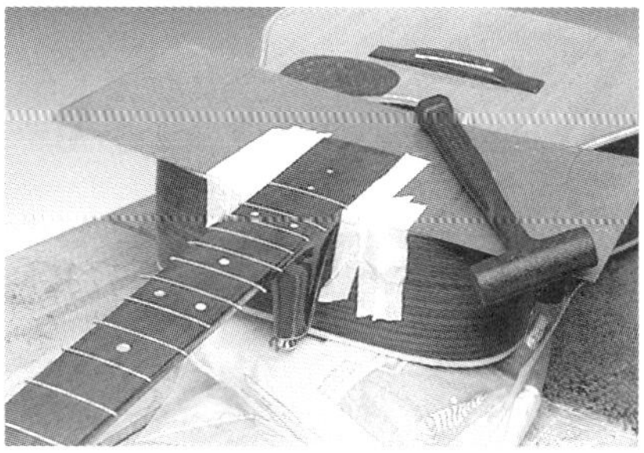

64 Set the heel area, neck block, and shoulders on the buckshot bag to make it more solid as you hammer—the tongue is delicate, and you can't just pound away...

65 If pounding on the tongue worries you, try a version of the "Teeter," or "epoxy" fret job pioneered by Don Teeter. Rout the fret slot wider with a small dental bit and a Dremel tool...

66 Widen the slot just enough for the fret to press in with finger pressure (some prefer a slight interference fit so that the barbs bite into the fret slot walls). Wax close up to the fret slot with paste wax on a Q-tip...

67 ...wax close to, but not on or into the slot—leaving a little dry area on each side of the slot...

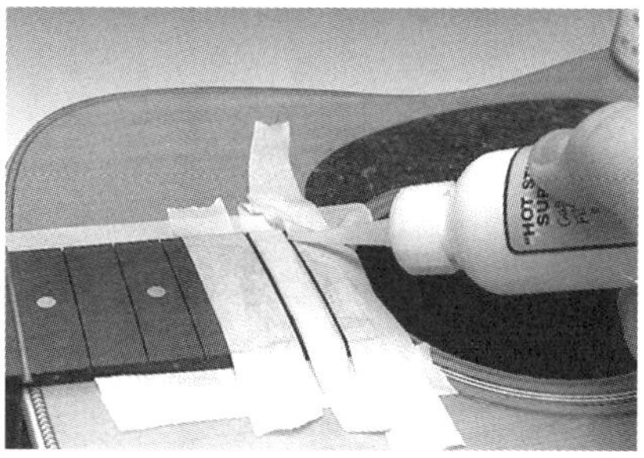

68 ...and tape off the fret slot and apply some glue—the traditional Teeter method uses 24-hour epoxy, but the 5-minute kind will do. We're using Hot Stuff "Super-T,"...

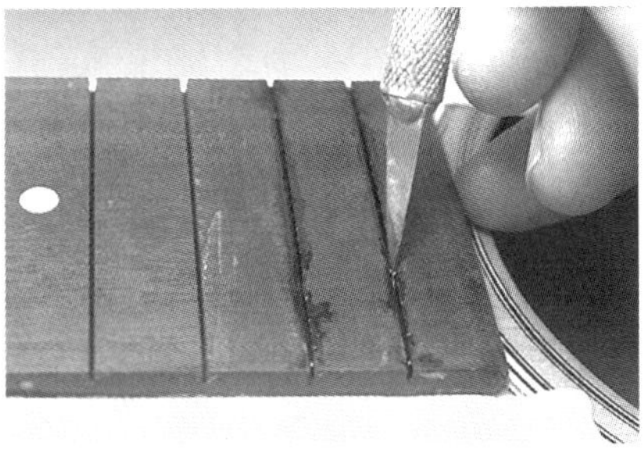

69 …moving and spreading it around in the slot (you've got to move fast with superglue)…

70 …and clamp the frets tight while the glue sets (in this case 2 or 3 minutes will do). The 16" radius sanding block makes a good gluing caul and "fret press"—with the fret slots widened, the frets press in without hammering.

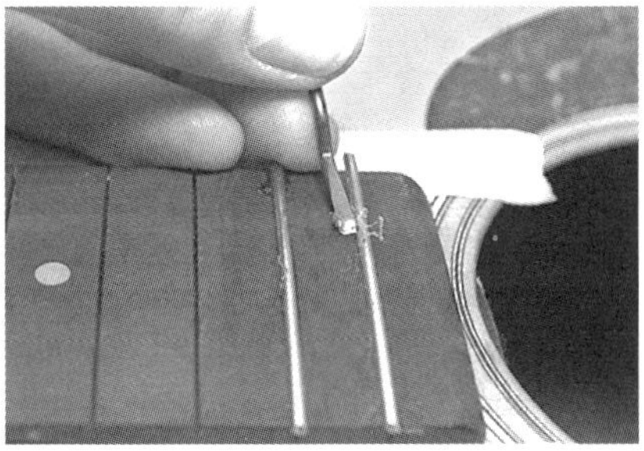

71 The glue squeeze-out trims off pretty easily because the fretboard is waxed—just another of the many uses for the small "Micro-chisels."

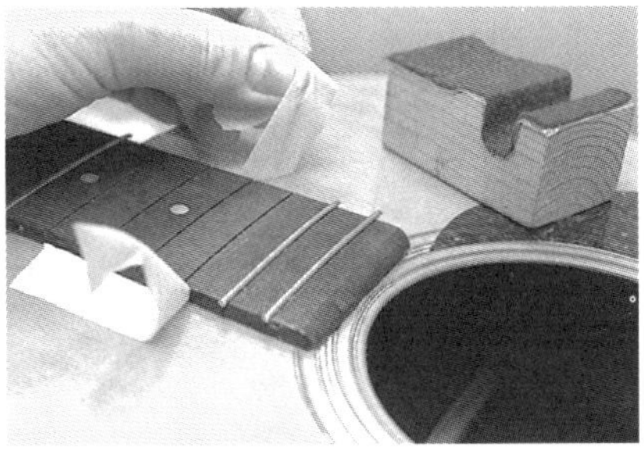

72 As always, use the low-tack draftsman's tape to avoid pulling away any finish (here's a good view of the interior clamping caul we used).

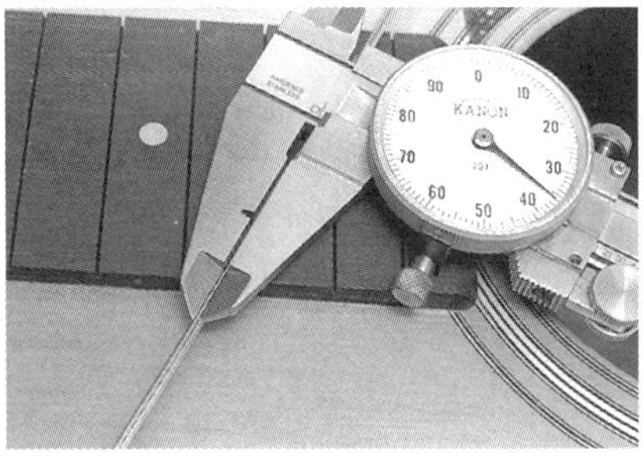

73 These barbs measure .037" but the tang matches, or is less than, the .022" slot (depending on which Martin wire you chose). *Another* tongue-fretting variation is to *narrow the fretwire* instead of widening the slot.

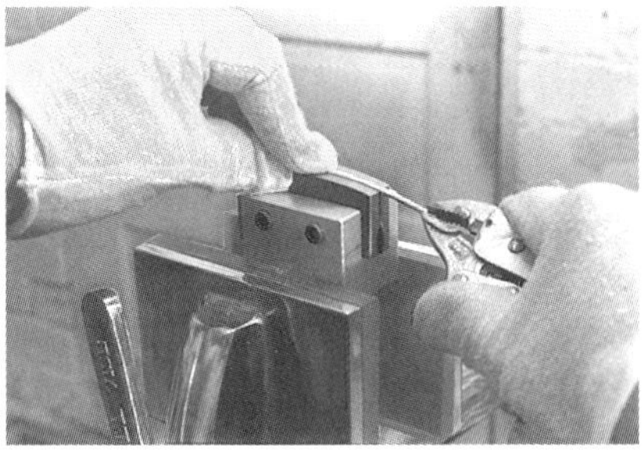

74 By drawing a length of fretwire through the homemade "tang-sizer" (see "Specialty tools"), you can shave down the barbs to any size you want (or even remove them completely).

75 With little or no barb, the frets can press in without hammering at all, and be held there with glue. In seconds you can drop a .038" tang down by .004" or .006" in one or two passes.

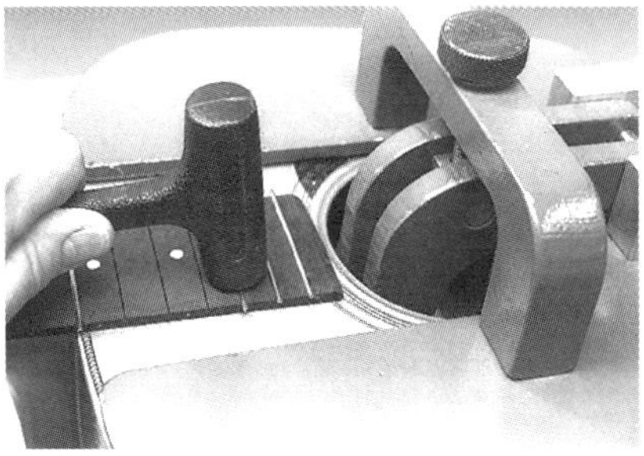

76 Here's another way to fret on the tongue—the cast iron "Fret Buck" tool, designed by Bob Taylor. Padded with cork, it sits on the shoulders and reaches through the soundhole to support the tongue and top…

77 …with the Fret Buck you can hammer almost any size wire you choose—in fact, the tool absorbs shock so well that some fretters install it at the outset of the job—even when fretting out on the neck.

78 Pre-cut only the tang before fretting, and the remaining crown will nip off easily without twisting. Don't pre-cut the whole fret to length because the overhang helps keep the fret ends down at the edges while you hammer.

79 If your knuckles hit the guitar while you're cutting, hold the nippers like this (or get nippers with longer handles just for nipping the tongue). Notice that the metal guard is in place.

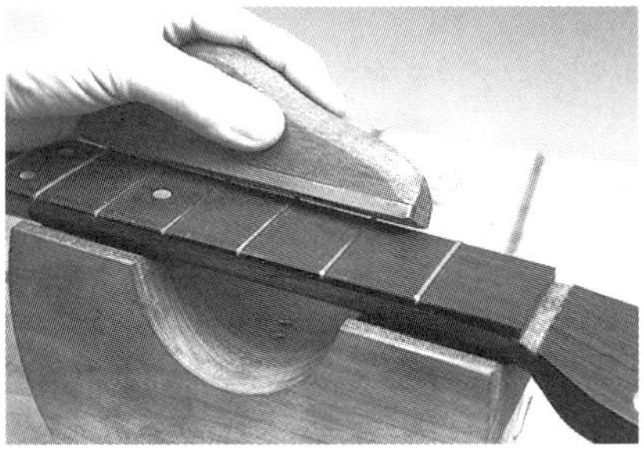

80 Don't "over-bevel" the ends—start by leaving them at a 60° angle—you can always remove metal, but you can't put it back!

81 We pre-cut the *tang* on all the frets (not just up on the tongue) to avoid unneccessary filing on the fretboard edge. But a few were missed, as you can see by looking down from overhead.

82 This neck is already worn and chipped along the edges, and any filing only makes it worse. Notice the hollow gaps in the fret slot below the fret...

83 These gaps look better if you fill them. The Martin company uses stick-shellac ("burn-in sticks"). Heat the right color (black for ebony, a brown or umber for rosewood) with a soldering iron...

84 ...and while it's still molten, press it into the gap—it'll harden instantly, so you'll need to re-melt it by touching it again with the hot solder tip.

85 Use a somewhat coarse file to "rough"-down the mound of hardened shellac...

86 ...and switch to something more gentle (3-corner file again) to smooth the fill. Stick shellac will chip like hardened finish, so you want to smooth it by degrees...

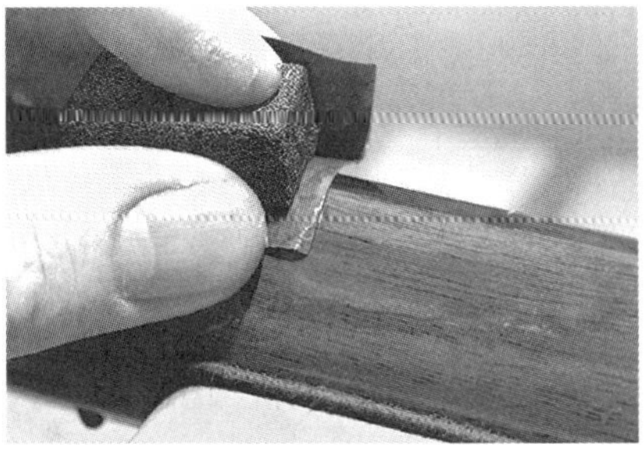

87 ...ending up with #800-grit wet-sanding sometimes, and even buffing it with Mirror Glaze and a small rag.

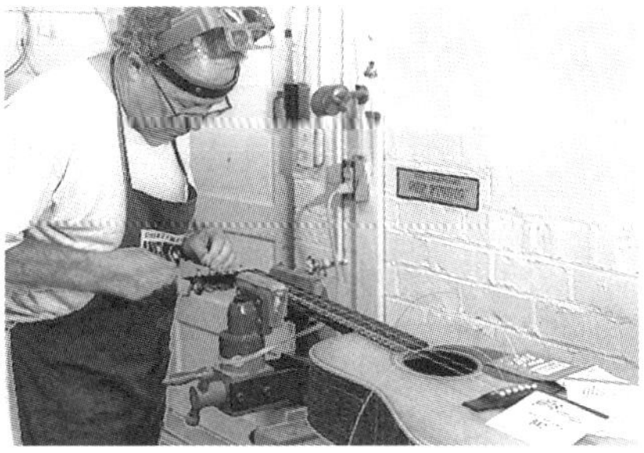

88 The real test comes with strings on. Will the neck still have too much relief? Will it stay backbowed from too heavy a tang?

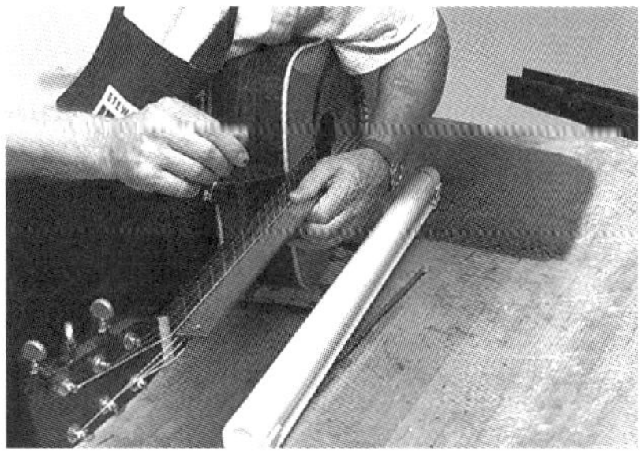

89 In playing position, strung to pitch, and using the notched straightedge to "read the board" we find .004" of relief—that's perfect! (The frets may not show the exact same relief as the board, since some frets could be high or low).

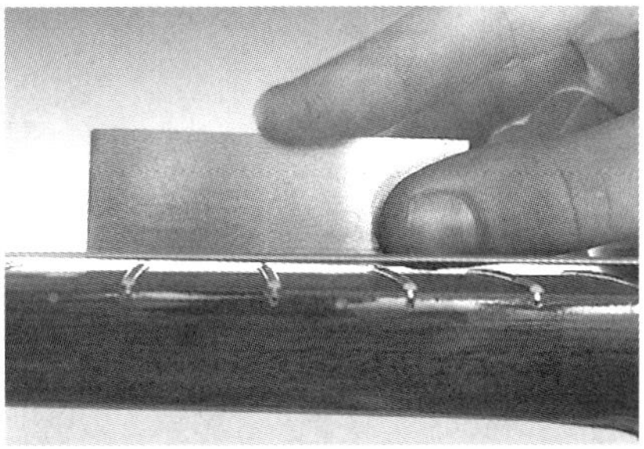

90 Check individual fret height with short straight edges looking for "rock" (a straightedge resting on any three frets will rock if the middle one is high—as this one is). If you find one...

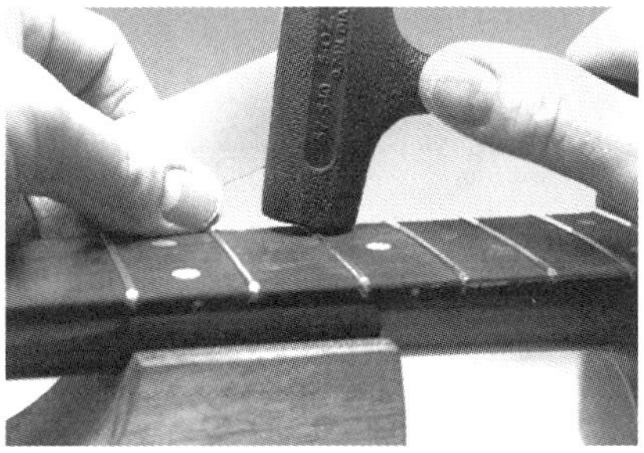

91 ...remove the strings and file down the high spot (or hammer it down)—sometimes you'll need superglue, a gluing caul, and a clamp to hold the fret down while it dries.

92 File, hammer, or glue down high frets (sometimes we pull them up if one fret is *lower* than its neighbors) until the straightedge touches all the tops.

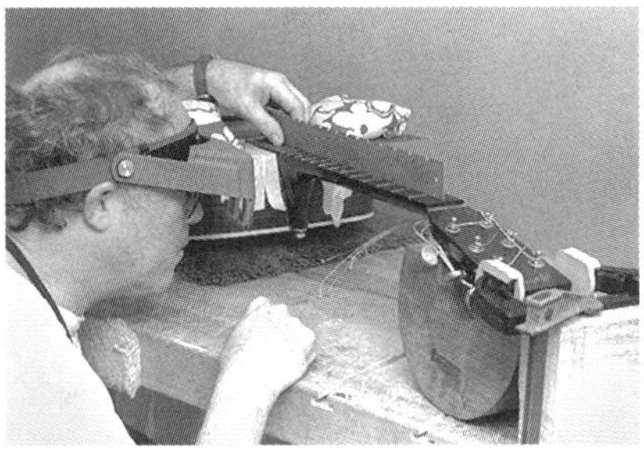

93 With the strings off, clamped back into the setup used earlier, and with the "string simulation" weights on, the straightedge reads dead flat—the .004" relief hasn't pulled in. That's OK, we'll level the frets with the neck "dead flat."

NOTE: It's nice to level the frets with the neck perfectly straight when possible, because it's so easy to be sure that all the fret tops are level with each other. If your neck isn't as nice and straight as this Martin—say it pulls into a significant relief at this stage when you're trying to level—remove some of the shoulder weight....

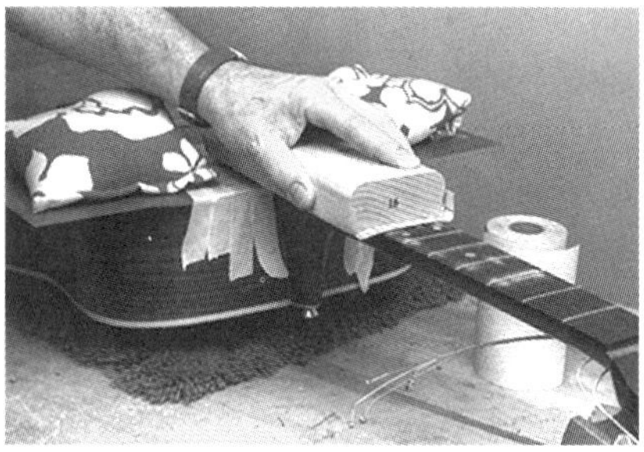

94 ...or add more. Either way, the relief will pull in when you string it up. Make a couple of leveling strokes with a radius sanding block and #220-grit paper to "rough-in" any high spots...

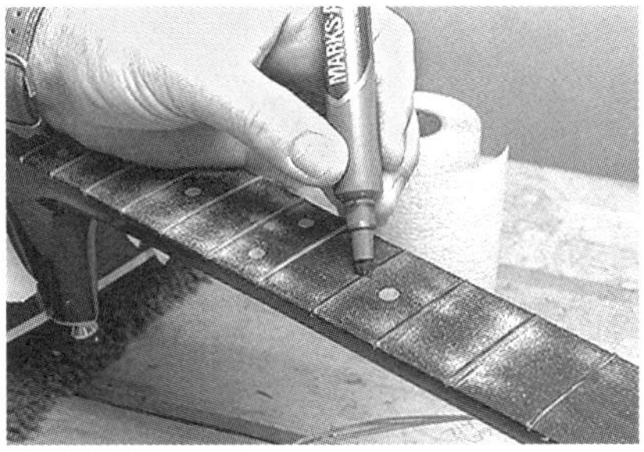

95 ...then highlight the fret tops with marker pen and repeat the process using #320, then #400-grit paper.

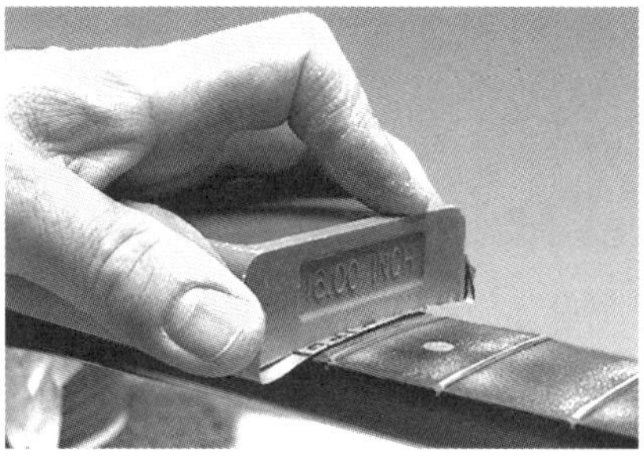

96 This is a "Deluxe" Radius Sanding Block—it *sands* the same as a wooden one (but it makes a better fret clamping and gluing caul because of its hardened casting resin composition—we'll use these as clamps later).

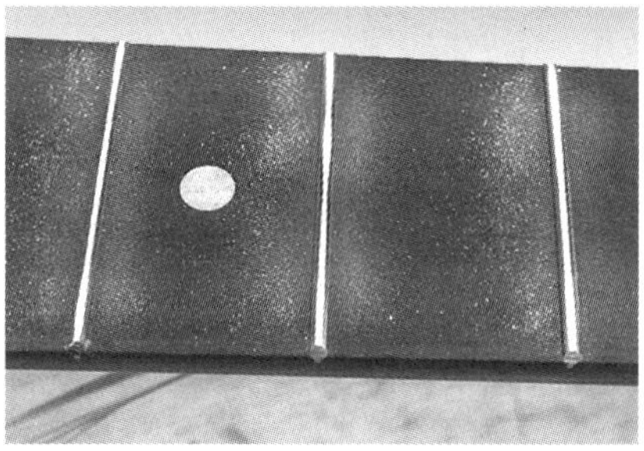

97 Several passes, changing the paper once, is all it took to powder the tops of those frets. We're ready for dressing.

98 A good selection of fret dressing tools, and the carpet scrap "toolbox" protects the guitar...

99 ...and it's OK to rest the carpet right on the body.

100 It's convenient and practical to be able to walk around the neck as you see here.

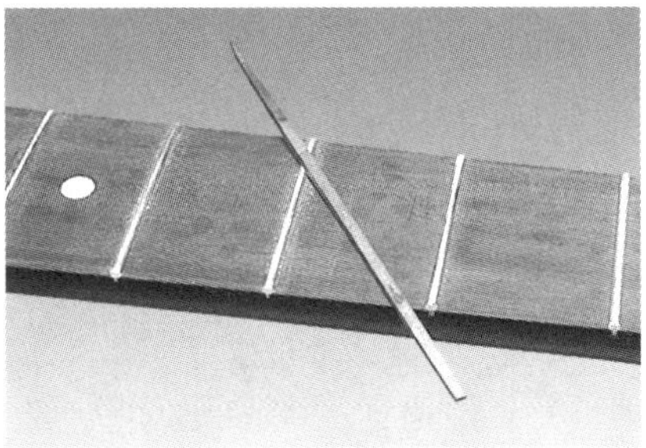

101 Though you're probably getting tired of seeing these tools, we'll run through them anyhow—any tip you might glean from a new or different shot is worth it. The 1/8" nut seating file...

102 ...is good for flattening, creating, or polishing the bevel (removing any marks left by the lengthwise beveling process).

103 One or two downstrokes...

104 …puts a smooth polish on the bevel face (sometimes we use upstrokes to make the wire-edged burr stand out)…

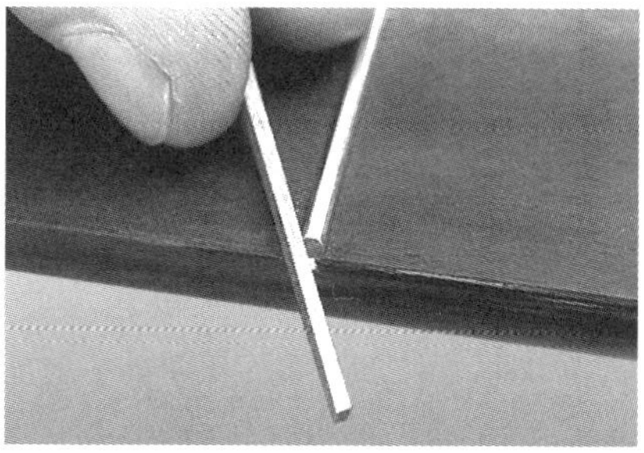

105 …so we can file it off with the same file used on its edge.

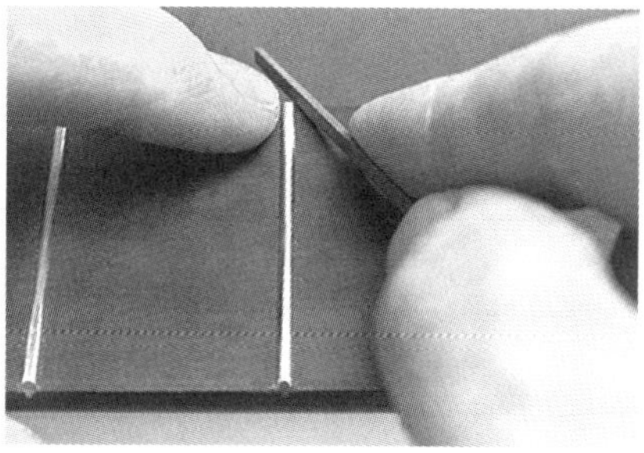

106 Use your finger as a guide to keep from slipping as you shape the ends.

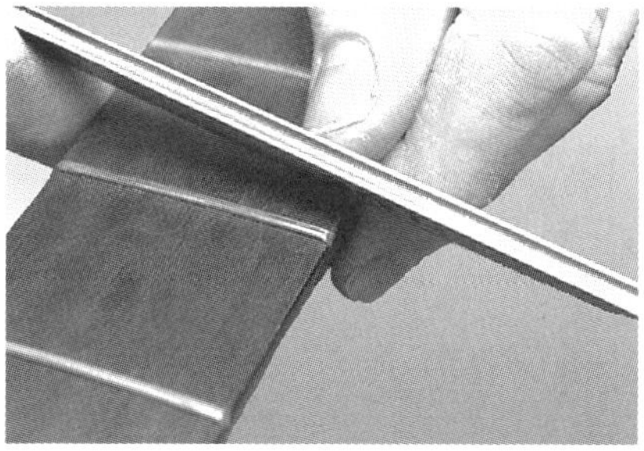

107 The small side of the diamond fret rounding file is good for Martin-size wire and smaller…

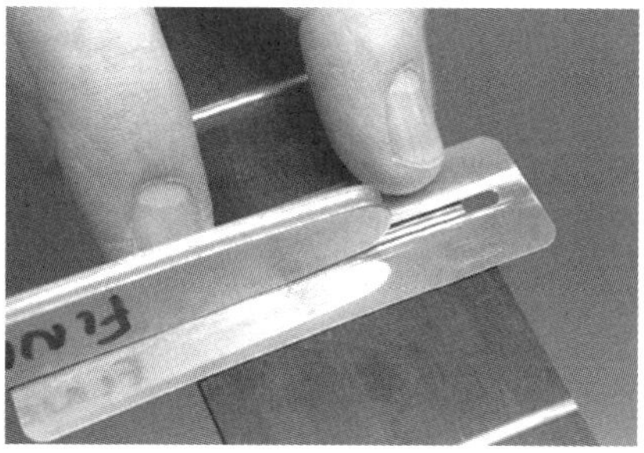

108 …and you should protect the fretboard with a stainless steel fret guard and/or tape, of course.

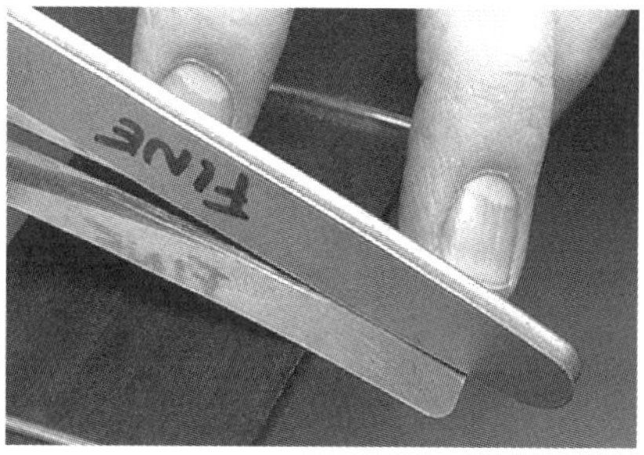

109 You can use the diamond file (with the fret guard) to shape the fret ends, too.

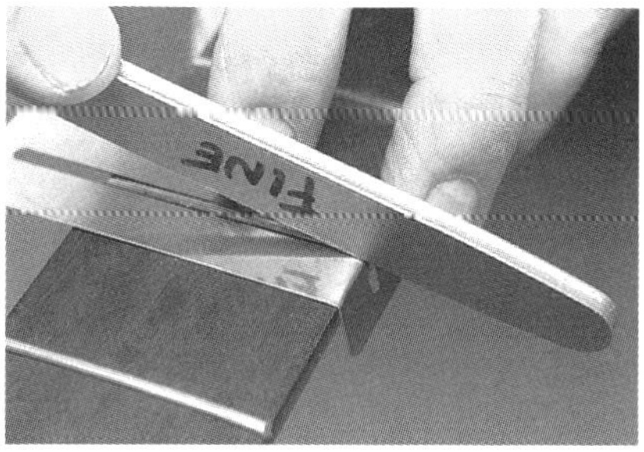

110 Try bending a guard to wrap over the end, to keep you from going too far…

111 …this is what we mean by "too far." Such marks in the wood on each side of the fret end could be inadvertantly made with *any* file, even when using the guard, so be careful!

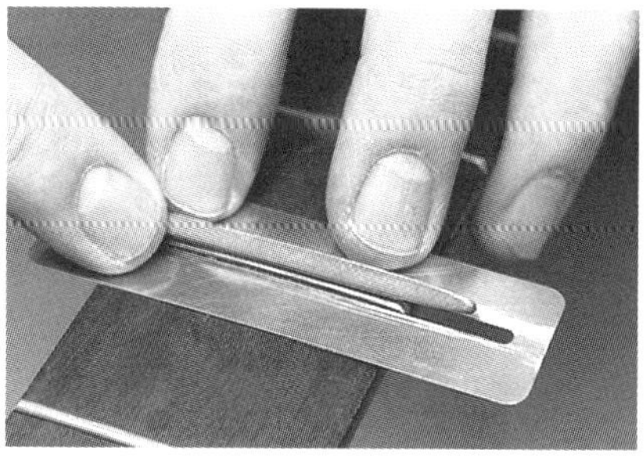

112 The small Waverly 3-corner file is still the safest of them all—especially if you don't have much rounding to do (a well-done fret job shouldn't).

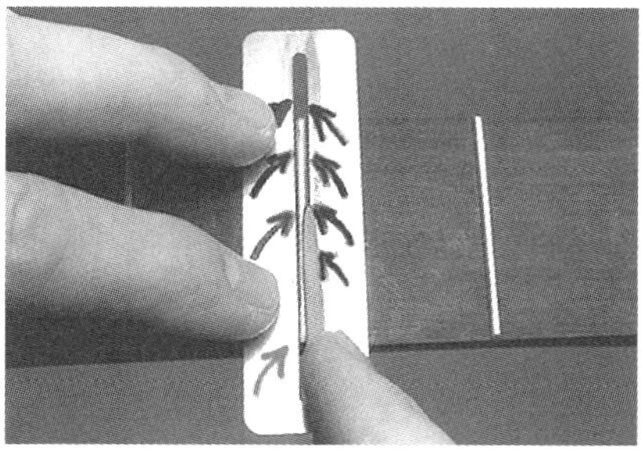

113 Round each side to center (just reviewing)…

114 …follow with the Sand-Sticks (#400 and #600-grit)…

115 …and finish with 0000-steel wool.

116 Can't wait to get this guard off and string 'er up.

117 The flex test can't budge this baby…

118 …a job well done!

LESSON 4

A COMPLEX REFRET JOB

(BOUND FINGERBOARD, "RUBBER NECK," & EXCESSIVE UPBOW)

This "European-style" Alvarez acoustic was a real nice axe until it spent a day locked in a car during August in southern Ohio. Not only did the "neck-set" angle change slightly (becoming underset with the strings too high), but the neck took on a huge upbow). It's surprising that the guitar stayed in one piece! Anyhow, thanks to that person's oversight, we had a fret job that covered more bases than any we could have hoped for: poor neck angle/action; bound fingerboard; heavy-duty fretboard planing; inlay removal and replacement; neck straightening with compression; notched fret ends (overhanging binding); and Dremel-routing the slots. All these problems were correctable with fretwork. Here's how...

1 Sighting the neck—it's plain to see that the fingerboard has a big rise or hump in the fretboard extension ("tongue").

2 The best way to check the neck is with the body laying on its side on the bench and with a strong backlight—these "Brite-Stick" fluorescent lights are great.

3 Using the notched straightedge and feeler gauge to measure the amount of upbow or relief in the neck.

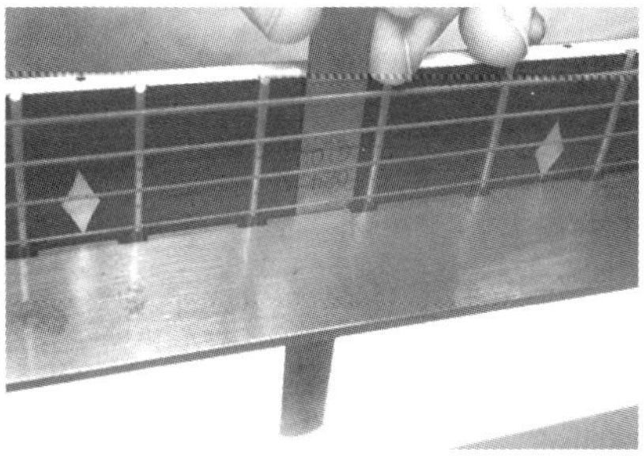

4 .024" is way too much relief!

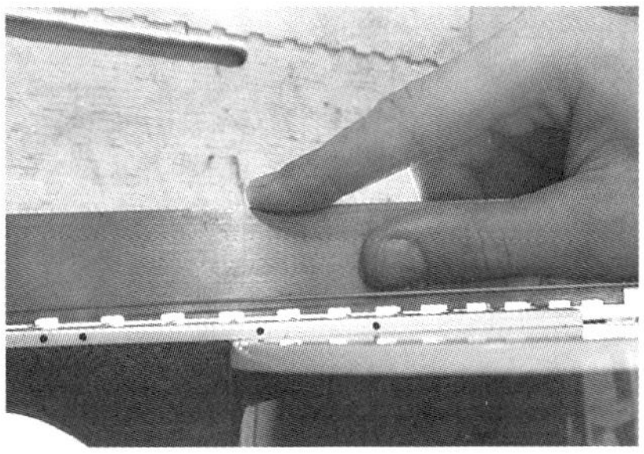

5 The culprit is this rising tongue...

6 ...that's how much relief there is in the 7th to 9th fret area.

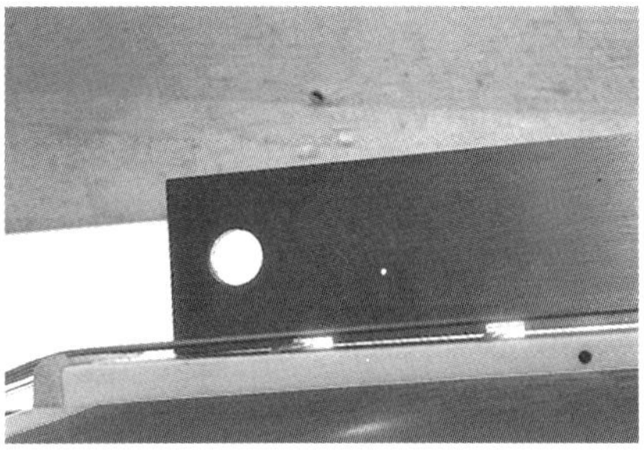

7 If the straightedge is a long one—starting at the 1st fret—you'll be reading relief from one end of the board to the other…

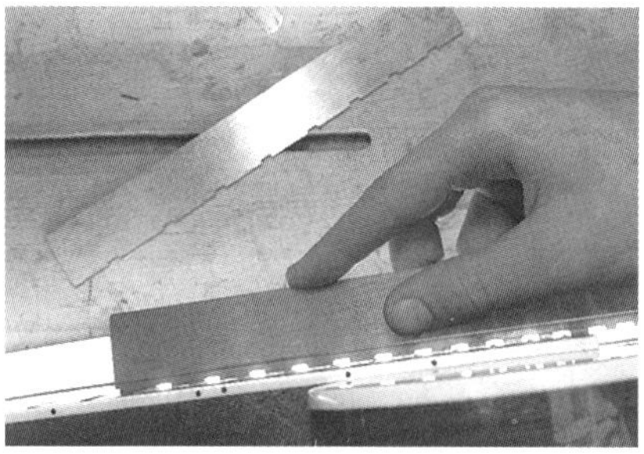

8 So, we cut one of the notched edges at the 9th fret (where you expect to see the fretboard start to level out) in order to read the tongue separately.

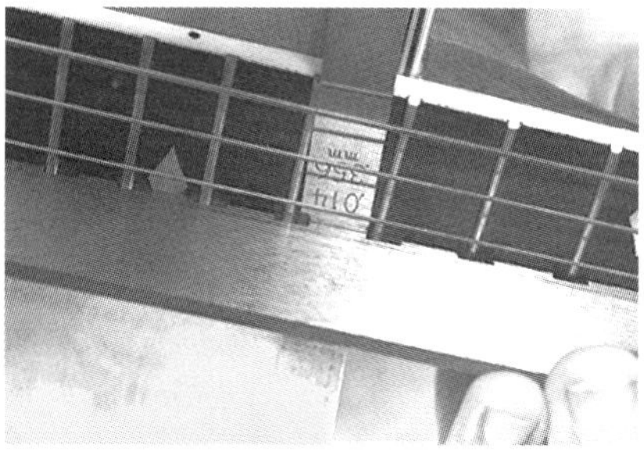

9 Where it should be flat, the notched straightedge shows .014" of gap (relief) on the tongue section alone (independent of the main part of the fretboard).

10 Even with the truss rod maxed out tightly…

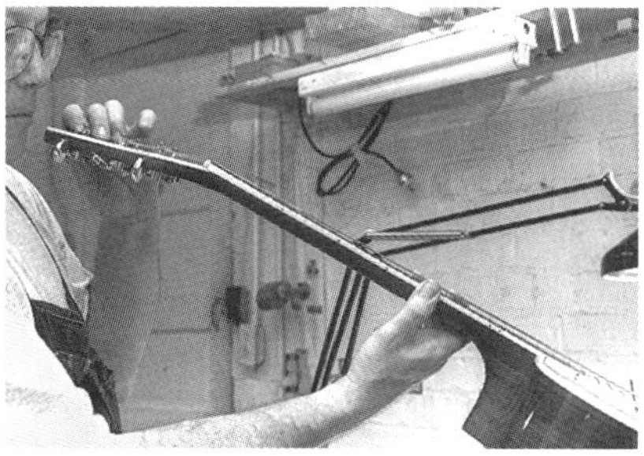

11… this neck has way too much up-bow; it wouldn't straighten out. In fact, upon giving it the "flex-test" for stiffness, we found it terribly weak—a "rubber neck," as they say.

12 That much weakness or "give" in a neck makes you wonder how well they matched the fret slot size to the fret tang size. Here's a quick way to find out!

13 The empty slot measures either .024" or .025"…

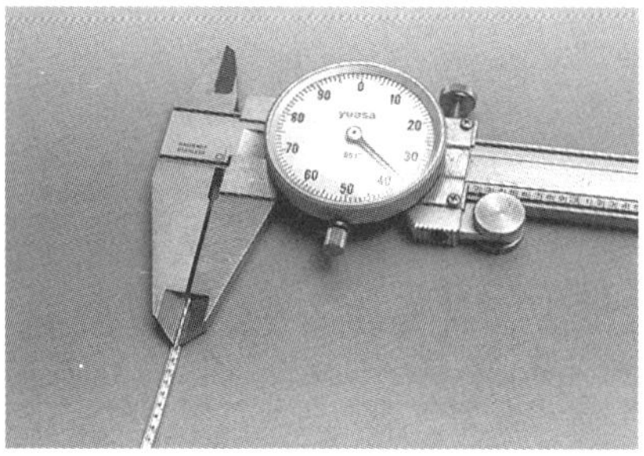

14 The outside of the tang "barbs" measured .037"…

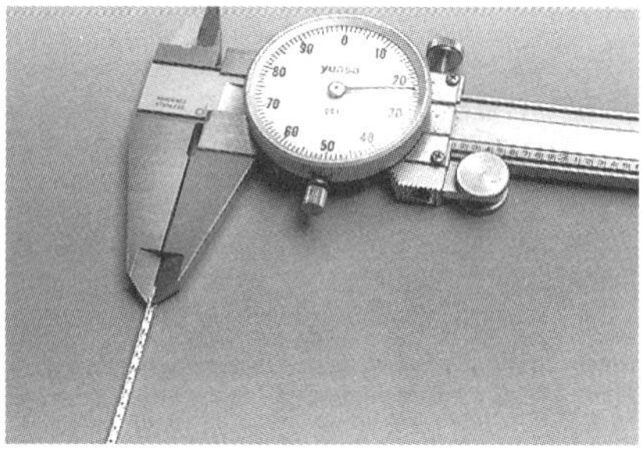

15 …the tang (measured in between the barbs) is .022"–.023"…

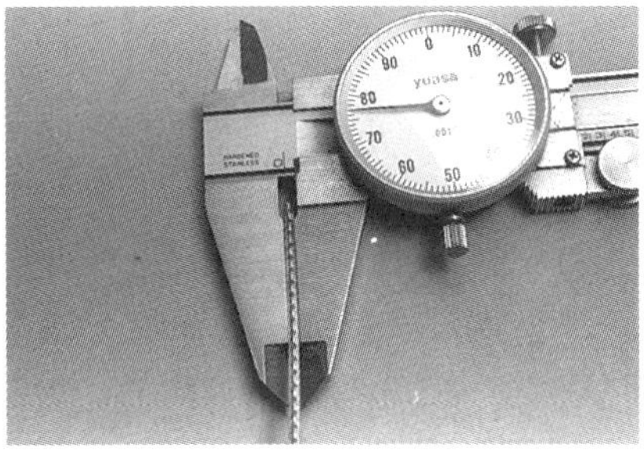

16 …the width of the crown is .078" (although there's no reason that we have to replace it with a fret of the same width).

17 To double-check, remove another fret…

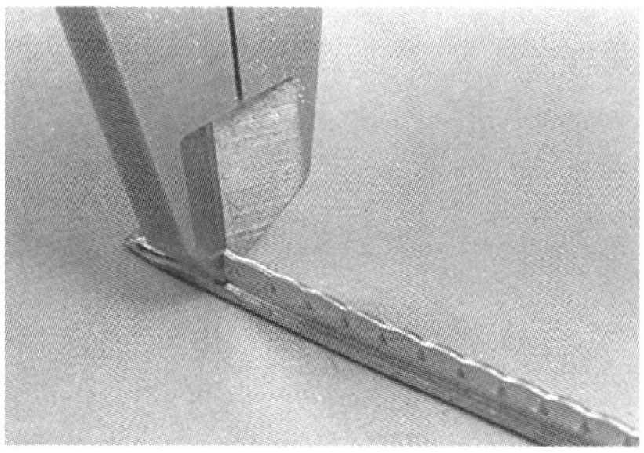

18 …but measure in between the barbs (a sharp bevel on the caliper jaw is a help)…

19 ...this one's a little thinner on the tang (.021").

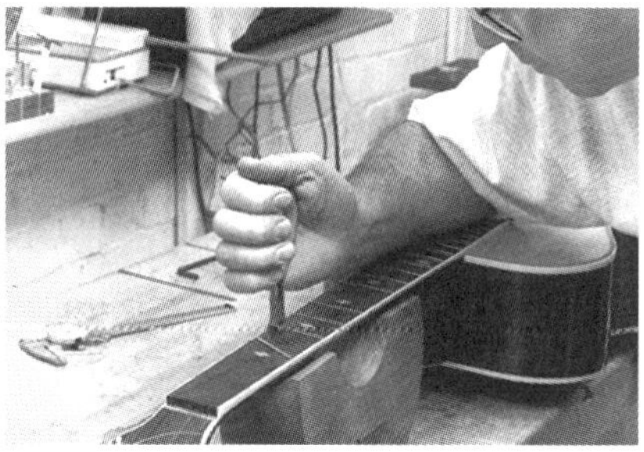

20 So there's a lot of slop between the tang and the fret slot walls—no wonder the neck's so weak. Remove all the frets.

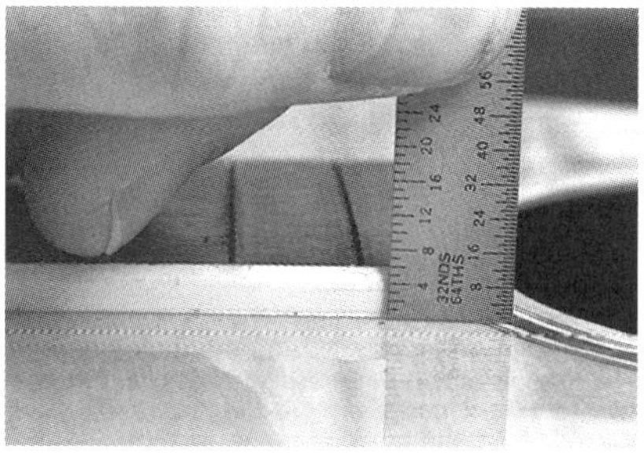

21 It's important to know the fretboard thickness—especially if you must remove a lot of wood to get the board straight. It's 3/16" at the end...

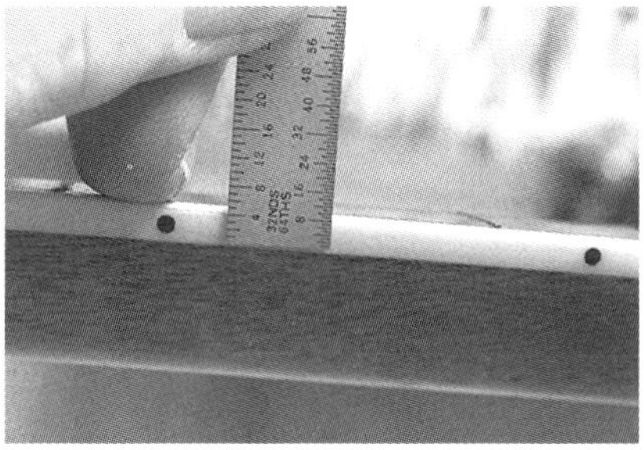

22 ...and 5/32" in the middle. Also pay attention to how close the side dot markers are to the surface.

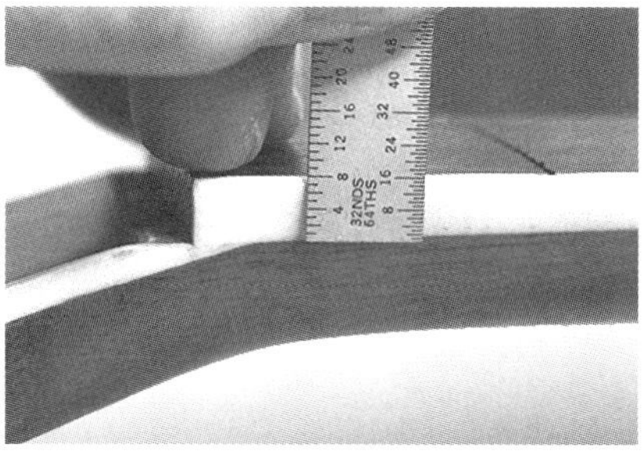

23 It's thick at the nut(1/4")! By choosing *where* the most wood gets removed, you can alter the action drastically—removing the most at the nut end will lower the action, much like a neck reset (see photo 43).

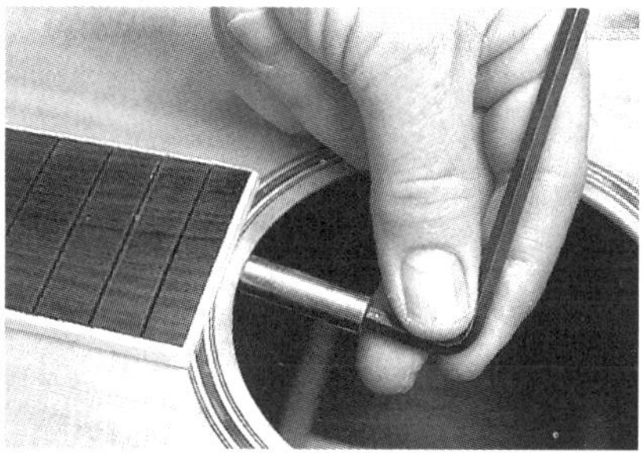

24 In hopes of gaining more truss rod adjustment of course, you should remove and lubricate the nut...

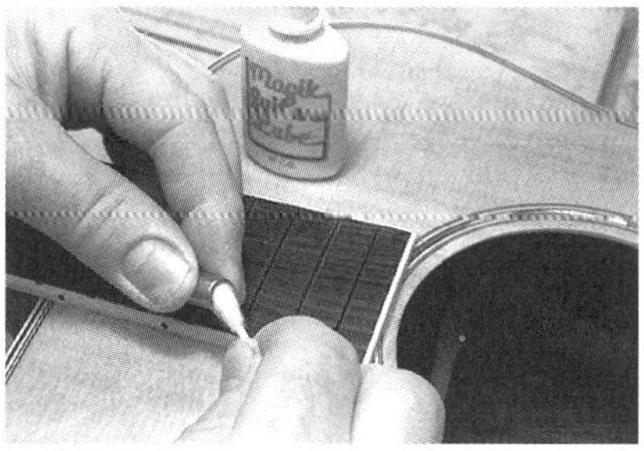

25 ...this always makes the rod work better.

26 Sitting on the neck rest, without strings (or frets), the neck shows a huge up-bow when viewed with a backlight. The truss rod is completely loose at this time.

27 The fret barbs probably helped a little in keeping the neck straight, but not much! With the frets removed, the upbow is a whopping .036"!

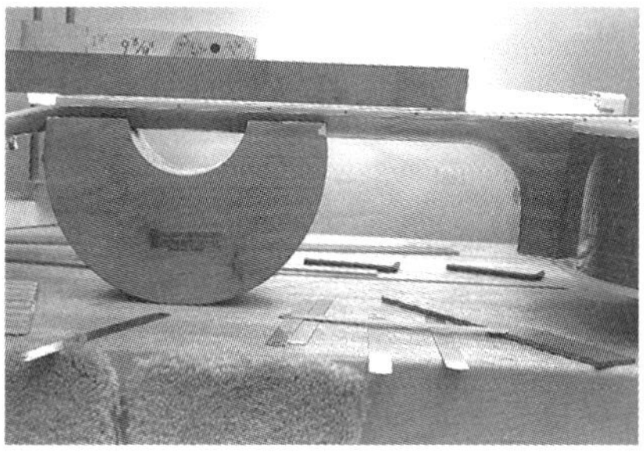

28 Here's looking at the fretboard length in two stages: the gap on the main fretboard (without the tongue) around the 7th and 9th frets...

29 ... is .020".

30 Up on the tongue (without the main fretboard) where it should be flat, there's a "secondary relief"...

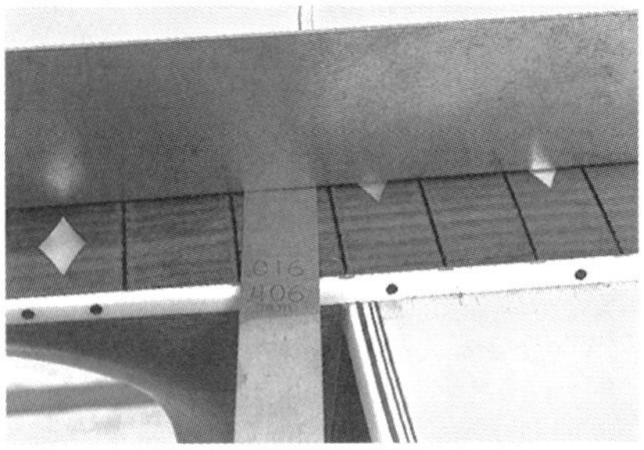

31 of .016". Then we tightened the truss rod to see how much of the gap it would remove, and it was…

32 …quite a bit! The truss rod wasn't doing much *before* the lubrication, but now it straightened the neck from the nut to around the 9th fret quite well.

33 Now it's time to smooth any fret-removal chips or burrs in order to get an accurate straightedge reading.

34 That main part of the board—at the 7th fret—only has .004" gap with the rod almost tight.

35 And the relief on the tongue measures .010" at the 14th fret (it had been .020" remember, before adjusting the rod)—so there's still a "rising tongue."

36 Another factor when "reading" a neck is that any portion of the fretboard between the 1st fret and the nut isn't part of the fretted playing surface…

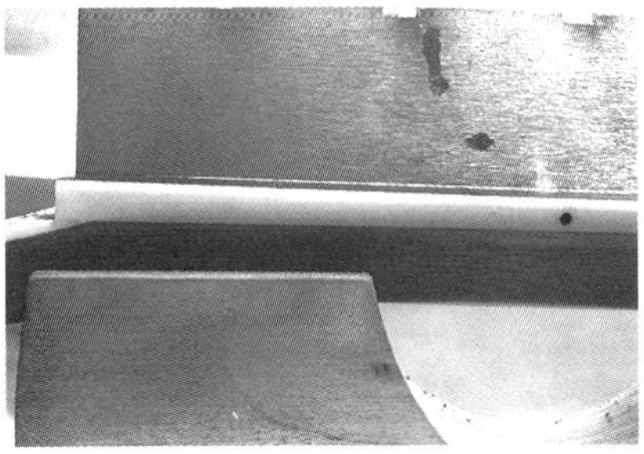

37 …so you're better off not setting the straightedge all the way to the end of the board if it makes the ruler show an increase in the gap. Read the first fret instead.

38 If you *removed* the excess wood here, the straightedge will show the true relief (a lot of wood will be coming off here in a moment).

39 If you lay a loooooonnnggg straightedge on this fretboard…

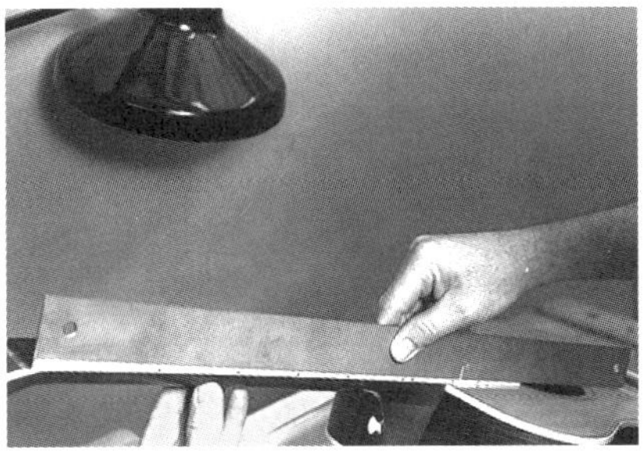

40 …and slide it back toward the bridge. It points down at the bottom of the bridge…

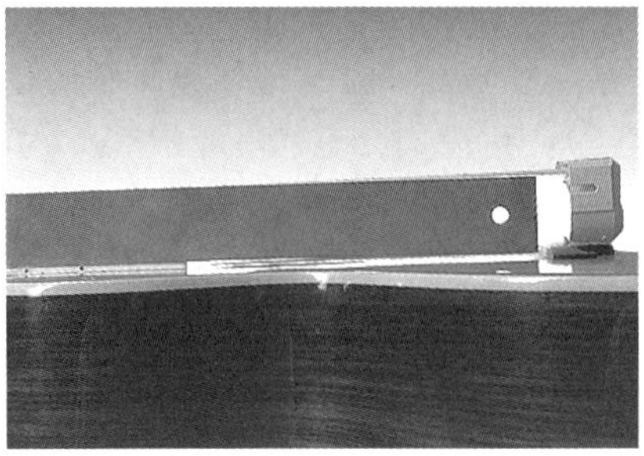

41 …almost touching the top—when it should point up toward the *top* of the bridge. Perhaps this neck came unset from the heat. It's "underset," and requires a very low saddle, but…

42 …by offsetting the straightedge 1/16" at the nut end on the fingerboard edge, we can accomplish much of what a neck set could do (as long as the fretboard is thick enough to accommodate heavy wood removal).

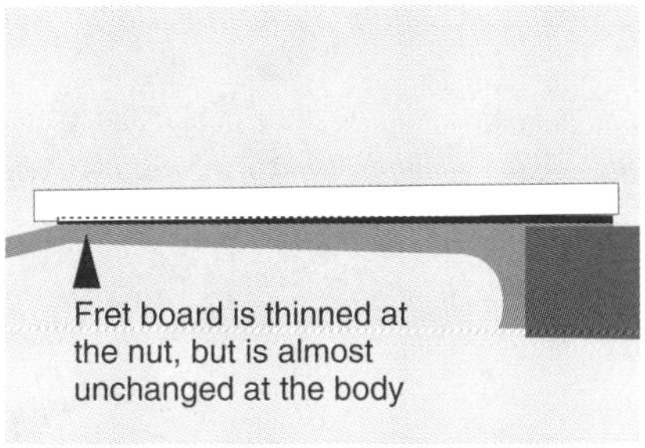

43 The straightedge is angled slightly downward at the nut for an "instant neck reset." (Shown from a different viewpoint in the drawing below.)

44 Then the straightedge would point where it should (at the *top* of the bridge).

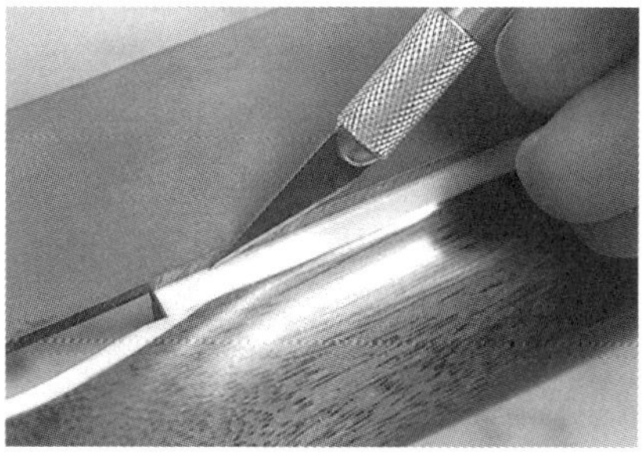

45 Scribe the offset into the finish lightly, but enough to see easily.

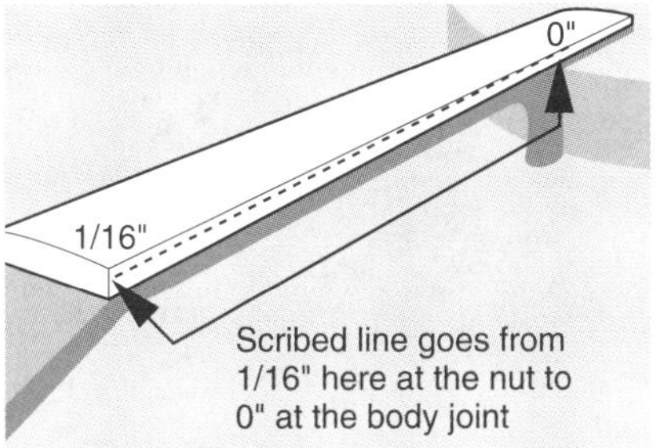

46 The scribed line runs from 1/16" deep at the nut on a long taper that diminishes to nothing at the body joint, accomplishing the "neck reset" mentioned above.

47 Checking the radius shows a "cylinder-shaped" fretboard with a 12" radius…

48 …at both ends of the fretboard.

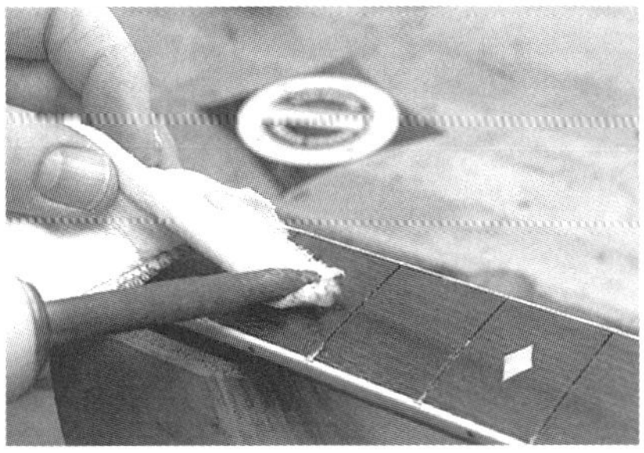

49 Since so much wood's coming off at this end, we used a damp rag and heat to loosen the glue, and then pried the pearl out carefully with sharp dental probes…

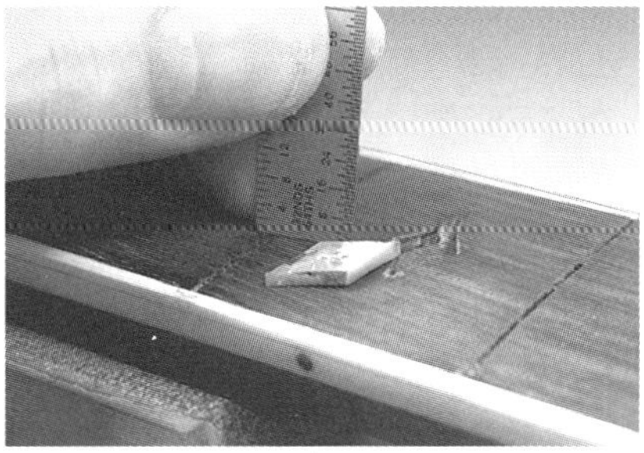

50 …these inlays were so thick, they might have been allright if we'd left them alone! *Plastic* inlays will catch on fire from heat—if they won't pry out you'd have to rout them out and make replacements.

51 A white pencil, grease-pencil, or chalk are good for highlighting the areas where wood needs to be removed.

52 Always check the slot depths if you need to remove a lot of wood (you're in trouble if they disappear during sanding, because they're hard to recut—especially with binding).

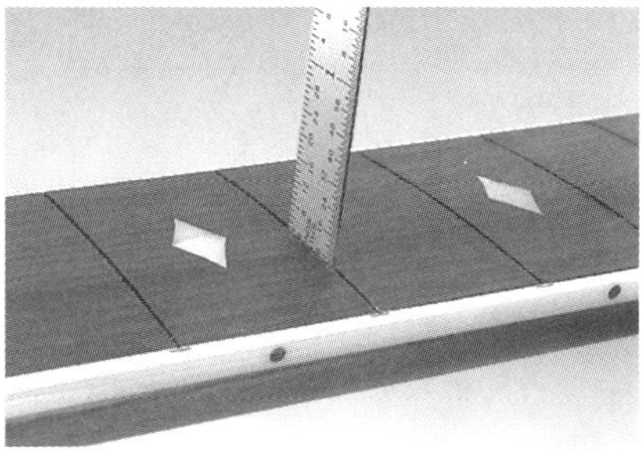

53 The nut end slots were 3/16", and up at the 5th they're 1/8"—that's deeper than they need to be. No wonder the neck is so weak and upbowed—these fret slots act like kerfing!

54 OK. Before taking away any wood which can't be replaced, it's time to think the whole job through and try a little experiment…

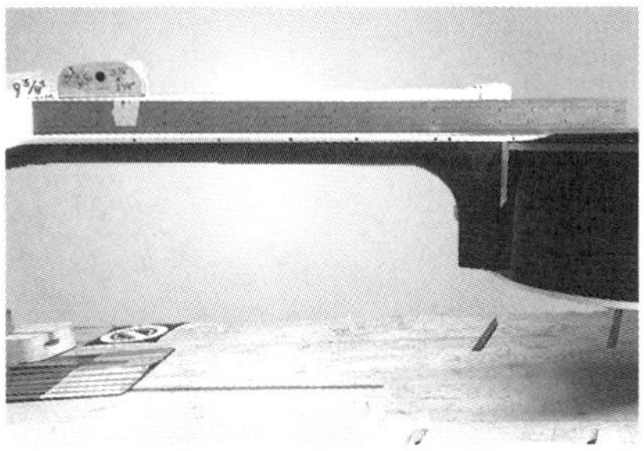

55 If a straightedge resting on the full length of the board…

56 …shows .022" of relief (we removed .016" from that original .038" by adjusting the truss rod),

57 …what would happen if we clamped the body onto the workbench, with the body held firm and the neck hanging free,

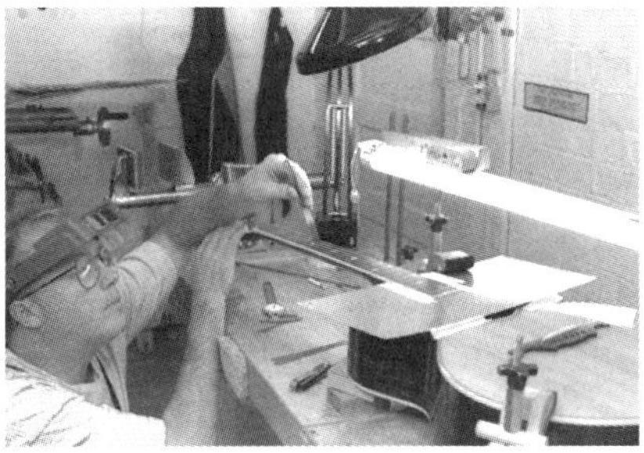

58 …pulled back on the neck (into severe backbow), and set a .026" feeler gauge into a fret slot, and let up on the neck? Would the fret slots "close-up" and hold the feeler gauge tight?

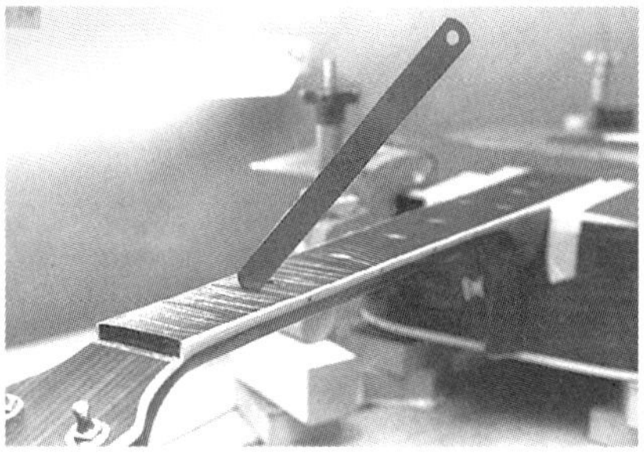

59 Yes!…

60 And by pulling back on the neck again, the feeler gauge falls free. We'll remove some of the excess (.022") upbow by bending the neck back, filling the slots with glued-in strips of wood…

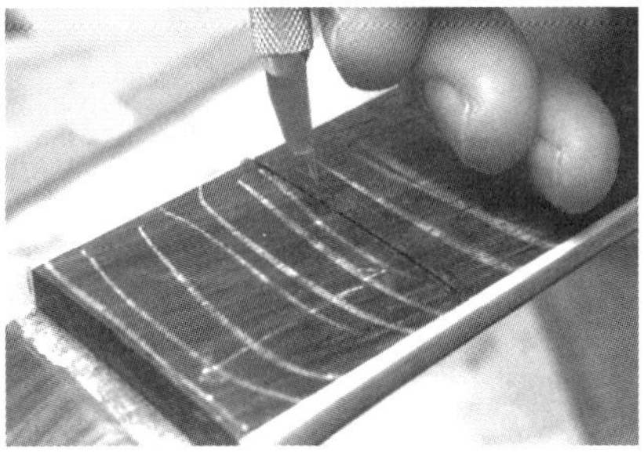

61 …and holding the neck straight by the wedging effect (similar to compression fretting with oversize tangs). We cleaned out any debris from the slots…

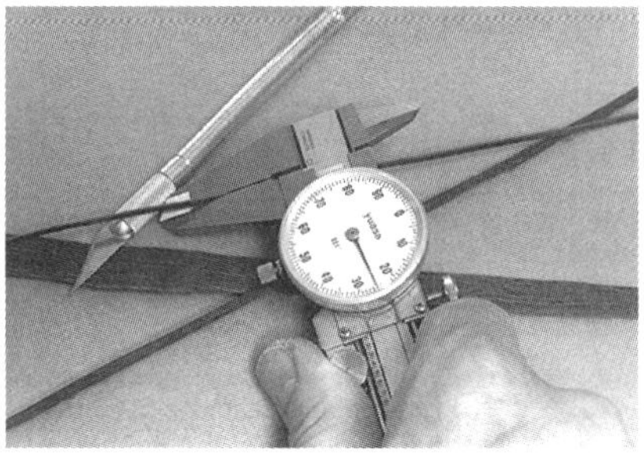

62 …this rosewood veneer just happened to measure .025" (± .0015")…

63 …and it stripped easily with an X-acto knife.

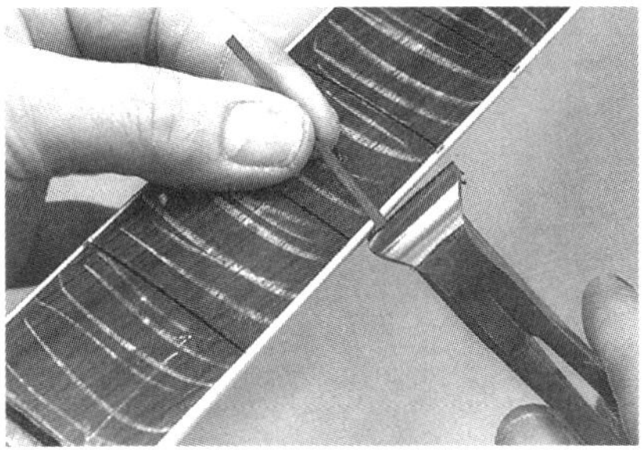

64 Trimmed to a length that fit inside the binding,

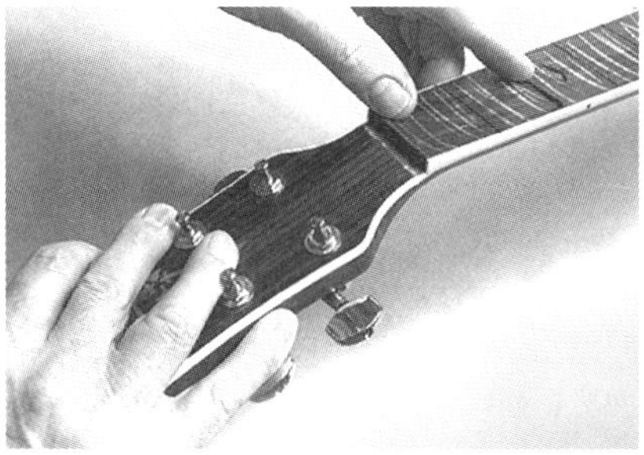

65 …the rosewood strips pushed easily into the fret slots if we pulled back on the neck.

66 You could get the strips well started with a fingertip…

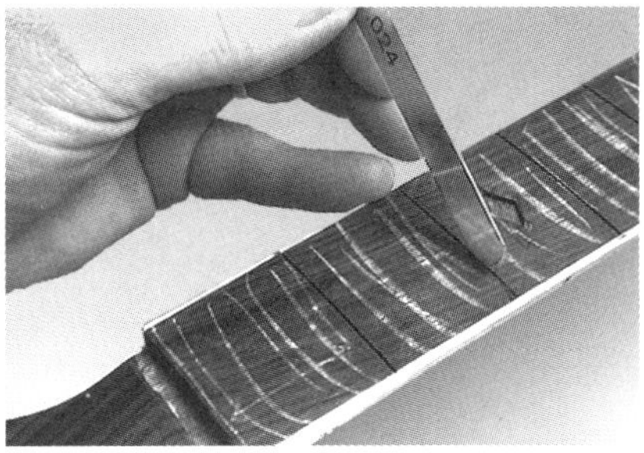

67 ...and finish by pushing them all the way to the bottom with a slightly undersized (.024") feeler gauge.

68 When some of the ends wouldn't go down as far as the center portion (arrow pointing at end)...

69 ...we supported the neck (the body is still clamped firmly in the workbench) with this little stand, and hammered the strips down into the slot with a short broken piece of feeler gauge as the driver...

70 ...that worked great.

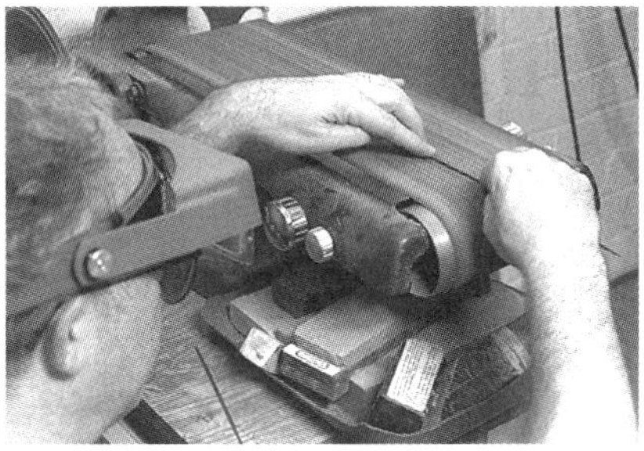

71 The height of each filler strip was custom-sanded to match the depth of each slot (the slots got shallower as the fretboard got thinner). You don't want to fill the slot completely.

72 After being filled with wood, the slots weren't deep enough to accept the fret tang, so we used a dental burr (with a re-ground outside diameter—see the tools section) to re-cut the slot (only cutting the bottom—not the walls).

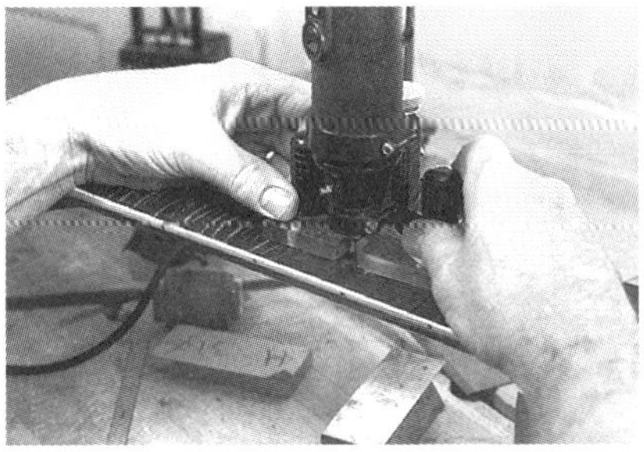

73 The filler strips fit so tightly that they could be Dremeled without having been glued (it seemed a better idea to superglue them after the routing so that the cutter bit wouldn't clog, burn, and stick with the superglue).

74 Once the slot depth was re-established, we ran water-thin "Hot-Stuff" down into each slot to saturate and immobilize each filler strip.

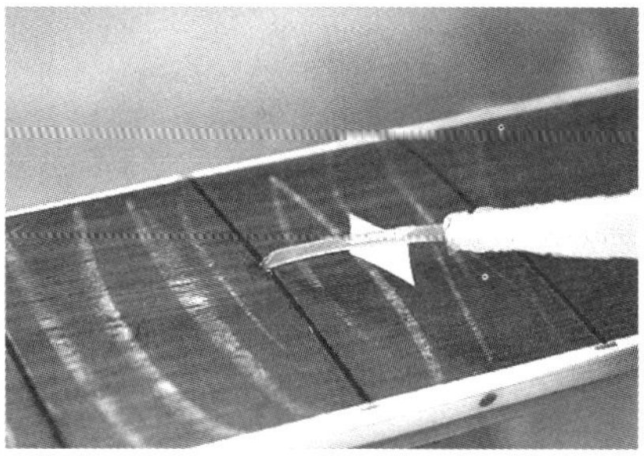

75 The teflon applicator-tip helped guide the glue into the slot—the superglue would fill right up to the top of the slot...

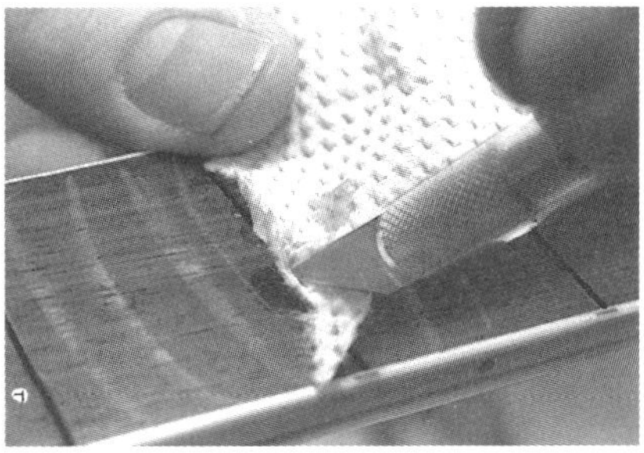

76 ...and we'd soak up the excess by using the X-acto blade to press a paper towel into the slot.

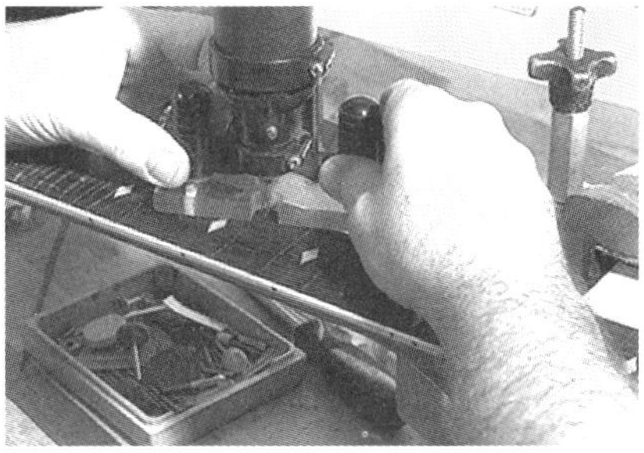

77 Even though the slots had been "depth-Dremeled" a few steps back (step 73), the superglue coating swelled them enough that a slight re-routing was required...

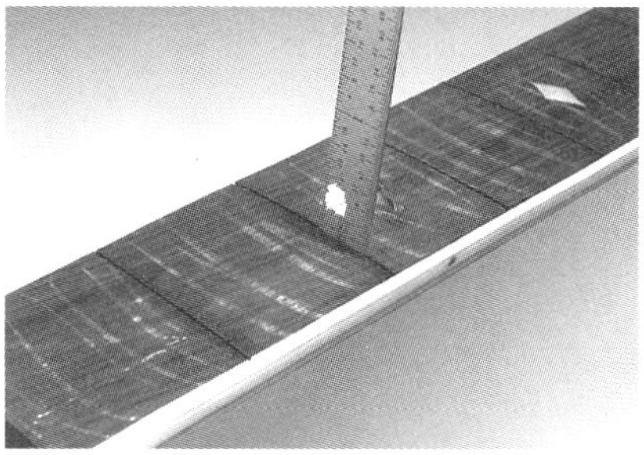

78 ...to assure the correct final depth. Now that the neck is somewhat stiffer, we'll continue by leveling the fretboard.

79 A scraper seemed the quickest way to remove a lot of wood in a hurry…

80 …until we got bored and went to the belt sander—creating a long flat taper from the nut to the 12th fret—*not sanding* from frets 12 to 17…

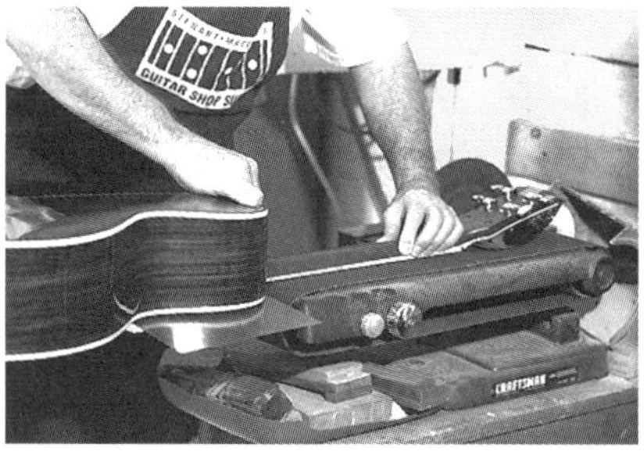

81 …and then knocking off the high end of the tongue (notice the protective sanding guard on the body). **CAUTION: Do I need to say that you could ruin the guitar by trying this trick? Be careful, or do it by hand!**

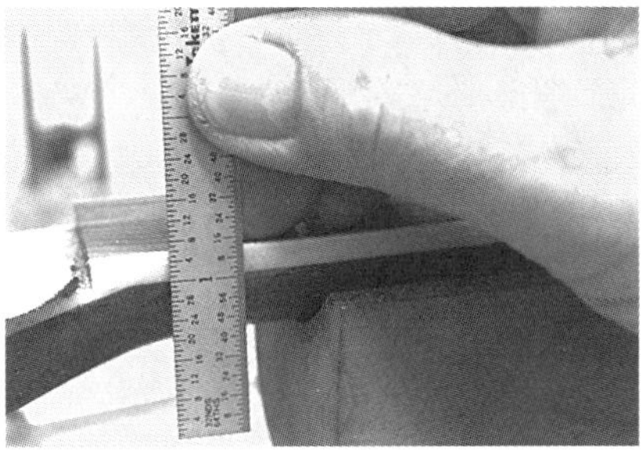

82 The sander removed the 1/16" maximum in a hurry.

83 …and those first few fret slots had to be re-cut…

84 …to a depth of slightly over 1/16".

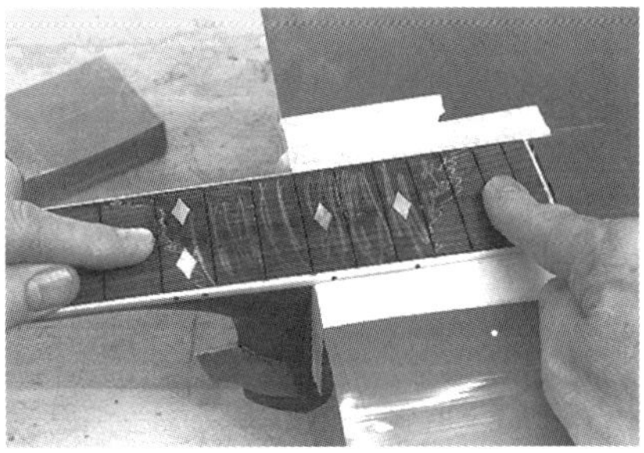

85 Here's the area which is original fret surface (untouched by the belt sander)…

86 …it was "blended in" to the belt-sanded areas, using the 6" fret leveling file wrapped with sandpaper.

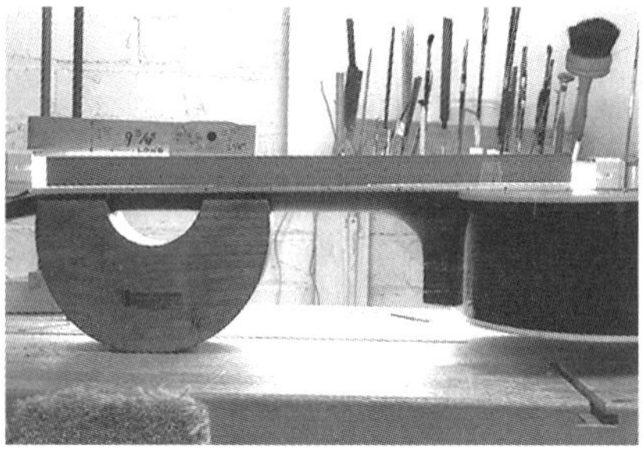

87 Now, after back-bending and gluing in the fret slot fillers, when a straightedge is set on the whole board you could see light at each end—the .022" unwanted relief is more than gone!

88 In fact we've .012" drop-off (back-bow) at the nut…

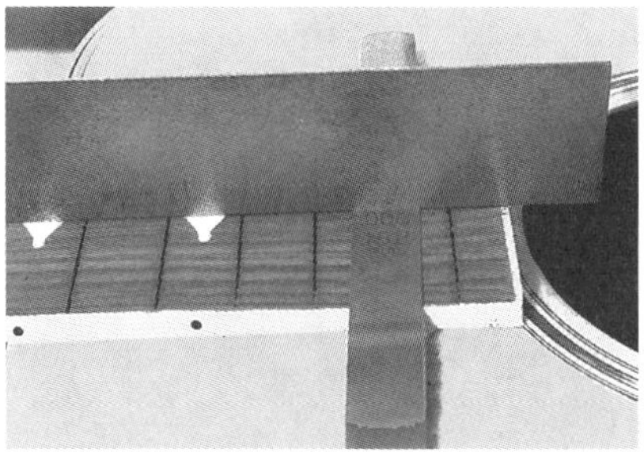

89 …and .006" "fall-away" on the tongue!

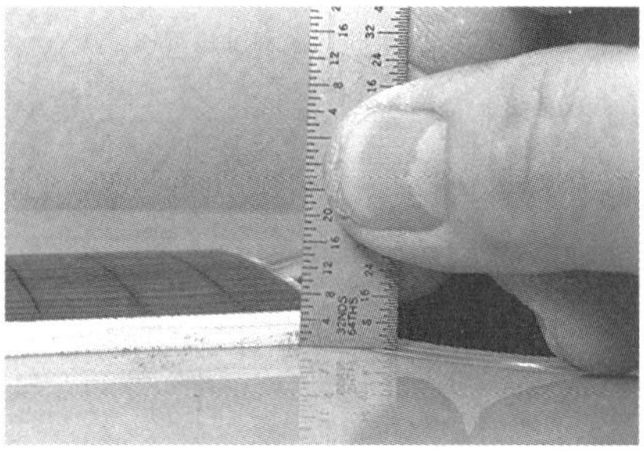

90 By straightening and stiffening the neck with the filler strips, less than 1/32" had to be removed from the 3/16" tongue, helping to preserve those dark side dot markers…

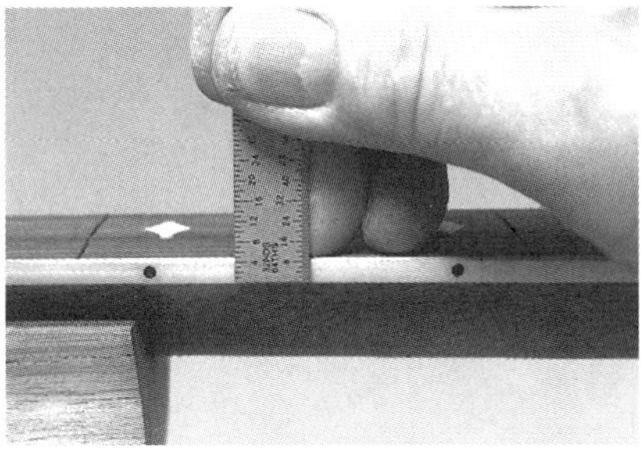

91 ...almost nothing was removed from the middle...

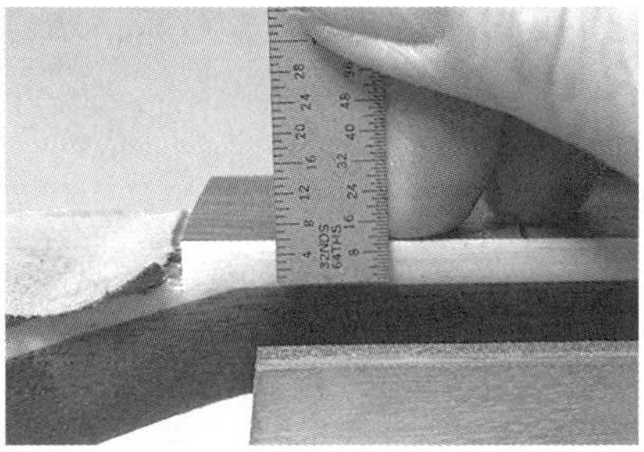

92 ...and the heaviest removal was at the thick end. The neck has been straightened and stiffened without undue loss of fretboard thickness, or top-to-bottom feel of the neck.

93 Time to deepen the inlay routs...

94 ...and glue the diamonds back in. We just pressed the inlays into place dry, and then ran water-thin superglue down into them.

95 A little rosewood dust and superglue helps fill any voids instantly.

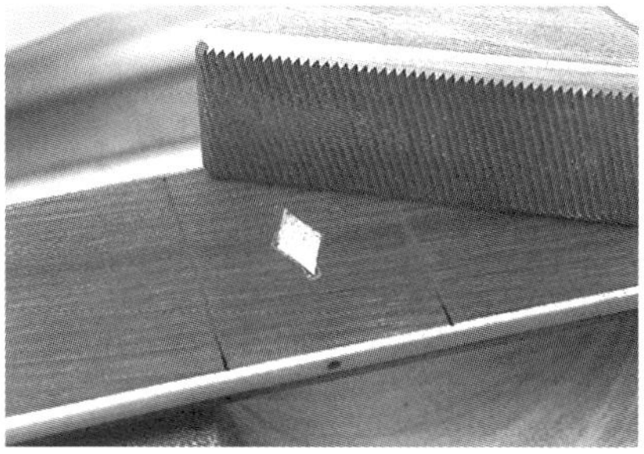

96 The "Fingerboard leveler" is ideal for leveling pearl.

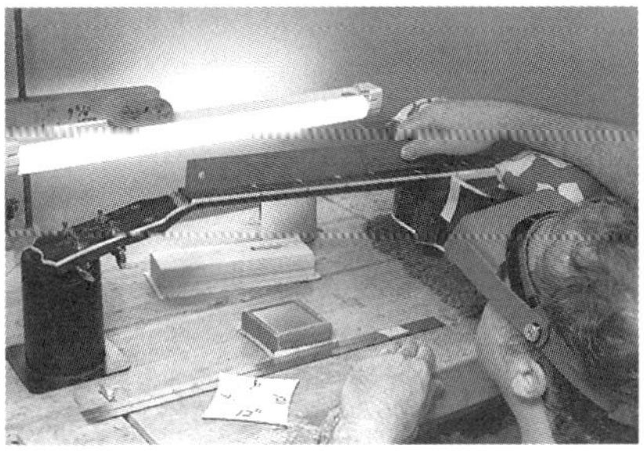

97 Now, with the peghead supported—not the neck—and some weight added to the shoulders for "string tension simulation," the neck is straight as an arrow (except for a little fall-away on the tongue).

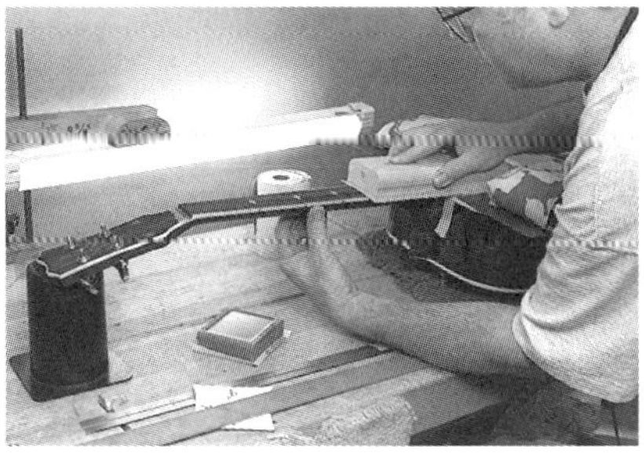

98 The 12" radius block blends the flat-sanded areas together and re-establishes a uniform fretboard radius.

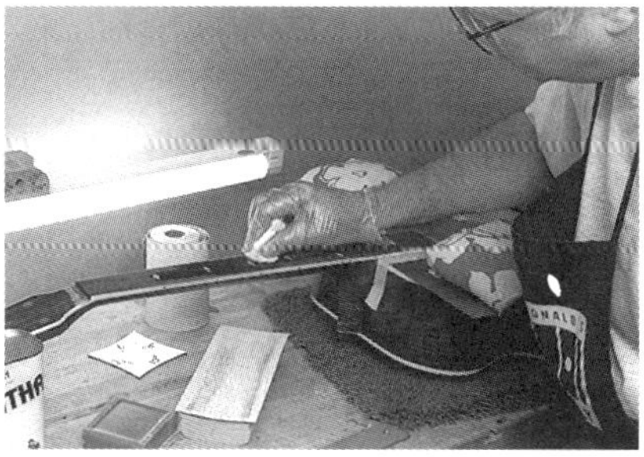

99 Wet-sand to raise the grain, and sand again. If you use naphtha, have good fresh air ventilation.

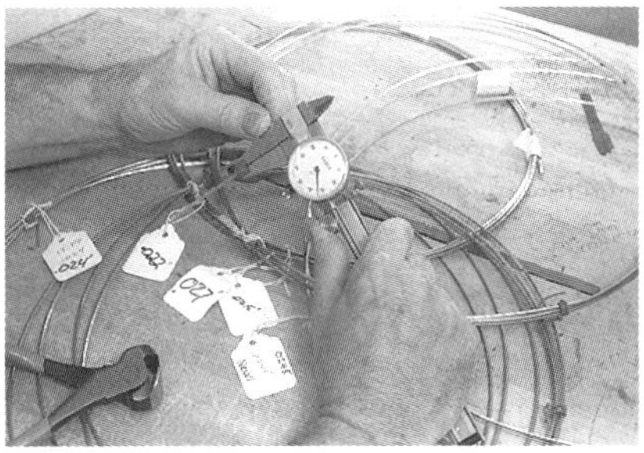

100 The wire we've chosen is a little thinner (.035" vs. .037") on the *outside* of the barbs than the original was...

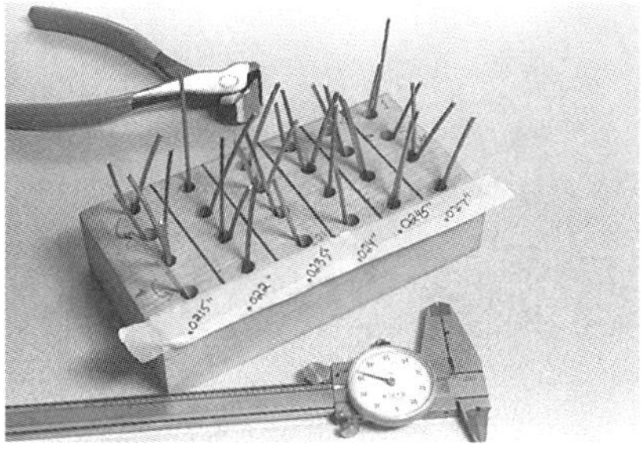

101 ...but not the tang. This wire was chosen from our selection of under-, and oversized tang fretwire. In this case we were only interested in an oversize tang in order to fill the wide fret slots.

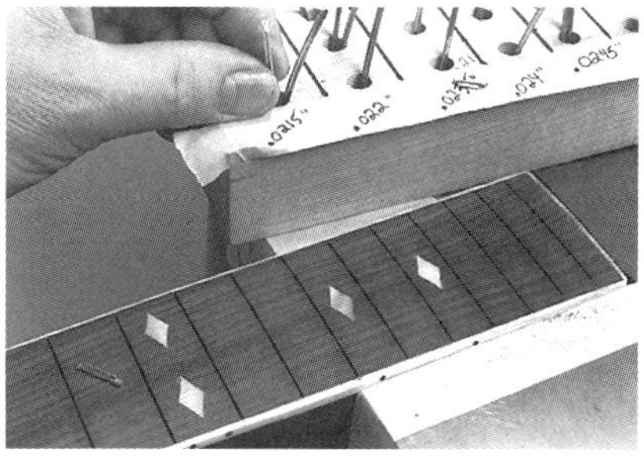

102 These six fret tang sizes should handle any of our needs for this job. We started with a piece of the narrow .0215" tang for the "tongue" since it has a wide enough barb to hold in the slot, but still hammers in easily.

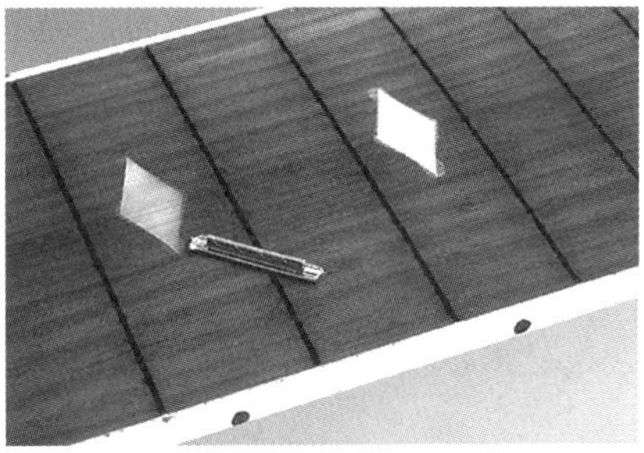

103 Use a short test piece, trimmed neatly so that any rough spots or burrs created by the nippers don't get in the way…

104 …and hammer it in as a test…

105 Then give it the fingernail or thumbnail test—this size wasn't good because it could be pried up easily with the fingernail. This was not good rosewood!

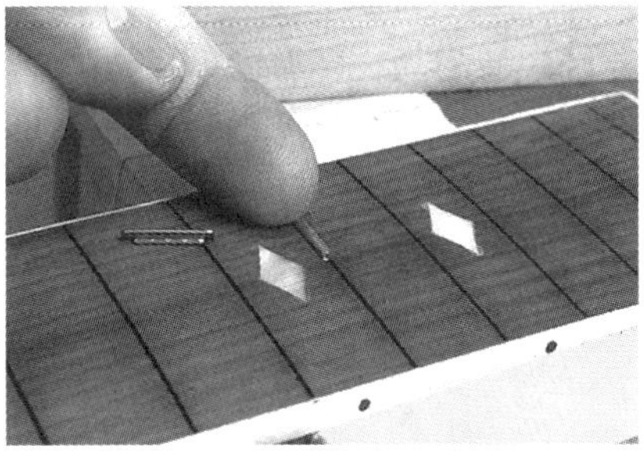

106 Two sizes up—the .0235" wire holds in well (but still hammers in easy since the tang is narrower than the slot).

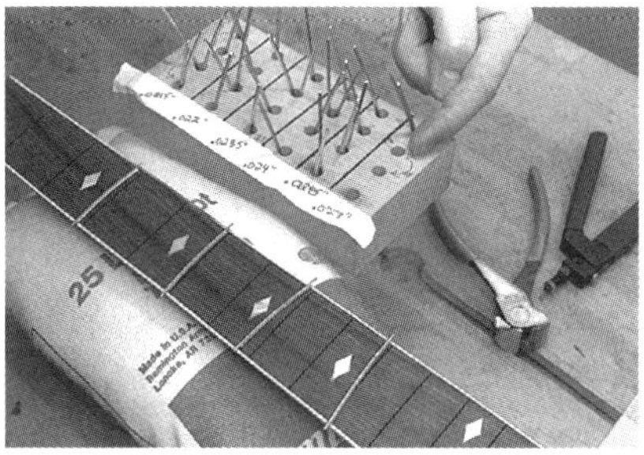

107 We used the .027" (the heaviest tang) wire on the main fretboard to stiffen it up (its tang is significantly larger than the slot). Start by using it at frets 3, 7, 5, and 9 and see how it goes.

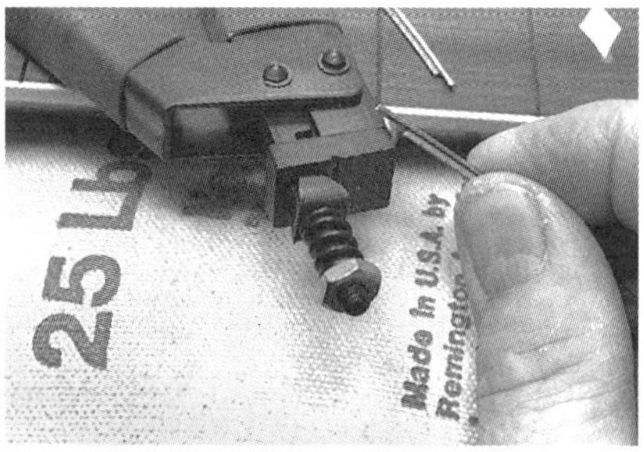

108 We're refretting with the fret ends overhanging the binding because the extra width gives a little more playing area. The tang nipper makes fret-tang notching a cinch.

109 After notching, it's still good to clean up any roughness with a file…

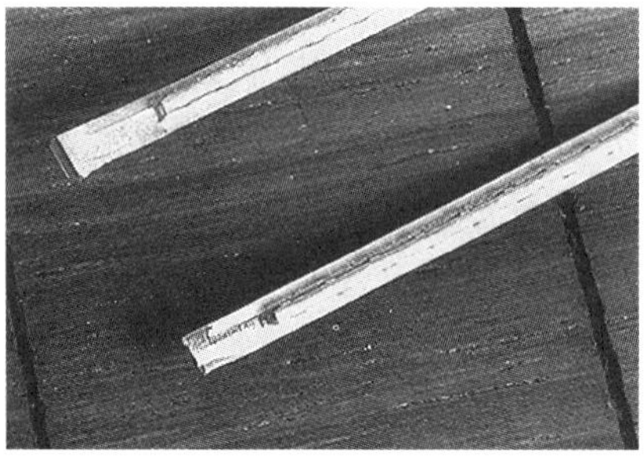

110 …one overhang has been filed, one hasn't.

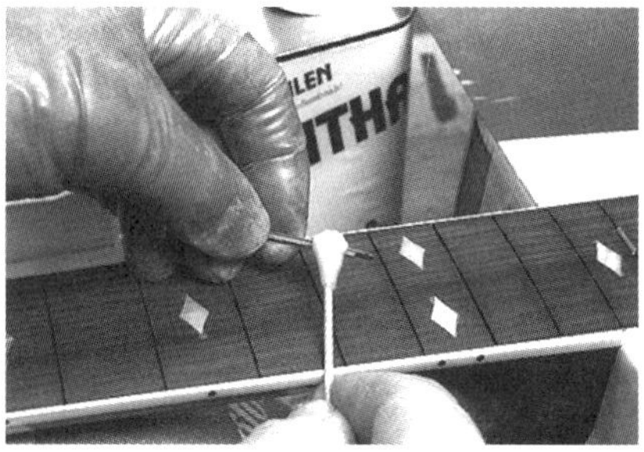

111 Remember, the fretwire should be thoroughly cleaned with Naphtha or other solvent degreaser until no black dirt and oil shows on the cleanup rag.

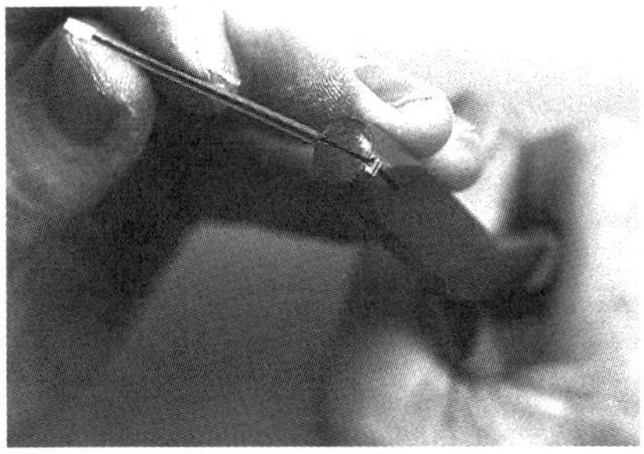

112 Most fretwire sold these days is pretty straight along the tang (viewed from the bottom), but sometimes it needs a little straightening with the fret bending pliers…

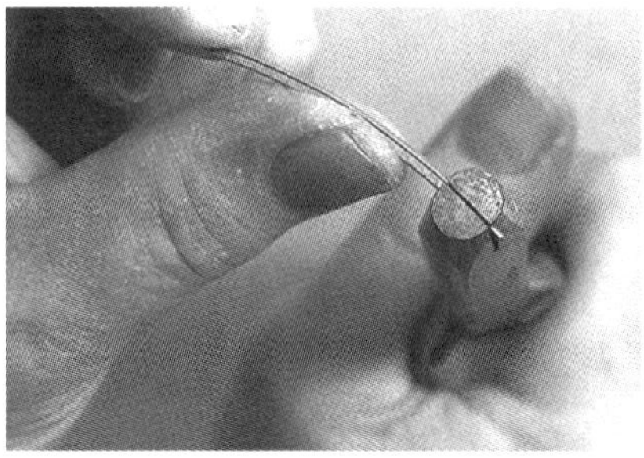

113 …and definitely you'll need to bend the wire to the curve (or over-curve) of the fretboard.

114 This much over-curve isn't too much if you'll be hammering them in.

115 The first couple of frets went in tough—perhaps there's still some sawdust or crud down in the slots. An X-acto blade makes a good "crud remover"—the slots must be clean!

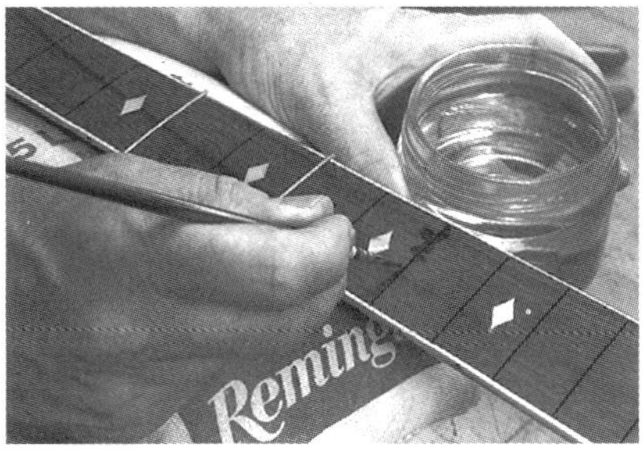

116 If you're not using glue (or even if you are using a water-soluble glue), paint a line of water along the slot to lubricate the wood and help the fret go in easier.

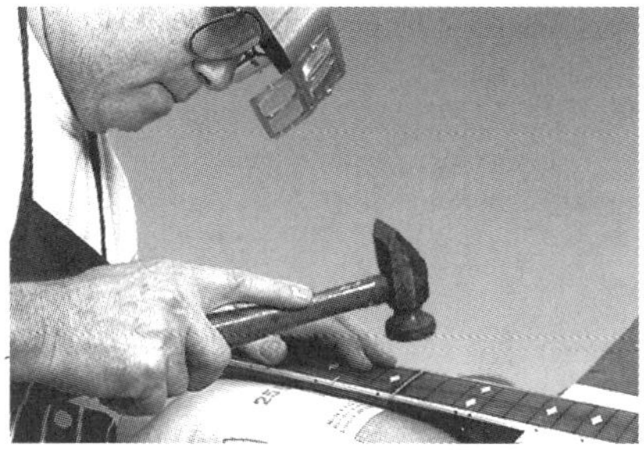

117 The 25 lb. bag of buckshot can be used all the way up to the heel/body joint.

118 The notched straightedge can check the neck-stiffening progress—even with frets installed. Even though the neck was perfectly straight earlier—with the two 6 lb. "string simulation" weights...

119 ...it could still pull up under string tension—maybe not more than the truss rod could adjust out, but who knows? We prefer to see the neck backbowing slightly from the wedging effect of the bigger fret tangs—we gained .002" here.

120 A little water in the slot...

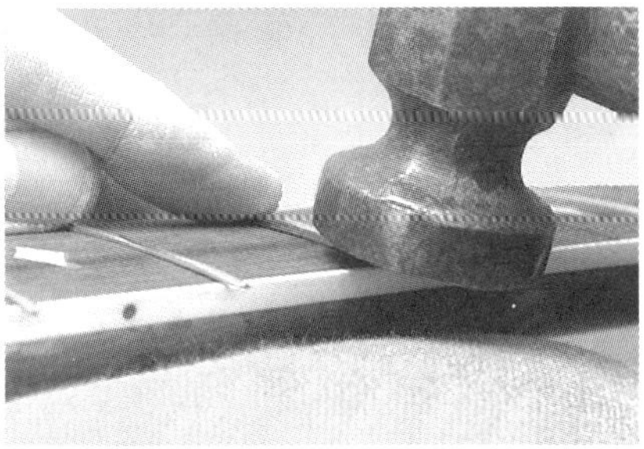

121 Pound one end down first...

122 ...then the other...

123 ...and then hammer from the center out to each end.

124 With 9 frets installed (.027" tang), we've now got .005" of backbow from the wedging effect. This means that when the truss rod is loosened (and it's pretty tight) the neck will hold fairly straight.

125 Here's a way of treating the fret ends *without* overlapping the binding—we didn't *use* this technique here, but we *might* have: Slightly undercut or back-bevel the tang...

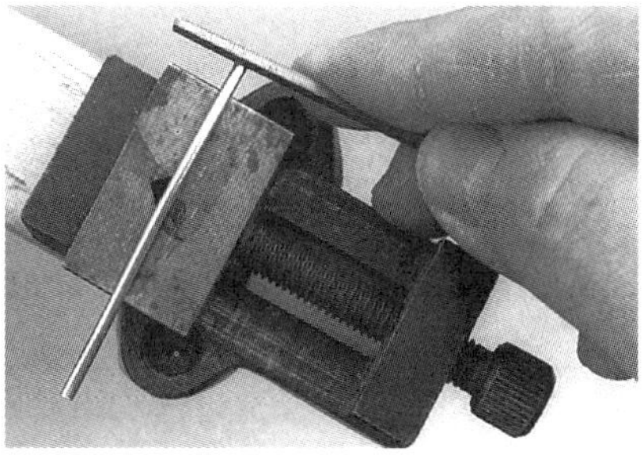

126 ...and then file the end of the crown to match the taper of the fretboard and binding (the taper results from the tapering fretboard width).

127 Can you see the slight bevel in the fret end to match the binding?

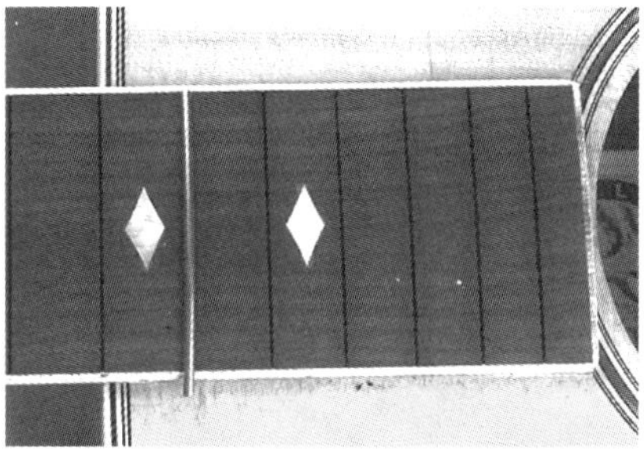

128 Leave the other ends long…

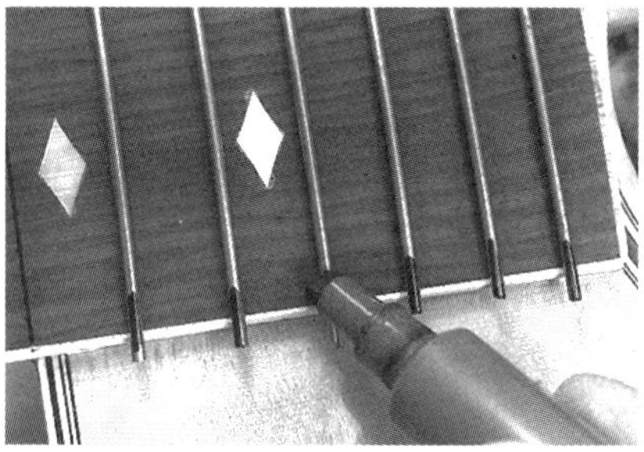

129 …and mark them with a blue marker after one side has been filed and fits the binding (the treble side in this case).

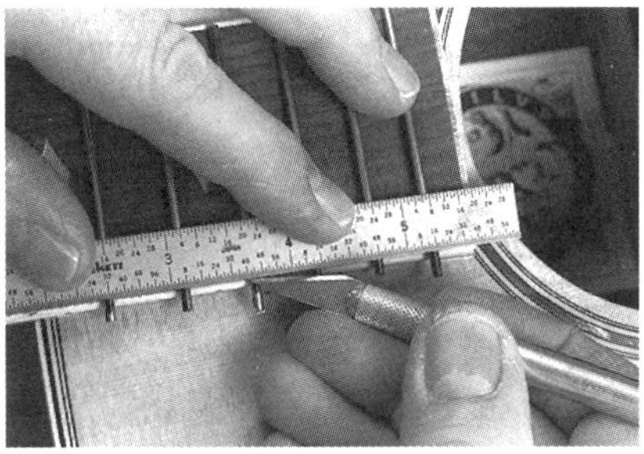

130 With a straightedge lined up to the plastic binding, scribe a mark in the blue-inked fret top…

131 …this shows exactly where the fret end should meet the binding, and matches the taper of the fretboard on this side.

132 Cut close to the line…

133 …and file the bevel…

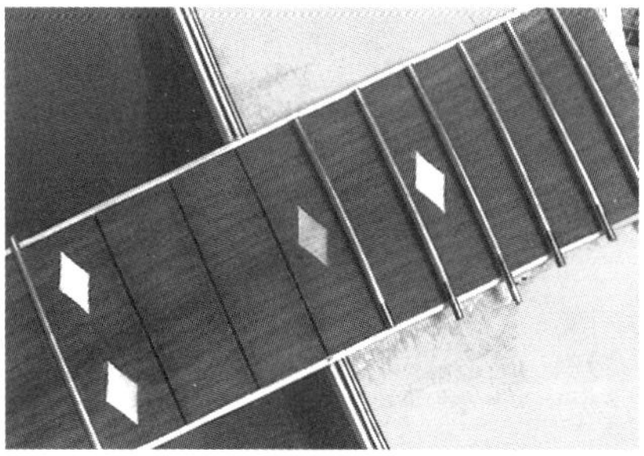

134 …until the fret fits within the binding and matches the binding taper on both the treble and bass sides.

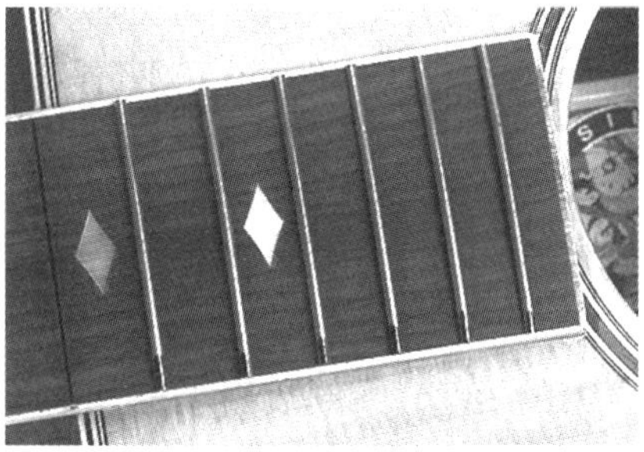

135 These would be ready to hammer in…

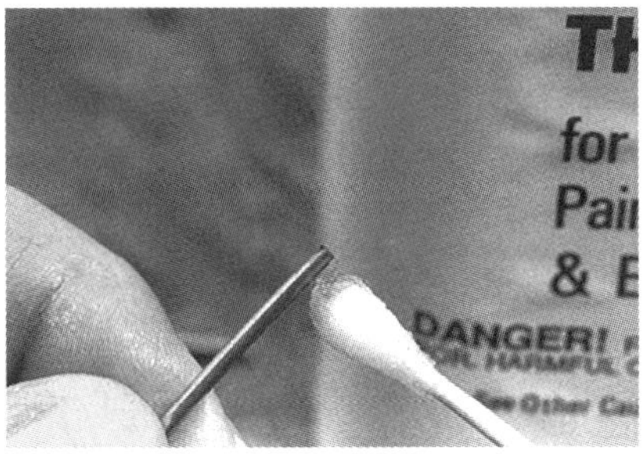

136 …except that the blueing should be cleaned off before it transfers onto the white binding. But we aren't fretting the neck this way…

137 …we're using the same overhang up on the tongue as we did on the main neck.

138 The .0235" wire is a good fit, remember?

139 Bevel the slot—but don't hit the binding!

140 A sandbag or shotbag held under the tongue, through the soundhole…

141 …makes it easier to hammer on the tongue.

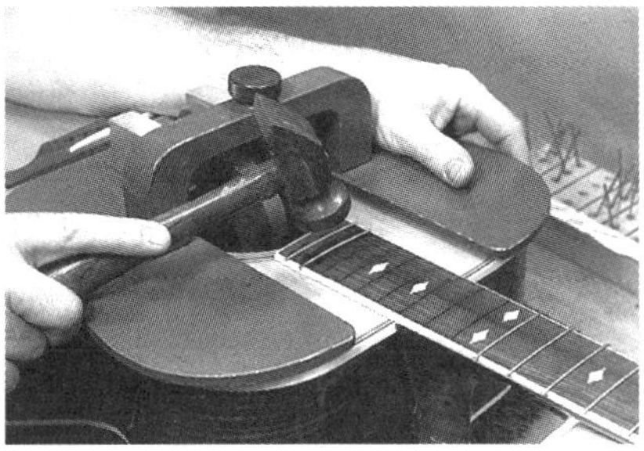

142 Of course the "Fret Buck" is the very best tool for this task…

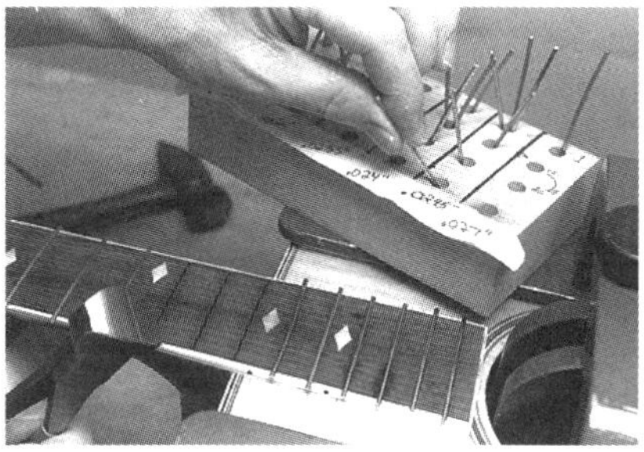

143 …and you can use a larger wire if you've got the "Fret Buck."

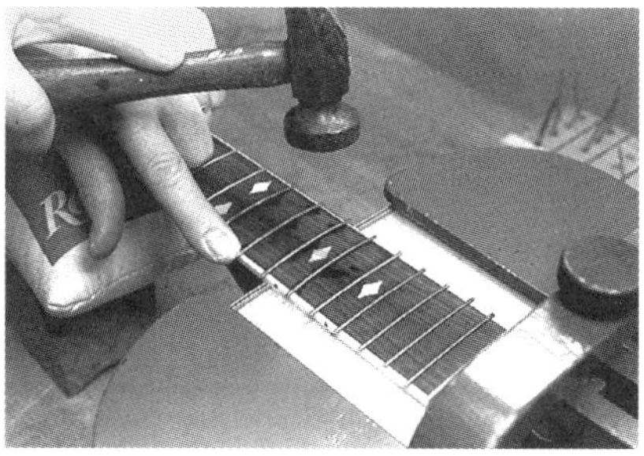

144 The .0245" is a good fit for these last couple of frets (over the neck block where it's solid)—not too big, not too small.

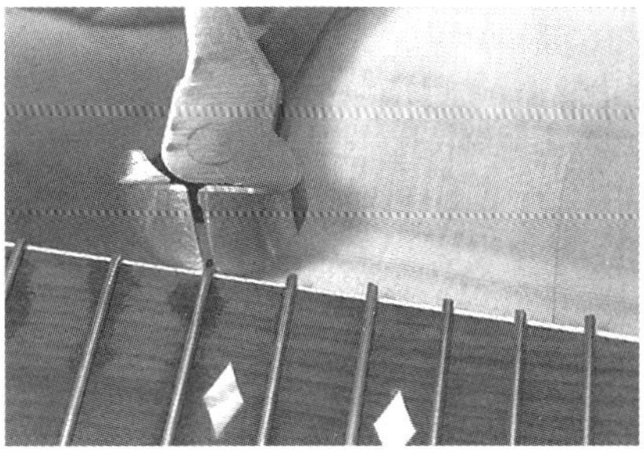

145 Whoops! Put down those nippers and tape off that delicate spruce top…

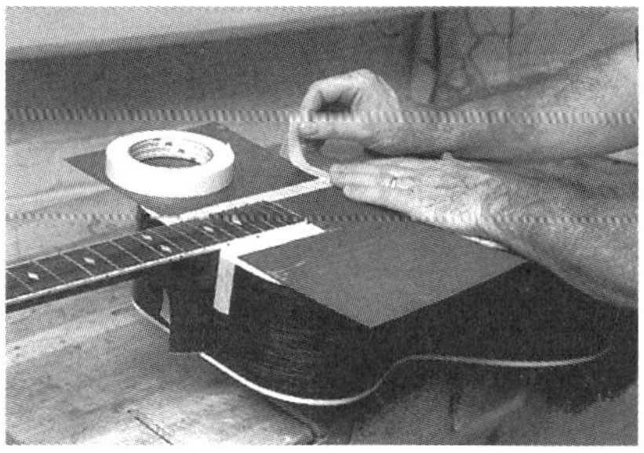

146 …like this. Before nipping the fret overhang, leveling the frets, or beveling the ends, protect the top! This is a stainless steel guard. Go ahead and bevel the fret ends as usual…

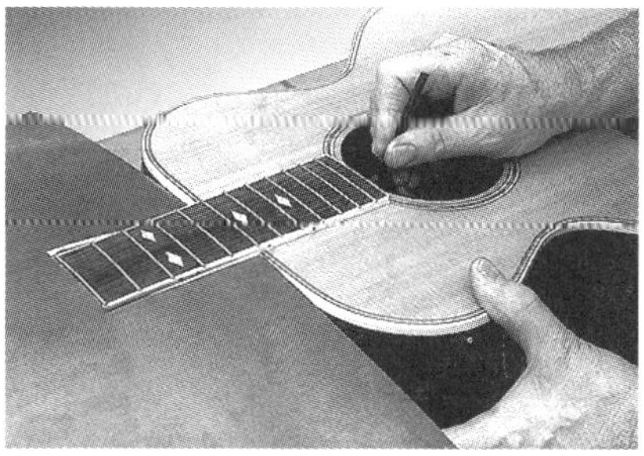

147 The fret ends are clipped and beveled, and we're ready to level. By loosening the truss rod slightly…

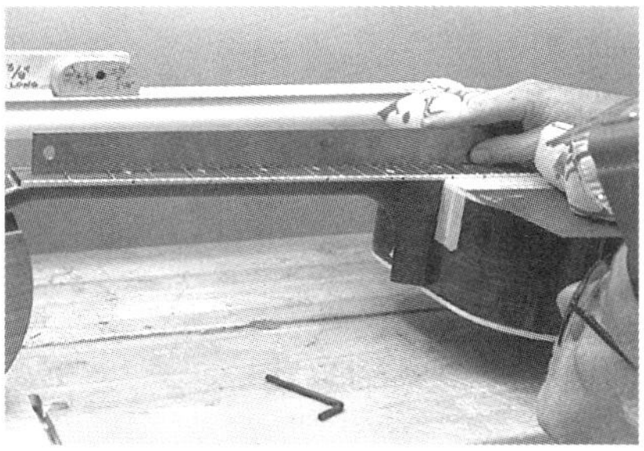

148 …and adding the "shoulder weights," the neck is perfectly straight from end to end with the peghead propped! This is very satisfying, considering what a "rubber neck" this was.

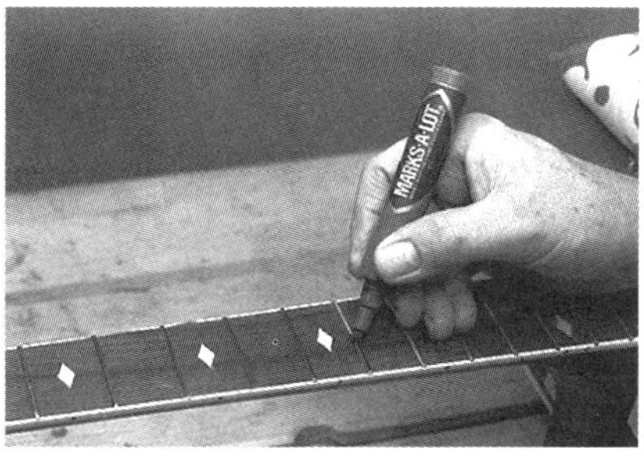

149 Mark out the fret tops with blue marker, being careful of the white binding (might be smart to tape off the entire board, don't you think?).

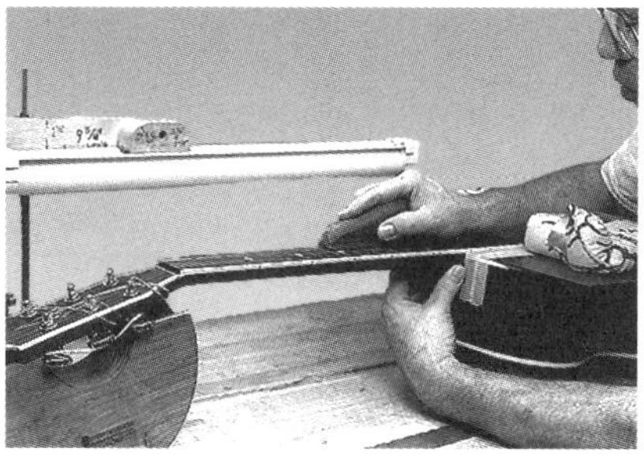

150 This neck is so straight that the short 6" fret leveler is all that's needed to knock down ("kiss-off") any high spots. I'm giving the neck a little support in the heel area to keep it from flexing.

151 It's OK to leave a few dips—you only want to file the high spots. In fact, you want to file as little as possible and get to the sandpaper as soon as you can (sandpaper doesn't leave marks like a file does).

152 Any file marks will remove nicely with #220-grit Stikit sandpaper and the 8" long radius sanding block.

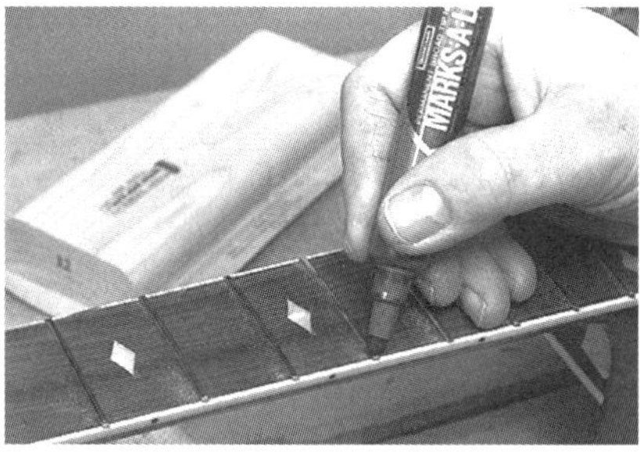

153 Give the fret tops another quick blueing...

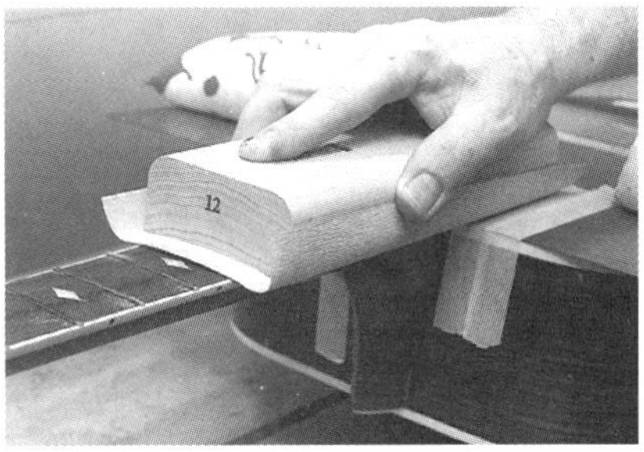

154 ...and sand from end to end with the block. The entire radius is hit at once with a radius block...

155 ...turning the fret tops to metal dust in a couple of passes. But remember, the radius blocks create (or follow) a cylinder!

156 The fret tops have been final-leveled with #320-grit sandpaper and are ready for dressing. Start by finishing up the fret ends.

157 You know by now that our 1/8" nut seating file is good for removing any rough file marks on the bevel. Start with a down-stroke...

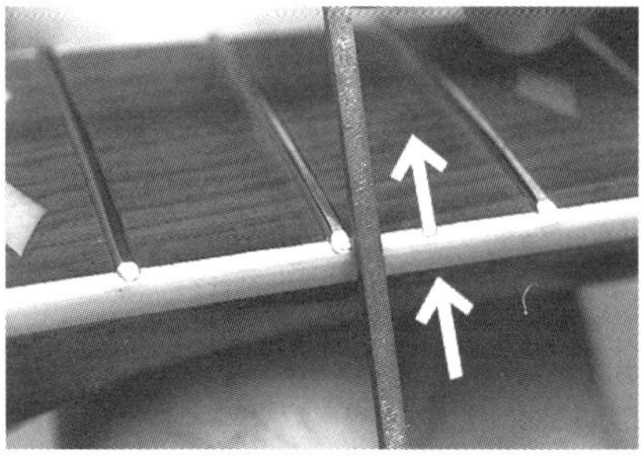

158 ...and sometimes an up-stroke is good for causing the wire-edged burr on each side of the fret end to stand up (or out)...

159 ...so that you can knock it off with the same file. This file is good for rounding the entire fret end if you like (although the small Waverly 3-Corner file is a little less coarse).

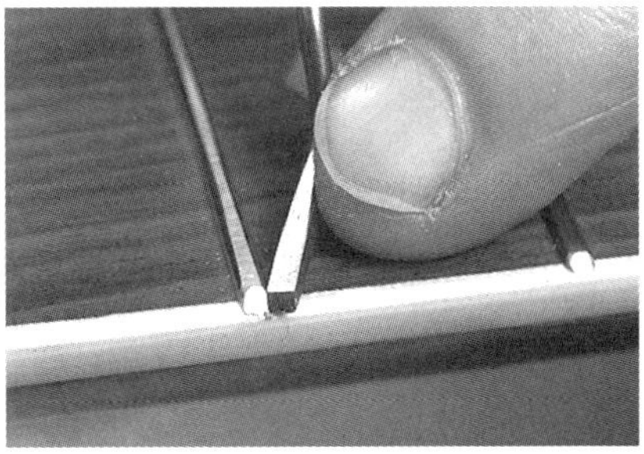

160 Sometimes you need a miniature chisel-edge to get the wire edge to stand up.

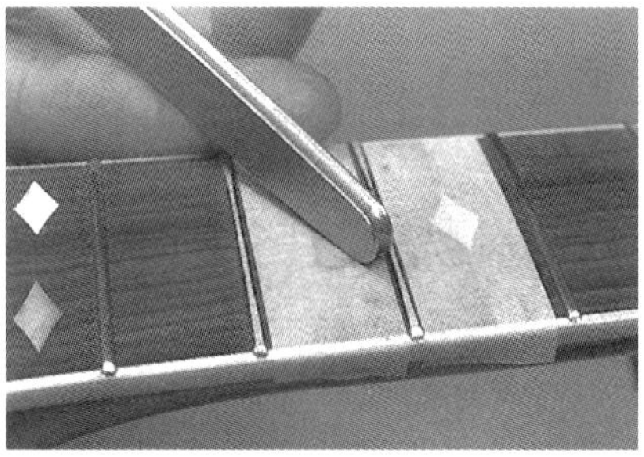

161 The diamond rounding files, as you've seen earlier, are great for bringing the "land" (flat fret top) to center. At the very *least,* you should tape off the frets before crowning them...

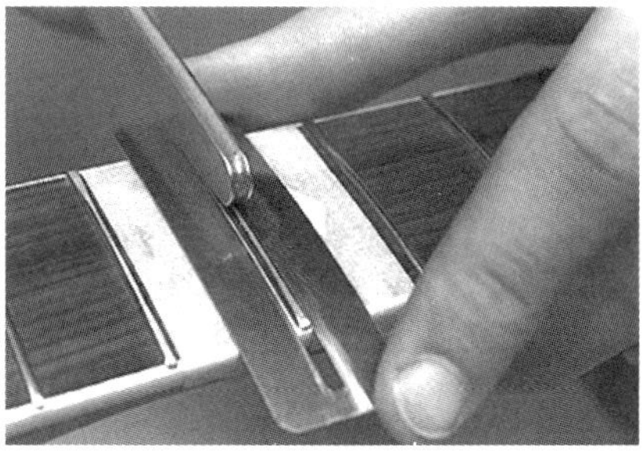

162 ...better yet, use a metal fret guard too (at least for any type of rounding file).

163 It's best to leave a thin bit of the "land" left in the very center...

164 ...to remove with the more gentle 3-corner file.

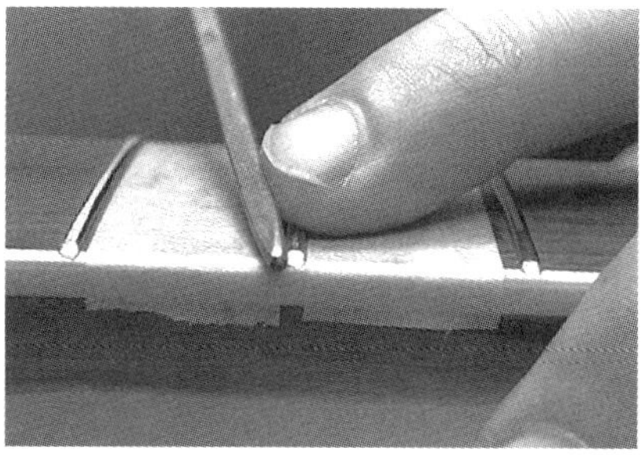

165 You can finish rounding and polishing the fret end at the same time (you'll need to turn the guitar end-for-end, or walk around the bench to finish the other side).

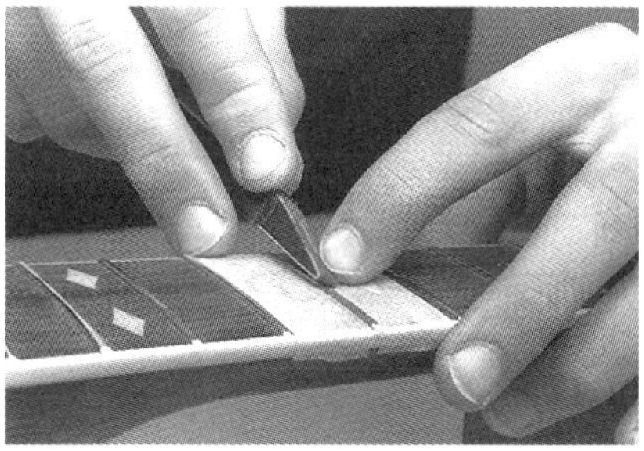

166 A #400 and #600-grit "Sanding-stick" makes a great final polisher, shaper, and mark-remover...

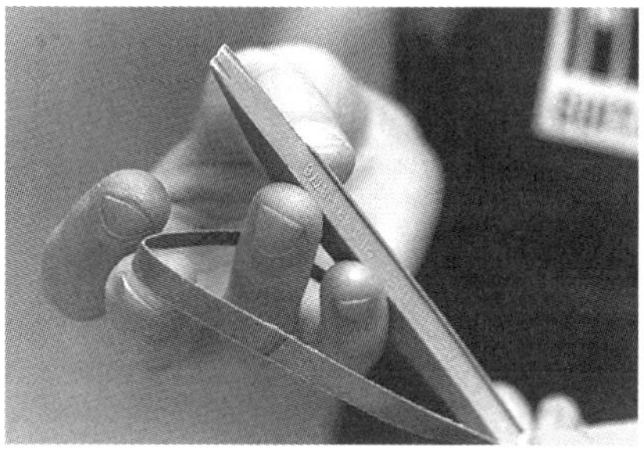

167 ...especially if you shape grooves in the plastic which will hug the fret's contour—two grooves on one side, and one on the other give an even coverage of the sanding belts.

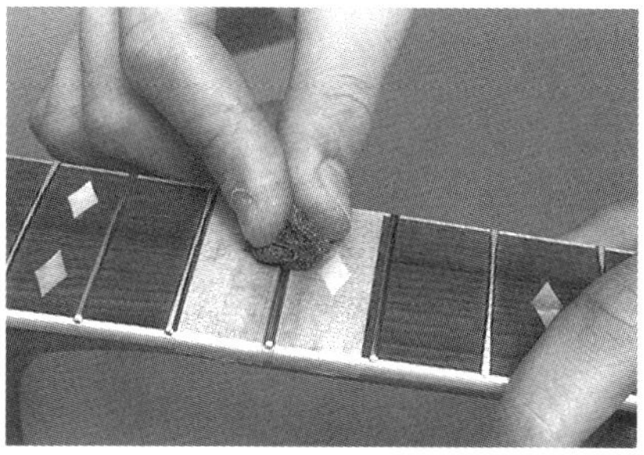

168 I still like to polish with 0000-steel wool as the final abrasive.

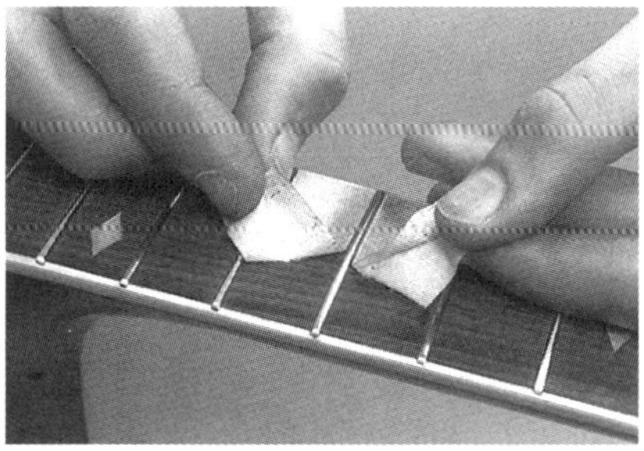

169 Remove any masking tape by peeling it from the edge inward—toward center—to avoid accidently pulling off finish along the fretboard edge.

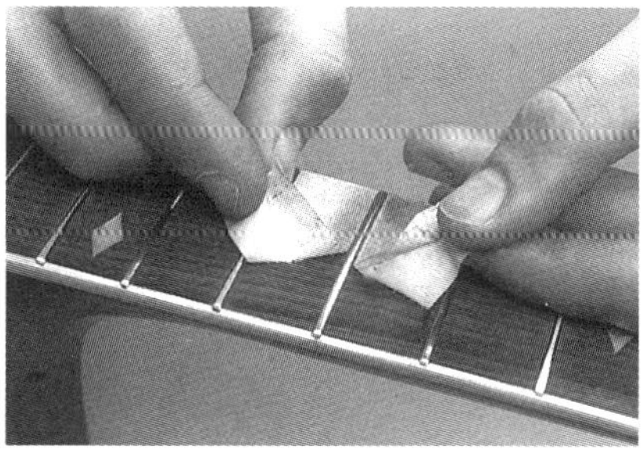

170 Go back to the beginning of the book to learn more about fret dressing. This one's done for now...

171 ...except for a final truss rod adjustment.

172 Checking the frets with the unnotched side of the notched straight-edge showed it came out perfect! Let's get on to something else...

LESSON 5
FRETTING A TELE NECK

(AN ADVANCED, YET STRAIGHTFORWARD BOLT-ON ELECTRIC GUITAR WITH A MAPLE FRETBOARD)

Along with learning the important aspects of fretting bolt-on necks, this chapter reviews all or most of the methods used in the previous chapters. Some methods are repeated to make sure you understand their importance, and how to perform them. To learn bolt-on fretting, you might as well make it a maple-neck because you have the finish to deal with as well.

For those interested, we're fretting this Telecaster in the "Neck-Jig." Read about the neck-jig in the Specialty Tools section. You don't *need* a neck-jig to fret a guitar—you don't *need* a FretBender to curve fret wire—but they're both great tools. We're using the neck-jig here just to give you a feel for how it works. This is not a lesson in the neck-jig, but the basics are covered. Every operation you see here can be done without the neck-jig. Along with the neck-jig, there are several "hi-tech" tools used for this fret job, such as "Jaws"—the fret machine from Hell.

As a general rule, don't touch the finish on vintage maple necks—it's better to use as tall a wire as you can and fret through the hills and valleys, humps and rises, and then level everything out during the fret dressing. But there are exceptions. Sometimes you'll have to remove some finish, or all of it, from certain maple-necks, more commonly those made during the '70s. You don't want to ruin a vintage instrument, but you'll have to decide for yourself what is and isn't "vintage." Let's begin...

1 Sight the neck in the playing position. You can balance the guitar by touching the peghead, but don't hold it!

2 Use some kind of light source or white background to read the neck with a straightedge (clean white paper or mat board). I'm using the notched straightedge which shows the fretboard—not the frets.

3 This neck is quite straight. The straightedge is touching flat at the 7th fret, or middle of the neck...

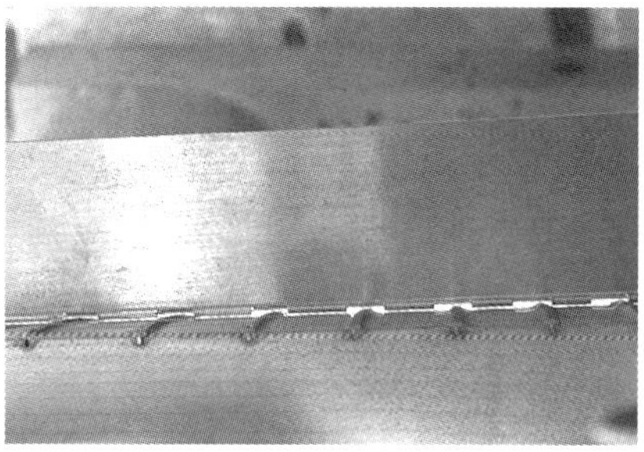

4 ...but up on the "tongue" (last 6-8 frets) we have a rise. A "rising tongue"—ugh!!.

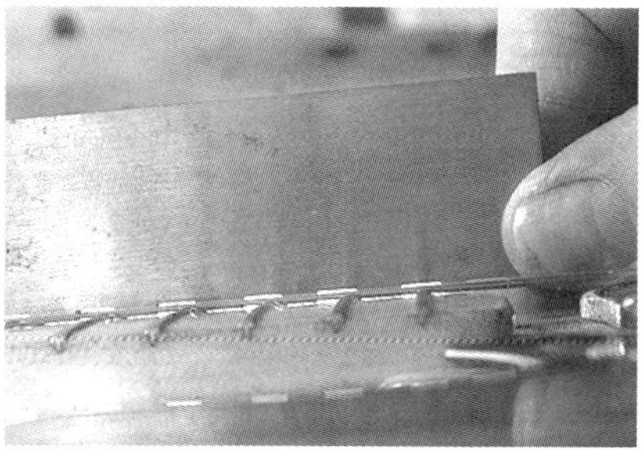

5 Look closely—most of the rise seems to be the super-thick build-up of polyester—if so, level the *finish*, not the wood, and fret on *top* of it this time!

6 Remove the neck...

7 ...and bolt it into the "surrogate body"—a block of wood which allows easy truss rod adjustment and avoids harm to the body.

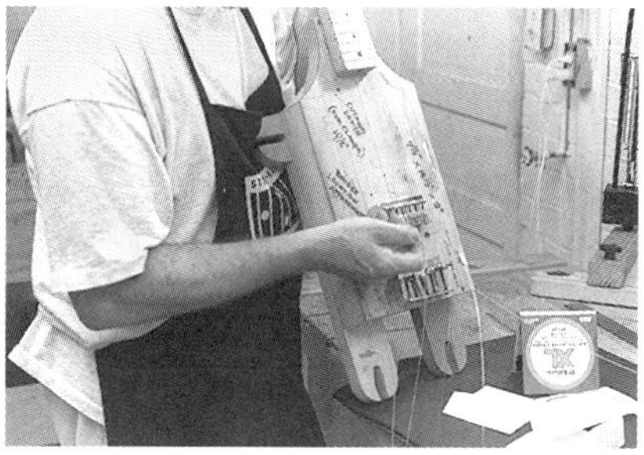

8 String to pitch with the correct gauge strings...

9 ...and set the action and radius correctly. You needn't worry too much about intonation.

10 Now read the neck again, and adjust the truss rod accordingly.

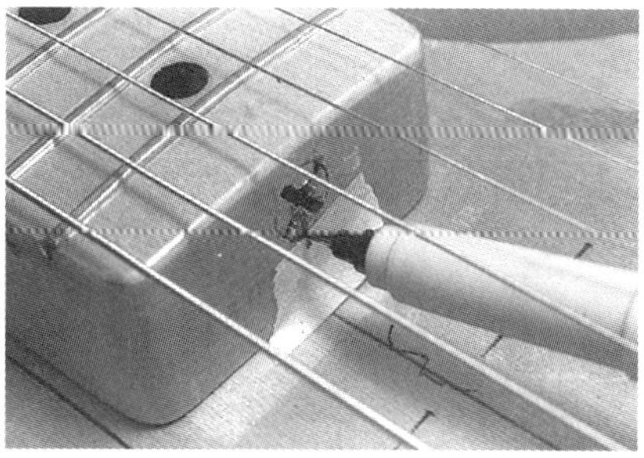

11 Make a mark on the truss rod nut before you turn it, so you know where it was when you started!

12 This is the neck-jig with the guitar resting in the "working" position. Now we'll tilt into the "playing" position to adjust the neck...

13 This neck is fighting the adjustment. The truss rod nut is quite tight, and it has sunk into the neck—compressing the wood ahead of it. This is common with some Fenders.

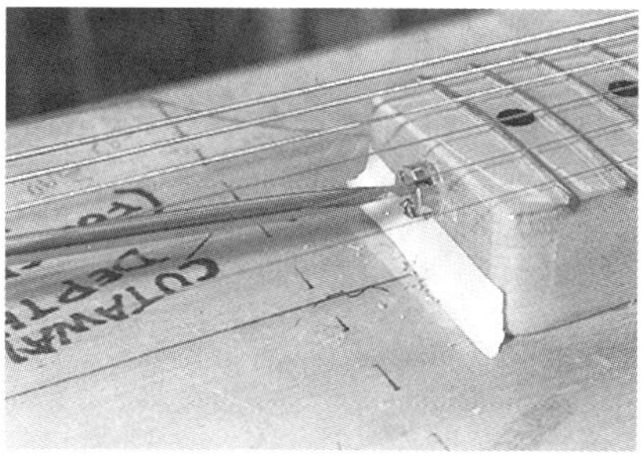

14 Remove and lube the truss rod nut; clean the male and female threads so the rod will adjust better. Also, slide a spacer on the rod to move the nut back where it should be to get a grip on the threads. (The nut may be "bottomed-out").

15 If you don't have the right size 3/8" washer as a spacer, *make* one out of something. I used a small threaded nut (the hex-sides were easy to grip while drilling/enlarging the clearance hole...

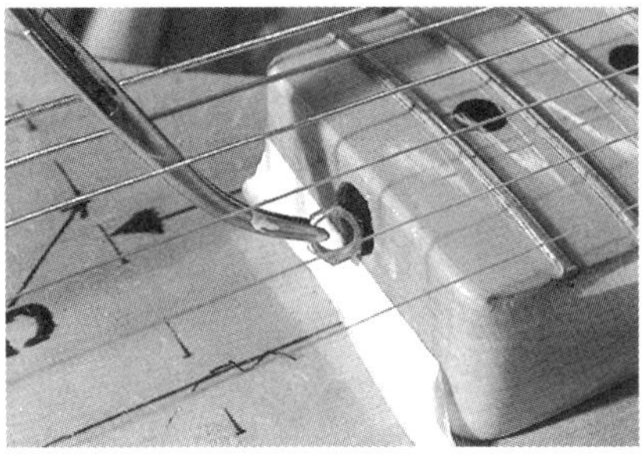

16 ...and smaller than the 3/8" diameter hole). Nobody will see it anyway.

17 Lubricate the threads! Don't soak anything, but clean the threads and put a fine coating of oil, Teflon, or graphite powder on them.

18 A quick adjustment in the level, or "working" position, to get the neck back in the ballpark...

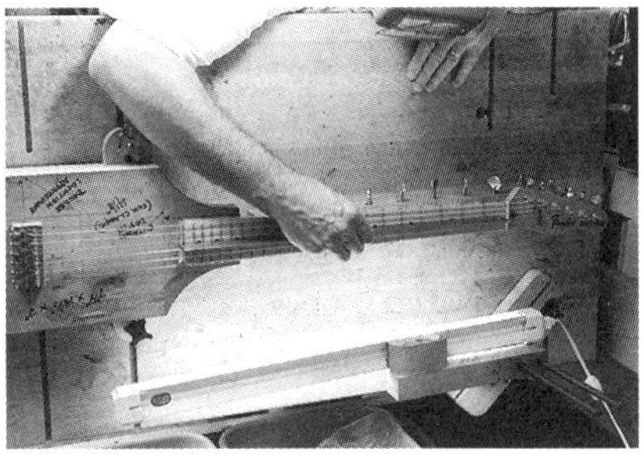

19 ...and then into the playing position for final neck adjustment. When the neck is straight, set the neck-jig rods until they touch and support the back of the neck (something to rest on).

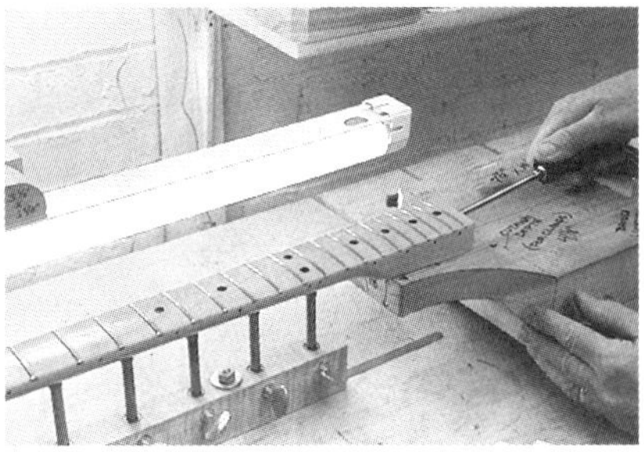

20 When the jig rods are set, remove the strings and loosen the truss rod to let the neck down onto the jig rods. Most necks go into backbow and rise up off the rods when the string pressure is removed.

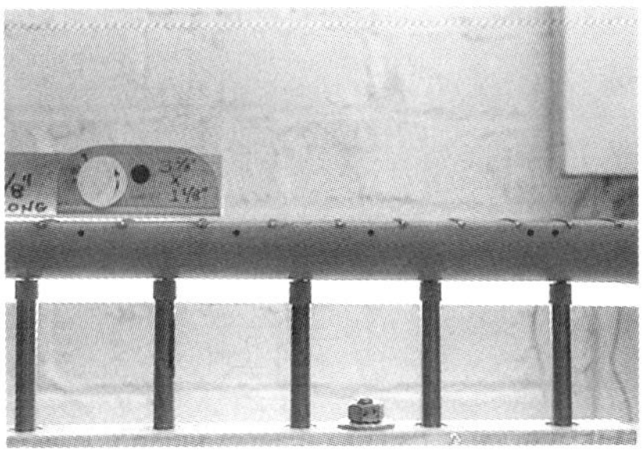

21 This neck sat back down nicely, resting on all the plastic-capped rods.

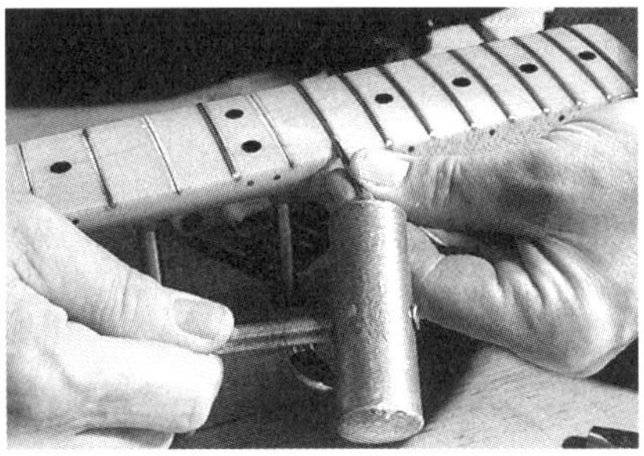

22 If the neck was made before '82, a great fret removal method is to drive them out sideways—toward the treble side—using a small machinist's scribe as a driver, and a hammer for power. (See "Trade Secrets"—Summer, '93).

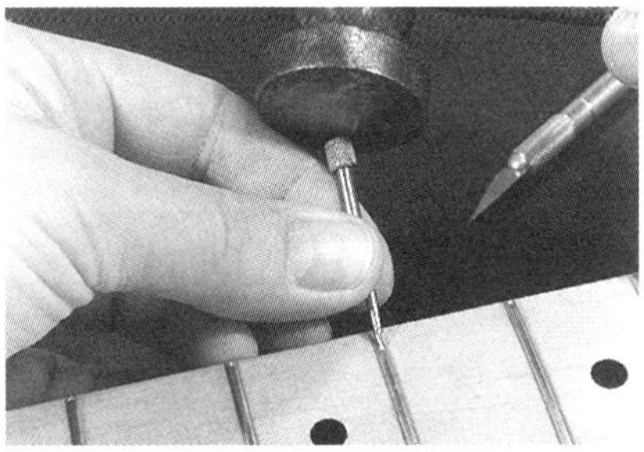

23 They'll also come out toward the bass side (if going toward the treble side gives you any trouble). We think the treble side is the best way to exit.

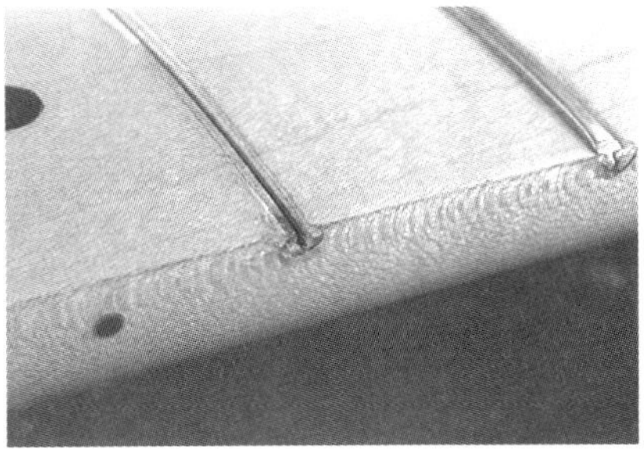

24 These chips on the side are from the expansion and contraction of the wood and the original frets. They're common, and were already there when the instrument came in.

25 This fret was pulled up and out in the normal way, with fret pullers. It's not that bad, chip-wise, although we've seen worse. We're not saying that removing Fender frets this way is bad...

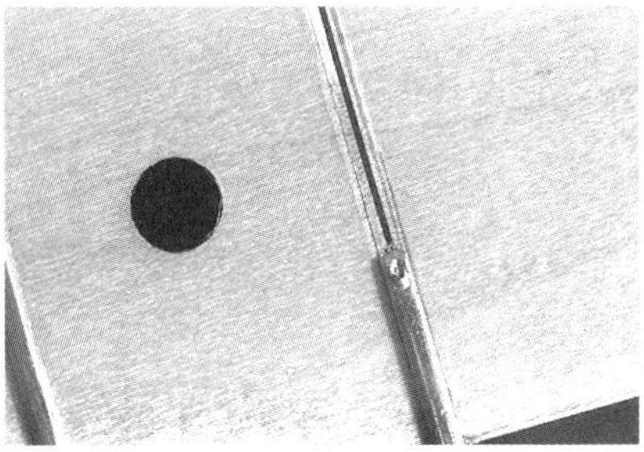

26 ...only that this way is cleaner. Lots cleaner! We heated these frets before driving them to loosen the grip of the thick polyester finish...

27 ...that's why you see the soldering iron. You're planning to save the finish, so don't make burn marks. Once the fret starts to move, grab the protruding end with your nippers and hammer on the nippers to pull the fret out.

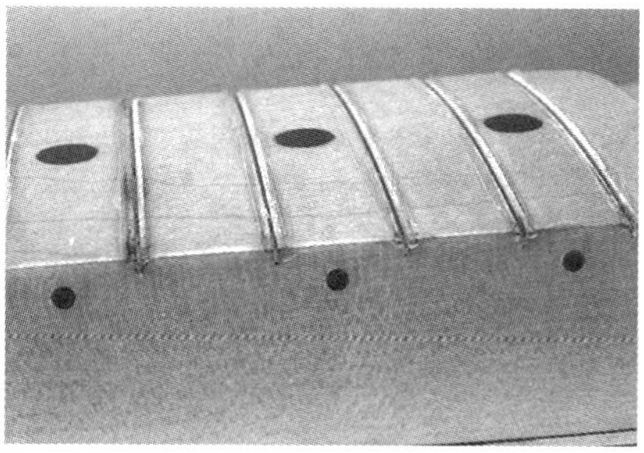

28 There's a slight burn mark on the left—if it were much more it would show later. The majority of the frets came out cleanly though, leaving the polyester finish almost perfect. You still can't "read" the neck...

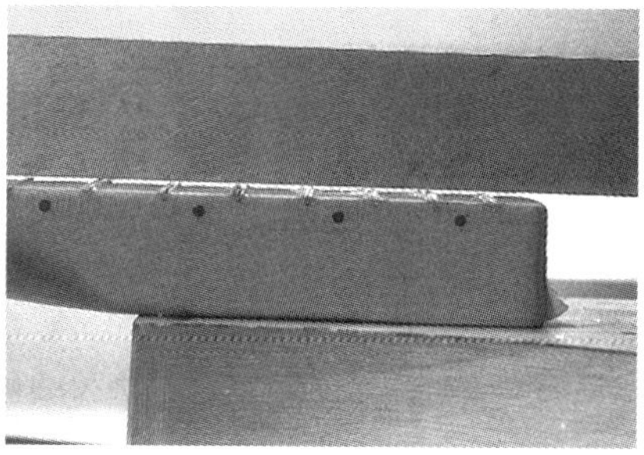

29 ...because the finish is "mounded up" to the fret slots—getting in the way of the straightedge. You're hoping to level the thick polyester as if it were wood, to get a flat enough plane to fret without messing with the finish.

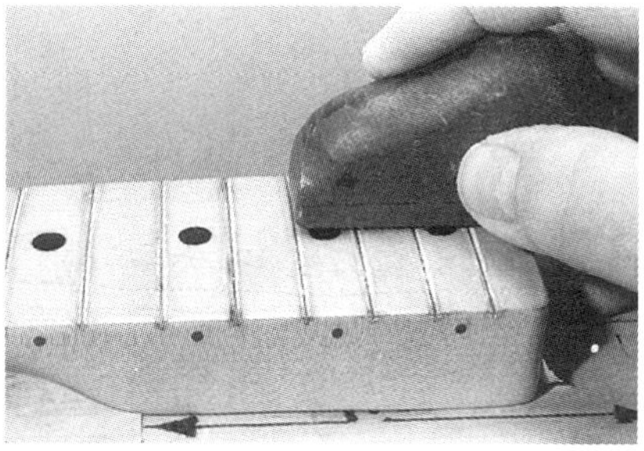

30 Remove the mounded finish with a short fret leveler file. (If the neck were perfectly straight and all "mounds" were level, you could fret on top of them. You'd have pretty tall frets, though, since these mounds are at least .012" tall!

31 A lot of finish has been "powdered" and the file is just starting to hit the finish on the main fretboard surface. Now lightly level the finish from end to end, to get a good reading with a straightedge.

32 These strips of tape demonstrate the "lie" of each string. You must choose between creating either a cylindrical or a tapered radius. If you prep the board along the string "lies," you are creating a tapered radius automatically.

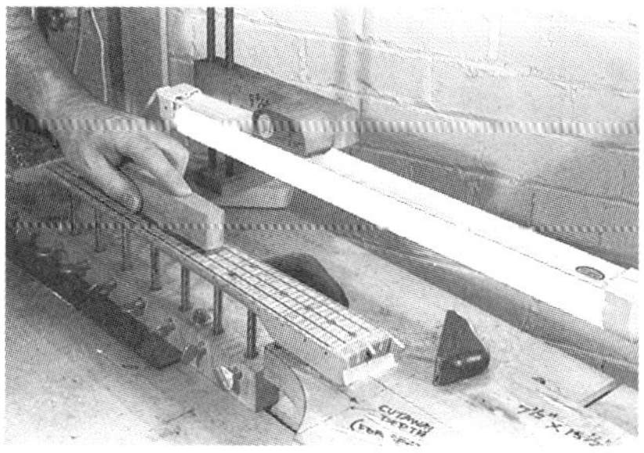

33 You can use fret leveling files to smooth the high spots, but don't dig into the finish or change the factory cylinder-shaped radius. Just glide along the surface and clean up those fret slot mounds.

34 Unlike the files and flat sanding blocks, the 7-1/4" radius sanding block follows the original *cylinder-shaped* factory fretboard—it contacts and sands the entire surface at once (see arrows). We're keeping the vintage radius.

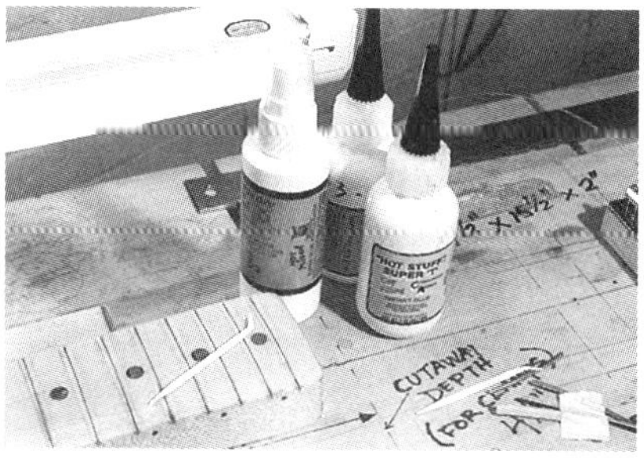

35 If the finish is lifting slightly along the fretboard edge (from expansion and contraction over the years between the metal fret, the wood, and the hard finish), touch it up with superglue.

36 The angled plastic toothpicks are good applicators...

37 ...and it's all right to let it mound up a little, because we'll file the glue level after it dries.

38 Use disposable cotton swabs to "paint" your way along every slot the full length of the board. That's a little beeswax "well" to hold the superglue for dipping into...

39 …beeswax holds superglue "well"—in a deep pool, superglue doesn't dry up or evaporate. Expect to use a number of cotton swabs.

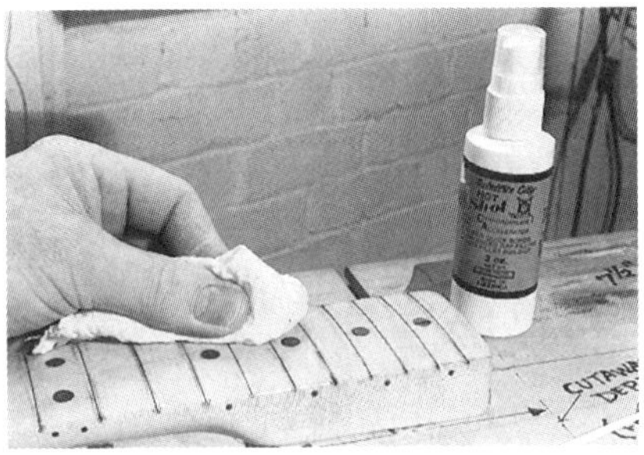

40 Even if the glue seems dry, wipe over it with a rag dipped in superglue accelerator, just to be sure.

41 Level the entire board with a small leveling file; this won't change the radius or dig into the finish, since it rides on top of the smooth finish and levels only the glue.

42 Short straightedges, or "fret rockers"—in lengths to span any three (but not more) frets—check flatness just as if the neck had frets in it. You're checking the tops of the bare fret *slots* for irregularity.

43 The main part of this neck is quite straight, and the different length straightedges show no high or low spots; they aren't "rocking."

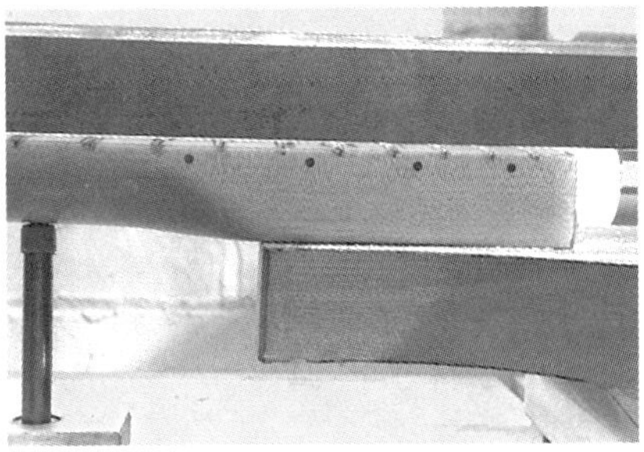

44 The upper register (tongue) however, still shows relief or light; it should be dead flat, or even have a slight fallaway, which is the opposite of relief.

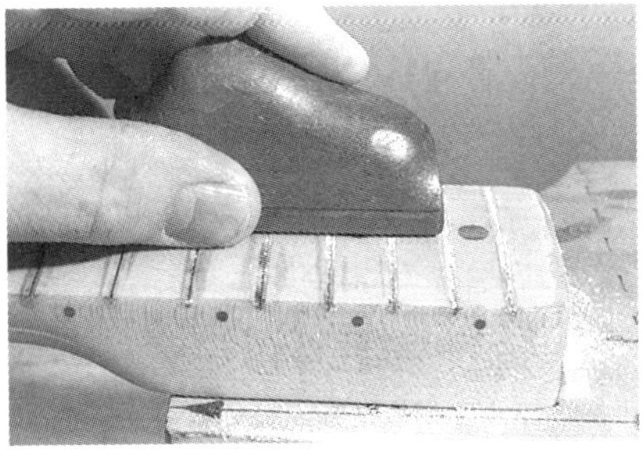

45 Taking off some more finish, and hoping not to "go through"—so far so good! If you do go through, you'll have to at least touch up that area, if not spray or refinish the whole fretboard.

46 As soon as the tongue begins to level out, switch to a 7-1/4" radius block with #220-grit sandpaper to smooth out and blend in the file marks. There's still plenty of finish. Man, they sprayed it thick in those days!

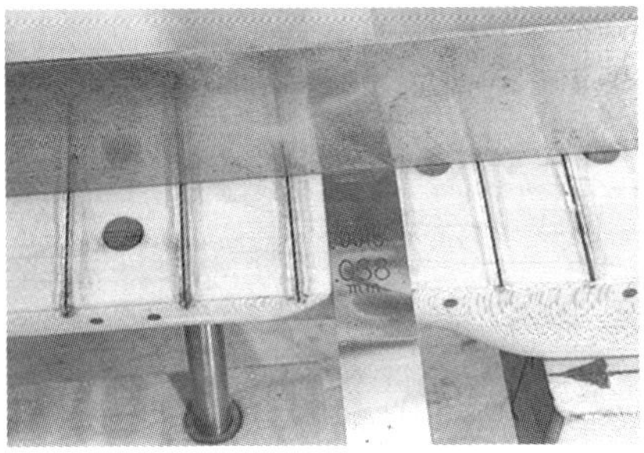

47 Now the "secondary relief" (light seen under a straightedge resting from the 10th fret to the end) is only .0015". You won't get any drop-off or fall-away on the last few frets, but that's OK; it's better than going through the finish.

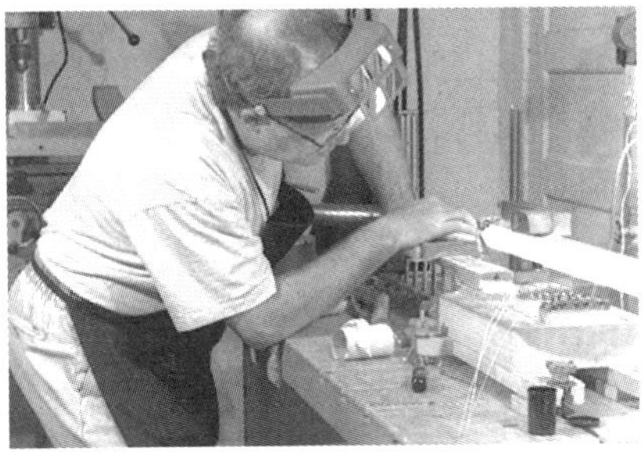

48 Now smooth-in the entire board. The radius block will follow the vintage cylinder-shaped radius. Sand with your whole upper body—legs braced, arms stiff, and the radius block mustn't move out of square to the center line!

49 Switch to #320-grit…

50 …then #500-grit…

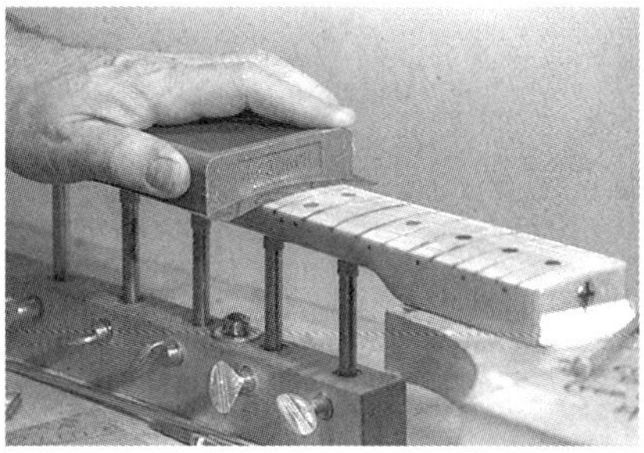

51 …and #800-grit to finish up.

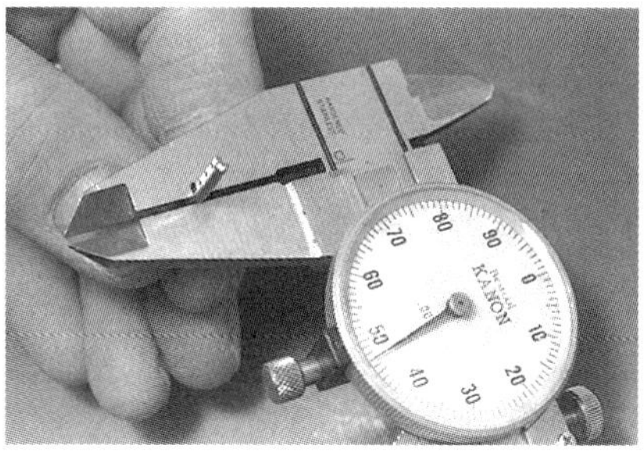

52 The wire we chose has a crown height of .048"…

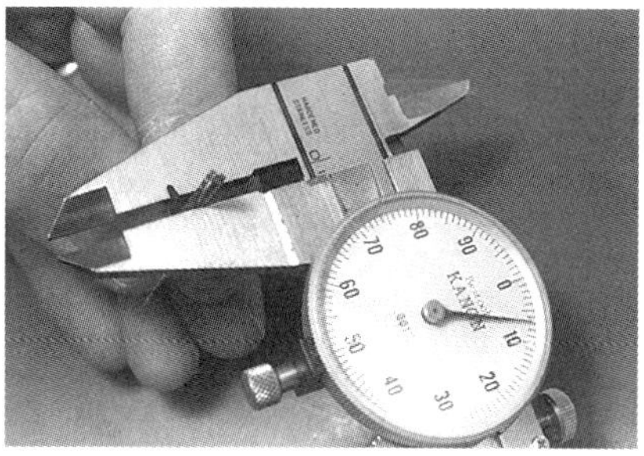

53 …and a total height of .108"…

54 …so the difference, or actual tang height, is .060".

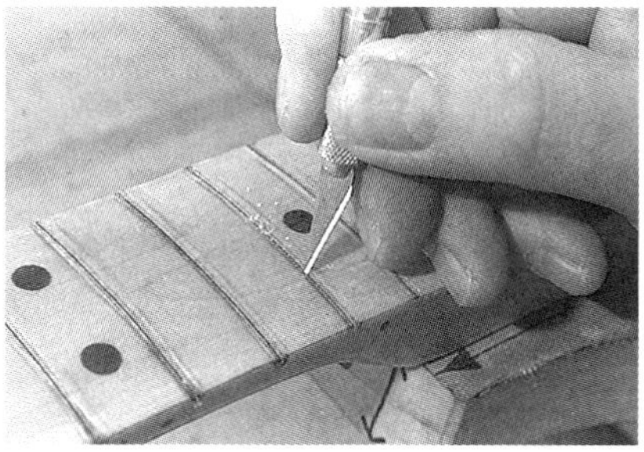

55 Use an X-acto #11 blade to clean the slots of dust and crud…

56 …before using the little Blitz saw (see Lesson Three) to further clean the slots, and more importantly, to guarantee that the fret slots are deep enough—slightly more than the .060" tang depth.

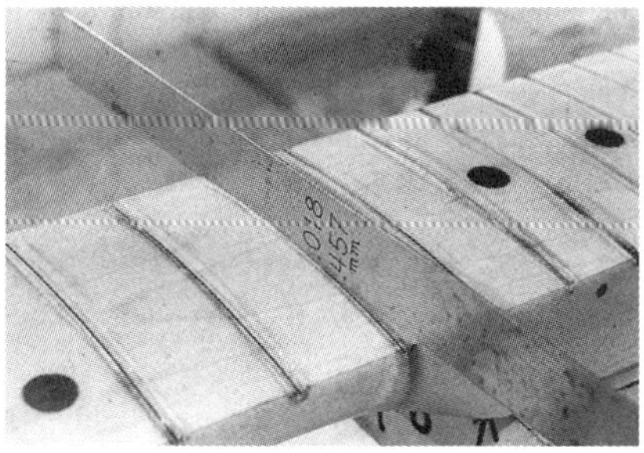

57 Some of these slots are hard to saw—they're measuring .018", when .020" is more normal for Fender. Maybe a little superglue got down in there.

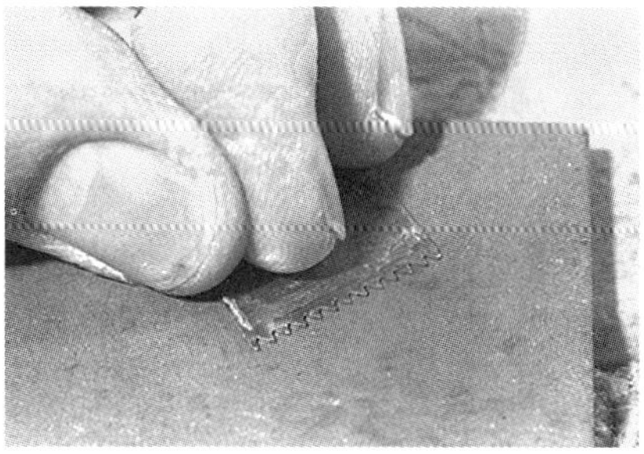

58 By rubbing both flat sides of a .020" blade on an "E-Z Lap" diamond-grit sharpening stone for several minutes…

59 …the blade thickness ended up at the desired .018" thickness to fit those swollen fret slots.

60 This blade is turned toward the operator—cutting on the pull stroke (Japanese-style). Note the somewhat crude but workable "depth stops." This in-between (.018") custom blade size is sure to come in handy again…

61 …it sure works great for those tight slots. Once the .018" blade cleared the way, the .020" blade cut without binding up.

62 The slot, when finally cleaned, now measures the proper factory size of .020".

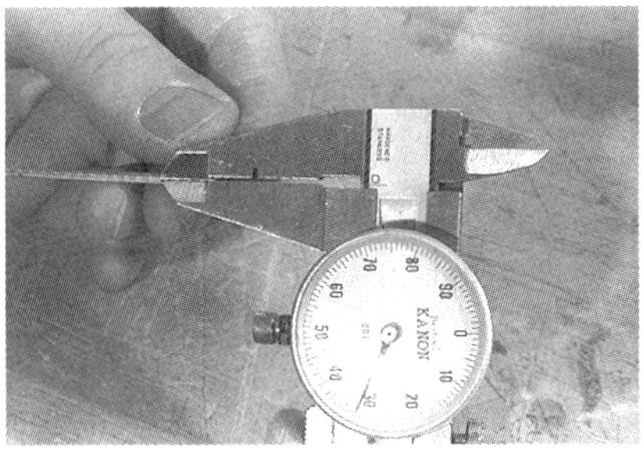

63 The original wire (always save at least one piece until you're done) measured .032" on the outside of the barb...

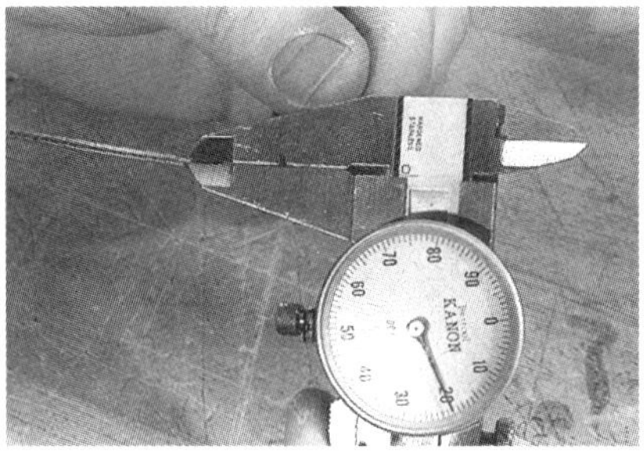

64 ...and .020" on the tang (if you can get in there to measure).

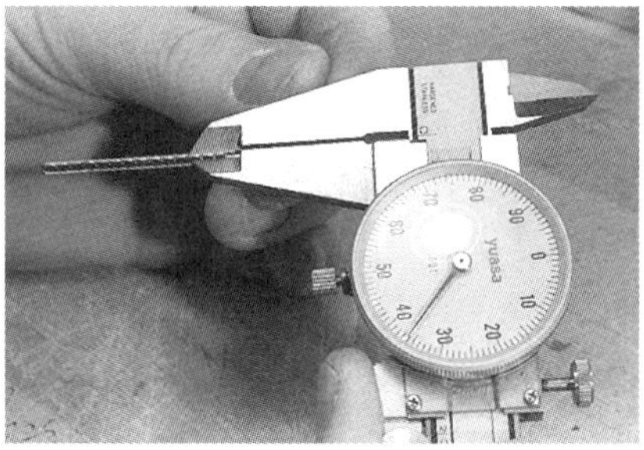

65 The new wire (our #3391) measures .036" to .038" on the barb...

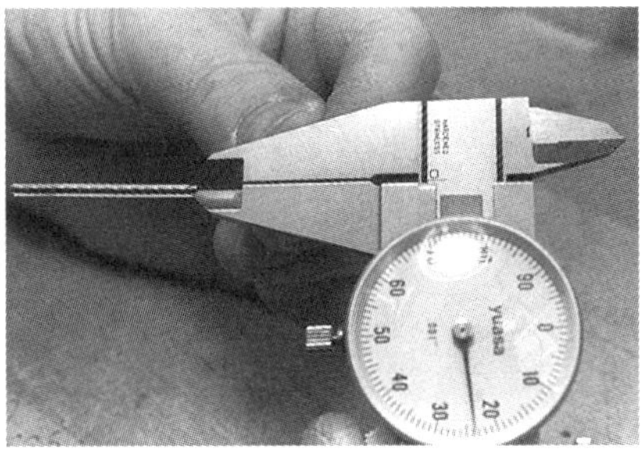

66 ...and between .023" and .024" on the tang (depending how hard you squeeze the calipers) respectively—this larger tang could easily cause the neck to backbow, especially if the maple is quite hard.

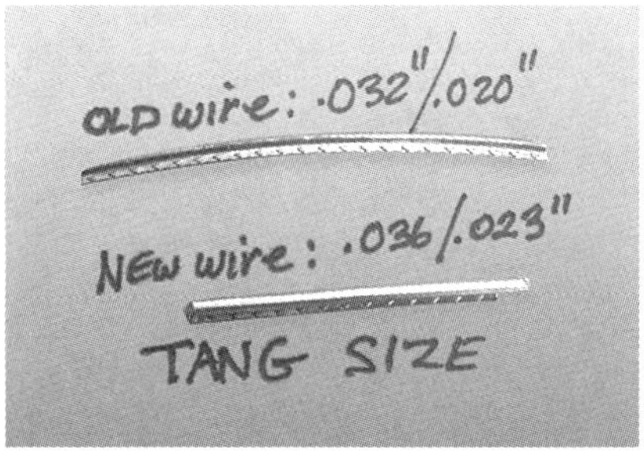

67 The old and the new...

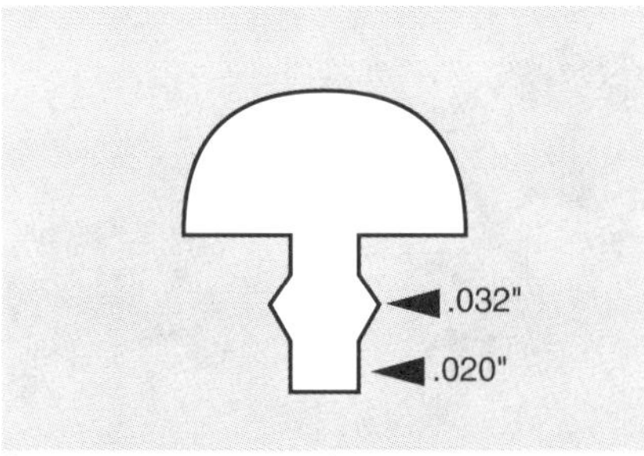

68 ...cross-sectional view.

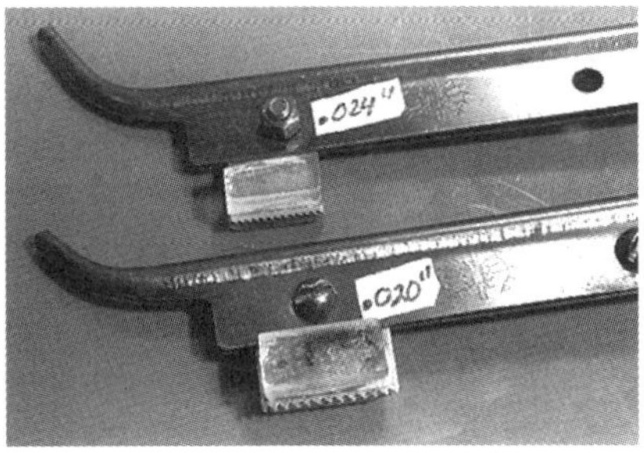

69 Even with the exactly correct-sized Blitz blade, trying to saw a slot that jumps only .004" in width is tough—what happens is that the new saw simply squeezes in and gets STUCK.

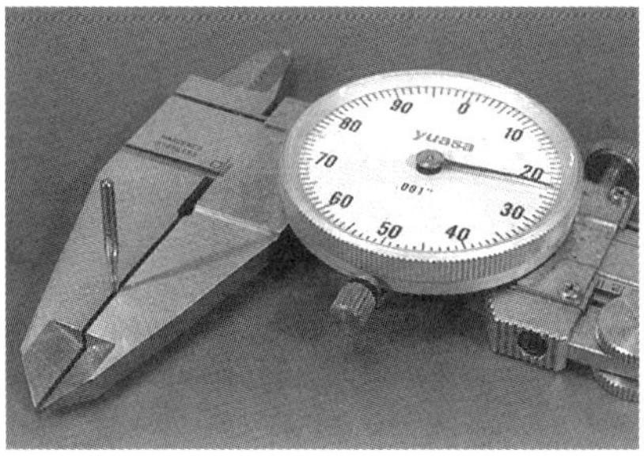

70 So, take a dental burr which measures say, .024" to .032"—our #1187 straight and #1189 tapered bits will do...

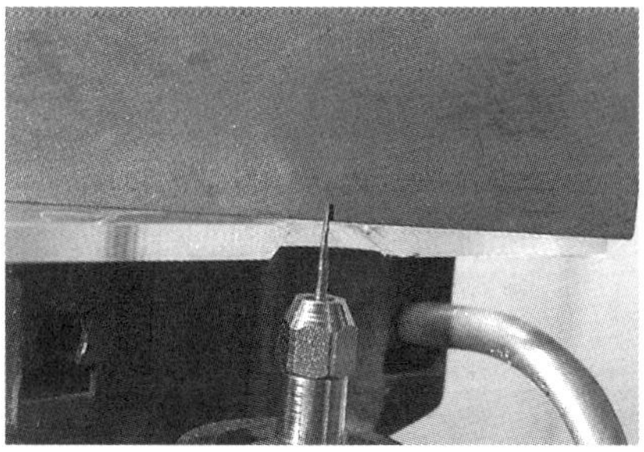

71 ...and run it against a diamond stone or whetstone to grind it down to around .020", .021", or .022" (use eye protection)...

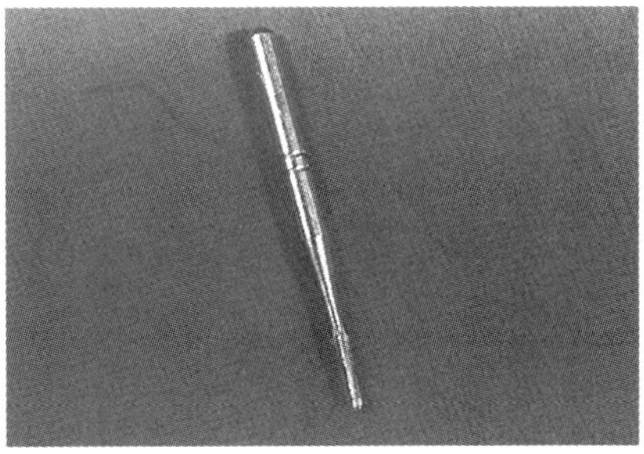

72 ...removing the taper at the same time.

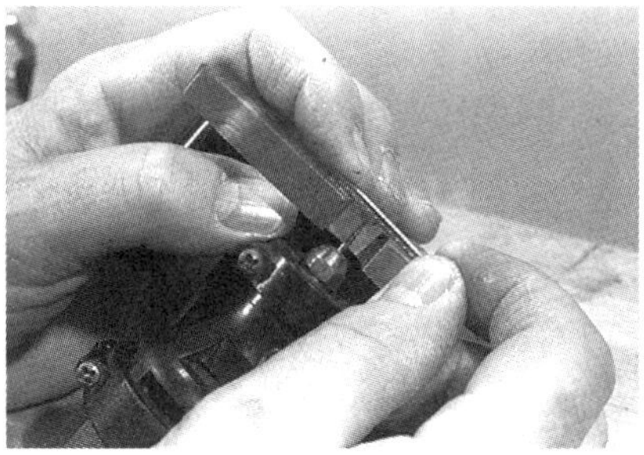

73 Set the dental burr to cut the right depth...

74 ...and run through the slots with that.

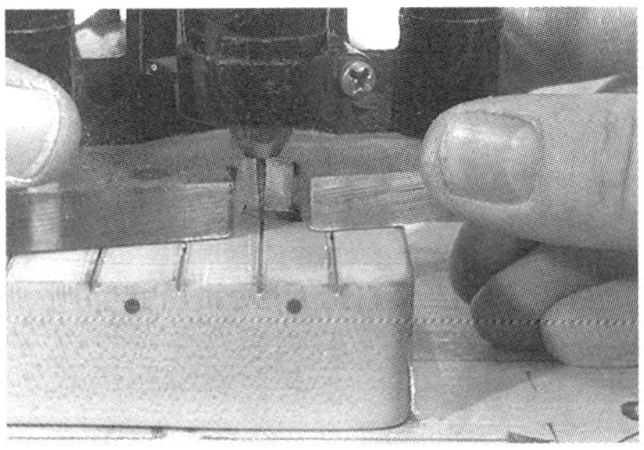

75 Another view of using the dental burr on the slots.

76 Any Dremel bit will cut slightly oversize, so the .021" bit will cut closer to .024", but the feeler gauge still fits a little tight.

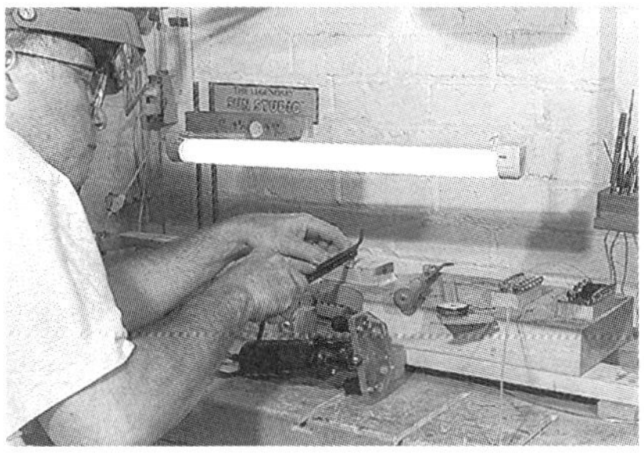

77 Follow the Dremel with your .024" Blitz saw (it'll saw without sticking now), squaring, cleaning, and final-sizing the slot.

78 Now the .024" feeler gauge will drop in without force.

79 Test a short length of your new wire…

80 …this goes in well, but it feels as if there's too much barb. These barbs are larger, relatively speaking, and of a different shape than the originals.

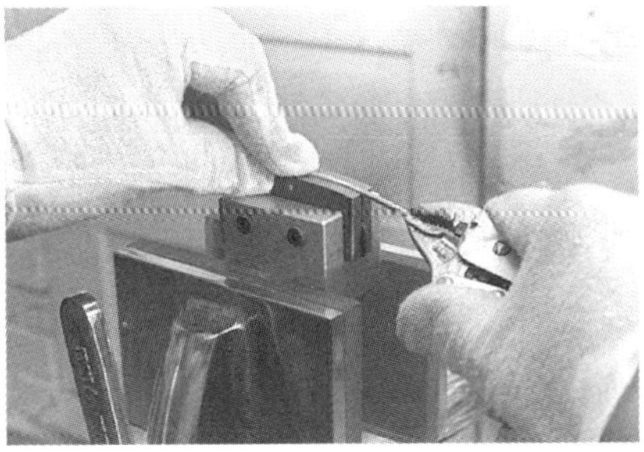

81 To keep from widening the slots, we can take off some of the barb using the "tang sizer" shown in Lesson Three.

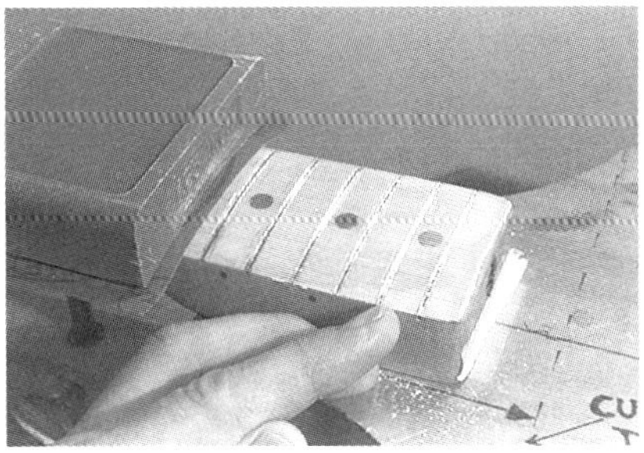

82 Uh-oh! While just kissing off any burrs made from the Dremel tool and Blitz saw, *I went through! Horrors!* There are just a couple of bare areas, and it's not worth refinishing the whole board. Here's a solution.

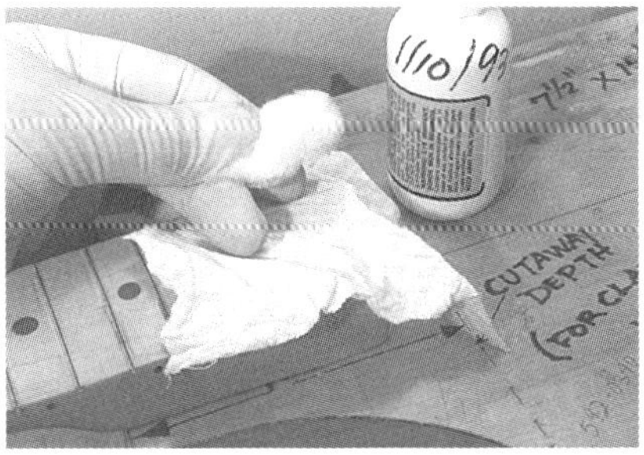

83 Make a "Frenching-pad" of a cotton ball and linen…

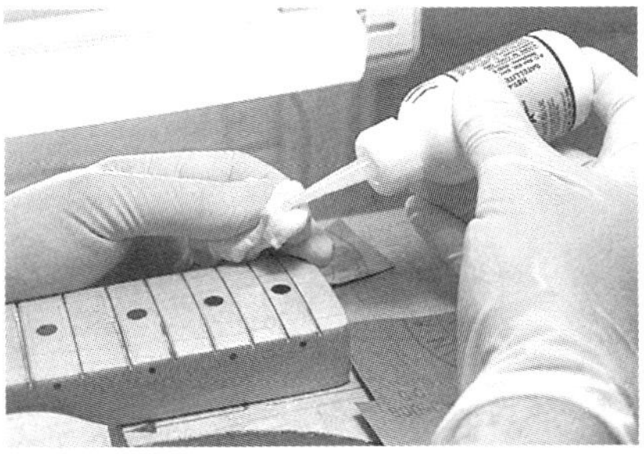

84 …and french-polish with superglue as if it were shellac. You must keep moving or you'll stick to the neck!

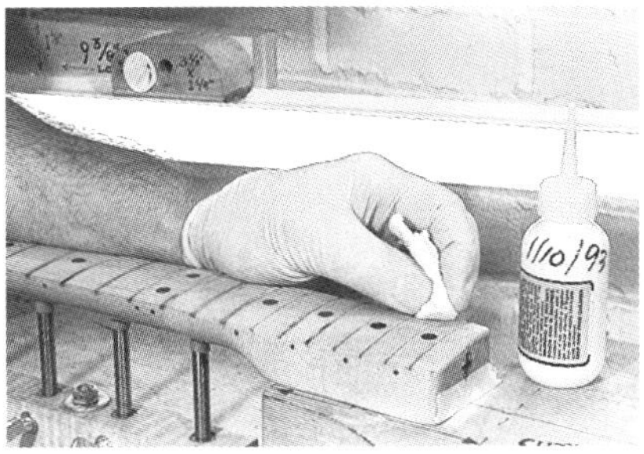

85 A couple of coats will dry in an instant. It's a good idea to write the date on your superglue when you open it, by the way.

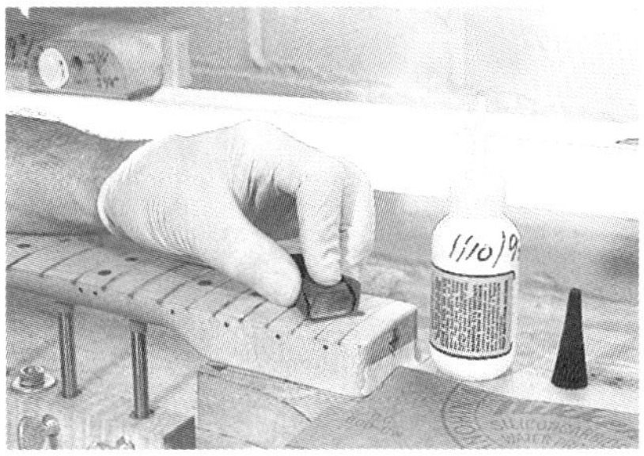

86 Use a small sanding block, run through the #500, #800, and maybe #1000-grits (dry) to level the "finish," and carry on with the job. The whole finish repair took 20 minutes.

87 Double-check the fingerboard radius (it's 7-1/4")...

88 And use the FretBender to pre-curve the fretwire. If you're hammering the frets in, overbend the wire so that its radius is more curved than the vintage 7-1/4" fretboard.

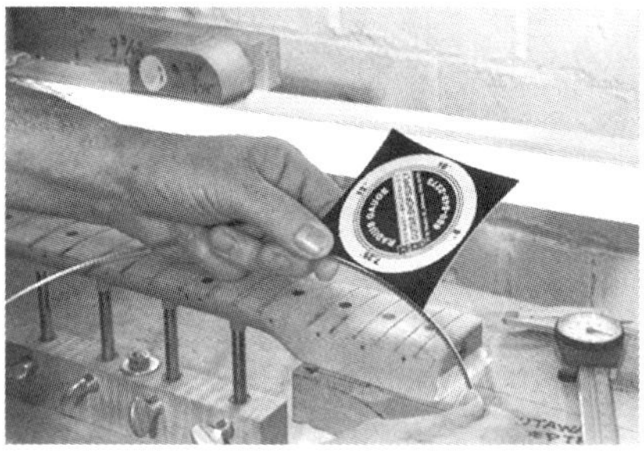

89 Use the radius gauge for comparing the curve of the fretwire while you adjust the FretBender.

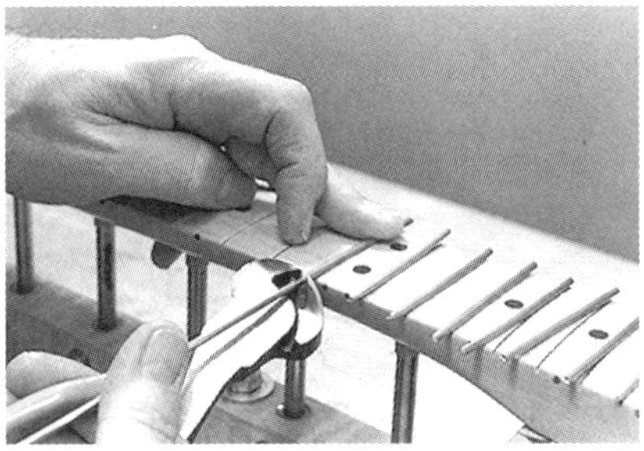

90 Cut each fret to length with about 3/16" overhang...

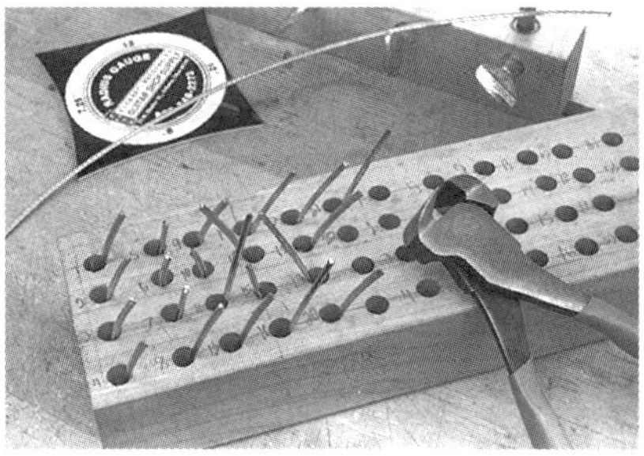

91 ...Store the frets in numerical order.

92 Use the Fret Tang Nipper to pre-cut the overhanging fret *tang* (even if there *isn't* any binding) because...

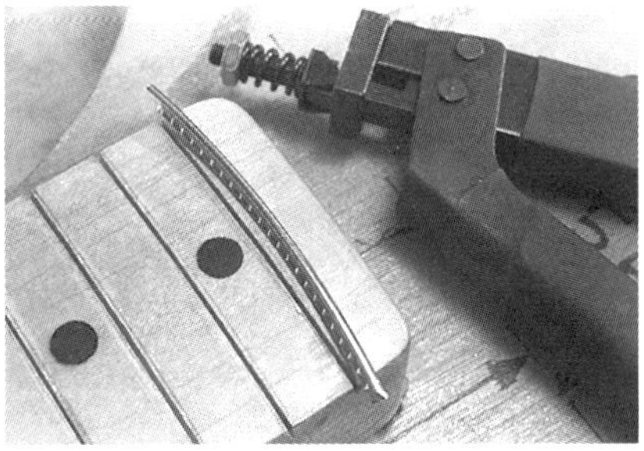

93 ...pre-notched frets won't twist from the nipping action when you cut the ends after installation (when a fret end twists it can become loose).

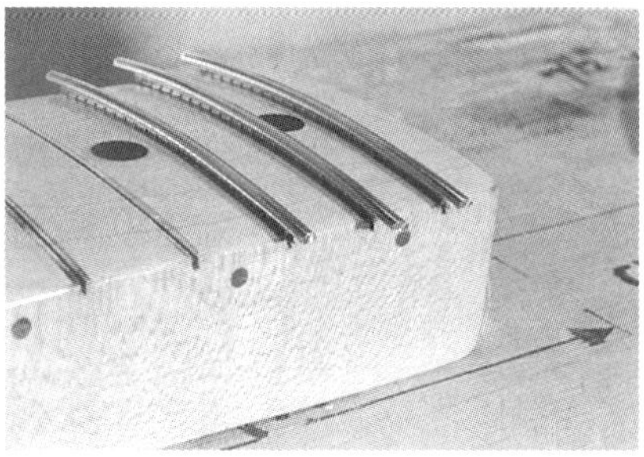

94 Also, if there's no tang to file flush to the neck, you won't mar the finish! You still need an overhang, however, to help "keep those ends down."

95 This little vise has a notch filed in the end. The unfiled portion of the jaw grips the fret tang, while the notched end allows the fret overhang to move...

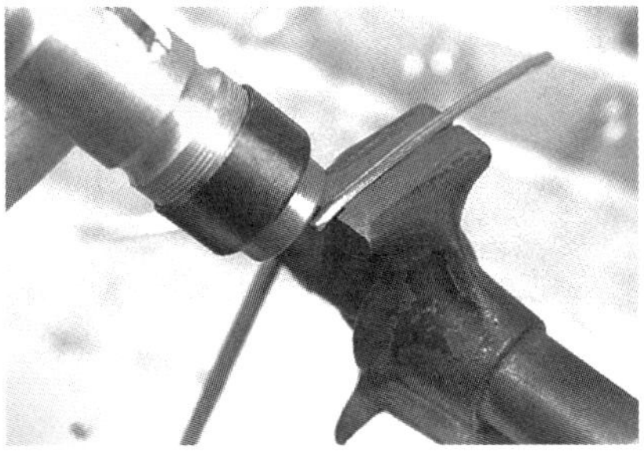

96 ...as you hammer it into an exaggerated "overbend." The jaws of the mini-vise have been ground to a round shape also, and it acts like an anvil as the hammer shapes the fret.

97 The overbends insure that the fret ends stay tucked down tightly.

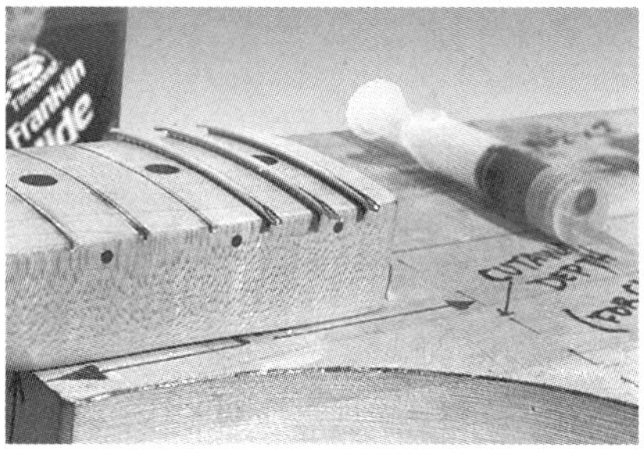

98 Frankly, these frets are a little underbent, so we'll give them a little extra bend with the fret bending pliers before hammering them in (I didn't have the FretBender adjusted pefectly).

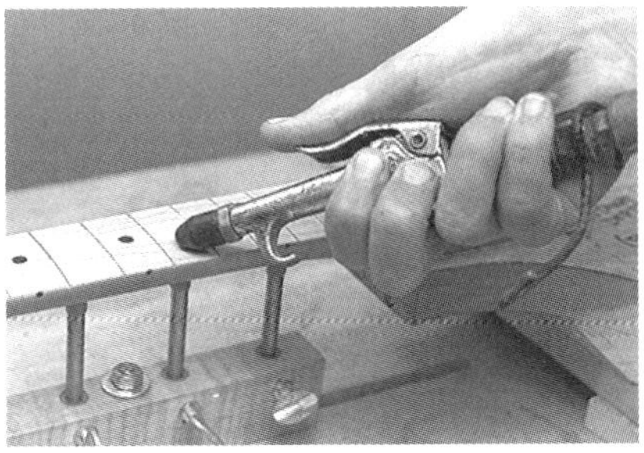

99 A final blow-out of any dust is important.

100 Try using hide glue, and be sure that the fretwire has been well cleaned with naphtha!!

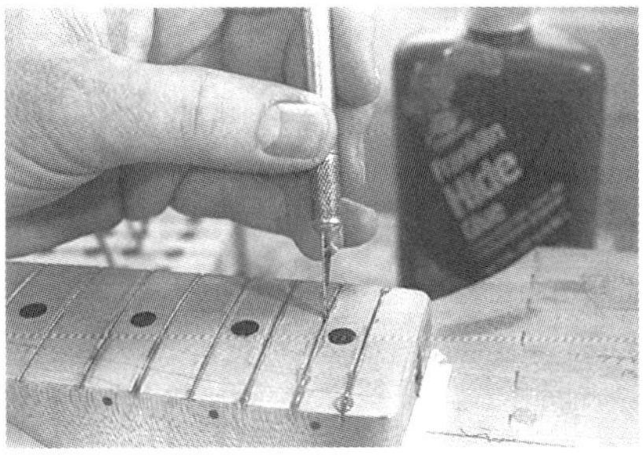

101 Move the glue throughout the slot...

102 ...and wipe up the excess with a rag dampened in hot water.

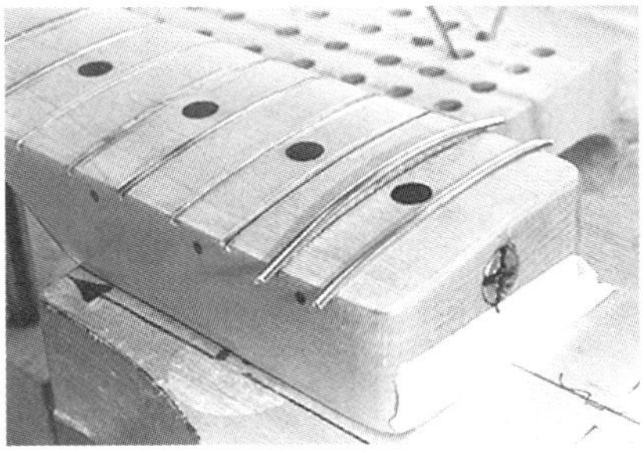

103 *This* is the amount of overbend you want. The fret will straighten out lengthwise as it's being driven in, and push the barbs sideways through the fret slot. This helps hold the fret (especially the ends) down.

104 Overbending seems to counteract the frets' tendency to "spring back" from the hammer blows—springback can cause fret ends to pop up.

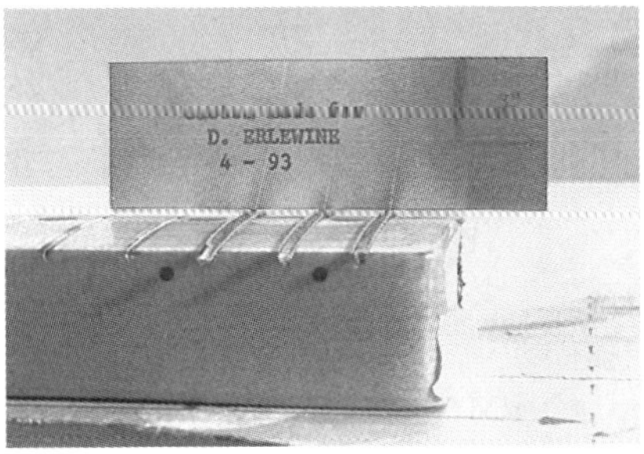

105 Once three frets are in, use a machined straightedge to see that each fret is level with the others—there's no way you can go wrong then!

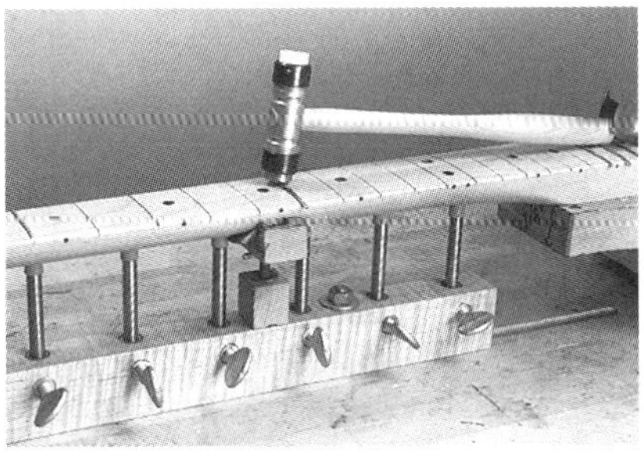

106 When hammering in the neck-jig, we use a support under the neck to avoid hammering the neck into the jig rods. That could "un-jig" the neck, or possibly cause small dents in the back of the neck.

107 Many neck-jig users would unjig the neck completely for the fretting part, and then re-jig for the fret leveling (See our "Don't Fret" video). This is a good overbend.

108 Tap down the outside edges first...

109 ...the edges needn't be driven completely home, but snugly. They'll keep the wire from tipping over and offer lengthwise resistance as you hammer the wire in...

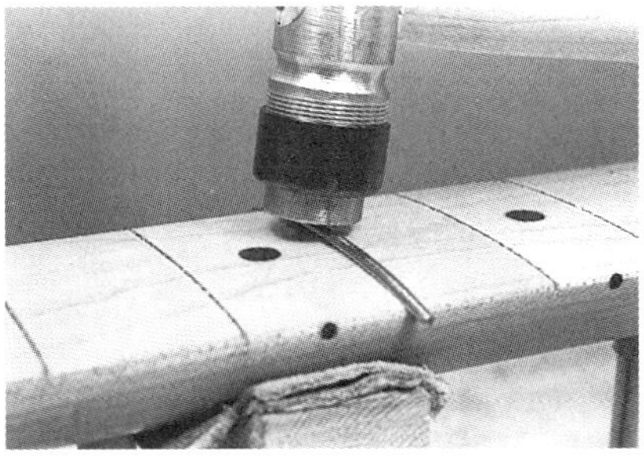

110 ...from the center to the outer edges. Hammer, don't pound!

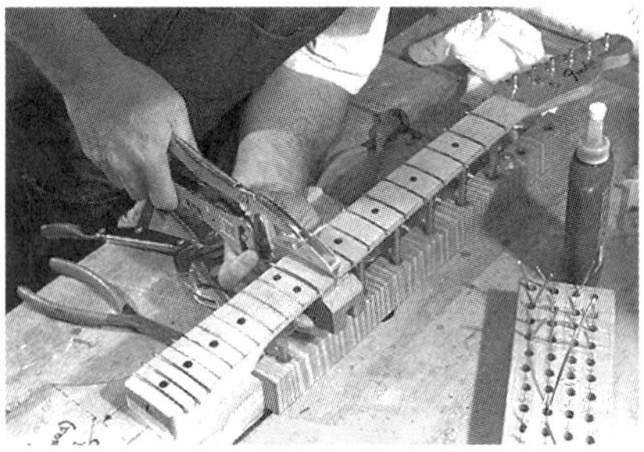

111 If you haven't seen this tool—"Jaws"—check out the Trade Secrets book for plans on how to make it. It was designed as a "mini-press" to work in the neck-jig.

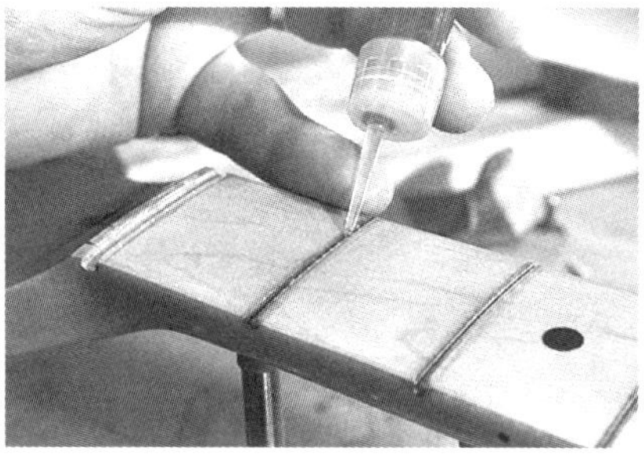

112 Hide glue...

113 ...and Jaws—what a combination! On vintage Fender (7-1/4" radius) fretboards, we'll start with a 7-1/4" pressing "shoe" in Jaws and...

114 ...sometimes follow with a 6-1/2" radius Jaws (it's nice to have two pair) to press down the edges only. Notice that there are four adjusting stops on Jaws.

115 All the while, check your progress with the straightedges. Keep each fret perfectly level with its neighbor, and you won't have much fret dressing to do, if the neck is straight.

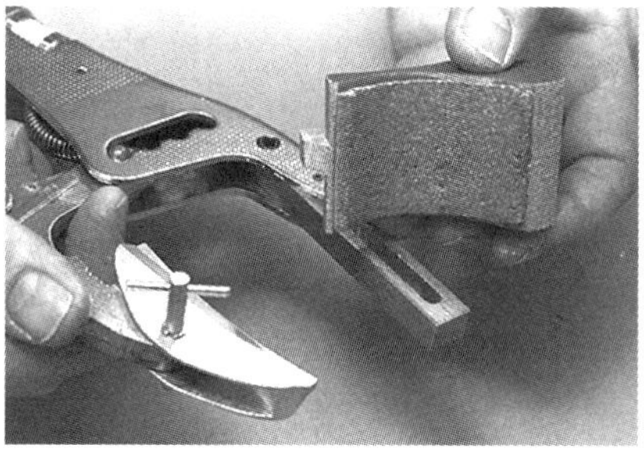

116 The bottom caul can be removed from Jaws to make more room...

117 ...for clamping on the body. (See the tools section for some other fret-pressing methods and clamping fixtures).

118 Between Jaws and a trusty hammer, the deed is done!

119 With the "Luthier's Workstation," while the hide glue sets, you can put the guitar out of the way and work on something else—and still remained "jigged." See you tomorrow!

120 The next day the glue has dried hard, crystalline, and full of tone. Hide glue will hold metal frets into wood slots quite nicely if the fretwire has been degreased. Nip the fret overhang.

121 Bevel the edges of the clipped fret overhang—hold your fingers against the edge of the neck to keep the file from slipping up onto the board.

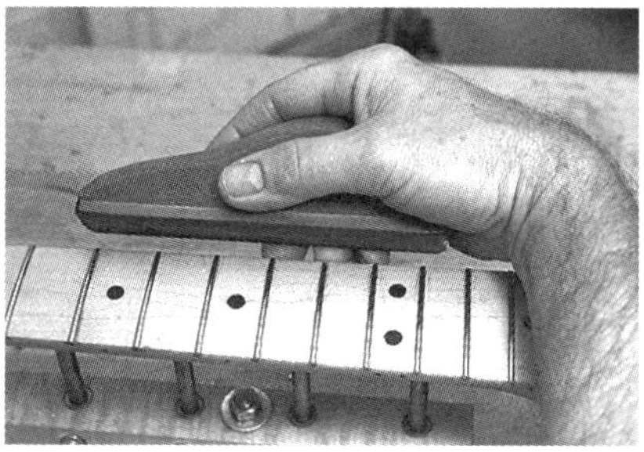

122 By holding your hand away from the neck, you can see the fingertips holding firmly in a line—the fingertips are your edge-guide.

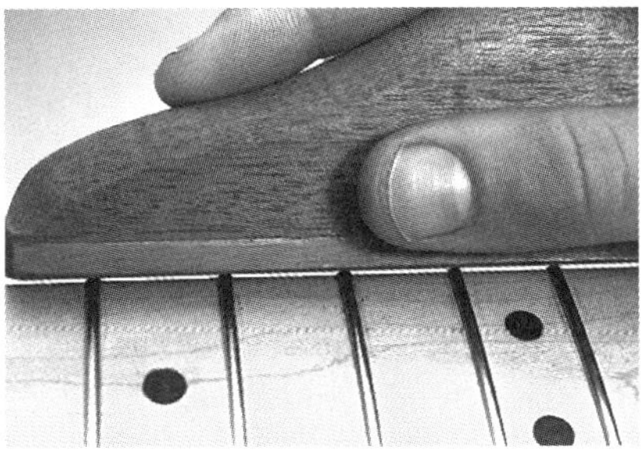

123 File the bevel of your choice until, with a light or a white background, the sliver of light that you see here disappears as the file removes the metal and comes flush with the neck. Going…

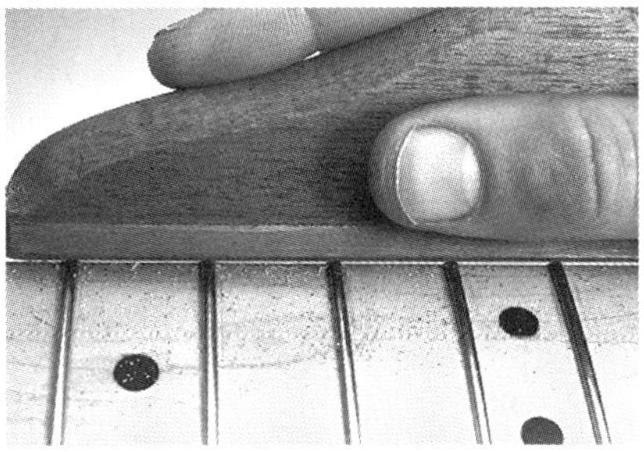

124 …going (watch the gap of light disappear)…

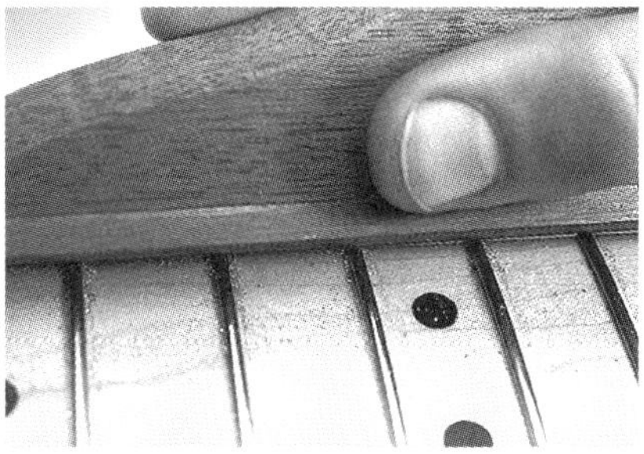

125 …gone!

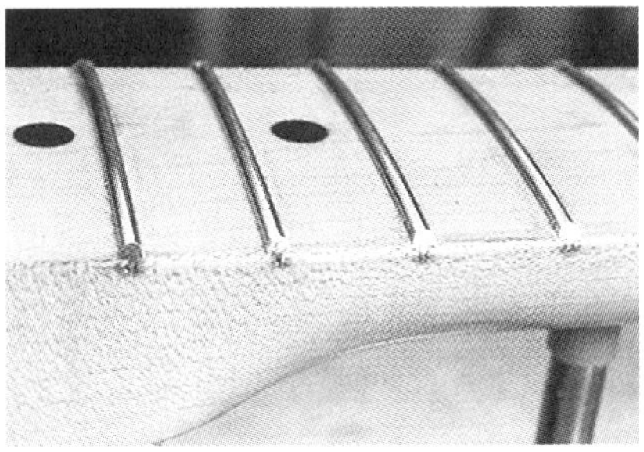

126 The beveled fret ends.

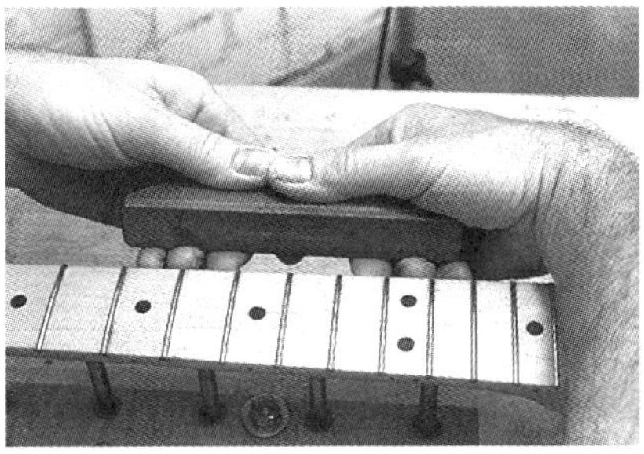

127 Actually, when you first start beveling, it's tough going, since the file gets caught up on the rough ends. Try starting with two hands (notice the fingertip guides of both hands)…

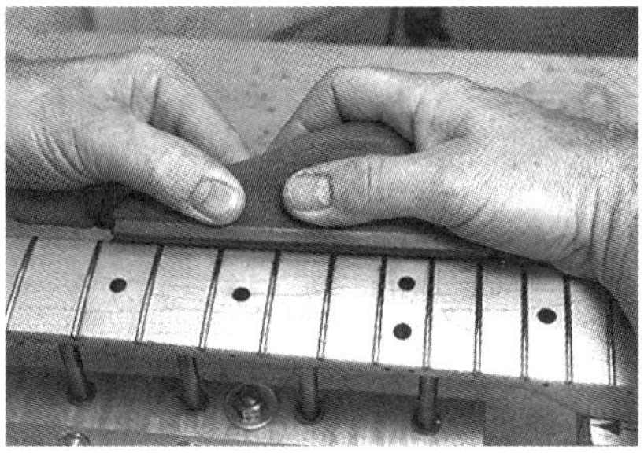

128 …hold firmly against the fretboard edge at the chosen bevel…

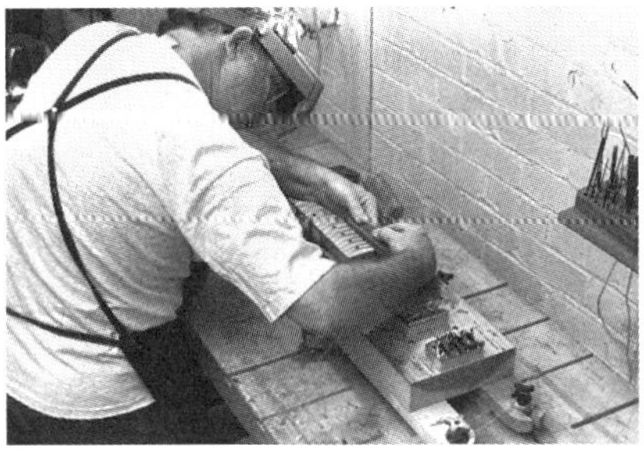

129 …and keeping your upper body stiff, use your whole upper body and shoulders to do the work. (Plenty of upper body there, boy!)

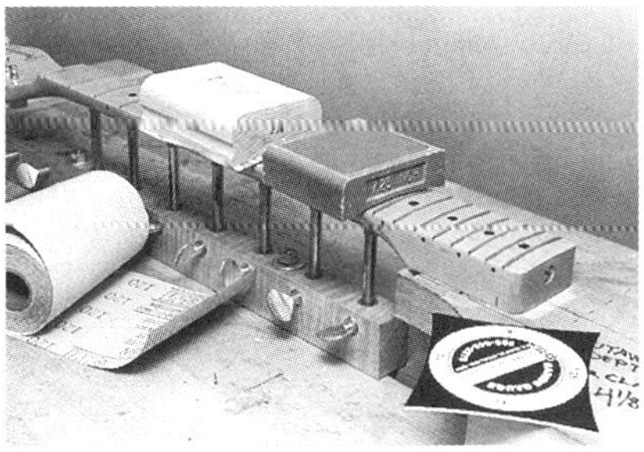

130 When the ends are beveled, you must decide between leveling with radius-sanding blocks, which create a cylinder-shaped radius and contact the whole fret surface at once…

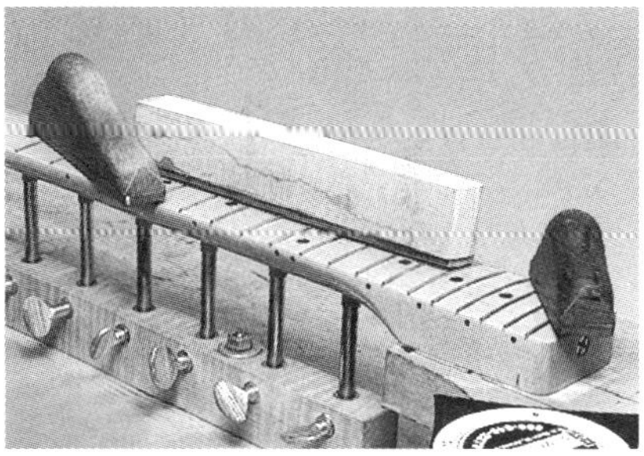

131 …or using flat tools and working the lie of the strings, creating a compound radius.

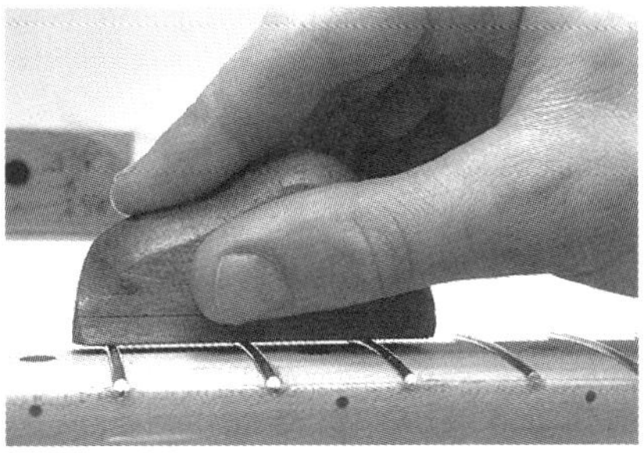

132 We chose the flat-bottomed tools just to remove any high spots…

133 …which were located by "rocking" with small straightedges.

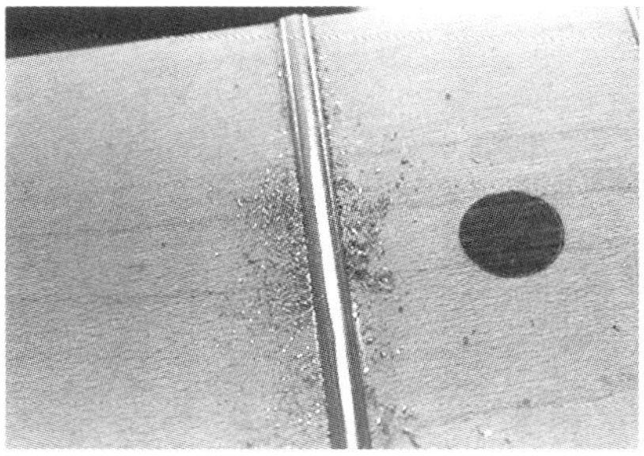

134 This slight flat was a high spot until the file knocked it down.

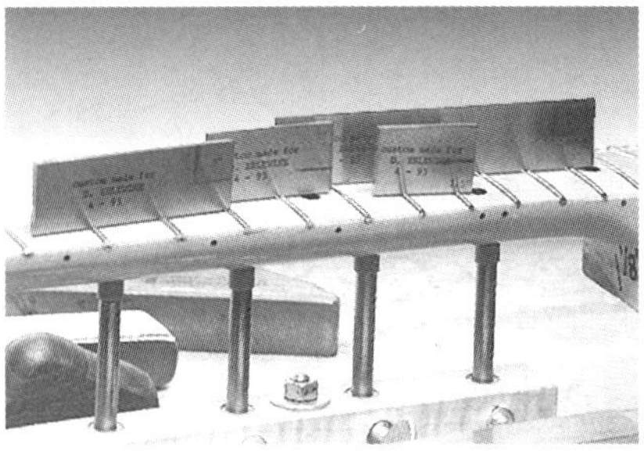

135 A set of different length straight-edges is important.

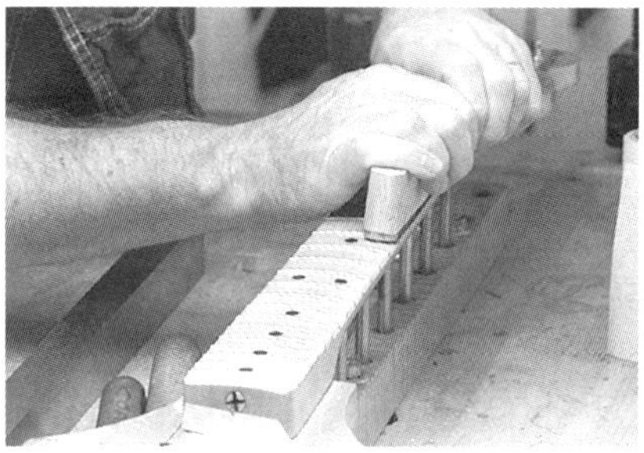

136 This is a longer (10") file, being used extremely lightly and parallel to the centerline, to gently level off high spots. By filing parallel to center, we're retaining the factory cylinder-shaped radius.

137 The filing was followed by a radius-sanding block in both #220- and #320-grits. This cylinder would be ready to "dress" except that we want to slightly alter it on the treble side—creating somewhat of a cone in that area…

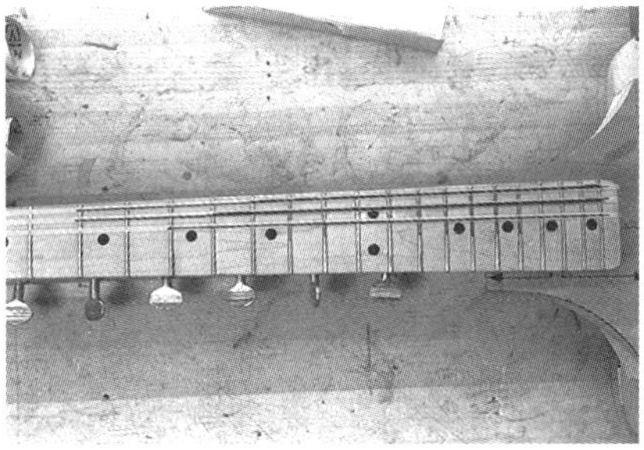

138 The trouble is from fret 3 to the end of the board—where a bent *E*-string notes out on a vintage 7-1/4" radiused board. With low or normal action, the *E*-string will buzz in the *B*-string area (the widest, darkest line in the photo).

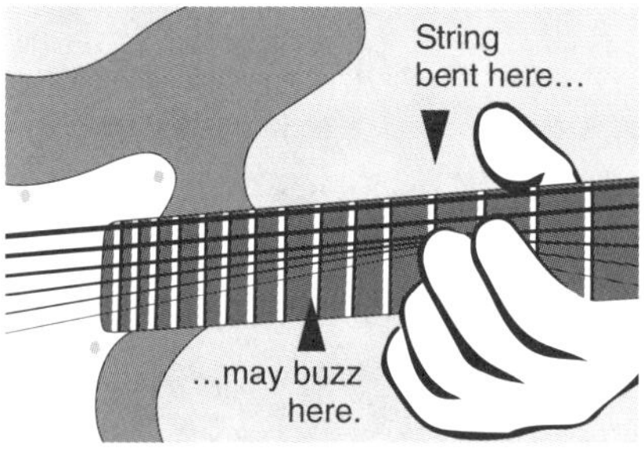

139 The buzz will become less as you go toward the *G*-string and then disappears toward the bass side. *(Drawing courtesy GPI Publications.)*

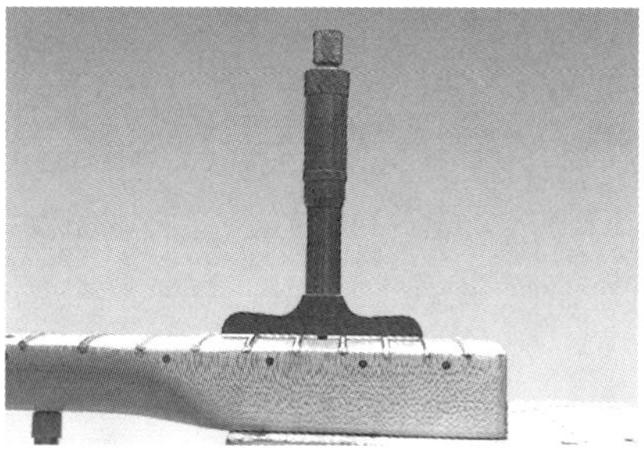

140 Measure the height of the frets in the upper register. Here we're really only concerned with the treble side.

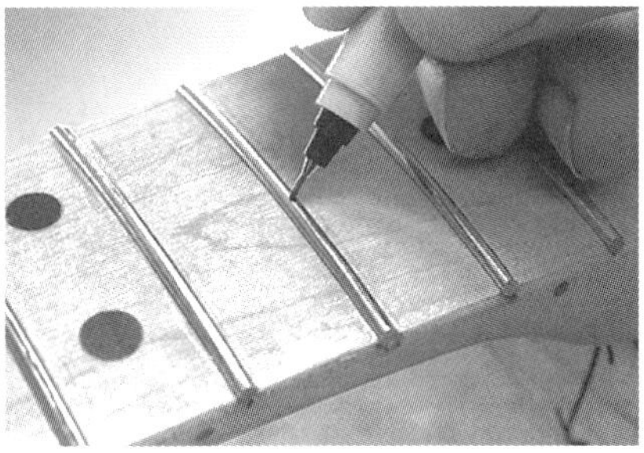

141 Put a tiny thin line of marker on the fret tops. There's no need to mark the bass side—it's just a habit. Use a careful thin line of ink because of the finish…

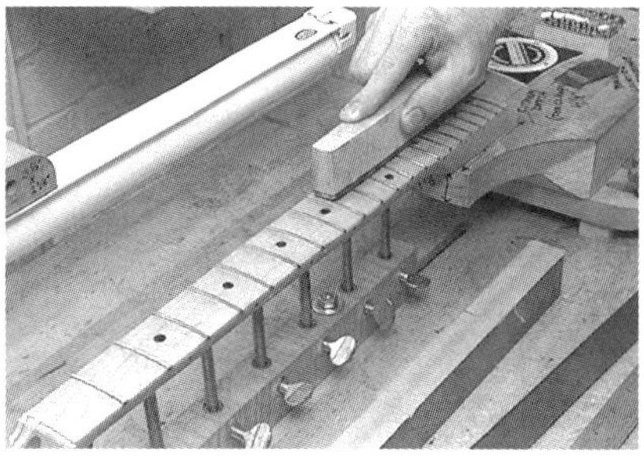

142 …then level the "noting-out" area with a file…

143 …followed by a sanding block (or a file wrapped with sandpaper)

144 …or use the long steel diamond-coated Fret Leveler to level and remove scratches…

145 …or use the fret plane.

146 I've flattened out the problem area (the shaded area in the illustration above)

147 …by removing .004" or .005" in that area alone. The fret*board* in this area may be a cylinder, but the *fret* has been slightly compounded by leveling in the "lie" of the strings. We created a slight cone on *top* of the cylinder.

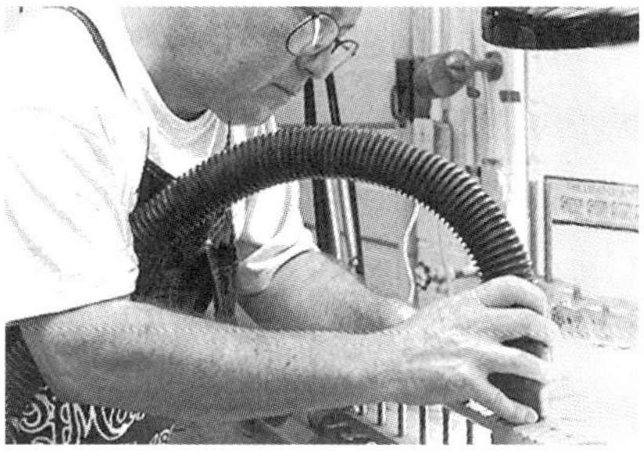

148 Vacuum up the metal dust…

149 …and re-check that area.

150 It looks great!

151 String back to pitch…

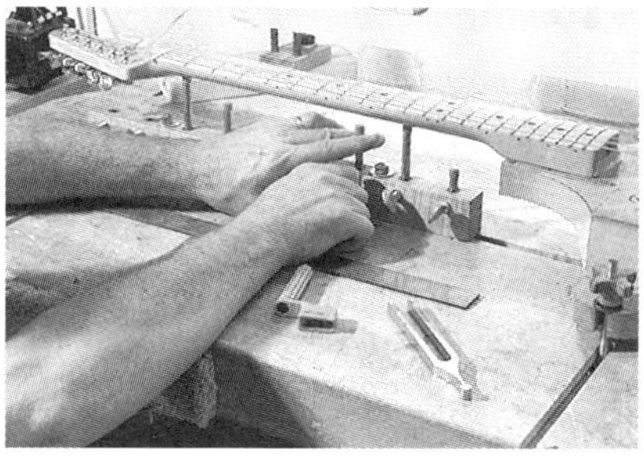

152 …drop the neck-jig studs…

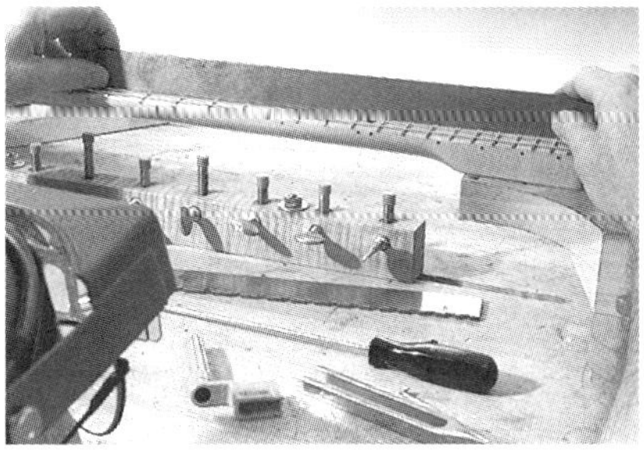

153 Check the whole neck with the strings on…

154 Needs to be straightened a little (truss rod tightened in the playing position).

155 *Playing* is the real test—the frets need to be dressed and smoothed for bending, but it isn't "noting-out"—the compound radiusing of just the one area worked great! *(Hey, Bo Diddley!)*

156 Clean up the area and get on to the fret dressing…

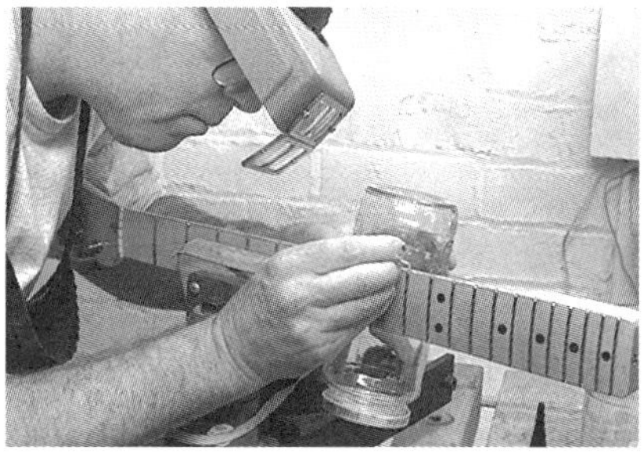

157 …but before dressing, you should touch up any finish irregularities. Often there will be small chips of finish along the fret edges, especially in the thick polyester finishes.

158 Use yellow and red label Hot-Stuff to fill in the chips instantly, with a little "accelerator" to speed things up. The bottoms of two glass jars make good pallettes—put the thin superglue on one, and the medium-viscosity on the other.

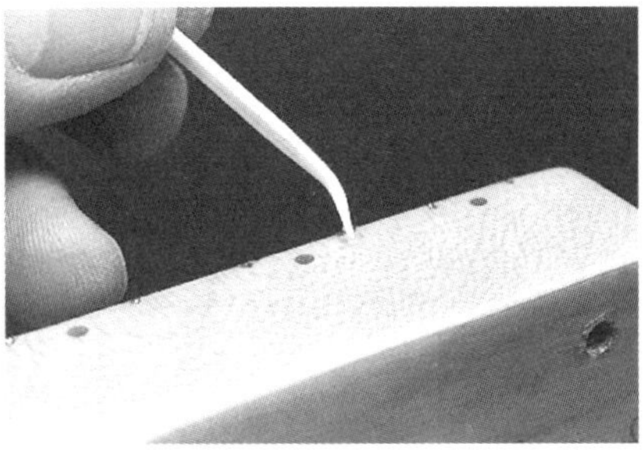

159 Using an angled plastic toothpick as an applicator…

160 …this is the result of several "drop-fill" applications and the wafting of accelerator over the area in between applications.

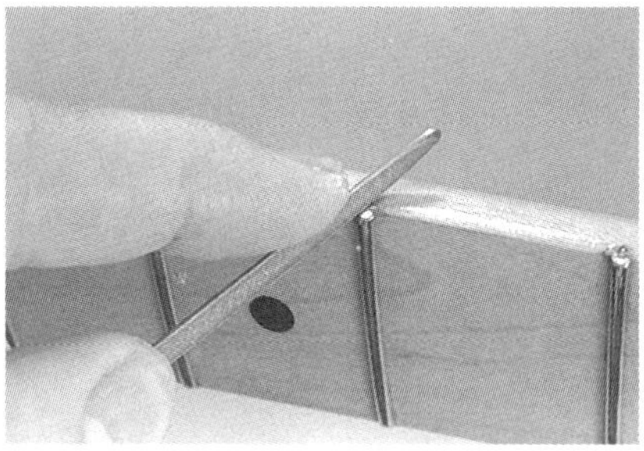

161 Shape the clear superglue fill with your fret-rounding tools—the 3-corner file is especially good…

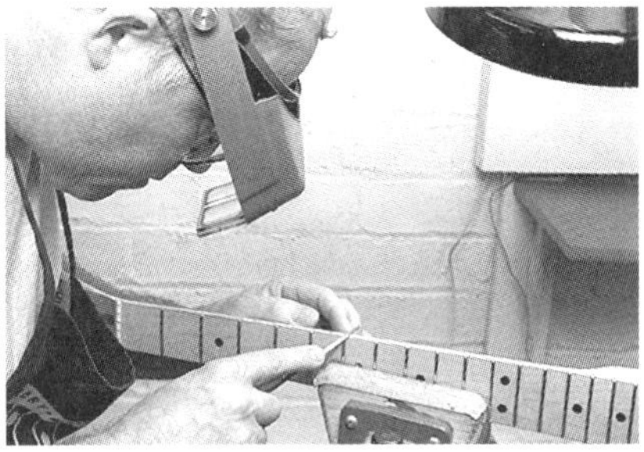

162 …you want to finish this work now before you final dress the frets or the fret ends.

163 Wet-sand with #800-grit Finesse sandpaper…

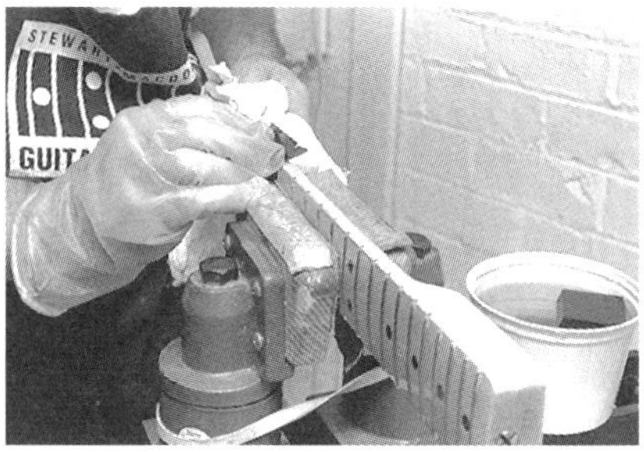

164 …you don't need a finer grit here because you're really just sanding on the edges…

165 …which rub-out easily with No. 2 and No. 9 Mirror-Glaze polishes.

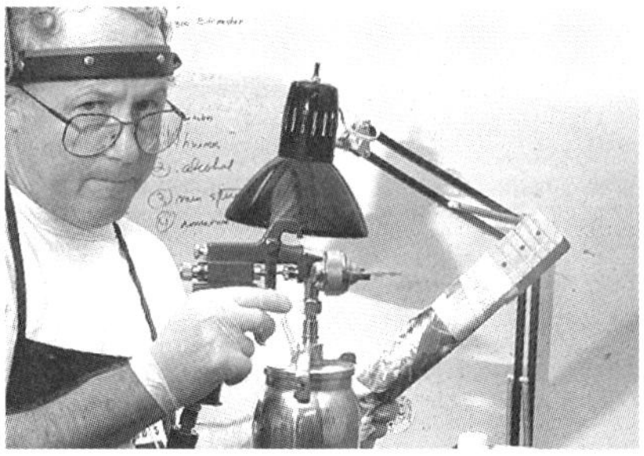

166 But we're not ready to dress yet. The superglue touch-up didn't match well enough in color. It needs to be touched up with clear lacquer and some color to hide the "sand-throughs."

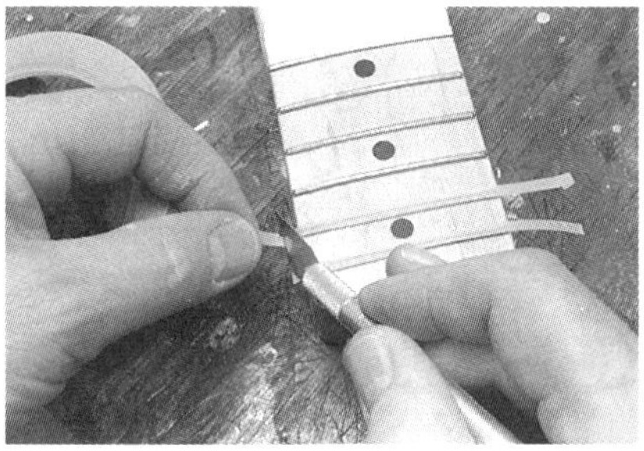

167 Tape off the frets just to make less lacquer to remove later (we used lacquer, even though it won't "melt-in" to the Poly finish. Doesn't matter, since we can spray right up to a fret and hide the line).

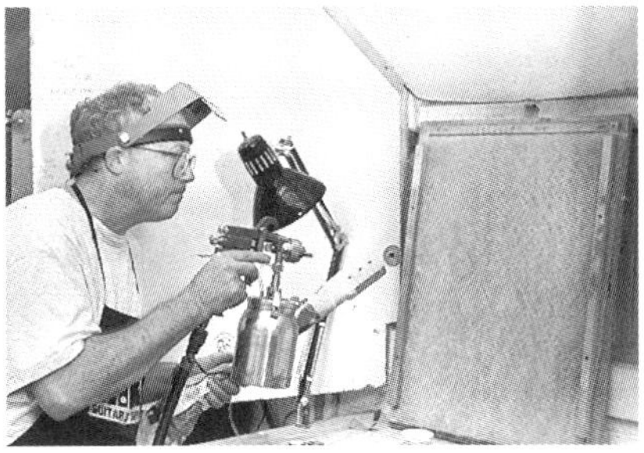

168 A couple of coats of clear lacquer…

169 And then we need a little color to match the slightly white, somewhat opaque look of the aged polyester. This is clear lacquer to which we're adding white lacquer…

170 …just to slightly opaque the clear.

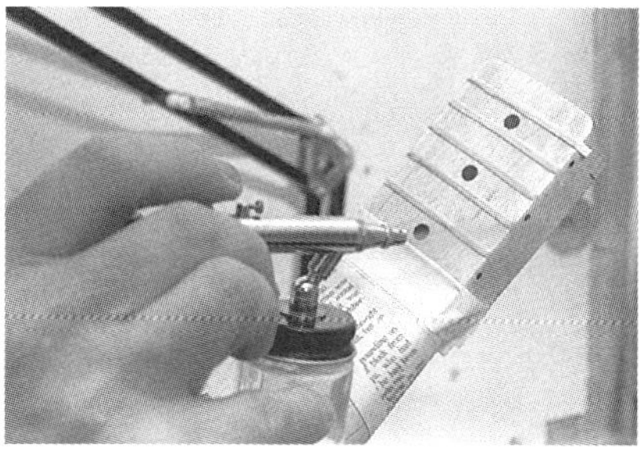

171 An airbrush is the best way to "tone" the neck...

172 ...close, but it still needs a little brown to amber the tone.

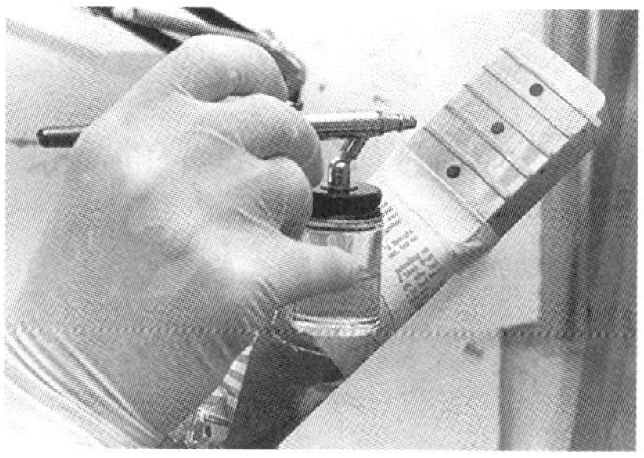

173 The slightest brown over the thinnest of white coats is a good color match.

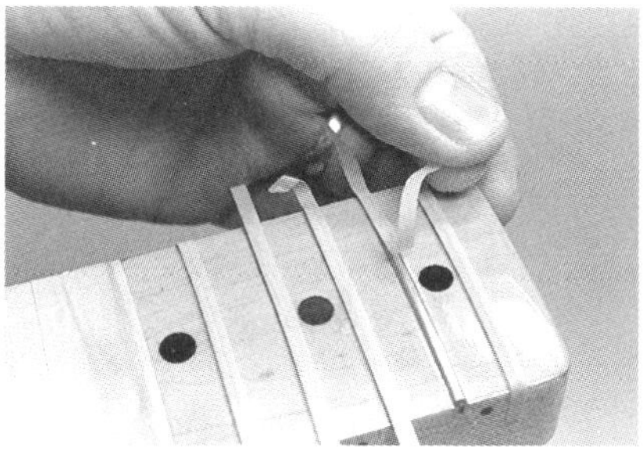

174 Remove the tape now so it won't dissolve into the final build-up of lacquer...

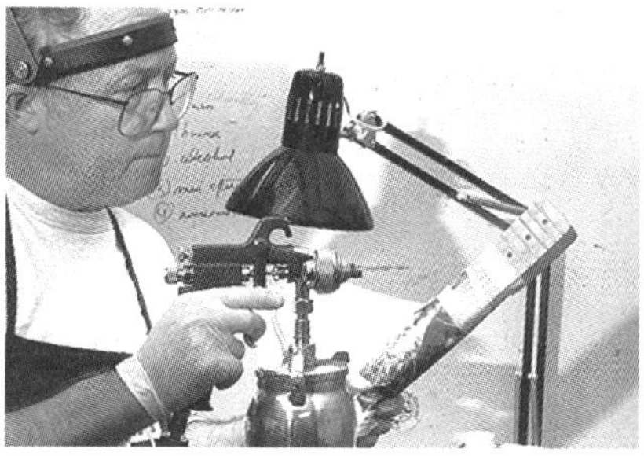

175 ...and spray a few coats of clear.

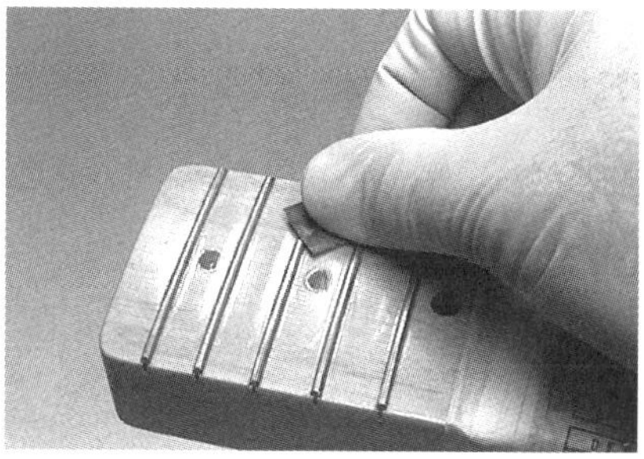

176 Sand in between coats with #500 to #800. Try to sand dry if you'll be spraying another coat or two.

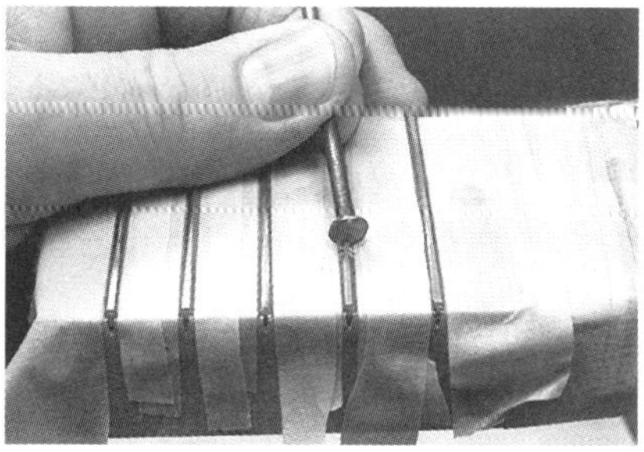

177 To remove the lacquer, use a nail with a groove ground into it. For more information, check out Lesson 7, the lesson on spraying a maple neck finish.

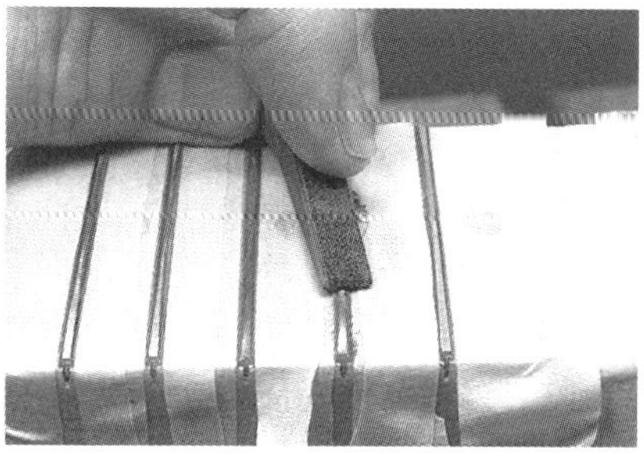

178 Notice that we've taped off the frets with draftsman's light-tack tape to protect it while removing the lacquer. The Sanding Stick will polish the lacquer off the sides of the frets. Now it's time to dress the frets.

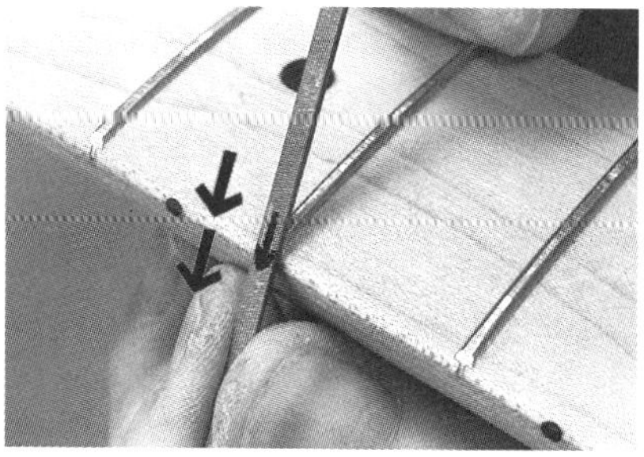

179 The fret ends were rough-beveled earlier. To remove any harsh scratches, and give the final bevel a polished face, once again use the 1/8" nut-seating file. Don't slip, and start with a couple of firm downstrokes...

180 ...or upstrokes are sometimes better; whatever it takes to smooth the bevel and get any wire "burrs" to stand out...

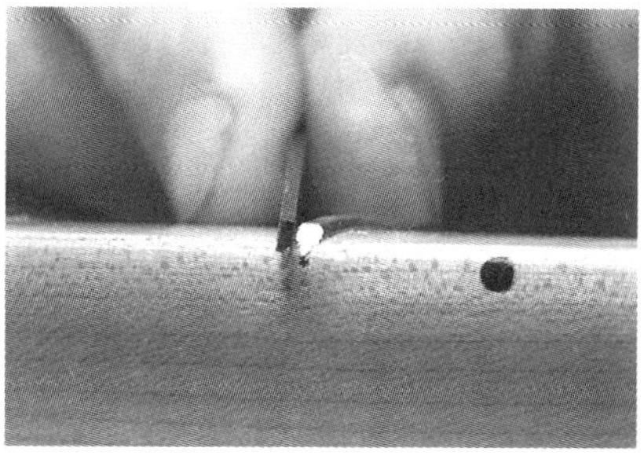

181 ...so that you can remove the burr with the same 1/8" file held like so...

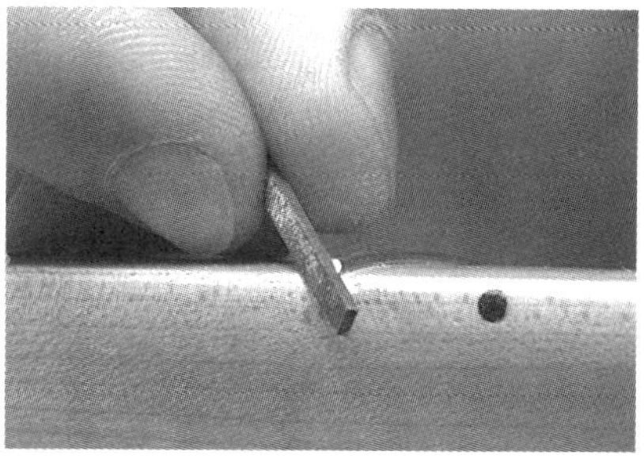

182 ...as you make the stroke with a rolling motion toward center. You may need to do this stroke several times.

183 Sometimes you'll need a small chisel (this is our Micro-chisel) to remove glue, remove excess or bubbled finish, or remove a wire burr.

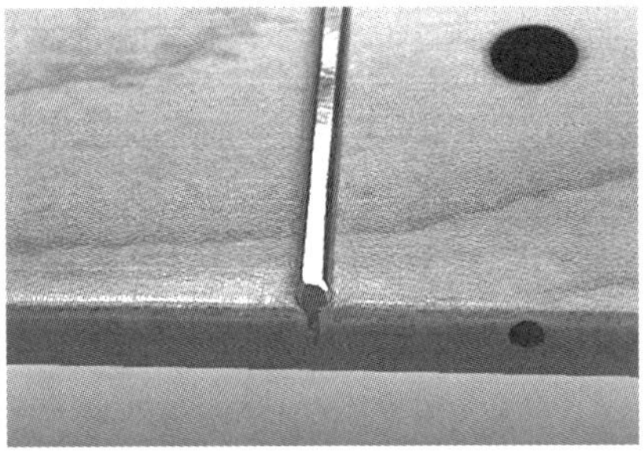

184 This is a nicely rounded end.

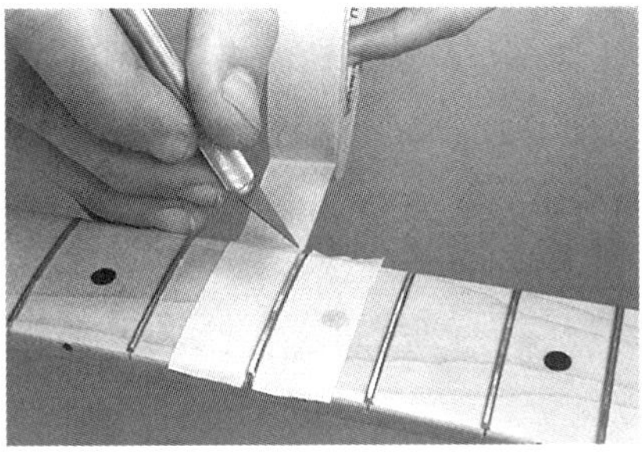

185 It's always safest to tape off the fretboard, especially on a maple neck, before dressing...

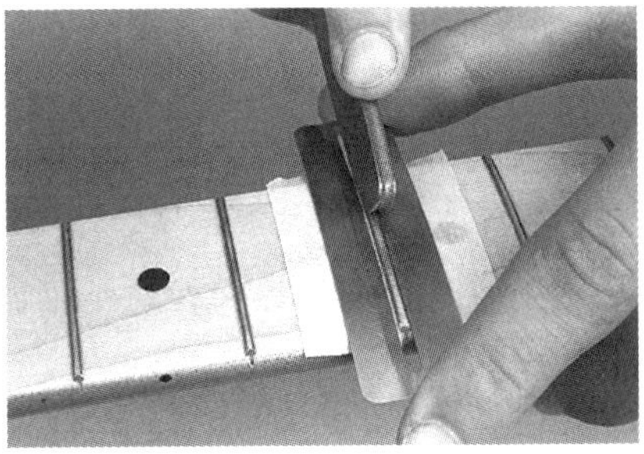

186 ...even if you plan on using the metal fret guard. On a properly done fret job the fine-grit diamond rounding file is all you'd need for bringing most of the flat tops to center...

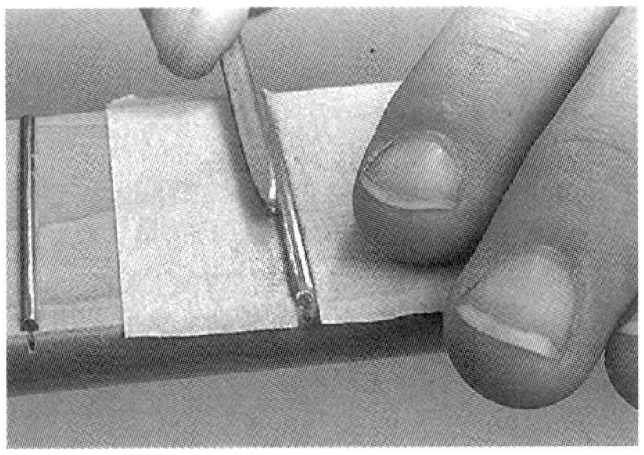

187 ...with the possible exception of a little clean-up with the 3-corner file. Use it to remove that last bit of flat spot or "land"...

188 ...and to final-shape the fret ends.

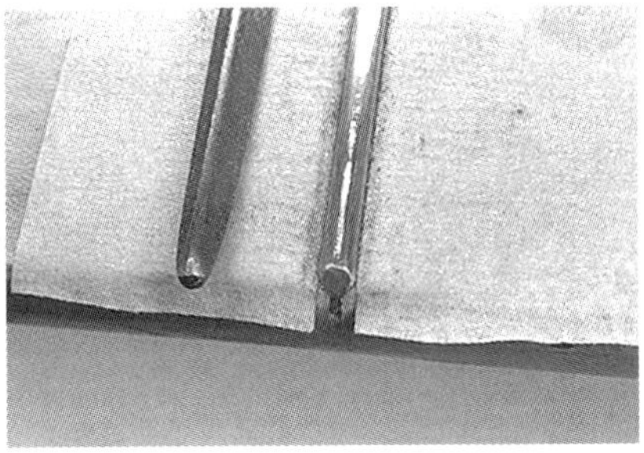

189 When there's the tiniest land left from the 3-corner file...

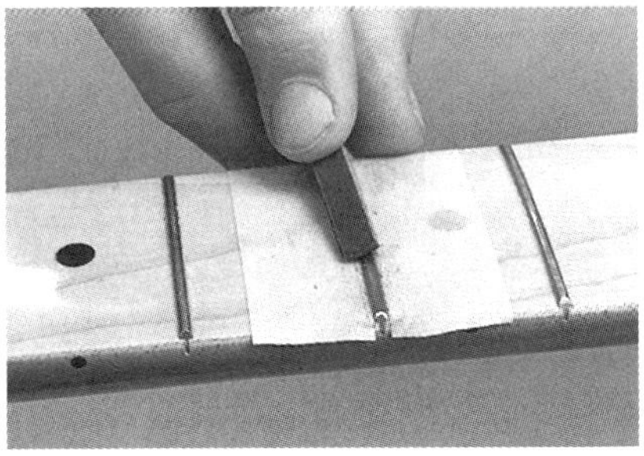

190 ...switch to the Sanding Stick in #400...

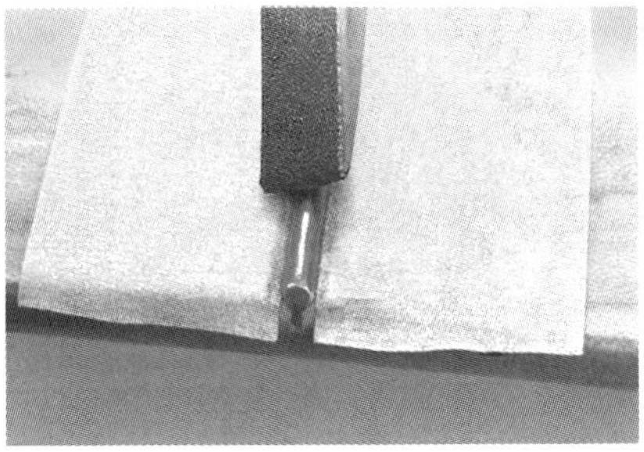

191 ...and #600-grits...

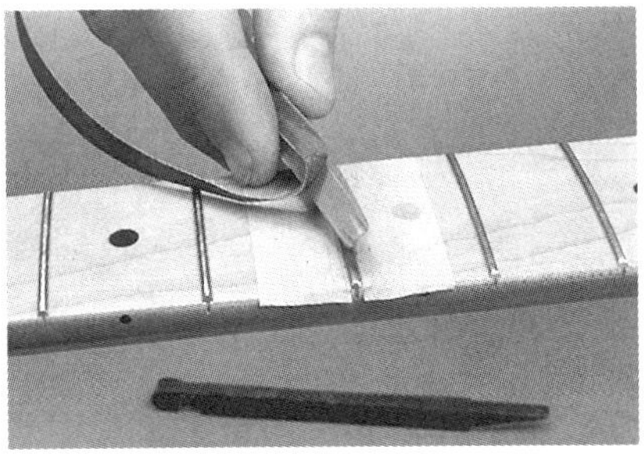

192 ...and be sure to file grooves in the Sand-stick that let the sanding belts hug the fret contour.

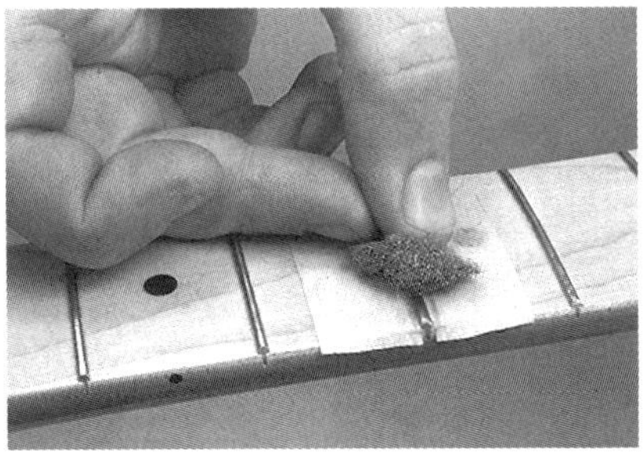

193 0000-steel wool...

194 ...and you're done...

195 …except for buffing the oversprayed lacquer on the last few frets. Using only the white wheel and buffing lightly, we can bring a shine to the lacquer in seconds.

196 Always buff from the center of the fretboard down, so that you don't catch the top edge and throw the piece. Of course, you can do the buffing by hand with Mirror-Glaze products, too.

197 Use the surrogate body for the final neck adjustment, to rough-in the setup, or to make a nut if needed. Here the neck's being set almost straight.

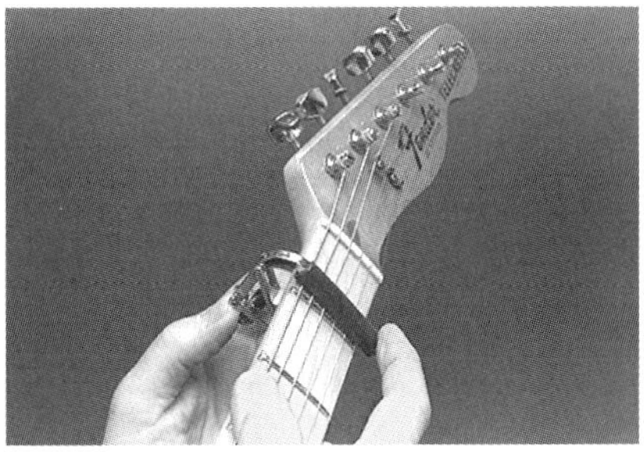

198 When they set the action at the Fender factory, they put a capo at the first fret to eliminate the nut as a factor when measuring relief and string height…

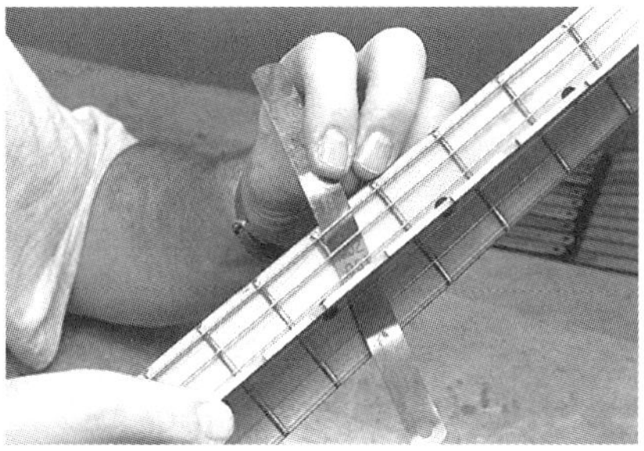

199 …then, instead of needing a straightedge to measure relief…

200 …they hold the other end of the string down and the *string* becomes a straight edge—freeing up one hand. This customer wants an almost straight neck (no relief)—.002" isn't much.

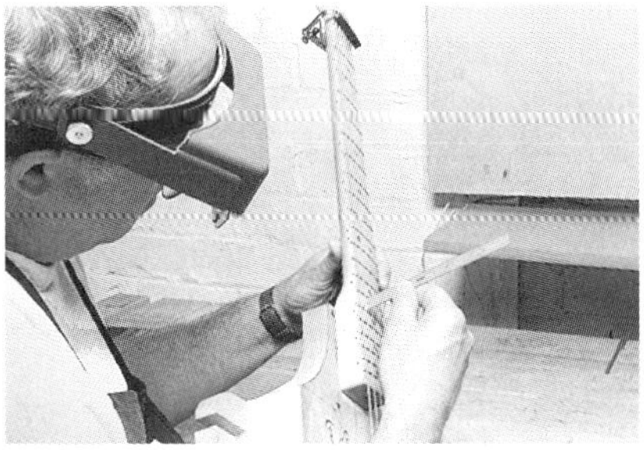

201 Also during a Fender factory set-up, the string height is measured at the 17th fret, with the capo still on.

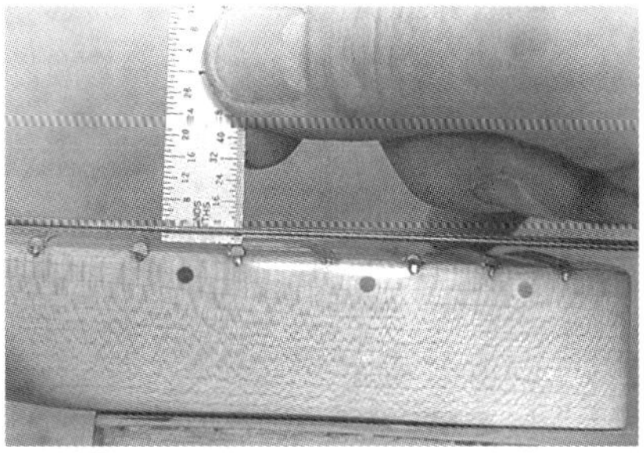

202 Set the outer two *E*-strings to a 4/64" gap between the top of the fret and the bottom of the string…

203 …raise or lower the bridge saddles until you get a 4/64" gap under every string at the 17th fret…

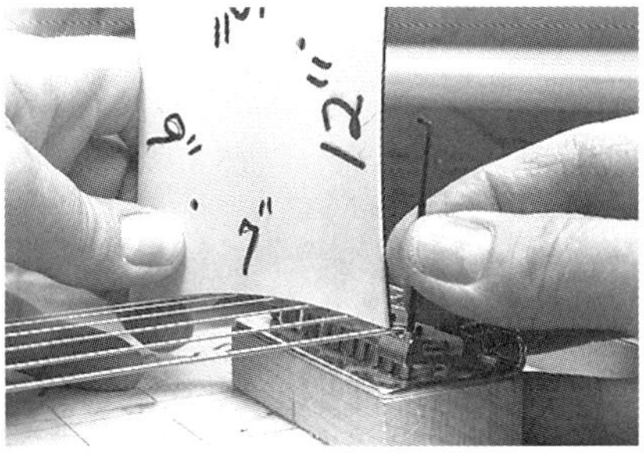

204 …or you could simply set the outer two *E*-strings to the right height, and then adjust the remaining strings until they touch the correct radius gauge (7-1/4").

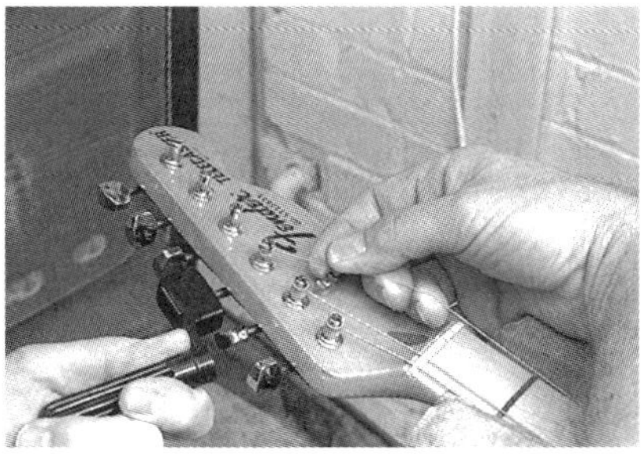

205 Now remove the strings, and put the neck back on the real body with a fresh set of strings…

206 …of course it'll feel even better on the actual guitar…

207 ...and it does!

We recommend saving any pieces of good fretwire that you remove (usually the last 8 frets on the tongue). Mark them by make and year, and you can use them later for single-fret vintage replacements.

LESSON 6

TOUCH-UP TRICKS FOR FRET SLOT ENDS

Here are some repair tricks for touching up chipped, worn, or too-deep fret slot ends in a maple fretboard (or *any* fretboard). This particular case was a '57 Strat that had been refretted at least twice. After the most recent fret job, it came in to have the poorly refinished fingerboard "made to look right." The fret job wasn't too bad, but the refinish was—whoever stripped and refinished the board used a powerful stripper which melted all the black fret markers; they were sunken and pitted. The finish wasn't very thick, and it stripped easily with small bits of rag soaked in lacquer thinner, right to the bare wood.

The black inlays filled in nicely with several built-up coats of thin (red label) and thick (yellow-label) "Hot-Stuff" superglue, which were carefully leveled with files and scrapers. I touched the bare fretboard as little as possible, and all the sanding and scraping was with the grain. After the dot inlays were level and flush with the fingerboard, it was ready for finishing—but first there was a little woodworking to be done on the fret slots.

During previous refrets the slots had been sawed much deeper than was necessary and never filled, except with years of dirt. This oversawing will happen if you don't use a depth-stop on your sawblade, but in this case it was every slot! It looked terrible. So before finishing, here's how you can approach filling a slot—if you should happen to saw too deeply by accident.

1 That was a very good year!

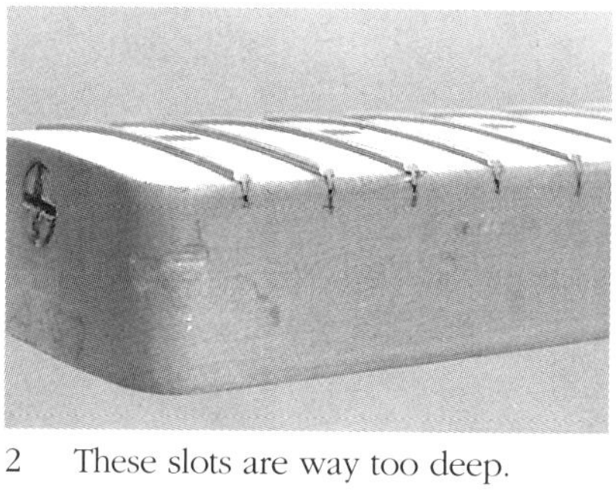
2 These slots are way too deep.

3 There's no excuse for this…

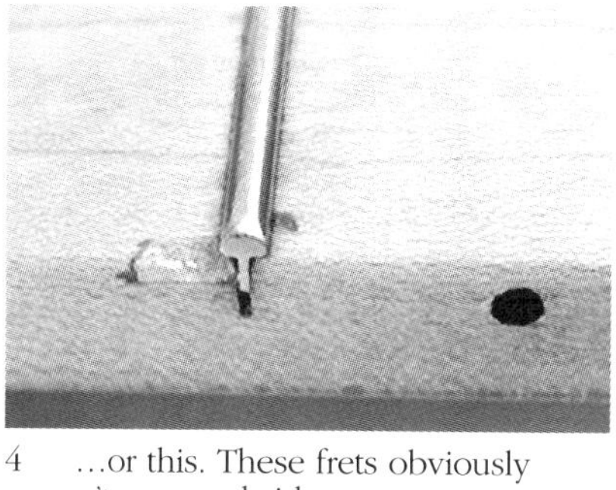
4 …or this. These frets obviously weren't removed sideways.

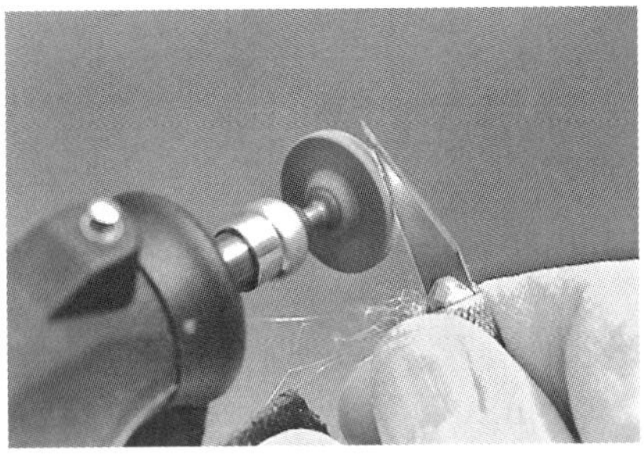

5 You must clean the dirt from the slots before you can fill them with a clean piece of maple. Try grinding a #11 X-acto blade to a custom shape...

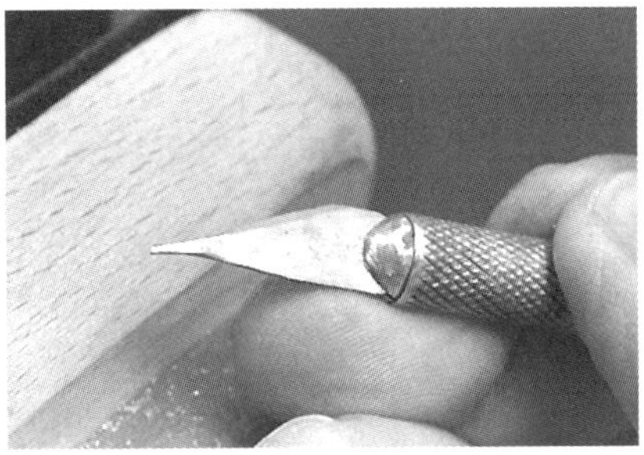

6 This little hook-shaped scraper was able to get into the slot without disturbing the fret tang...

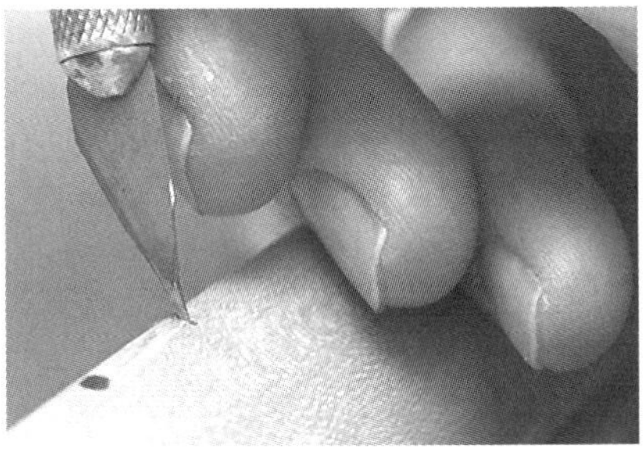

7 ...and pull out crud, while the scraper action squared-up the slot walls.

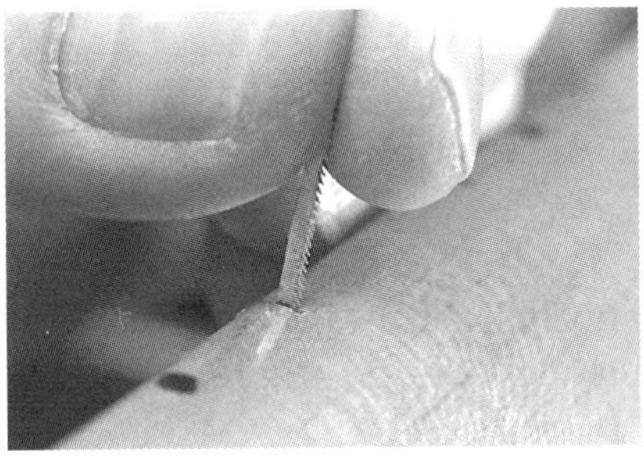

8 This little jeweler's saw blade helped too...

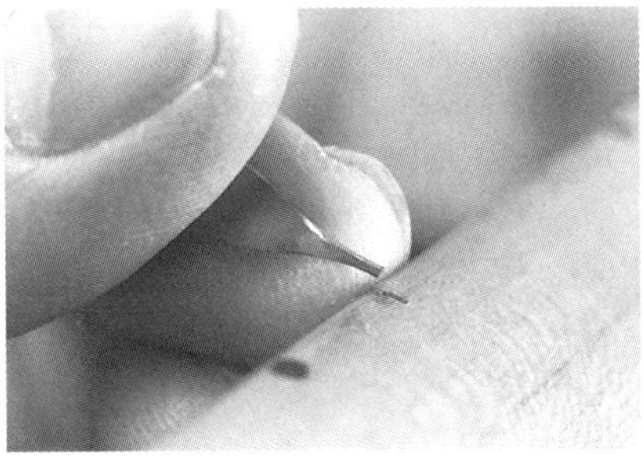

9 ...but it was this scraper-tip that really squared up the walls.

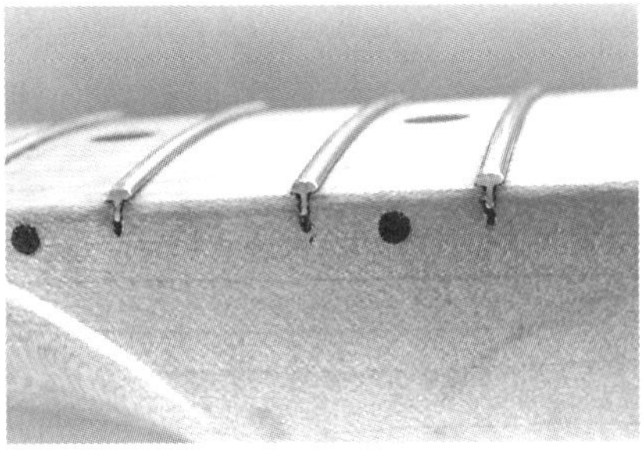

10 Start by studying the grain of the maple...

11 ...and find a board with similar color and grain.

12 This piece had an appearance on both the end and side grain...

13 ...which was similar to the neck.

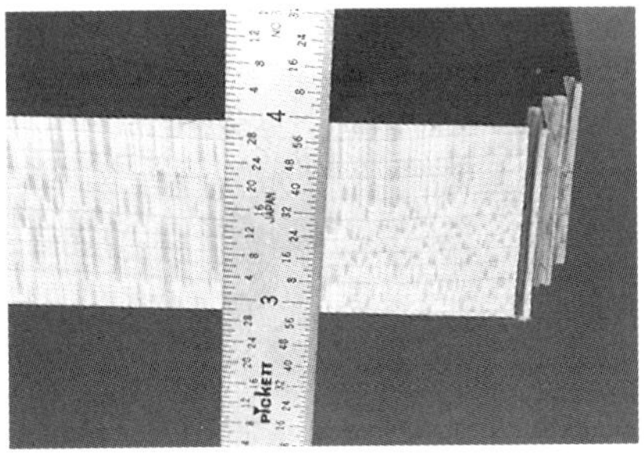

14 By measuring the grain lines...

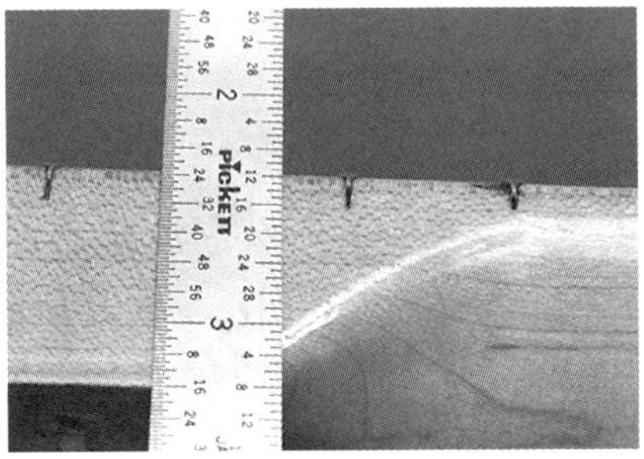

15 ...and comparing it to the neck, you can cut a piece that will have a dark grain line running through it in the right area.

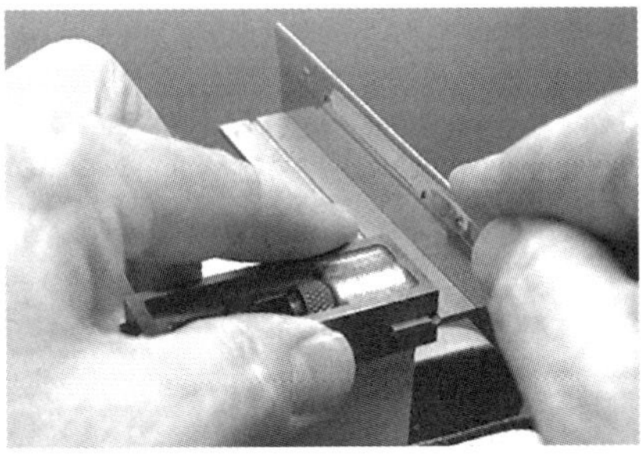

16 Use a square to guide your saw...

17 ...a thin X-acto saw...

18 ...and saw a sliver of wood...

19 ...that you can break loose by wiggling it with your sawblade.

20 See how the grains line up?

21 This is a bar of aluminum with a ledge, or "rabbet," milled into it. The ledge, which is shallow, holds the maple piece...

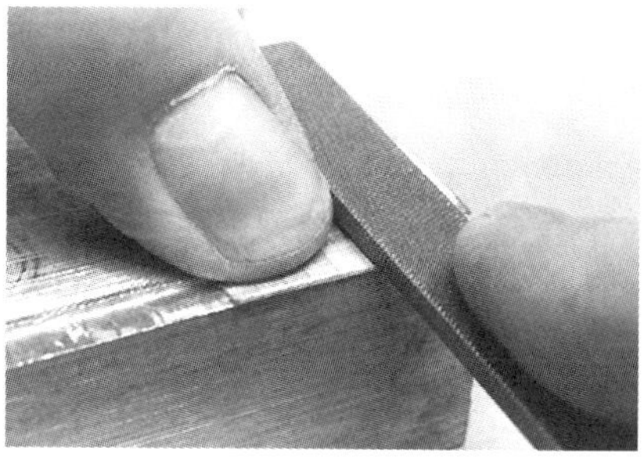

22 ...and acts as a stop, so that you can file it to shape or thickness.

23 In this case I'm slightly tapering the piece.

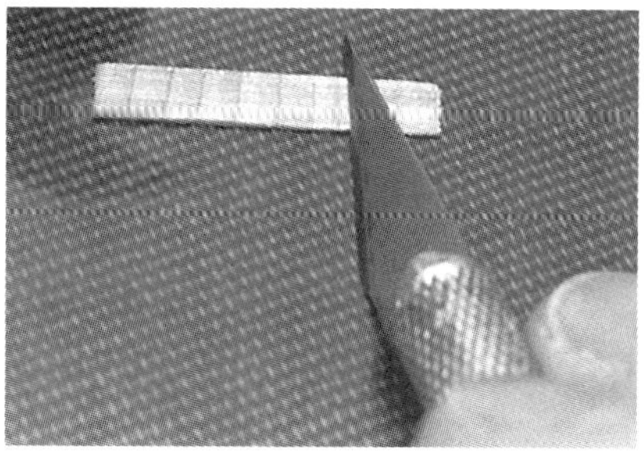

24 Cut out the matching piece...

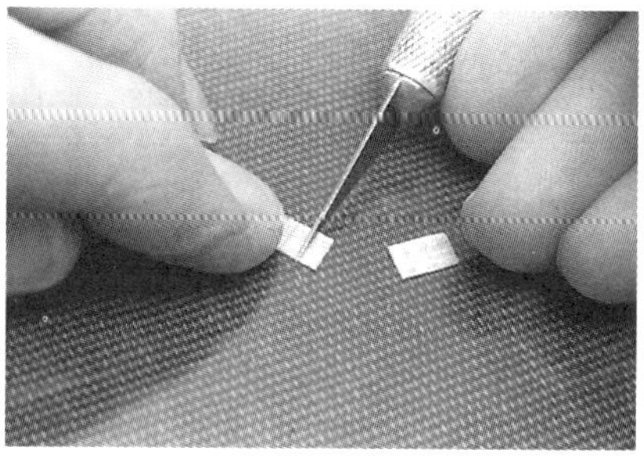

25 ...trim it to size...

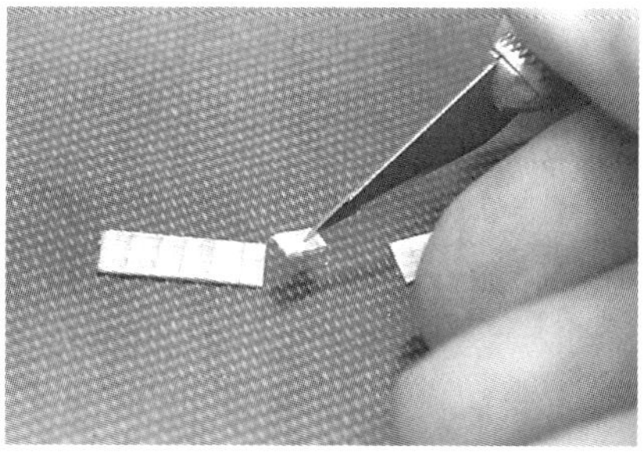

26 ...spear it with a sharp #11 X-acto blade...

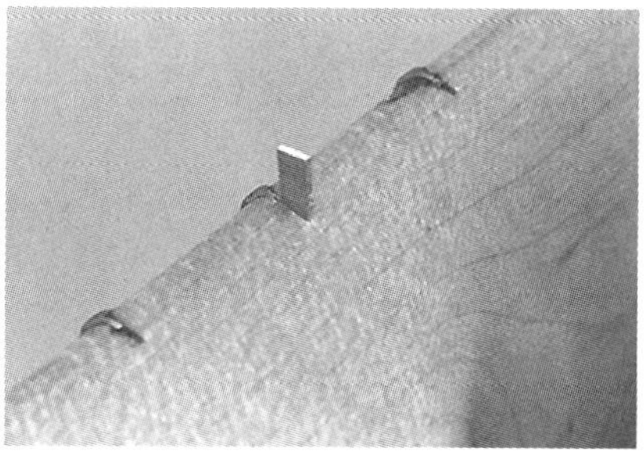

27 ...and see how it fits (there's a drop of hide glue in the slot already).

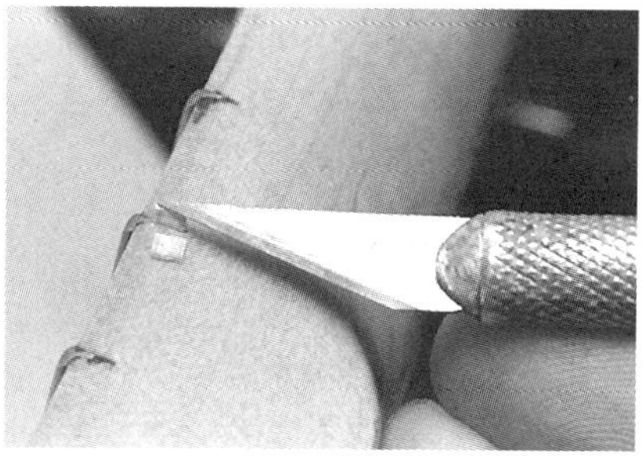

28 Cut off most of the overhang...

29 ...and lightly tap in the remainder...

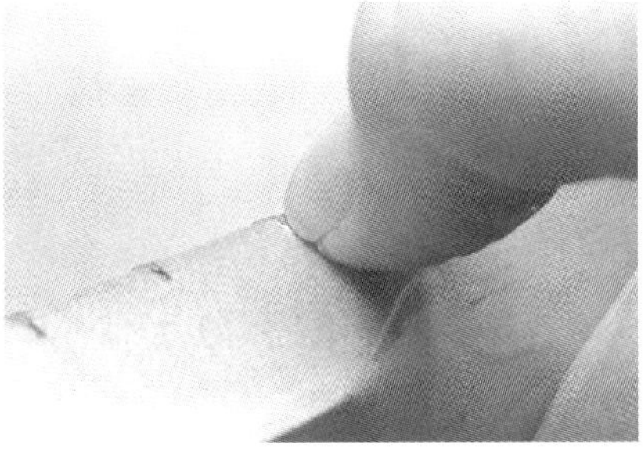

30 ...or press it in with your thumbnail.

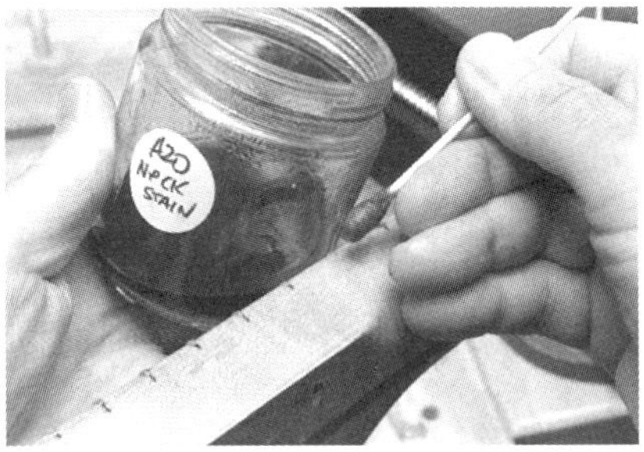

31 A touch of Lockwood aniline water-stain helps to hide it.

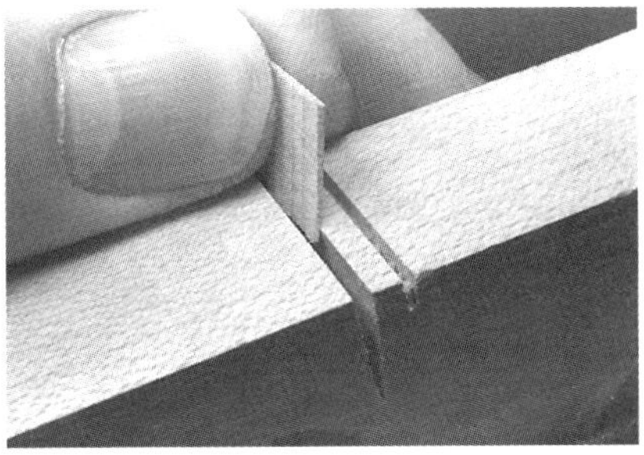

32 This piece had grains that ran at an angle...

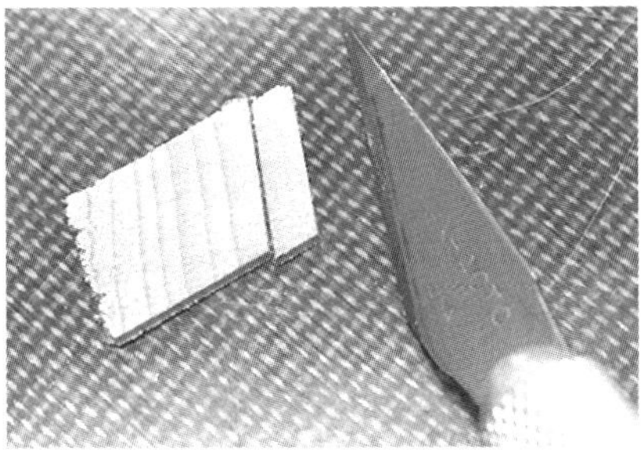

33 ...so trim the fill at an angle...

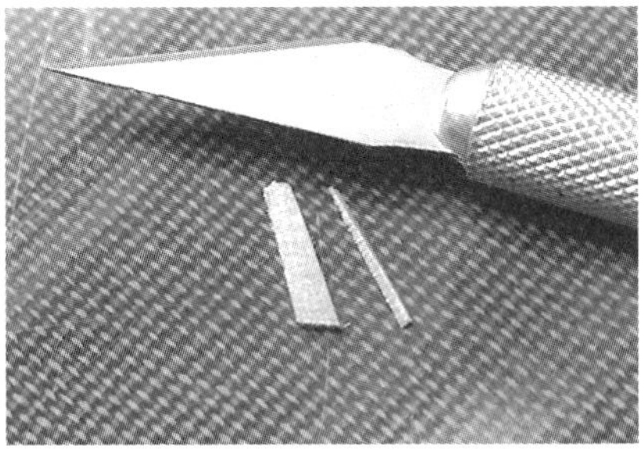

34 ...and a slight taper is a help...

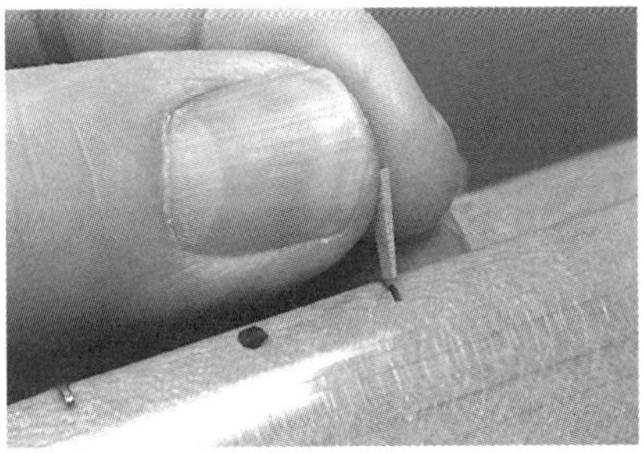

35 ...for sliding the piece in until it stops.

36 This is a "dry run" to see how it fits.

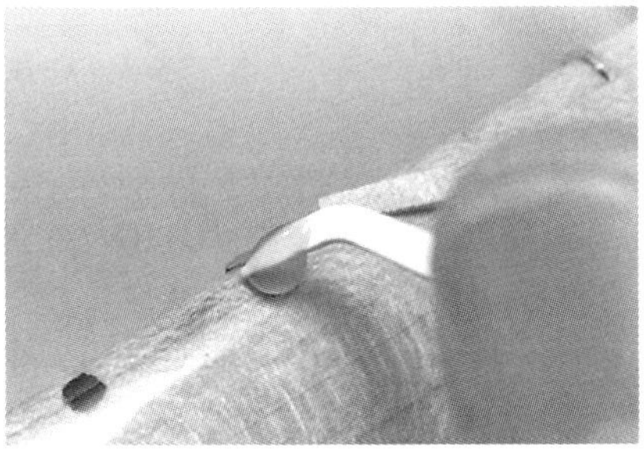

37 Let the hide glue run into the slot and get it wet. Sometimes it helps to lay a drop of warm water in the slot end to draw in the hide glue and swell up the wood...

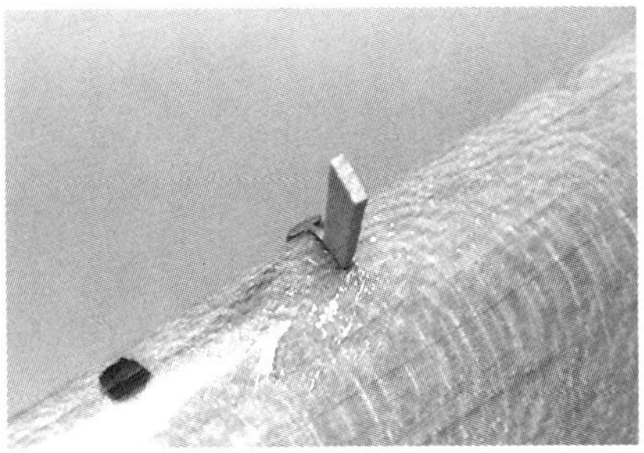

38 ...for a tight fit.

39 Trim the overhang, and let it dry. Now on with the refinishing (Lesson Seven)...

LESSON 7
"SPRAYING OVER" A MAPLE NECK

Here's a good way to put a finish on any maple fretboard. Use this method for new work, or after a refret where the finish was removed during the leveling of the fretboard.

In the vintage market, "spraying over" actually refers to finishing on top of the old finish—whether it is on the fretboard or anywhere else (body, peghead, back of the neck, etc.). In this case the neck finish was left original, but the fretboard surface was stripped to the bare wood before the refret (and after several previous attempts—as mentioned on page 117).

1 Use the less-sticky "drafting tape" for any taping-off done directly onto the original finish, to avoid pulling off brittle finish.

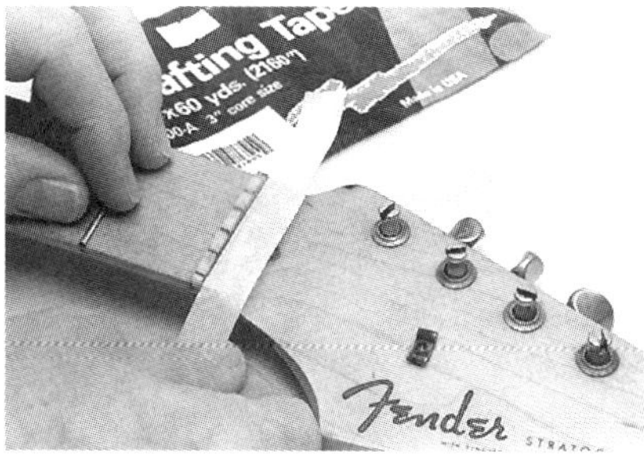

2 Even with drafting tape, use as little as possible. This one strip—near the nut—gives an area to *tape onto* with stronger tape.

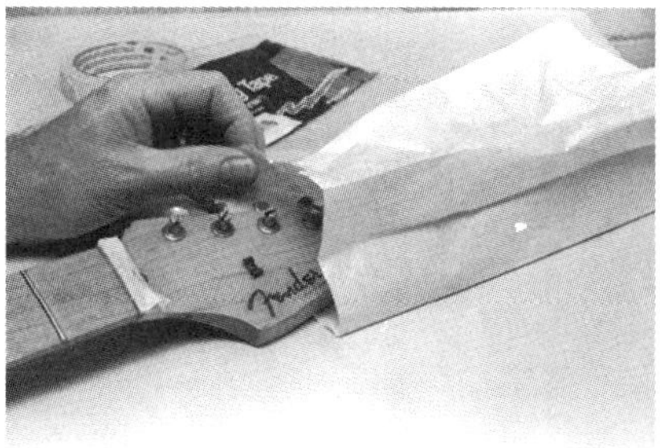

3 A paper lunch-bag makes a quick peghead cover...

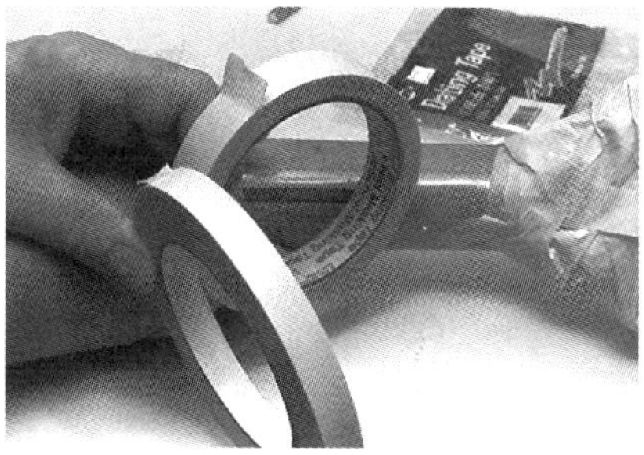

4 ...and we use the wider "regular" tape to secure anything which isn't touching the brittle vintage finish.

5 A 7/16" dowel-stick, tapered to fit the 3/8" hole and then drilled and tapped to screw onto the truss rod...

6 ...makes a good spraying "handle."

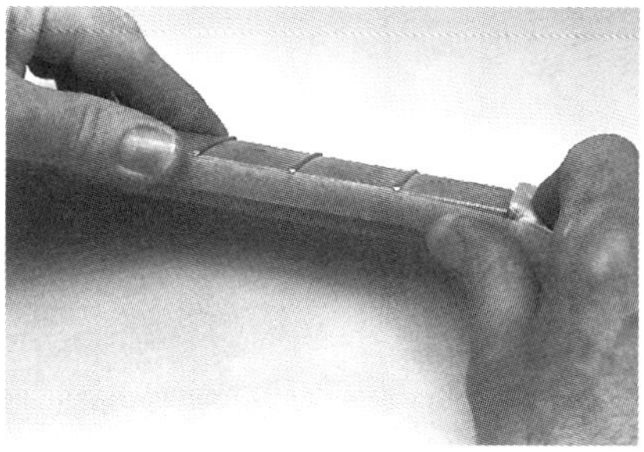

7 Drafting tape laid carefully along the fretboard edge...

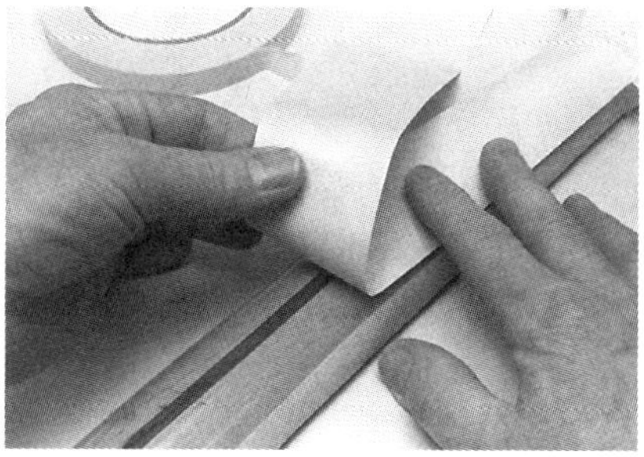

8 ...gives something to tape onto. Use regular masking tape to fasten clean paper over the exposed finish and onto the drafting tape.

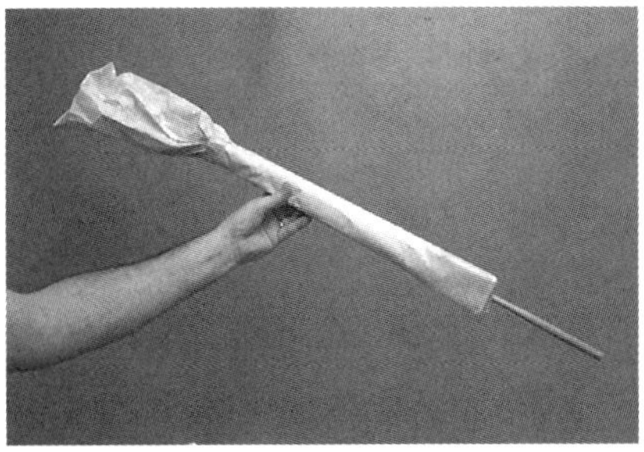

9 Ready to spray. PHOTO: J. O'BOYLE

10 We stained the bare wood of the fretboard with Lockwood water-soluble aniline (red, yellow, and brown) mixed with clear water to weaken the strength.

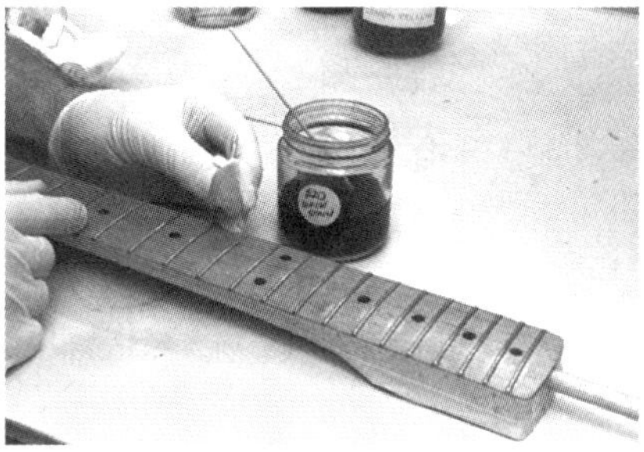

11 One or two applications, made with a rag, will give the color you're after. Practice on scrap.

12 We used Behlen's lacquer mixed as follows: one part lacquer...

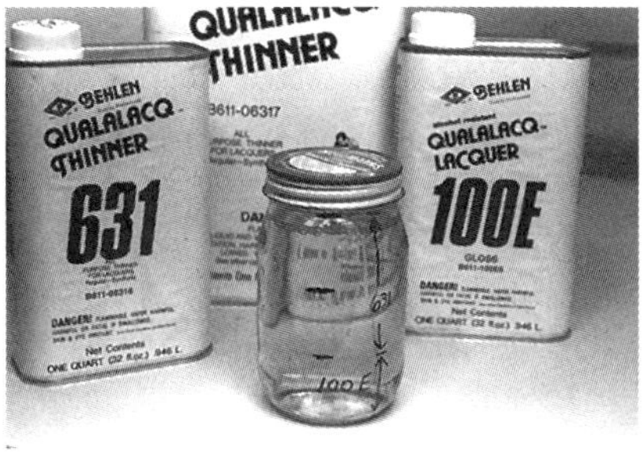

13 ...with two parts thinner.

14 Spray a good wet coat.

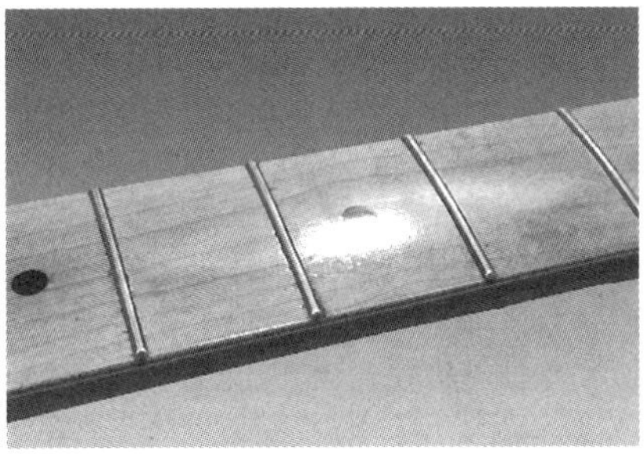

15 It'll look like this when it's wet...

16 ...but soon it soaks right into the maple, until you get a build, and then you're done. When finishing maple, don't put it on too thick—a key is to get the build *into* the wood, but not too much *on* it.

17 "Dry-sand" (no water or other lubrication), using small pieces of #500-grit sandpaper. We prefer the "Nikken" brand—a well known Japanese water-sanding paper of exceptional quality.

18 If you sand sideways, in the direction of the fret, the scratches may not always "melt-in" as well as you might hope, especially in the early stages when they could actually mark the wood itself...

19 ...so, circular sanding motions—done at any stage of the finish—eliminate sideways scratches, much like a random-orbit sander.

20 Use small pieces, dry, and discard them often. Only sand the first coat or two, to get rid of any fuzz or bumps and to give the rest of the coats a smooth surface to build on.

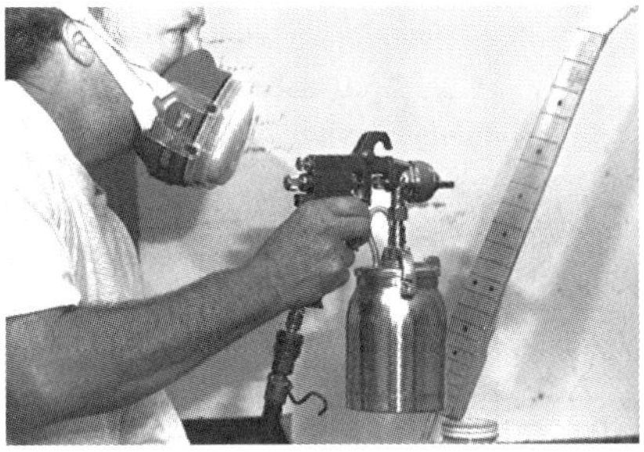

21 Another wet coat (coat #2). Don't sand this, or the next couple of coats.

22 However, when the finish starts to build on the fret, you can scrape it off while it's still a little soft, using a 12-common nail that has a semi-circular groove ground into it.

23 Most finishers probably don't do this—it's a little time consuming—but it does make removing the final lacquer from the frets easier, since there isn't much buildup.

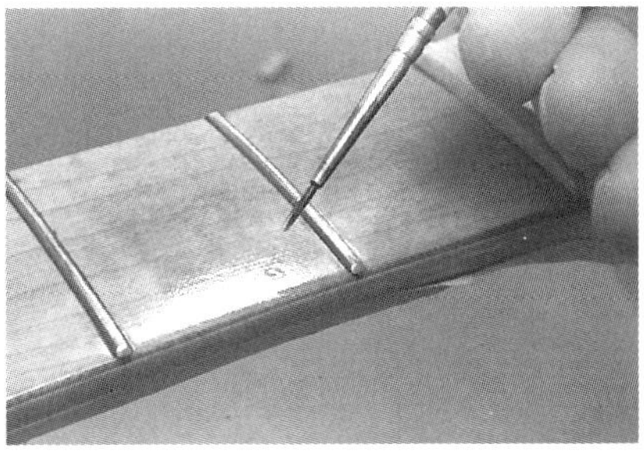

24 Spray another coat or two, and if you find any pits, touch them up with a brush and a drop of clear lacquer or sanding sealer. Don't sand.

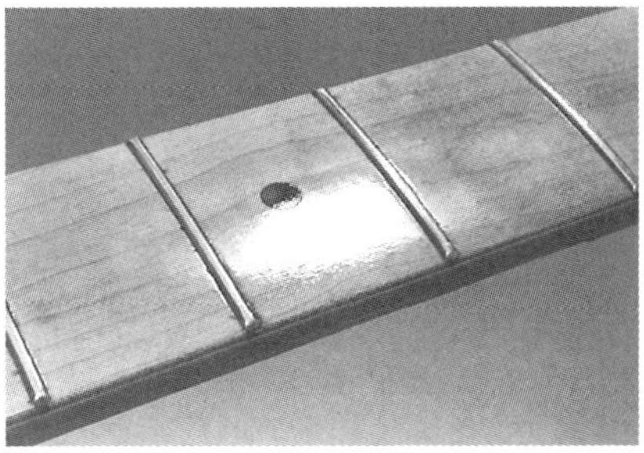

25 We've sprayed about 3 or 4 coats of lacquer at this point, not sanding the lacquer, but occasionally scraping off the fret. The sideways scratches have disappeared, and any touched-up pits have melted in.

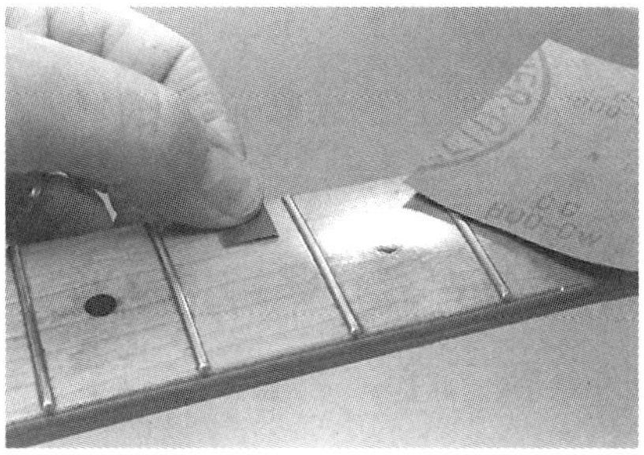

26 Dry-sand now (you can do it wet if you like) with #500, and then #800-grit Nikken paper. Sideways sanding is OK with this much lacquer built up. Sand until the shine is dulled (as you see here) and spray another coat.

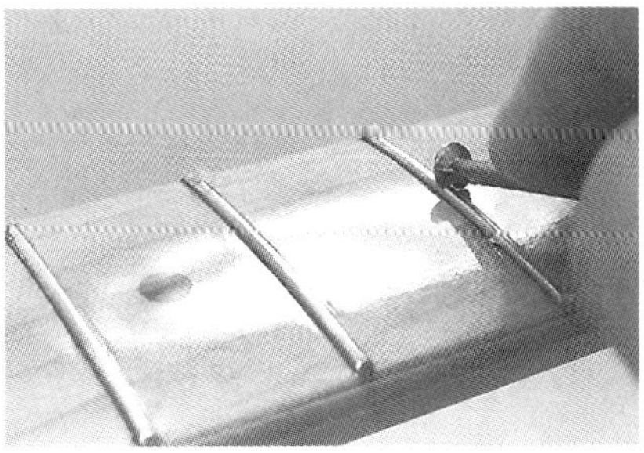

27 Scrape the fret again; don't worry about getting it *all* right down to the bare fret, just get most of it.

28 This is a good smooth finish with very little "orange peel" and no pits. You can buff it now, or sand before you buff. Avoid water-sanding, because you'll be spraying one last coat.

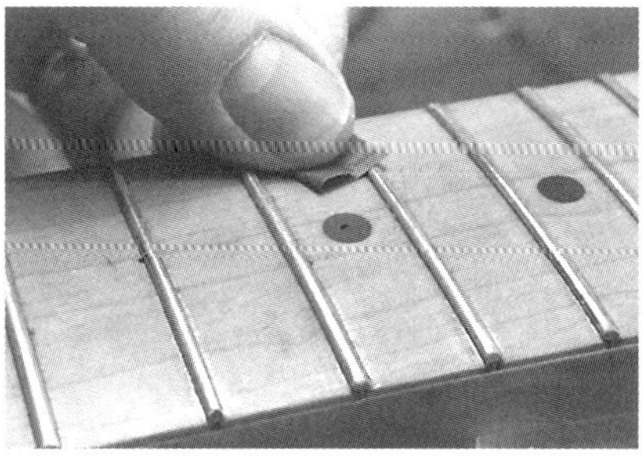

29 We sanded with #800-grit Nikken, dry. We *didn't* scrape the finish off the frets this time, so that the thin coat of lacquer on the frets will keep the buffing wheel (especially the "white" wheel) from turning black.

30 Any sideways scratches made with #800-grit at this stage won't leave marks that can't buff out.

31 Use #1500 or #2000-grit Nikken paper to remove the tiniest "lacquer line" along the fretboard edge (the lacquer coat rolled slightly over the edge).

32 This buffing rig clamps onto the finishing table and the buffing residue floats right out on the breeze. We keep our explosion-proof fan running while we buff. When buffing frets we only use the right-hand (brown) wheel…

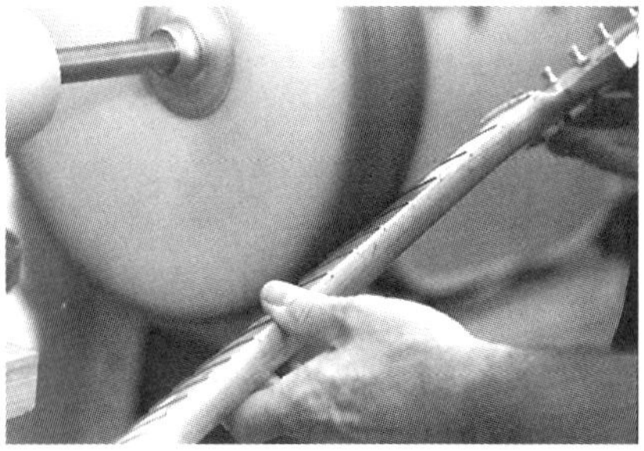

33 …but here we're buffing the lacquer and not the frets, because they're covered with lacquer. Buff from the center down; never catch the upper edge of the piece, or it may get thrown—at you!

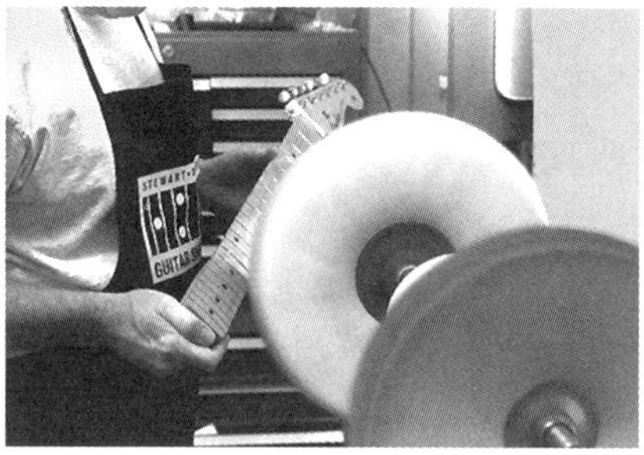

34 The white wheel removes the brown-wheel scratches—leaving a perfect gloss. Hopefully it hasn't cut through that last film of lacquer on the frets. We use the white wheel for lacquer and bone—you can't polish bone on a blackened wheel.

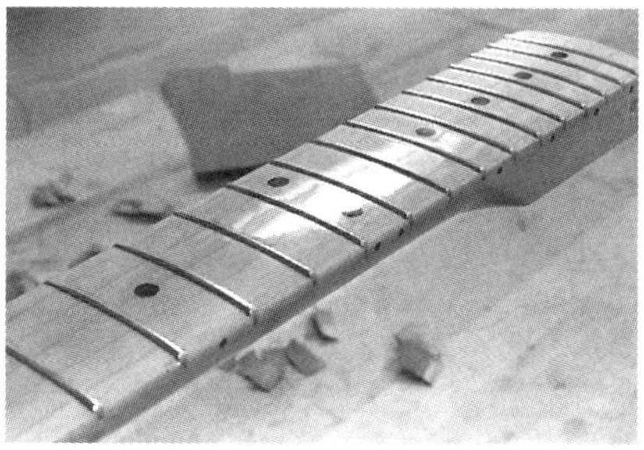

35 The final high gloss! Too high actually—Fender has always mixed a de-glosser (flattener) into the lacquer to keep it from shining this much. The more it shines, the more you can see imperfections.

36 One treatment some finishers give to a new maple neck finish is to spray a 4:1 ratio (4 thinner:1 lacquer) "finish" or "melting-in" coat over the buffed fretboard.

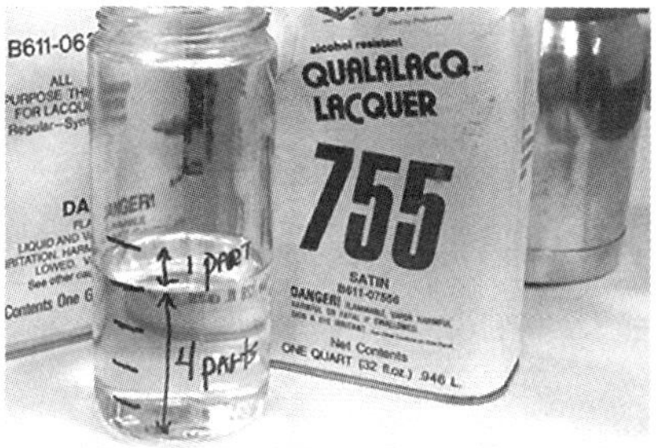

37 By substituting "Satin" or "Dull-rub" lacquer for the gloss lacquer you can reduce the sheen, as Fender does.

38 Another choice is to use 4 parts thinner, 1/2 part lacquer, and 1/2 part "flattener" to reduce the sheen. You can even use thinner and flattener *only*, with no lacquer at all. Practice on scrap!

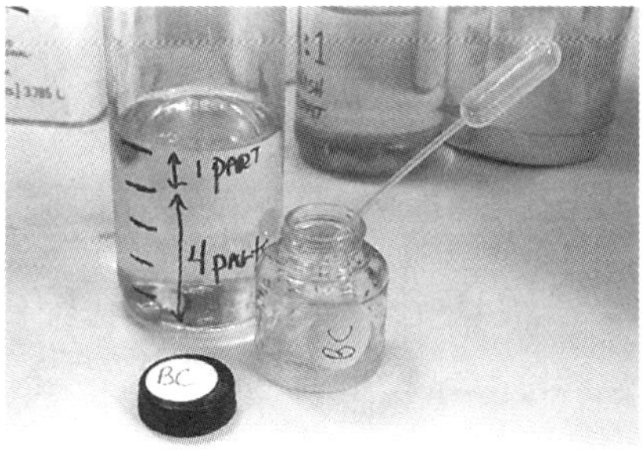

39 Add a thimble-full of lacquer retarder to the mixture to help everything flow well and "melt-in" together.

40 Sprayed carefully over the sanded and buffed high-gloss coat, a smooth, *slightly* satiny, used or "vintage" look is produced. This was thinner and flattener only.

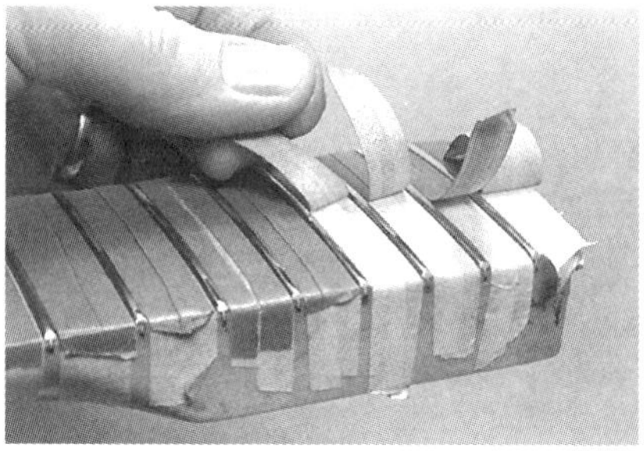

41 Once dry, tape off the fretboard with drafting tape, then put the brown, heavy-duty "flatback" tape *over that* for extra protection. Don't put the brown tape directly onto fresh—or vintage—lacquer.

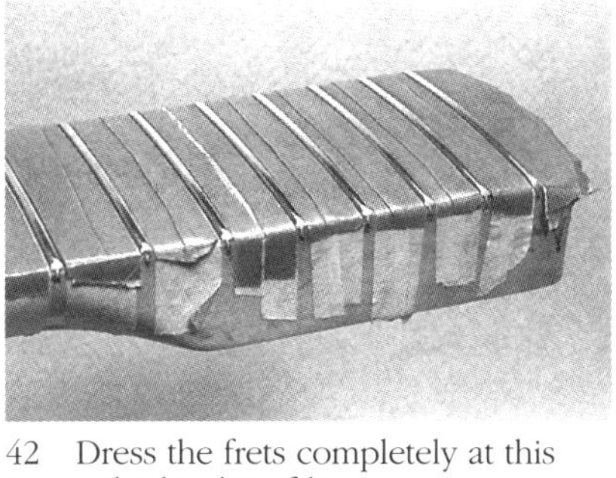

42 Dress the frets completely at this time—the last bit of lacquer removes easily with a fret file or the sand sticks. After dressing, while the tape's still on, buff the frets, by hand or on the wheel.

43 The buffed frets—carefully remove the tape, and you're done!

IN CLOSING. . .

We hope that you've enjoyed this book and that you'll do better fretwork because of it. Remember, there's never just *one* way to do anything when it comes to fretwork—so learn all the methods that you can. Then you'll have a big bag of tricks to draw from. Don't ruin a good axe learning, either—always practice on scrap! If you want more information on fretting, look into the following:

BOOKS

These books have good information on fretting.

The Acoustic Guitar, Vol. 1 and Vol. 2 by Don Teeter (Oklahoma Press)

Complete Guitar Repair, by Hideo Kamimoto (Oak Publications)

Guitar Repair, by Irving Sloane (Bold Strummer)

Guitar Repair Repair Guide, by Dan Erlewine (GPI/Miller Freeman)

PERIODICALS

Stewart MacDonald's Guitar Shop Supply quarterly catalog of tools, parts, and supplies includes an eight-page section titled "Trade Secrets" which is loaded with fretting facts. To receive your free catalog, call (800) 848-2273, or write us at Box 900 B, Athens, OH 45701.

Guitarmaker, the quarterly trade journal of the Association of Stringed Instrument Artisans (ASIA). For subscription and member ship information, contact: ASIA, P.O. Box 341, Paul Smith's NY 12970.

American Lutheri, is a trade journal published quarterly by the Guild of American Luthiers (GAL). Contact GAL headquarters, 8222 S. Park Ave., Tacoma, WA 98408.